MEXICAN
MASCULINITIES

CULTURAL STUDIES OF THE AMERICAS

Edited by George Yúdice, Jean Franco, and Juan Flores

MEXICAN MASCULINITIES

Robert McKee Irwin

Cultural Studies of the Americas

VOLUME 11

University of Minnesota Press
Minneapolis
London

Poetry by Xavier Villaurrutia is reprinted by permission of the Fondo de Cultura Económica, Mexico.

Portions of chapter 1 previously appeared in "Altamirano's Studs: Male Beauty in Nineteenth-Century Mexican National Literature," *Nómada* 5 (2000): 95–99; reprinted by permission of *Nómada*. Portions of chapter 2 previously appeared as "The Famous 41: The Scandalous Birth of Modern Mexican Homosexuality," *GLQ* 6, no. 3 (2000): 353–76; reprinted by permission of Duke University Press. Portions of chapter 3 previously appeared as "The Legend of Jorge Cuesta: The Perils of Alchemy and the Paranoia of Gender," *Hispanisms and Homosexualities*, ed. Sylvia Molloy and Robert McKee Irwin (Durham, N.C.: Duke University Press, 1998), 29–53; reprinted by permission of Duke University Press; and as "As Invisible As He Is: The Queer Enigma of Xavier Villaurrutia," *Reading and Writing the Ambiente*, ed. Susana Chávez-Silverman and Librada Hernández (Madison: University of Wisconsin Press, 2000), 114–46; reprinted by permission of University of Wisconsin Press; and as "La homosexualidad cósmica mexicana: Espejos de diferencia racial en Xavier Villaurrutia," *Revista Iberoamericana* 187 (1999): 293–304; reprinted by permission of *Revista Iberoamericana*; and as "*La Pedo Embotellado*: Sexual Roles and Play in Salvador Novo's *La estatua de sal*," *Studies in the Literary Imagination* 33, no. 1 (2000): 125–32; published by the Department of English, Georgia State University; reproduced by permission.

Published by the University of Minnesota Press
111 Third Avenue South, Suite 290
Minneapolis, MN 55401-2520
http://www.upress.umn.edu

Library of Congress Cataloging-in-Publication Data

Irwin, Robert McKee, 1962-
    Mexican masculinities / Robert McKee Irwin.
      p. cm. – (Cultural studies of the Americas ; v. 11)
    Includes bibliographical references and index.
    ISBN 0-8166-4070-X (HC : alk. paper) – ISBN 0-8166-4071-8 (PB : alk. paper)
    1. Mexican literature–20th century–History and criticism. 2. Mexican
literature–19th century–History and criticism. 3. Masculinity in literature.
4. National characteristics, Mexican, in literature. 5. Homosexuality in literature.
I. Title. II. Series.
    PQ7155 .I79 2003
    860.9'353–dc21

                  2002013887

Printed in the United States of America on acid-free paper

The University of Minnesota is an equal-opportunity educator and employer.

12 11 10 09 08 07 06 05 04 03   10 9 8 7 6 5 4 3 2 1

Contents

Acknowledgments

I gratefully acknowledge my dissertation committee (Sylvia Molloy, George Yúdice, Jennifer Wicke, Gerard Aching, and Ana María Dopico) for their suggestions, interrogations, commentaries, and loyal support over the past several years. Of this group, Jennifer Wicke deserves special mention for her always thoughtful and sound advice, as does George Yúdice for his enthusiastic encouragement of my work, particularly as manifested in his interest in having my book included in the Cultural Studies of the Americas series.

Others who have given me guidance and encouragement include Maarten van Delden, Kristin Ross, Kathleen Ross, Richard Sieburth, and Avital Ronnell, my professors at New York University. In addition, José Quiroga, Daniel Balderston, Licia Fiol-Matta, Oscar Montero, Rebecca Biron, Francine Masiello, Gabriel Giorgi, Gorica Majstorovic, Estelle Tarica, Camilla Fojas, and Victor Macías González in the United States, and Carlos Monsiváis, José Serrato Córdoba, Pilar Alberti Manzanares, Gabriel Medina, Miguel Rodríguez Lozano, Ana María Salazar, and the late Irma Isabel Fernández Arias in Mexico, along with Juan Gelpí and Diana Palaversich, have provided me with important dialogue, feedback, and tips concerning my research and the development of arguments. I must also mention that Carla Locatelli and Ruth Rogaski have been inspirations to my work, each in her own way.

The annual conference of Mexicanists at the University of California, Irvine, formerly organized by Carl Good and José Villalobos, as well as the annual Jornadas Metropolitanas at Casa Lamm in Mexico City, put together by Lilia Granillo Vázquez, Manuel Medina, and Javier Durán (among others), has been an invaluable proving ground for many of my ideas. I must especially thank Lilia Granillo Vázquez and Fernando Huerta for helping me to see the practical importance of this project.

Regarding my years of research in Mexico involving often semi-annual extended trips to Mexico City, I am grateful to Dubravka Suznjevic for generously allowing me to operate out of her home and always ensuring that I would get enough *chiles poblanos* and, on occasion, *chapulines*. So many of my Mexican friends, going back to the years I enjoyed living in la Colonia Puebla in Mexico City in the late eighties, helped in their own way to incite my interest in this project. My friends and colleagues in New York City and New Orleans, particularly my various tennis teammates, rivals, and playing partners, have helped me keep my sanity through years of endless research, formulations, translations, edits, and rewrites.

I am indebted to Tulane's Roger Thayer Stone Center for Latin American Studies, to New York University's Center for Latin American and Caribbean Studies, to the Dean's Office of New York University's Graduate School of Arts and Sciences, and to the New York University Department of Comparative Literature's Anaïs Nin Fellowship for research and travel funding that allowed me to carry out this lengthy project promptly and effectively. Key research facilities have included Mexico's Biblioteca and Hemeroteca Nacional, particularly its Fondo Reservado for older materials, along with New York University's Bobst Library and Tulane University's Howard-Tilton Memorial Library, most particularly its Latin American Library, where I have benefited greatly from the personal attention of its director Guillermo Náñez and senior librarian Paul Bary.

The latter stages of this project owe much to the wise and generous advice of Jean Franco and the encouragement of George Yúdice, as well as to positive reinforcement from my colleagues on the faculty and among the graduate students in the Department of Spanish and Portuguese at Tulane University. I also greatly appreciate the professionalism of Richard Morrison, my acquiring editor at the University of Minnesota Press, and of copy editor John Eagleson.

Despite her demanding professional schedule, Sylvia Molloy has given me steadfast support over the years in so many ways. Without her wise and thoughtful suggestions, I would never have been able to produce this opus. In her role as mentor, she has shown me how to be a professional in academia, and she has been both a role model and a true friend.

Finally, for his patience, his help with the translation of so many *mexicanismos*, his honest and often brutal criticism, and his unyielding belief in me, even in the roughest of times, I dedicate this book to Gerardo Espinosa.

Broadside, "Los 41 maricones: Aquí están los maricones, muy chulos y coquetones" [Here are the pansies, very cute and coquettish]. Artwork by José Guadalupe Posada, 1901. Courtesy of Harry Ransom Humanities Research Center, University of Texas at Austin.

Introduction

The Hidden Vices of
los Hijos de la Chingada

El Antro Inmoral de Envilecimiento

> ¡Qué desgracia vivir degradado, señalado, repudiado por todas las ge-
> neraciones, hundido en el cóncavo maldito de los desprestigios sociales,
> cerrando los ojos á las leyes divinas del progreso, y los oídos á los
> acentos sublimes y conmovedores de la moral!

> What a disgrace to live degraded, singled out, repudiated for all genera-
> tions, sunken into the accursed crater of social discredit, closing eyes to
> the divine laws of progress and ears to the sublime and moving accents
> of morality![1]

Who have angered the above writer so tremendously that he would
unleash such invective against them? What have they done that is so
terrible that they are to be "repudiated for all generations"? How have
they simultaneously threatened progress and morality? The above
narrator goes on to accuse them of having committed a horrible vice:

> y el vicio, ese vicio que rebosa en la copa de la prostitución más desen-
> frenada, es el que hace esclavos á los hombres y los denigra, hasta caer
> en el antro inmoral del envilecimiento y de la corrupción, que rompe
> sus lazos en mil añicos, para no purificarse nunca.

> and the vice, that vice which overflows from the cup of the most un-
> bridled wantonness, is that which makes slaves of men and denigrates
> them, to the point that they fall into the immoral den of vilification and
> corruption, which breaks their shackles into a thousand bits, so they
> may never again become pure. (Castrejón 165)

Novelist Eduardo Castrejón is scandalized by the behavior of the
"famous 41,"[2] a group of transvestites arrested in 1901 when their
private ball was raided by the Mexico City police. Men dressed as

women, men dancing with men threatened rigid notions of masculinity and male sexuality in Mexico. This outrageous defiance of social norms caused an uproar and introduced male effeminacy and homosexuality as both the other that would define a macho heterosexual national model and an other that in fact was itself intrinsically Mexican, and that from that moment on would be viewed, albeit reluctantly by many, as an undeniable element of national culture.

Castrejón's editors, in the introduction to his 1906 novel, *Los 41*, carefully insert the scandal and its colorfully queer and very Mexican characters into a Mexican literary history of picaresque, *costumbrista*, romantic, and *naturalista* novels (*modernismo* is conspicuously ignored), drawing parallels in particular to Fernández de Lizardi's landmark *El Periquillo Sarniento* (iii–vii). Yet Castrejón, whose prose resembles more that of yellow journalism than that of his more acclaimed literary predecessors, was and still is utterly forgotten by Mexican literary criticism. Likewise, Mexican literary history has consistently ignored the important symbolic role of masculinities and male sexualities in the numerous grand literary constructions and reconstructions of Mexico since independence. The 41 (the great mythic figures of Mexican homosexuality)[3] are, as Castrejón's editors posit, the sons of el Periquillo and Manuel Payno's *bandidos del Río Frío*. They are the forefathers of both la Pedo Embotellado and the other colorful personalities of Salvador Novo's memoirs as well as Octavio Paz's *hijos de la Chingada*.

Los Hijos de la Chingada

Paz's well-known allegory of *mestizaje* proposes Mexicans to be the sons of the rape of indigenous Mesoamerican cultures by the invading Spanish *conquistadores*. This allegory coincides with much Mexican literature whose heroes are frequently young *mestizo* men, Mexico's sons. Moreover, it is not romances between white Spaniard *galanes* [gallant romantic heroes] and lovely indigenous maidens that symbolize national unity, but much more commonly homosocial bonds among young Mexican men, *los hijos de la Chingada*.

From the errant young Periquillo, ever in search of father figures; to the inseparable buddies Arturo and Manuel of Payno's *El fistol*

del diablo; to Luis Inclán's *hermanos de la hoja,* the tobacco smug-
gling heroes of *Astucia;* to Vicente Riva Palacio's pirates of the gulf; to
the queer *modernista* alliances between Rafael and Andrés in Amado
Nervo's *El donador de almas,* and between Claudio and José in Rubén
Campos's *Claudio Oronoz;* to the ragtag troops of Azuela's *Los de
abajo* and other novels of the revolution; to the more problematic
male alliances in the later novels of José Revueltas, Rosario Castellanos and Juan Rulfo; to the male bonding in the early proto-Chicano
literature of María Amparo Ruiz de Burton and foundational Chicano
literature of Américo Paredes and José Antonio Villarreal: Mexico is
protagonized by young men, and national unity is allegorized by male
homosocial bonding.

This study traces the history of Mexico as constructed through
its literature and its male protagonists. Masculinity and male sexuality have historically been key components of national identity
constructions. As conceptions of masculinity change over time, so
change notions of *lo mexicano.* Despite Paz's attempts to make essential historic links between Mexicanness and the conquest through
the allegory of *los hijos de la Chingada,* history proves more complex.

A New Literary History: Masculinity and Nation

However, this is not a history of Mexico; it is a history of literary
constructions of Mexico. From the era of independence to the early
1960s, just prior to the rise of feminism,[4] it delivers a new reading
of Mexican literary history through its shifting constructions of masculinity and nation, investigating not just the well-known stereotypes,
but also more marginalized discourses that challenge them. Moreover,
it reveals the many contradictions among mainstream discourses as
they evolve (or degenerate) over time and as they become entangled in
constructions of other key components of national identity including
race, class, and particularly sexuality.

Recent feminist scholarship has examined representations of women
prior to the rise to prominence of the feminist movement in Mexico.[5] Despite noble efforts by early feminists such as Laureana Wright
de Kleinhans,[6] the limited success of novelists Refugio Barragán de

Toscano, María Enriqueta, and Nellie Campobello, and the nonliterary fame of writers Antonieta Rivas Mercado and Guadalupe Marín, between national literary heroine Sor Juana Inés de la Cruz in the seventeenth century and Mexico's first canonized *autoras* Rosario Castellanos and Elena Garro in the fifties and sixties—there were no major female writers in Mexico, largely due to persistent sexism within national literary institutions. Indeed, the best-known women to have written in Mexico during its first 150 years following independence from Spain are Scottish visitor Frances Calderón de la Barca and Chilean guest Gabriela Mistral.[7]

It is no surprise then that literary constructions of nation by canonized male writers should have been about men and masculinity. With only a few exceptions, the most important being Federico Gamboa's Santa, the literary personages who represent Mexico are men: Lizardi's Periquillo Sarniento; the various *bandidos,* good or bad, of the nineteenth century from the novels of Inclán, Payno, and Ignacio Altamirano (*El Zarco*); revolutionary leaders like Demetrio Macías of Azuela's *Los de abajo;* Martín Luis Guzmán's postrevolutionary *caudillo;* and Rulfo's Pedro Páramo and his sons. This study is inspired by and complementary to the above mentioned feminist projects; it links the growing body of work on masculinity and homosexuality in Mexico to literary constructions of the national:[8] by rereading the rhetorical uses of masculinity in canonical texts; by offering complementary readings of lesser known texts by relatively well-known authors such as José Tomás de Cuéllar, Ángel de Campo, Nervo, Xavier Villaurrutia, Novo, Francisco Rojas González; by including texts, often little known, by women writers such as Barragán de Toscano and María Luisa Garza, along with better known works by Campobello and Castellanos; and by searching out forgotten texts, often read in their day as popular fiction (and therefore not serious literature) including Castrejón's *Los 41*, along with science fiction novels of eugenics and androgyny.

The types of texts under consideration are literary, then, but in a broad sense. While there is no doubt that the institution of "high" literature strove to construct a shared notion of Mexicanness during the entire period covered here, the effectiveness of this enterprise must not be overestimated. As Ángel Rama has made clear, *la ciudad letrada* is not the nation. In Mexico, it has always been a small group of erudite intellectual elites who have had access to and control over discourse on a national level. Canonized national literature, then, cannot be considered to represent the thinking of any but a very particular minority of Mexicans, nor could this literature reach the majority of Mexican citizens since literacy was a major issue throughout the years under consideration here. This is not to say that the project of literary nation building was utterly ineffective. As José Joaquín Blanco states referring to Mexico's greatest promoter of national literature, Altamirano: "Acaso sólo el propio Altamirano y su tribu de amigos y seguidores podían llenar en su tiempo el paradigma de mexicanidad que establecían para la nación entera. Pero el paradigma quedaba establecido, por imposible que pareciese" [Perhaps only Altamirano himself along with his tribe of friends and followers could in their day fulfill the paradigm of Mexicanness that they established for the entire nation. But the paradigm remained established, as impossible as it may have seemed] (*Crónica literaria* 43). And as it came to be studied in school, emulated, and expanded upon, "la cultura nacional se fue volviendo menos 'imposible' al paso de las generaciones" [national culture gradually became less 'impossible' with the passing of generations] (42).

Nonetheless, high literature alone cannot tell the whole story of constructions of nation. For this reason, this study makes use of a broader range of texts including newspapers, broadsheets, pop literature, and scientific (and pseudoscientific) studies, for example, of criminology and social psychology. The idea is not to attain an impossible goal of achieving complete and accurate representation, but to present a variety of alternatives to the hegemonic visions of Mexican masculinity of Mexico's *letrados,* a Foucauldian web of gender discourses that complicate and contradict each other and themselves and represent a broader view of Mexicanness than could the canon by itself.[9]

Moreover, what counts as a Mexican text here includes not just those written by Mexicans and published in Mexico. Numerous perspectives on what defines Mexicanness are considered. Of interest

are works written about Mexicans by foreigners, works often published abroad and in other languages. Certainly, many Mexican novels
by Mexican authors were first published abroad, sometimes in other
languages, including not just books by marginalized authors such as
Enriqueta (*El secreto*, Spain) and Garza (*La novia de Nervo*, United
States), but also novels by canonized authors such as Nervo (*El
bachiller*, France, in French) and even Azuela (*Los de abajo*, United
States). John Reed's *Insurgent Mexico*, according to such an epistemology, is as much a novel of the revolution as Rafael Muñoz's
¡Vámanos con Pancho Villa! and Villarreal's *Pocho* is as valid an exploration of Mexicanness as Paz's *El laberinto de la soledad*—and it
is telling that the proto-Chicano archetype of the *pachuco* is key to
both works.

Mexico here is defined in neither political, nor geographical, nor
racial, but cultural terms.[10] Mexican literature, by this definition, includes any texts that grow out of, examine, shape, or reflect (correctly
or not) Mexican culture,[11] whether in Mexico or elsewhere. Thus,
even though the Mexicanness of citizens of Mexico City may differ
in many ways from the Mexicanness of second- or third-generation
immigrants in Southern California, both groups largely believe they
share a common culture as Mexicans. Critics such as Gloria Anzaldúa
have argued effectively that the border produces its own fragmented,
hybrid culture, but this does not imply that Mexicanness does not
seep into the borderlands of the southwestern United States: "Deep
in our hearts we believe that being Mexican has nothing to do with
which country one lives in. Being Mexican is a state of soul—not
one of mind, not one of citizenship" (62). This Chicano-inspired
vision of Mexicanness shapes this study, allowing Mexicanness to
escape the artificial confines of geographic, linguistic, and political
borders.

Moreover, notions of Mexicanness described by foreigners also
contribute to national gender stereotypes. Oscar Lewis's *The Children
of Sánchez* is an obvious example. And while such texts inevitably
display biases, as Julio Ramos has argued, the biases of the foreigner
in his or her constructions of another culture are often quite similar
to those of the native.[12] No text provides unbiased insight into an

authentic national essence. Every text (including this one), whether written by a native citizen or a foreign visitor (or anyone else), must be read with a critical eye toward the ideologies from which it arises and the power relations between the author, his or her objects of study, and the text's readerships.

The focus on gender, sexuality, and nation is meant to problematize historical constructions of Mexicanness, to "fisurar lecturas estableci-das" [to fissure established readings] (Molloy, "La flexión del género" 56), to reconstitute Mexican literary history, to recast it as a history of discourse on gender, sexuality, and nation, three themes that intersect repeatedly in literary works of 1810 to 1960. The overwhelming abundance of texts, canonical or otherwise, that link these particular thematics suggests a need to map out a genealogy of their intersections, a task that neither Mexican literary histories nor genealogies of *lo mexicano* have undertaken to date.[13]

As Matthew Gutmann states, by the time of the Mexican revolution, "Mexico came to mean machismo and machismo came to mean Mexico" (24), but masculinity had played a key role in national constructions from the beginning of the national period. It is a central theme in Mexico's first novel, *El Periquillo Sarniento,* and remains a focus throughout the nation-building literature of the nineteenth century. The imagined communities constructed in nineteenth-century literature were communities of men.[14] It is no accident that Samuel Ramos's landmark 1934 study of Mexicanness, *El perfil del hombre y la cultura en México,* used Alfred Adler's notion of masculine protest as a major premise.

The Meanings of Macho

Since nationhood is frequently constructed as a "virile" institution, a brotherhood of men, a key ideological factor to consider is the particular notions of sex and gender incorporated into texts that represent national culture. Two terms of importance are, then, "maleness" and "masculinity," the former referring to a set of physical characteristics shared by men, the latter indicative of a collection of behaviors, attitudes, and attributes that men may or may not exhibit (but that, perhaps, they ought to). Oftentimes masculinity is seen as a natural product of maleness. On the other hand, only maleness is natural, while masculinity is learned or acquired, and only by some men (or even some women). Thus, maleness is usually seen as an absolute (one must be either male or female) while masculinity is envisioned more as a range of positions along a continuum (one may be more or less masculine than others). In many cases, the gender ideology behind a text may be conflictive in and of itself.[15]

A well-known definition of Mexican masculinity will illustrate. It is provided by Manuel, one of Oscar Lewis's informants in *The Children of Sánchez*:

> Mexicans... admire the person "with balls," as we say. The character who throws punches and kicks, without stopping to think, is the one who comes out on top. The one who has guts enough to stand up against an older, stronger guy, is more respected. If someone shouts, you've got to shout louder. If any so-and-so comes to me and says, "Fuck your mother," I answer, "Fuck your mother a thousand times." And if he gives one step forward and I take one step back I lose prestige. But if I go forward too, and pile on and make a fool out of him, then the others will treat me with respect. In a fight, I would never give up or say, "Enough," even though the other was killing me. I would try to go to my death, smiling. That is what we mean by being "macho," by being manly. (38)

Manuel Sánchez's definition is perhaps typical. It makes vague biological links (having balls), but then goes on to describe not how a man naturally behaves, but how he "has got to" act in order to be seen as manly by others. Masculinity, then, is not internal; it is determined more by the judgments of others than by an intrinsic quality. Moreover, in this case, it is a status that is at constant risk. In the confrontations Sánchez describes, presumably only one participant can emerge looking manly. Masculinity would then seem to be a relative concept, not about whether or not one has balls, but about relative degrees of gutsiness, bravery, competitiveness, or whatever the determinant quality (or qualities) of masculinity is seen to be. These conflictive aspects of masculinity are not the product of Sánchez's marginal social status, his lack of education, or his irregular family situation (his mother had died and he was raised by his father); we shall see during the course of this study that, although with numerous historical variations, these very same conflictive ideas regarding masculinity resound through the history of Mexican literature. For Sánchez, masculinity is a natural aspect of maleness, yet it must be learned and may be lost. It is at once an absolute category, the binary opposite of femininity, and a category to be measured in degrees and compared against the masculinity of others.

Conflicts of this sort pass unnoticed because, while masculinity is not easy to define, everyone knows what it is. Everyone recognizes masculinity, and therefore it need not be defined. It is, in fact, a key component of the national *habitus,* to borrow Pierre Bourdieu's term.[16] Subjects buy into certain learned "truths" that then rule their own actions and that they coerce others into learning and following as well, without even being conscious that they are doing so. Notions of gender are frequently among these "truths."[17] This system of gender not only affects how individuals see things, but also confines their actions.[18]

The assumed natural link between sex and gender binaries is, in fact, quite problematic. Biological sex is not a strictly binary phenomenon. It is not possible to divide all humankind neatly into the two categories of male and female. There are simply too many biological anomalies.[19] A study by Julia Epstein finds more than a dozen different classifications of physical anomalies ranging from irregularities in chromosomes with minor visible sexual ambiguity to full-blown hermaphroditism (104–16) and notes that "estimates place the incidence of sexually ambiguous births at from 2 to 4 percent" (100).[20] Moreover, biology is not the only factor at work in determining perceptions of sex and sexual difference. Judith Butler sees sex itself as "a regulatory ideal whose materialization is compelled, and this materialization takes place (or fails to take place) through certain highly regulated practices" (*Bodies* 1).[21]

Against the Binary

Given the above interrogations of the biological model of sex as a simple male/female binary, it would seem that there is little to support a binary vision of gender as a simple either/or equation of masculine and feminine. In fact, while such a binary vision often is applied in Mexican discourse, it is not the only model at work. A simultaneous contradictory model exists as well, a model suggested in the common Mexican expression, "ser muy hombre" [to be very manly]. This model implies that gender is a continuum ranging from very masculine to very feminine with all sorts of degrees of difference in between. This thinking along a gender continuum usually goes along with a detachment of gender from sex, i.e., the gender ideology at work allows that a man may be very manly, not very manly, or even not manly at all. A biological man might be feminine just as a biological female might be masculine. While such gender nonconformism is often disapproved of, it is not necessarily viewed as being against nature. Some men are naturally macho, while others are naturally effeminate, while still others might seem to be both.[22]

This study means to remain aware of both how different ideologies of gender simultaneously exist and how they shift in importance over time. Gender is, as Gail Bederman puts it, "a historical, ideological process" (7), which is culturally specific, dynamic, multifaceted, self-contradictory, and always changing. At different historical moments (and sometimes at the same historical moments) in Mexican discourse, gender is and/or isn't linked to notions of biological sex, it is a binary system and/or a continuum, it is fixed and/or shifting, it is a natural phenomenon and/or an ideological construct. All these competing discourses fade in and out over time and accumulate into the messy web of contradictions that is Mexican masculinity.

Men are men, and yet they must become men. They must perform certain acts that make them men. However, if performance of acts is key to masculinity, then masculinity is essentially a performance, and no one is really authentically masculine. While the word "performance," with its contemporary theoretical implications, has only recently been adopted by Latin American feminists,[23] the recognition of the performative aspects of masculinity is not new and has been an important component of discourse on Mexican masculinity for decades. Adler argued in 1910 in a series of essays that were to be highly influential in Mexico that a man's doubts about his own masculinity often lead to an overcompensation in masculine behaviors that he termed "masculine protest." This notion of hypermasculinity emphasizes that masculinity, particularly in its most strident (most masculine) manifestations, is merely acted out or performed. While neither Adler nor his Mexican followers (the most prominent being Samuel Ramos) used the term "performance" in their writings on masculinity, they presaged contemporary discourse on gender performance in many ways.

Butler finds that certain "acts, gestures, enactments, generally construed, are *performative* in the sense that the essence or identity that they otherwise purport to express are *fabrications* manufactured and sustained through corporeal signs and other discursive means" (*Gender Trouble* 136). While it is unlikely that Adler and Ramos would give up entirely on the idea of masculinity in fact being a natural condition of men, their attention to its exaggerated manifestations calls attention to its being less a fixed identity or an inherent set of traits than a process that must be enacted and reenacted, asserted and reasserted constantly.

Similarly, although Simone de Beauvoir is famous for proclaiming that one "becomes" a woman, it is perhaps more often masculinity that is viewed as a rite of passage. Manhood is often achieved through certain competitive or ritual acts; men who do not perform these acts properly are seen as immature at best, or, more often, effeminate.[24] Such rites of passage do occur in Mexico, and it is clear that failure to perform them properly might cause one to be regarded as effeminate. In Lewis's *The Children of Sánchez,* the ritual of having sex with a prostitute seems to be a major factor in deciding young Manuel's masculine identity. When he resists going to a whorehouse out of a fear of venereal disease, he is taunted: "This trembling idiot doesn't seem to be a man" and "Are you a queer or what? It's about time you went." Finally, Manuel does go and successfully fulfills the rite of passage: "I didn't like it at all. But the boys were satisfied with me and so that was over with" (39–40).

Gender practices may be learned or absorbed and performed subconsciously as if they were natural, or they may be play-acted.[25] In the latter case, an individual consciously follows a gendered script, perhaps for the purpose of entertaining those around him or her, knowing full well that he or she is merely performing gender. In either case, the gendered script, the prescribed actions and behaviors associated with a given gender, cannot just be invented by the individual, but there is nothing to say that one script (i.e., the script that is performed subconsciously versus the one that is performed consciously) is more authentic than the other. Of course, within the *habitus,* an individual will follow a particular gendered script, usually the one associated with his or her assigned biological sex, and that prescribed gender performance is seen as the authentic one. However, the fact that one can play-act, can experiment with gendered scripts that he or she has not assimilated as part of his or her identity, can choose to draw from sources not prescribed by institutions of ideological norms (school, family, religion, etc.), or can select from among conflicting ideological norms (what one learns at school may not be the same as what one learns on television), points to the possibility of agency, an ability to resist and perhaps even subvert, an ability that helps account for historic change. Whether or not the transvestites of the famous "41" ball of 1901 intended to subvert gender norms and instigate wide-reaching social change in Mexican culture, the fact remains that the link between gender and sexuality that they so firmly established in the Mexican popular imagination arose out of their unexpected choice of gender scripts.

Historic Shift: 1901

In Mexico a decisive shift in this direction occurred around the turn of the century. Prior to that point, homosexuality was not much discussed (although it had been in colonial times),[26] and effeminacy in men was abhorred, but never assigned a sexual dimension. Meanwhile, acts of affection between men, which might be read as homoerotic today, passed unnoticed as long as those men involved appeared to be masculine. However, as homosexuality became a hot topic around the *fin de siglo*—and with the "41" ball, the attention of a scandal-hungry public found homosexuality in the heart of Mexican culture—effeminacy quickly came to be associated with transvestitism and homosexuality to the point that male effeminacy was for much of the twentieth century largely considered synonymous with male homosexuality in Mexico. While this circular logic (in which effeminacy seems to cause homosexuality and homosexuality seems to cause effeminacy) quickly took its place within the *habitus*, its historic specificity belies its naturalness or universality.

In any case, notions of homosexuality came to be crucial in defining masculinity during the first half of the twentieth century in Mexico, and many of the stereotypes that became prominent in those years continue to exert influence today, even in scholarly discourse. Contemporary investigations of Mexican male homosexuality frequently cite *El laberinto de la soledad* not just because it contains Mexico's first significant attempt to characterize homosexuality in a national context, but also because Paz's notion of homosexuality in Mexico turns out to be a central factor in defining Mexican masculinity (and, therefore, Mexicanness itself). For Paz (in perfect accordance with the less erudite Manuel Sánchez), Mexican masculinity is a precarious state that can only be attained and that must be constantly reaffirmed through competitive trials. One cannot be a man in a vacuum in Mexico; masculinity can be achieved only through interaction. Paz's key terms are "rajarse" [to crack] and "chingar" [to fuck or fuck over]. Women are seen as open, penetrable beings, and their femininity is a sign of weakness, while men are closed beings who show their power over others by penetrating them. Men must never allow themselves to crack and must flaunt their power by fucking others over, in one way or another. Heterosexual sex, under this scenario, becomes crude rape. However, Paz's vision of gender is not based only upon material sex acts, but is determined in a largely symbolic scenario.

In this way, masculinity is frequently put to the test among men. Contests of wit, authority, or brute force produce symbolic relations of sexual penetration, in which the loser cracks, gets fucked, and is feminized by the winner, who, in this way, enhances his masculinity. In terms of material sexual relations between men, homosexuality takes on a distinct form in which one participant anally penetrates the other, with the latter being a true homosexual and effeminate, and the former retaining his masculine heterosexual identity. Homosexuality, according to this scenario, always involves anal penetration, and always takes place between one homosexual and one heterosexual man. Moreover, this homosexuality is not defined by a desire for a particular sexual object as it is in some other cultures. In contemporary U.S. gay culture, it is generally assumed that any man who desires another man is a homosexual. In Mexico, according to Paz, it is not the sexual object that matters, but the sexual aim, i.e., male homosexuality is based on a man's aim of being penetrated, with the aim of penetrating considered heterosexual no matter whether the sexual object is male or female.

This scenario, which Paz elaborated to demonstrate how machismo functions symbolically among a certain class of Mexican men (and not to define Mexican male homosexuality), has been taken as gospel by many researchers who look for and find such belief systems among homosexuals in Mexico. Joseph Carrier, pioneer sociologist of male homosexuality in Mexico, cites the famous line from Paz, "masculine homosexuality is regarded with a certain indulgence [in Mexico] insofar as the active agent is concerned" (Carrier 17) to support his idea that only male homosexual relations that follow the active/passive dichotomy based on anal penetration are authentically Mexican and that any variations (reciprocal fucking, fellatio, penetration by self-identified homosexuals) come as a result of the influence of international gay liberation discourse and contact with homosexuals from abroad (192–95).

The difficulty with Paz is that he did not purport to be an expert, nor indeed to have any first-hand knowledge, about male homosexual practice. The model he proposes undoubtedly does have some degree of validity, perhaps a substantial degree of validity, but the fact that it was authored by a presumed heterosexual and that it models homosexuality after heterosexuality makes it less than persuasive. What is lacking among many of the contemporary studies of male homosexuality in Mexico is a critical reading of Paz, or an examination of other historical sources, particularly those written by homosexuals, to determine whether or not they support Paz's claims. In fact, we shall see that they largely do not. For example, in Castrejón's novel, when it is revealed that protagonists Mimí and Ninón are homosexual lovers,

their girlfriends do not care which of them plays the man. They ab-
hor and reject both men equally, even though Ninón is seen as more
masculine. His girlfriend, Judith, in fact, assumes that he plays the
masculine role with other men, but exhibits no "indulgence" at all toward him. Nor does it occur to her that a man can fuck men or women
and still be heterosexual (Paz's sexual aim paradigm); she assumes
that since he is interested in men, he is not really interested in women
and that his apparent heterosexuality had been a mere pose (i.e., she
clearly believes in a sexuality defined by sexual object). Later representations of male homosexuality by Villaurrutia and Novo provide
further evidence that Paz's scheme is of only limited worth.

Sociologist Annick Prieur is much more circumspect in her treatment of the topic of Mexican views on male sexuality and reaches
different conclusions from those of Paz.[27] Explicitly addressing Carrier and other researchers of homosexuality in Mexico, she states:
"My observations indicate that male bisexuality in Mexico is neither
socially accepted nor stigmatized; this polarization does not grasp the
complexity of what is happening" (188). Further, she argues,

> As long as a man is the penetrator, or at least is perceived as such,
> having a homosexual relationship will not be threatening to his self-
> image, or to the images others have of him. But since nobody other
> than a direct witness can really know what happens in bed, there will
> always be a doubt connected to homosexual encounters, and, thereby,
> the risk that a man's masculinity may be perceived as impaired. This is
> a reason for treating such encounters with so much discretion. (206–7)

It is difficult to know, even under such a bipolar system as the one
laid out by Paz, where heterosexuality ends and where homosexuality
begins. Given that male-male relations, with male homosexual relations being but one manifestation, are so important in the achievement
of masculine identity in Paz's Mexico, this blurry boundary between
heterosexual and homosexual becomes important to understand.
Even Paz sensed the quandary when he wrote, "No sería difícil
percibir ... ciertas inclinaciones homosexuales" [It would not be difficult to perceive certain homosexual inclinations] in the Mexican
macho (*El laberinto* 74), and it is essential that all the vagaries and
variations regarding male homosexual practices, desires, and belief

systems be considered when broaching the topics of homosexuality or masculinity in Mexico.

Eve Sedgwick, in quite a distinct context, notes that there are competing models of homosexuality that coexist in the minds of many individuals, which she calls the "minoritizing and universalizing views of sexual definition" (*Epistemology* 86). Many seem to believe that homosexuality can be defined as the polar opposite of heterosexuality and that everyone is either one or the other (homosexuals are a distinct minority), and yet at the same time believe that heterosexuality is under constant threat of contamination by a homosexuality that lurks everywhere, just waiting to be activated or exposed (everyone is homosexual to some degree) (*Epistemology* 84–90). In Mexico, the heterosexual man who fucks another man is considered fully heterosexual, and yet, as Prieur points out:

> Through the representations of the homosexual and of the "manly" man a fundamental difference is created between two kinds of men who biologically speaking are the same; and when the homosexual and the mayate[28] are together, they usually cooperate to maintain this difference. But there is always the possibility that the other at any moment could turn out to be the same as oneself, since only an appearance separates the two. (253)

The two kinds of men are distinct, but only superficially so; boundaries are drawn, but not always trusted.

An alternative vision is that of Mexican homosexuality as a carnivalesque subversion of social convention, a rebellious destruction of (or at the very least vandalism against) the symbolic barriers defining gender and sexuality.[29] The carnivalesque atmosphere of the entire "41" event, along with Villaurrutia's image of homosexual sex not as an act that defines a man's identity but one in which identity is lost, and also the spirited aggressive queerness that Novo describes in his memoirs (*La estatua de sal*) all support this alternative notion of Mexican homosexuality not as a rigid imitation of heterosexual norms, but as an exuberant rejection of them.

While I do not purport to all out repudiate Paz's observations on Mexican ideological constructs of homosexuality, I aim to question the weight they have been given in academic discourse on Mexican homosexuality. I believe that Paz has brought to light just one of several visions of male homosexuality that have come into play at different historic moments and in different contexts of Mexican cultural history. While they fall outside the scope of this study, it is significant that none of the early novels that address the theme of male homosexuality (Paolo Po's *41, o un muchacho que soñaba en fantasmas* [1963], Miguel Barbachano Ponce's *El diario de José Toledo* [1964], Alberto X. Teruel's *Los inestables* [1968], José Ceballos Maldonado's *Después de todo* [1969], Luis Zapata's *El vampiro de la Colonia Roma* [1979], to name a few) are at all reminiscent of Paz's ideas, instead concerning themselves with such issues as pederasty, prostitution, homophobic violence, and social repression.[30]

The Homosocial and the Homosexual

Homosocial relations between men, then, are highly contentious. At the same time, they are essential to the construction of the Mexican nation. Doris Sommer has argued persuasively that the symbolic construction of nation as an imagined community occurred in nineteenth-century Latin America through romantic literature's use of heterosexual bonds (usually across differing social classes, regions, races, etc.) as an allegory for national integration. However, Sommer neglects to explore a parallel allegorical strategy for constructing nationhood: male homosocial bonding. In many cases, women's role in such symbolic nation building is little more than as an object of barter between men, and this very patriarchal version of forging a nation is a symptom of what Gayle Rubin has called "the traffic in women." Moreover, as Sedgwick has argued, "in any male-dominated society, there is a special relationship between male homosocial (*including* homosexual) desire and the structures for maintaining and transmitting patriarchal power." She adds, "this special relationship may take the form of ideological homophobia, ideological homosexuality, or some highly conflicted but intensively structured combination of the two" (*Between Men* 25). In the Mexican context, the impossibility of keeping male homosocial bonds free from homosexual connotations (even when they take the form of egregious ideological homophobia) makes this symbolic relationship enormously conflictive.

Masculine Paradox

In this way, notions of both Mexican masculinity and male homosexuality are riddled with paradox. Masculinity is achieved and bolstered through symbolic (or real) homosexual acts, which do not imply a homosexual identity. However, the fact that the positionality of the participants in such acts is unstable and always suspect, with the fucker always a hair's breadth away from becoming the fucked, implies that homosexuality is always lurking beneath the surface of this masculinity. Meanwhile, male homosexuality is equated with effeminacy. And this symbolic vision, which carries over into even contemporary discussions of corporeal homosexual acts between men, is based upon assumptions of exceptional rigidity. Male homosexuality is anal penetration and the roles played by men (top, bottom) must be fixed as male homosexual relations reinforce cultural definitions of gender and sexuality. And yet male homosexuality is also associated with carnival, orgies, an anything-goes libertinage that breaks down definitions of gender and sexuality.

Additionally, seduction theory, another historically popular idea in Mexican culture, implies a loss of sexual difference. A heterosexual is seduced by a homosexual into becoming more and more homosexual, more and more like his seducer. This danger is seen, for example, in Villarreal's *Pocho* when young Richard's father worries about his son hanging around with homosexuals. Degeneration theory provides another trope in which homosexuality is just one of many vices to which inferior classes of the human species are likely to succumb. A degenerate might easily become a serial rapist, a promiscuous satyr, a pederast, a child molester, or all of the above, with gender identity not necessarily being a factor at all. Castrejón's *Los 41* and other turn-of-the-century works often seem to operate under the premise that the sexual degeneration of homosexuals leads inevitably to the criminal and physical degeneration of society. Finally, the trope of narcissistic homosexuality explored in the writings of Xavier Villaurrutia implies sameness on the part of homosexual partners. A wide variety of tropes of homosexuality appear in Mexican cultural production over the years, tropes that often contradict Paz. Mexican homosexual writers, in particular, appear singularly unwilling to conform to stereotypes, as homosexual poet Salvador Novo's nickname attests: "el más macho de los poetas jotos" [the most macho of queer poets] (Barrera López 40).

Similar paradoxes emerge when the paradigms of masculinity are crossed with notions of civilization and barbarity. The ideology of progress implies a cultural virility bound up in the technological and military superiority of a nation, but at the same time, progress leads to civilization, and in civilized society, men no longer need to work hard and become soft.[31] In Mexico, the rhetoric of race and class frequently intersects with that of gender in complicated ways. Blacks and *indios* are often portrayed as savage, almost like animals. As such, men of these races are at certain moments more masculine than their white counterparts for their brutishly aggressive nature and raw sexuality, and at others less masculine for their state of subordination and inferiority. Similarly, lower-class Mexicans are both less civilized (more brutishly masculine) and less powerful (more passively feminine) than upper-class Mexicans. The gendered rhetoric of race and class shifts and twists, sometimes within the same text, to suit the goals of the author. Contradictions, however, tend to go unnoticed. Gender, as a main element of the Mexican national *habitus,* goes unquestioned even as it becomes entangled in blatantly racist stereotypes.

Paradigms of Male Homosocial Bonding

While contradictions abound in the treatment of masculinity, there are several trends that show interesting developments over time. Chapter 1 treats the nineteenth century, an epoch in which liberal ideals of liberty, equality, and fraternity were guiding principals of the modern state, the era of Mexican independence from Spain in which national brotherhood came to symbolize national coherence. Mexico came to be an imagined community of Mexican brothers, of men. For this reason, the early nation-building novels of Mexico so frequently make use of male-male relations in their allegorizations of national integration.

However, I argue for going a step further, and looking at the erotics—in this case, the homoerotics—of nation-building. While homosocial relations do not necessarily point to homosexual relations (or even to homosexual desire), nor does the fact that homosexuality was not a concern in nineteenth-century Mexico mean that there was not an element of homoeroticism in the nation building literature of the era. Nor is it surprising that there is a consistent male homoerotics at work during the entire century.

From Lizardi to Altamirano, male homosocial bonding is the key allegory of national integration in literature. Furthermore, the national protagonists had to be in many cases not only physically strong, but also handsome and charismatic. The Mexican romantic heroes of nineteenth-century novels were frequently Herculean, well-built studs. It is only natural that such men should inspire a spark of erotic desire in their relationships with their countrymen. In fact, it is often just this homoerotic desire that solidifies the adhesive (to borrow Whitman's locution)[32] ties of patriarchy that bind the nation.

These canonical literary representations of Mexican masculinity dialogue with their contemporary texts by women such as Barragán de Toscano, non-Mexican visitors such as Calderón de la Barca, and border texts in which Mexican masculinity is represented in English for a U.S. audience (e.g. Ruiz de Burton's *The Squatter and the Don*). Interestingly, while many of the themes and assumptions regarding gender coincide in texts written by women and men, it is those produced by male authors that tend more to eroticize the masculine.

If homoerotics went unnoticed in nineteenth-century literature, effeminacy in men was a major worry throughout the century. But effeminacy was not linked to homosexuality until the turn of the century, and eroticized male bonding did not imply effeminacy—let alone homosexuality, a nonexistent concept—in those times. While in colonial times, certain acts (sodomy) had been seen as a problem, homoerotic desire in the nineteenth century went largely unnoticed. What all this means is that to today's readers, perhaps inclined to see the world in terms of straight and gay, there is an undeniably queer element to nineteenth-century Mexican literature and therefore also to early constructions of Mexicanness.

Around the turn of the century, when sexual scandals abroad, including the trials of Oscar Wilde, and the scandal of the 41 in Mexico made headlines, the homoerotics of male homosocial bonding became all too apparent, as is seen in chapter 2. Moreover, as homosexuality came to signify effeminacy in men, the civilizing, nation-building homosocial bonding of the nineteenth century took on new meaning.

It must be added that male homosocial bonding in the nineteenth century not only served to unify and civilize. Male bonding when not allied with civilizing projects such as education or national defense could be destructive. Bandits, pirates, gamblers, and other criminal types symbolize the barbaric side of male homosocial bonding, a side that is equally virile, equally erotic, and equally queer. Issues of social class did not quite entangle themselves with questions of masculinity yet. Upper-class men were *hombres de bien;* lower-class men were *muy hombres;* all were masculine, at least until century's end.

The turn of the century is the era of the government of Porfirio Díaz, an era of political and economic stability, but of literary change. After a very unstable nineteenth century, with numerous political assassinations and coups d'état, constant battles between liberals and conservatives, regional strife, indigenous uprisings, an invasion by the United States and occupation by France, Mexico at last was beginning to prosper under the leadership of Díaz. If the nineteenth century was a period of nation building, the turn of the century was one of national consolidation. And while its literature tended to focus less on explicitly national themes than in the past,[33] it did begin to reflect on and even criticize nineteenth-century assumptions regarding such key elements of the national *habitus* as race, class, gender, and sexuality.

Class tensions were a major inspiration for a growing discourse on crime at the time, a discourse appearing in literature, journalism, and scientific investigation. This criminal discourse focuses explicitly on a subject barely broached and certainly never directly confronted in earlier nineteenth-century literary production: male sexuality, including both savage and unbridled displays of heterosexuality and excessively refined and utterly perverse manifestations of a new Mexican institution, homosexuality.

Gender itself falls into crisis, as seen in the "intellectual hermaphrodism" of the protagonist of Nervo's *El donador de almas,* or in the biological hermaphrodism that surfaces in Roumagnac's scrutiny of Mexico City prison life. Similarly, Castrejón's novel and José Guadalupe Posada's engravings celebrating the "famous 41" ball bring the carnivalesque underworld of male transvestism and homosexuality to the forefront of the national imagination. The growing discourse on sexuality had come to equate effeminacy with homosexuality. Thus, while the barbaric masculinity of the lower classes maintained its macho cachet, upper-class masculinity and particularly upper-class male bonding tended to be seen as more and more suspect, more and more queer. And paradoxically, homosexuality was as barbaric as bestiality.

Let me add a caveat here. At no historic moment is there a monolithic discourse on Mexican masculinity. There is always a cacophony of often contradictory ideas in circulation, and this is particularly true at the turn of the century, a moment of change that generated a proliferation of discourse on gender and sexuality in Mexico and, as such, a moment of chaos. Many texts do not so much draw conclusions as raise questions. What is clear, however, is that there came to be a greater consciousness about class difference and sexuality in Mexico at this time.

Concerns with social class, race, and nation become more pronounced and more tightly interlinked with gender rhetoric after the revolution of the 1910s, as seen in chapter 3. Debates on virile literature spelled out ideas that were just being toyed with at the turn of the century. While bourgeois writers of the *porfiriato* had looked down on the barbarous masculinity of the lower-classes, the socialist and sometimes hyperbolically nationalist spirit in the milieu of Mexican letters following the "proletarian" revolution promoted a literature that glorified lower class masculinity and male homosocial bonding as prototypically Mexican. It likewise rejected civilized bourgeois masculinity as elitist, effeminate, patently homosexual, and decidedly un-Mexican.

In this period of often intense nationalism, debates on the virility of national literature contribute both to the discovery of Mariano

Azuela's *Los de abajo* and the subsequent advent of the novel of the revolution as a major literary genre, and also to the controversial and sometimes notorious rise to fame of a clique of writers who resist nationalist prescriptions of what Mexican writing and Mexican masculinity should be: the Contemporáneos. Chapter 3 focuses on both the "virile" literature of the revolution and the "effeminate" literature that opposed it. Ironically, as with the literature of the nineteenth century, the hypermasculine homophobic literature of the revolution turns out to be quite homoerotic in spite of itself. Meanwhile, the "literatura jota" [queer literature] of the maligned Contemporáneos poets turns out to be anything but anti-Mexican, in fact, fitting neatly into Mexican intellectual history as descendents not only of the queer *modernistas,* but also of the "straight" Ateneo de la Juventud, the anti-positivist intellectuals who were seen as the intelligentsia of the revolution and who would later play a major role in establishing postrevolutionary Mexico's cultural politics and institutions. While it was the Contemporáneos poets (including Villaurrutia and Novo, both open homosexuals, along with polemicist Jorge Cuesta, among others) who would lead mainstream Mexican literature, often against its will, in new directions with regard to discourse on gender and nation, minor writers of the age including several women (Garza, Enriqueta) and also science fiction and other pop genre writers (Eduardo Urzaiz, A. Izquierdo Albiñana —a woman writer herself) developed imaginative new scenarios in gender discourse, often going beyond even those proposed by the most daring *modernistas* in their treatment of controversial themes such as androgyny, transvestitism, and eugenics.

By the 1940s and '50s, the time period treated in chapter 4, male homosocial bonding as an institution had really become an impossibility. The ever threatening erotics of relations between men became more and more obvious as male relations of all kinds came to assume sexual overtones. Someone had to be the *chingado* and someone the *chingón.* All kinds of male-male interactions came to imply homosexual rape and a constant shuffling and reinforcing of hierarchies between men. Homophobia became a major guiding principal in Mexican culture.

Homosexuality was now seen as a barely erotic, utterly unaffectionate form of sexual violence that not only reinforced (or occasionally reversed) hierarchies, but also reinforced gender difference with one man, the *chingón,* always masculine and dominant, and another, the *chingado,* always subordinate and effeminate. The idea was to use male-male relations to *chingar* as much as possible to achieve an ever more pronounced masculinity, without becoming tainted with homosexuality, as only the *chingado* was made homosexual by homosexual contact. Ironically, this vision of homosexuality came from ostensibly heterosexual observers.

After the intense nationalism that reached its peak with the presidential term of Lázaro Cárdenas in the late 1930s, the next twenty or so years see the novel of the revolution play itself out in sometimes unexpected ways in novels such as Rojas González's *La negra Angustias* about a black revolutionary heroine. Mainstream novels such as Revueltas's *El luto humano* and Rulfo's *Pedro Páramo* play out the demise of the Mexican male homosocial, while early Chicano texts such as Villarreal's *Pocho* and John Rechy's *City of Night* continue to elaborate on the same obsessive themes (e.g., the proving and reinforcing of masculinity, the often hostile yet eroticized realm of the Mexican male homosocial) of their contemporaries in Mexico. And while the United States had been a monstrous and threatening northern other since independence, by the mid-twentieth century ever growing migration, tourism, and trade relations between the two countries made Yankee culture an ever more important opposing counterpoint to *lo mexicano.*

In addition, the growing body of literature by women writers and the increasingly complex representations of women in literature also brought about some important shifts in notions of gender. Of course these strands go back to at least the nineteenth century and can be seen particularly in the noncanonical works of early women writers, but not only there. Women—traditionally saintly mother/wife/virgins or sexy whores—by mid-century came to take on different roles, more active roles, and to assume more masculine traits. With cultural constructs of masculinity and femininity less essentially linked to biology, national gender stereotypes themselves came more and more into question.

The "national" aspect of these constructions becomes especially apparent in early border literature. Prerevolutionary Mexican culture remained a battleground between remnants of colonial ideology stressing racial purity and difference, and newer liberal ideologies of egalitarianism and *mestizaje* as the trope for national integration. After the revolution, the latter won out as José Vasconcelos promoted *mestizaje* as a global ideal. However, a competing ideology spelled out by Paz shows *mestizaje* to be an allegory for the conquest of indigenous Mesoamerica by Spanish invaders. In each case, Indians are denigrated if not excluded altogether from national culture as either too uncivilized to count as citizens or a mere phantasmatic reminder of a glorious nearly forgotten past. In gendered terms, indigenous Mexicans are passive, feminized. Real Mexican men are at first white *criollos,* and later *mestizos.*

Border texts define Mexicanness through cultural contrast with the United States. Interestingly, in the context of the U.S.-Mexican border, masculinity is again a focus, and the erotics of both idealized hypermasculinity and male homosocial bonding clearly come into play in the context of a Mexican masculinity that must define and assert itself not in terms of racial purity or *mestizaje,* but in terms of national difference and contemporary power struggles in North America. Once again, integration, that is, unification now across borders, is allegorized through male homosocial bonding. However, by the early 1960s, the erotics of such bonding cannot be ignored. Border culture is inevitably and unequivocally queer.

Conclusion

This study presents, then, a homoerotics of nation, a homoerotics that is specifically Mexican in this case, but one that always in its own local forms can be found in many other places. The queer slant to democracy of Walt Whitman and the heady virile erotics of *la literatura gauchesca* of Argentina[34] come immediately to mind. The hypermasculinity and intense male homosocial bonding common to national constructions inevitably produce an unintended homoerotics that often later engenders fierce homophobia. When the homoerotics of typical virile national constructions is sensed, homophobia in the national arena is to be expected. A deconstruction of national stereotypes of gender and sexuality and an incisive incursion into the national *habitus* are meant to combat and undo whatever racism, sexism, and homophobia have engrained themselves in the national psyche over time.

Los hijos de la Chingada, Mexican men, according to one stereotype, experienced from 1810 to the early 1960s a roller coaster of trials and tribulations. One crisis moment occurred in 1901 when the 41 were being repudiated as "pestilent sewage." Meanwhile, other Mexican men were being reviled for just the opposite, for being too manly, with the "macho bravo" not being a valiant he-man, but a "fiera hambrienta" [ravenous beast] (Urbina, *Crónicas* 4–5).

This genealogy of Mexican masculinities is meant to debunk stereotypes and reveal the degree to which gender is employed rhetorically in ways that twist and pull *los hijos de la Chingada* until they are mangled. The goal here is to pull some key bricks out of their labyrinth of solitude and let these guys escape. We have reached the centenary of the ball of the famous 41. Let the party begin.

Chapter 1

Early Paradoxes of Masculinity and Male Homosocial Bonding
The Nineteenth Century

Notions of Masculinity and Male Sexuality in the Early Years of Independence: *El Periquillo Sarniento* and *Costumbrismo*

Building a Virile Mexico

In 1868 when Ignacio Ramírez complained about the "hermaphrodite literature" that was contaminating national expression[1] in Mexico, his rhetorical employment of gendered terms to allude to a flaw in what he called "the patriotic mission" of literature is not as odd as it might seem. Isn't the very word "patria" [fatherland] a lexical hermaphrodite in Spanish ("patria" from *pater*, "father," but a feminine father, "*la* patria"—often "la madre patria" [the mother fatherland]) (Franco, *Plotting Women* 79)? In fact, gender is employed with great frequency in the Mexican literature of the nineteenth century, allegorically—and sometimes rather queerly—in numerous attempts at forging a notion of Mexico as an autonomous nation and a distinctive culture. In a country whose most important national icons were female (the Virgin of Guadalupe, symbol of Mexican independence; la Malinche, emblem of the conquest and *mestizaje*), it was necessary to establish a truly virile culture in the newly independent Mexico. Mexico could not regress to its colonial status as a subjugated, morally and physically weak, even effeminate territory. In fact, there was a struggle throughout the nineteenth century to assert and sustain, through literature, an image of Mexico as virile.

At first glance there is one aspect of nineteenth-century Mexico's gender rhetoric that is particularly striking today: the utter lack of references to sexuality. It might seem strange at first because recent sociological investigations on sexuality in Mexico insist that gender in Mexico is defined through sexuality and vice versa (e.g., effeminate men *are* homosexual, and homosexuals have to be, by tautology, effeminate men).[2] It is also notable when we take into account the vitriolic colonial rhetoric on the sodomy of native Mexicans a few centuries earlier, which seems to have disappeared from Mexican gender discourse in the nineteenth century.[3] The term "homosexuality"—which appeared for the first time in Europe in the mid-nineteenth century and helped to enforce a stable definition of normative heterosexuality—did not yet exist in Mexican discourse. In Mexico, gender had no implications with regard to sexuality for practically the entire century; no one accused effeminate men of homosexuality and, similarly, the ideal of virility did not point to an essential heterosexuality, simply because such concepts did not exist.[4]

In those years, then, the ways of delimiting gender difference were not the same as those that have been utilized since Freud and European sexology arrived in Latin America. In *Astucia* by Luis Inclán—one of the most read novels in nineteenth-century Mexico and a book that, according to Salvador Novo, "ningún mexicano debería desconocer" [no Mexican should be unacquainted with] (*La vida...Manuel Ávila Camacho* 626)—to affirm sexual difference, the author resorts to crude biology (although not presenting it as an absolute). His hero—nicknamed Astucia and identified by Novo, in his introduction to the novel upon its rerelease in 1966, as "el arquetipo ideal del mexicano" [the ideal archetype of the Mexican male (xvi)—informs us, "porto calzones porque sé sostenerlos" [I wear breeches because I know how to hold them up] (71). The possession of a sizeable member makes masculinity possible, but a certain complementary masculine knowledge is required in order to realize manhood. However, nowhere is it implied that women are needed; heterosexual desire is not part of the formula. Furthermore, there exist beings dressed as men who presumably have men's bodies who, in fact, are not male, but who are by no means homosexual. At another moment, the same young hero worries that his friends will think that he is a "Mariquita con calzones, un amujerado" [Nelly in breeches, a womanized man] (8) because he cries upon saying goodbye to his father. Gender and not sexuality is clearly the issue. In that epoch when homosexuality was not spoken about, and not even the old demon sodomy was mentioned anymore, masculinity (or femininity) was defined not via sexual desire, but instead through other traits or behaviors such as bravery, stoicism, or sexual (specifically defined as neither homo- or hetero-) prowess.[5]

I do not claim that there was no norm of heterosexuality in the nineteenth century, but only that the heterosexual paradigms that can be identified at that time in Mexican culture are not precisely the same as the stereotypes that we know today and that are often utilized to define sexual difference (i.e., through the above mentioned tautology that equates effeminacy with homosexuality). Nineteenth-century heterosexuality is, in contrast, a more fluid sexuality in which heterosexual desire is assumed as a norm, but a norm that is not necessarily opposed to nor exclusive of homosexual desire. Male desire was assumed to be directed toward women, but this did not preclude male desire for other men. The latter form of desire, perhaps because it had in colonial times been so utterly shameful ("the nefarious vice"), had disappeared from Mexican discourse and remained unformulated in early independent Mexico. When political cartoonist Santiago Hernández satirized president Benito Juárez's unbridled ambition by portraying him kissing Sebastián Lerdo de Tejada on the lips, it did not unleash any sexual scandal even though the two men were unattached to women at the time; it is likely that the Mexican public did not know what to make of such an image.[6]

The former, male desire for women, whether shameful or not, presented more pressing social problems, and therefore needed to be regulated through marriage in order to maintain an orderly system of procreation and child rearing.

Foundational Heterosexuality

Doris Sommer, in her seminal work, *Foundational Fictions,* speaks of "national romance" as a nineteenth-century Latin American liter-ary genre in which there is a conspicuous pattern: heterosexual love relationships that challenge boundaries of class, race, or region to allegorically forge an idea of *patria,* of an imagined national commu-nity and shared national culture. I agree with Sommer (along with innumerable other critics)[7] that the literature of the nineteenth cen-tury played a fundamental role in the construction of a specifically national culture and a concretely Mexican ideology. And I agree that heterosexual romance often played an important symbolic role in na-tional discourse. Certainly most of Altamirano's works, as well as those of Payno and Riva Palacio, to name but a few, rely on the al-legorical paradigm of heterosexual romance to construct an image of a unified, or unifying, nation. However, in the case of Mexico, many of the novels most pivotal to nation-building discourse do not make significant use of the heterosexual romance paradigm. For example, while it predates the texts of Sommer's study, the picaresque foun-dational fiction, *El Periquillo Sarniento,* along with the later rural picaresque adventure *Astucia,* despite inevitable subplots of hetero-sexual romance, are simply too focused on the world of men to fit Sommer's schema. This is clearly the case in other parts of Latin Amer-ica as well (the *gauchesco* tradition in Argentina comes immediately to mind).[8] Novels of heterosexual romance are examples of but one rhetorical strategy of nation building employed in nineteenth-century Latin American fiction. While gender, particularly masculinity, was uniformly a key term in this discourse, notions of nation were not constructed only through allegories of male-female bonding.

Mary Louise Pratt argues convincingly of "how particularly limited and repressive the bourgeois republican era has been in producing and imagining women as historical, political, and cultural subjects" (48–49). She goes on, "women inhabitants of modern nations were not imagined as intrinsically possessing the rights of citizens; rather, their value was specifically attached to (and implicitly conditional on) their reproductive capacity" (51). For this reason, heterosexual bonds may have been invoked as national allegories, but always with the greatest care as the nation they symbolically produced could not reproduce itself haphazardly. Even if women were used to cement bonds across lines of race, class, religion, political party, etc., it was the relationships between men that really mattered because only men were citizens. Male homosocial bonding, with or without women as intermediaries, is the major means of allegorizing national integration in nineteenth-century Mexican literature. It is the national *fraternité* that men would aspire to or identify with as they began to conceptualize the imagined community of Mexico.

This is not to say that women were not part of the equation. As nineteenth-century authors dating from Lizardi were aware, women as well as men read. And women's role as mothers was of great importance to national projects.[9] For this reason, whether or not they were to allegorize national integration, women's relations with men were to remain of great concern in Mexican literature for the entire century. However, it was the adhesiveness of male homosocial bonding through which authors from Lizardi to Altamirano forged the nation.

Heterosexual Panic

First, let us look at the myth that heterosexuality represented an ideal in nineteenth-century Mexican culture. Desire between men and women in the literature of the era, as a matter of fact, was not an ideal. Heterosexual restraint may have been an ideal, but heterosexual desire represented the most pernicious of dangers. Heterosexuality was taken for granted, but it was feared as a necessary evil and regulated as a sinister force, a threat to civilization itself. While sex between men (or between women) lacked a name and apparently did not challenge society with any social risk, heterosexual desire threatened all kinds of disruption.[10] Heterosexual desire could contaminate racial purity, blur barriers of social class, corrupt virgins, destroy the institution of matrimony by means of adultery, incite the sin of incest, or even engender the infamy of pregnancy out of wedlock. Women had to be protected from the "dangerous [male] seducer," from the "bestial sensualism" of men, to borrow a few phrases from Altamirano—in *Clemencia* (6) and *El Zarco* (20), respectively.

In fact, this peril of heterosexuality has a rather lengthy history, as Lizardi reminds us in *La Quijotita y su prima:* "La primera asociación que hubo en el mundo fue de dos individuos, Adán y Eva, y ya vemos lo que sucedió. El primer hombre acaso no hubiera prevaricado si la mujer primera no le hubiera seducido" [The first association that came to pass in the world was that of two individuals, Adam and Eve, and we already know what happened there. The first man might not have erred had the first woman not seduced him] (95). Lizardi's point of view clearly differs from Altamirano's in that the danger is not the man, but the woman; however it is still the desire between the sexes that imperils civilized society.

As José T. de Cuéllar puts it in his 1890 novel *Los mariditos,* "¿No es acaso la misión de la especie humana sobre la tierra, crecer y multiplicarse?... el creced and multiplicaos, obedecido literalmente, es para las bestias de los desiertos" [Is it not by chance the mission of the human species to grow and multiply?... grow and multiply, obeyed literally, is for the beasts of the deserts] (97). Heterosexual desire is not part of civilized society, but instead is a barbarous force that society must attempt to civilize.

Bonds of matrimony (heterosexuality's civilized form), moreover, do not last, not because of competing homosexual relations, but because of the inconsistency of women (or sometimes men, depending on who is making the argument), i.e., because of the inadequacy of heterosexual desire in maintaining its own institutions. According to Cuéllar in his earlier *Historia de Chucho el Ninfo* (1871), "La gravísima cuestión de la felicidad doméstica, en la que tanta parte tiene la mujer, suele ser arrojada por ésta al basurero en un tumbo de dados. La falta de prudencia en la mujer, está convirtiendo todos los días los nidos de palomas en pequeños infiernos" [The very serious issue of domestic happiness, for which women have so much responsibility, is often thrown in the trash by these same women with a toss of the dice. The lack of prudence in women turns doves' nests into little hells on a daily basis] (220).[11]

Thus the institutions that promote heterosexuality and attempt to civilize it are under constant threat from heterosexuality itself, which is not a monogamous force, at least in some women,[12] as we see above, nor in men, as Payno makes clear in "Memorias sobre el matrimonio": "el matrimonio es la tumba del amor.... Una querida la divinizamos, la vemos como un ángel, mientras en una mujer propia vamos descubriendo diariamente multitud de pequeñas humanidades que arrancan hoja por hoja las flores de la ilusión" [marriage is love's tomb.... A mistress we make into a divinity, we see her as an angel, while in our own woman, day after day, we discover a multitude of small human foibles that pluck, petal by petal, the flowers of the illusion] (117). The savage force of heterosexual desire is contained by the civilizing structure of marriage, which is supported, precariously, by the illusion of heterosexual romance. A nation founded upon heterosexual romance, as Sommer proposes, would have been quite distressing to the major authors of nineteenth-century Mexico.

Cuéllar frets a great deal about the perils of heterosexuality, dedicating an entire book to his anxieties about men who lose their youth and wreck families by marrying too young in *Los mariditos*. In it, he traces historical roots of heterosexual paranoia: "El amor precisamente, y sus escándalos, fue el que hizo exclamar a nuestros antepasados: *entre santa y santo pared de calicanto,* y comenzaron a levantar paredes entre santas y santos... se instituyó el noviazgo de balcón, la prohibición de aprender a escribir, y el retraimiento exagerado y malicioso entre uno y otro sexo" [It was precisely love, and its scandals, that made our ancestors exclaim: *between saintly young boys and girls must go a big stone wall,* and they began building walls between saintly young boys and girls... balcony courtship, the prohibition on learning to write, and the exaggerated and malicious aloofness between the sexes were instituted] (15).

Cuéllar goes on to blame the errors of heterosexuality in part on the inadequacy of homosocial bonding in Mexico:

En México le faltan al pollo dos elementos indispensables en la formación del hombre: la escuela social y la educación varonil. Le falta en relación con los hombres, el club, los ejercicios atléticos y los entretenimientos varoniles; y en relación con el bello sexo, el contacto sincero y cordial, a que se llega en todas partes por el refinamiento de las costumbres. Por eso el pollo no sabe resistir el atractivo engañoso de la mujer.

In Mexico, lads lack two elements indispensable in the education of a man: social schooling and manly instruction. In terms of their relationships with men they lack social clubs, athletic exercise, and masculine entertainment; and in terms of their relations with the fair sex, they lack sincere and cordial contact, which is achieved everywhere through refinement in customs. For this reason, the young lad does not know how to resist the deceptive attractions of the woman. (15)

Civilized heterosexuality in men, for Cuéllar, benefits from intensive and exclusively masculine social activities. It would seem that more athletic contact with other men would raise men to a loftier level of cultivation and erudition appropriate for domesticated heterosexuality.

Greek Models of Heterosexuality

Ironically, Cuéllar, along with a number of Mexican authors of the period, appeals to the Greeks and Spartans as better examples of how to manage ties between men and women. Cuéllar contrasts Spartan "models" with the hapless Mexican *mariditos* [little husbands] (98–99). Ramírez, in that essay ("Poesía erótica") in which he complains of a literary hermaphroditism—"que confunde al mismo tiempo los sexos y el lenguaje" [which simultaneously confuses the sexes and language] (480)—in Mexican romantic literature, defends a well-defined heterosexuality in which men are "active" and women "passive." Yet for him, this paradigm is not self-perpetuating; it needs to be watched over assiduously to prevent the crucial gender barriers from breaking down. The queerest irony in the essay comes up when Ramírez, intending to unveil a model of moral (i.e., not hermaphrodite) literature, furnishes the example of Sappho.[13]

Years later, the example of the Spartans (and their institutionalized intergenerational homosexual pedagogy) is utilized in an argument quite different from that of Ramírez in a polemical book that was avidly read in Mexico, André Gide's *Corydon*. Gide's thesis quite possibly follows from the appendix to Arthur Schopenhauer's chapter on the metaphysics of sexual love in *The World as Will and Representation*, a book contemporary with Ramírez's essay. The system proposed by Gide—in which mature male mentors, bored with their wives, maintain pedagogical and sexual relations with young men who are unable to control their sexual impulses but who are not yet ready to marry women—would quite easily resolve the problem of Cuéllar's *mariditos,* along with the social ills of prostitution, adultery, premarital sex, etc.

This Greek world of male bonding, which is not necessarily homosexual but rather fraternal, with its male homosocial spaces and institutions and exclusion of women from public life, also recalls Mexican literature of the nineteenth century. From bands of robbers (*Los bandidos del Río Frío, Astucia, El Zarco*) to pirates (*Los piratas del Golfo* by Riva Palacio) to soldiers (*El fistol del diablo* by Payno) to governmental institutions (*El fistol, El Zarco, Los bandidos,* etc.) to simple friendships (*El fistol, El Periquillo Sarniento, Astucia, Clemencia*), in nearly every *costumbrista* or nationalist novel of nineteenth-century Mexico, some purely male homosocial group stands out.

Fraternity and National Culture

Beyond the usual arguments of nation building being an enterprise of, by, and for men, in the case of nineteenth-century Mexico, formalized all-male cultural associations and fraternities played a key role in constructing national culture. As Cuéllar urges, " 'Debemos asociarnos, fraternizar y trabajar con fruto en una empresa noble y grande': la creación de la literatura nacional" ["we must associate, fraternize, and work fruitfully in a grand and noble enterprise": the creating of national literature] (quoted in Schneider, *Ruptura* 79). In fact, during the years following the French occupation, José Luis Martínez reports that there were at least 124 cultural fraternities in Mexico, five times more than in the earlier part of the century (40).[14]

Ramírez, in a speech at a meeting of one such association, recited a poem convoking the fraternal gathering of men, greeting each other with "amorosas manos que se estrechan ardiendo en impaciencia" [amorous hands that grasp each other, burning with impatience] (*Obras* 4) and passionate embraces. He promulgates an effusively affectionate brand of brotherly fervor as "la primera entre las esperanzas e ilusiones que cultivan los siglos y las naciones" [the foremost of

hopes and dreams cultivated by centuries and nations] (5),[15] calling to
mind the religious devotion that the pirates of the Gulf of Mexico (in
Vicente Riva Palacio's novel) feel for their leader, Juan Morgan: "Juan
Morgan era más que el jefe de aquellos hombres, era su Mesías" [Juan
Morgan was more than the boss of those men, he was their Messiah]
(vol. 1, 37). Intellectuals such as Ramírez idealized male bonding as
key to nation building, and his followers such as Riva Palacio translated this national ideal into their literature. And while *Los piratas del
Golfo* may not have been strictly a national romance,[16] as we shall
see it is but one example of many in nineteenth-century Mexican literature that places greater emphasis on male homosocial bonding than
on heterosexual love.

In *Los piratas,* the hero, Brazo de Acero, has to choose between
heterosexual love (marriage to the lovely Julia) and homosocial devotion in the form of a life shared with the pirates and the charismatic
Juan Morgan. "Durmió un rato, y soño que Julia y Morgan echaban
suertes sobre su corazón. Despertó sobresaltado y volvió a la reali-
dad. Era que el pirata había ganado la partida" [He went to sleep for
a little while, and dreamed that Julia and Morgan were casting competing spells over his heart. He awoke, shaken, and returned to reality.
The pirate had won the contest] (vol. 1, 73). Needless to say, Brazo
de Acero became a pirate. While Riva Palacio may not have been
aware of what B. R. Burg calls "[t]he predominance of homosexual
methods of sexual expression" among colonial era pirates (xxxix), in
Mexico, the battle between homosocial camaraderie and heterosexual
romance was being won by the former.

It is interesting to note that it is the same Riva Palacio who shows
that literature can be sexed, though not in a biologically determined
way. Hélène Cixous would have been quite disappointed to learn that
the much admired poetess Rosa Espino—about whom it was said:
"Para escribir como Rosa Espino, se necesita tener alma de mujer
y de mujer virgen. Esa ternura y ese sentimiento no los expresa así
jamás un hombre" [To write like Rosa Espino, it is necessary to have
the soul of a woman, and of a virgin. Such tenderness and sentiment
could never be expressed by a man]—was, in actuality, General Riva

Palacio demonstrating what Lilia Granillo calls "cierto afán travesti literario" [a certain transvestite literary ardor] ("Las tretas" 90–91).[17]

The Boys of Costumbrismo

Still, it was not the authors of Mexican literature (including literary transvestites such as Riva Palacio) who provided the models of gender in national discourse, but the characters they created in their foundational fictions. Another important author who favored the homosocial over the heterosexual was Payno (although his endlessly complex plots make ample use of both), master of the *novela folletinesca* [novel published in installments]. For example, the amusing plot of *El fistol del diablo* (with its dashing and ambivalently evil devil) begins at a party where, after meeting two attractive women, the hero, Arturo, finds himself pursued by another suitor of one of the women. His romantic rival quickly proclaims, "Yo detesto a usted con toda mi alma" [I detest you with all my soul], and challenges Arturo to a duel. The second man, a military captain named Manuel, strikes fear into Arturo with his apparent passion and volatility, but it turns out that his fierce hatred is not to last for very long; during the duel, he suddenly changes his attitude and decides that Arturo is to be his "best friend," an invitation that Arturo accepts without hesitation. Manuel unexpectedly offers to confess to him his most intimate secrets: "Por ahora...nos iremos al *Progreso* a comer y a beber una copa de champaña" [For now...let's go to the *Progreso* to eat and drink a glass of champagne] (37). And with a casual toast, their fraternal friendship is sealed and goes on to last the entire book. Arturo's (and in a parallel form, Manuel's) quest for heterosexual love remains out of his grasp for much of the novel while his affectionate bonding with Manuel is what holds its long, messy, and always lively plot together. Meanwhile, the two men, one a spoiled civilian, educated in Europe, who nonetheless shows himself to be valiantly patriotic when the occasion arises, the other a tough and swarthy military man, bonded in a friendship, "representa[n] perfectamente el carácter mexicano" [perfectly represent the Mexican character] (297), and their Mexicanness is sealed when they take up arms in the war against the

United States in the last part of the book. In this case there is no obvious eroticism. However, it is queer that their homosocial bonding turns out to run much deeper than the heterosexual bonds that permitted it to occur in the first place. Their feelings toward the various female protagonists are also strong, but as honorable men, they would never dare seek the level of personal intimacy with a woman that they cultivate in their friendships.

Another queer example of male bonding occurs in Florencio M. del Castillo's 1854 novel *Hermana de los ángeles*. A bizarre plot full of numerous intersecting love triangles centers on the relationship of Manuel and Rafaela (and Lorenzo who queerly completes their *ménage à trois:* "eran una joven y dos hombres, quienes... formaban una sola familia" [they were a young woman and two men who... formed a single family] [21]). The two protagonists, born in the first years of Mexico's independence, were raised both as brother and sister and as a queer means of homosexual procreation.

Their fathers had been best friends since childhood: "vivían unidos como hermanos, con esa amistad que llega a convertirse en un lazo de sangre" [they lived united like brothers, with that kind of friendship that manages to be transformed into a blood bond] (32). Nowadays the exchange of bodily fluids that the term "blood bond" might imply is decidedly on the queer side, and the heterosexual development of these two blood brothers only supports this impression: "se querían de tal modo, que cuando el primero se casó, el segundo formó la resolución de hacer lo mismo para que entre sus hijos sobreviviera y continuase su fraternidad" [they loved each other to the point that when one of them married, the other resolved to do the same so that among their children their brotherhood could survive and endure] (32). Their adventures into heterosexuality prove fruitful; the son of one "brother" (Manuel) and the daughter of the other (Rafaelita) ultimately fall in love and marry. Their marriage can be read as a political allegory of early independent Mexico with Manuel, a musician, symbolizing liberal cultural ideals and Rafaelita, his very spiritual wife, representing conservative Catholic morality. However, the fact that Manuel dies without fathering a child with Rafaelita indicates the ultimate failure in the procreative efforts of their fathers.

Meanwhile, the queer spirit of the original brotherhood lives on as Manuel is not satisfied by Rafaelita alone. The narrator comments at one point that "el verdadero amor no es ese sentimiento a que el mundo da ese nombre, porque las almas no tienen sexo" [true love is not that sentiment to which the world gives that name, because souls have no sex] (44). Sure enough, soon after marrying, Manuel takes after his father in finding himself attracted to a young melancholic man named Lorenzo: "¿La causa?—No sabré decírosla porque las leyes de la simpatía son oscuras y desconocidas" [The cause?—I do not know how to put it into words because the laws of affection are murky and unknown] (51). Of course the narrator is unable to identify the cause of attraction between men since there was no concept of such an attraction in nineteenth-century Mexico, even though it seems that such attraction pervades its literature. The fact that "entre Manuel y Lorenzo no tardó mucho en desarrollarse una amistad verdaderamente fraternal" [between Manuel and Lorenzo there was little delay in developing a truly fraternal friendship] (51) is perhaps more consistent with carrying on the spirit of his father than his marriage with Rafaelita. And later, after a series of amorous conflicts leads to the deaths of Lorenzo (in a duel) and Rafaelita (of a broken heart), one wonders whether Manuel, should he love again, will choose a woman or another man.

Such heterosexuality, which seems to be valid only "between men," recalls Eve Sedgwick's readings in her book of the same title. Once again, it is male homosocial desire that dominates. However, as Sedgwick makes clear, such homosocial bonding is never perfectly distinct from homosexual bonding. It is never quite clear where to draw the line between male-male relationships that are purely social, and those that contain an element (whether acted upon or not) of homosexual desire.

In Cuéllar's *Los mariditos,* friendship reaches an even more ardent level. A future *maridito*, Ernesto, after a quarrel with his fiancée, Rebeca, ends up in a *cantina* in the company of an immoderately amicable shoemaker "que estaba...dispuesto a todo" [who was...ready for anything] in an atmosphere presided over by "el mofletudo Baco" [chubby-cheeked Bacchus]:

El alcohol que tiene la rara virtud de torcer, sin arte, las clavi-
jas del alma, pone en inusitada actividad algunas facultades, muy
especialmente las del amor.

Por medio de esta discordancia, el borracho suele ser la criatura
más amorosa del mundo. Todas las facultades afectivas del zapatero se
consagraron a Ernesto; se sentía ardiendo de amor por él, queriendo a
toda costa probarle su cariño y su amistad.

Llevaba bastante dinero en los bolsillos; de manera que Dios los crió
y el diablo los juntó aquella noche hasta la madrugada del día siguiente.

Alcohol, which has the rare virtue of artlessly twisting the pegs of the
soul, casts certain faculties into uncommon animation, especially those
of love.

By means of this discordance, a drunk tends to be the most amorous
creature in the world. All the faculties of affection of the shoemaker
were devoted to Ernesto; he felt himself burning with love for him,
desiring at all costs to prove his affection and friendship to him.

He had plenty of money in his pockets; so God created them and
the devil joined them that night until the wee hours of the following
day. (52)

We might ask in vain just how "the devil joined" two drunken guys,
"ready for anything," that night. But what we do observe most clearly
is that the amorous ardor between Ernesto and Rebeca never reaches
such levels; despite the danger of which Cuéllar warns us with respect to heterosexual desire, for Ernesto, it is the love between men
that leads to passion, albeit a fleeting one. It is also curious that
Ernesto's night of "los funestos aturdimientos de la crápula" [the
baneful bewilderment of debauchery] (52) occurs not only following that brief altercation with Rebeca, but also very soon after his
definitive split with his "amigo predilecto" (favorite friend), a young
German haberdasher, after an argument about Ernesto's marriage at
the local swimming pool where they met every Sunday. The young
German reappears only at the end of the novel as a device in the narrator's preachy concluding rhetoric regarding the dangers faced by men
who marry too young. He continues swimming alone in Ernesto's absence, and one can only conclude that Ernesto would have been better
off having never married Rebeca (who deceived him for money and

led him to his tragic end, incarceration), and instead continuing his former life of idyllic Sundays swimming with his loyal blond buddy.

Los Hermanos de la Hoja: Homoerotic Rites of Virility

Interestingly, it is the novel that is perhaps the most masculine (in terms of its idealized homosocial milieu) of the century, *Astucia,* that presents us with the queerest scenes of homosocial ambiance.[18] For example, in a rite of initiation in which the young Astucia (Lorenzo) enters the group called "los hermanos de la hoja" [the brothers of the (tobacco) leaf],[19] a struggle occurs that can only adequately be described as homoerotic:

> —Entonces —dijo Pepe a sus compañeros a la vez que les hizo una seña muy significativa— le quitaremos sus pistolas. Y al instante todos se le abalanzaron, cual si fueran hambrientos lobos sobre su presa; al oír Lorenzo aquella amenaza, desenganchó al momento los trabucos y trató de cubrir su espalda, defendiéndolos vigorosamente. Ruda y tenaz fue la lucha, pero mucho más la resistencia; pues sirviéndole a Lorenzo sus fuerzas hercúleas, sólo a empellones se los quitaba de encima, llevándose ellos entre sus manos lo que podían agarrar, hasta que dejándolo casi en cueros y convencidos de su energía, pujanza y sobre todo sangre fría, dijo Pepe lleno de sudor y jadeando de fatiga:
> —¡Basta¡— A su voz todos se pararon; y Lorenzo, con toda la ropa hecha pedazos, con mucha tranquilidad volvió a engancharse los trabucos, se limpió la frente y se cruzó de brazos sin hablar una palabra.

"So," Pepe told his companions while he gave them a very significant signal, "let's get his pistols off him." And at that instant they all threw themselves upon him, as if they were starving wolves leaping on their prey; upon hearing the threat, Lorenzo immediately unfastened his guns and tried to cover his back, defending them vigorously. Rough and tenacious was the battle, but only by shoving did he get them off of him, with them grabbing whatever they could get their hands on, to the point of leaving him practically naked; and now convinced of his energy, might, and above all sang-froid, Pepe, all sweaty and panting with fatigue said:
"Enough!" At the sound of his voice, everyone halted; and Lorenzo, with all his clothes torn to pieces, putting away his guns with complete tranquility, wiped his brow and crossed his arms without speaking a word. (82–83)

In what sort of rite do men turn into "starving wolves" to strip the clothes off their new mate? Perhaps this intimate hands-on initiation rite is called for in this case because young Astucia is about to be named leader of the group. On the other hand, according to David Gilmore's cross-cultural study on masculinity, it is not necessarily unknown for rites of passage into manhood to have a sexual or even homosexual component.[20]

After reading of this rather erotic initiation rite, it is not very surprising to learn that the same *hermanos de la hoja* punish their enemies in another scene by pulling down their pants and spanking them (339). Nor should it shock us when the incarcerated Astucia, his cell infested with bugs and reeking of "filth," decides to strip off his clothes (like his cellmates, "ocho o diez infelices que me parecieron demonios, ... casi desnudos" [eight or ten wretched guys who looked like demons ... all practically naked]) (274) and remain naked until they release him. This last episode, with its homosocial nudity in jail, in fact, is practically a commonplace in the literature of the century, as we will see when we look at *El Periquillo Sarniento*.

El Periquillo Sarniento, Filthy and Disgusting Embryo of Narrativity

El Periquillo Sarniento [The Itching Parrot] is known as the first Latin American novel and widely recognized for its role in the construction of an imagined national community in Mexico;[21] Sonia Marta Mora Escalante calls it "el embrión de toda narratividad decimonónica y, más allá de ella, la ventana abierta a la cultura hispanoamericana posterior" [the embryo of all nineteenth-century narrativity and, beyond that, a window opened to all subsequent Hispanoamerican culture] (13–14). The novel's uniquely Mexican character is seen not only in the settings, the types of characters, and the local customs, it is manifest in the novel's language, its local slang. Fernández de Lizardi, a journalist who wrote novels only when he became frustrated at the censorship of his newspaper and pamphlets,[22] did not so much strive to produce high literature as to attract a broad readership. As Jean Franco puts it, "The possibility of teaching the masses under the guise of entertainment was the motive that inspired Lizardi to write *The Itching Parrot*" (*Critical Passions* 484).

This motive also explains the "vulgarity" of Lizardi's language and subject matter. Luis Urbina finds that while "en ninguna página... llega a ser inmoral; en bastantes... es sucio hasta el asco" [on no page... does he actually become immoral; on many... he is filthy to the point of being disgusting] (*La vida literaria* 126). Still, his critics usually admit that "si hubiese usado otro [estilo], ni el pueblo le habría comprendido también, ni habría podido retratar fielmente las escenas de la vida mexicana" [if he had used another style, neither would the public have understood him as well, nor would he have been able to faithfully portray scenes of Mexican life] (Altamirano, *La literatura nacional* 42). Moreover, it is precisely Lizardi's mix of vulgar and "correct" language that makes the novel truly national in an Andersonian sense, i.e., it helps to forge an imagined community. Nancy Vogeley describes Lizardi's use of "plain style as well as the bits and pieces of snobbish usage, garbled speech, argot and jargon of the *Periquillo*'s characters" as follows: "In presenting his reader with a kind of linguistic union in the body of the text, Lizardi offers psychological solace in the suggestion that political harmony may also be possible" ("Defining" 789).

It is just this "vulgar" aspect to Lizardi, then, that makes the novel so important nationally, and additionally makes it vital and "hirsuto" [hirsute] as Agustín Yáñez put it in 1940 ("Estudio preliminar" xxxvvi). The application of a signifier of masculinity (*hirsuto*) to the novel makes sense in the context in which Yáñez wrote, that of a "virile" literary nationalism that will be discussed in detail later. Still, the term is also fitting in a way that Yáñez did not intend: to refer to the very masculine focus of the novel.

Along with *Los bandidos del Río Frío, Los piratas del Golfo, Astucia,* and *El Zarco, El Periquillo* focuses much less significance on heterosexual relations than on fraternal friendships and pedagogical bonds between men: in fact, its main character is a model of Mexicanness, a distinctively male Mexicanness. El Periquillo Sarniento, nickname of Pedro Sarmiento, recounts his life from his childhood and errant ("perverted," as he often puts it) youth until his ultimate moral reform several decades later. At each step of his life, the influence of his male relatives, friends, teachers, and employers is abundantly demonstrated while only occasionally does a woman of any significance appear in his life. Let us examine how gender functions in the Mexican vision of Lizardi, "el Pensador Mexicano" [the Mexican thinker].

The story commences with a description of the early childhood of *el Periquillo* under the title, "Mi patria, padres, nacimiento y primera educación" [My fatherland, parents, birth and early education] (20). The priority, as we see, is given to the fatherland, but the narrator speaks little of it while worrying a great deal about the last item mentioned, his education, which he finds not to have been sufficiently masculine, at least in terms of the instruction he received at home. He first criticizes his aunts, grandmothers, and, as he puts it, "otras viejas del antiguo cuño" [other old women of the old fashioned mold], for having taught him "superstitious paganism" such as the use of deers' eyes or alligators' fangs as charms (21). Then he vehemently reproaches his mother for having hired a wet nurse to suckle him "porque es una cosa que escandaliza a la naturaleza" [because it is something that is a scandal to nature] (22).[23] But he reserves his greatest ire for his father for having allowed his well-intentioned but "indulgent" and "extravagant" mother to take on too big a role in his education. As he says, "me pervertía más mi madre; y mi padre tenía que ceder a su impertinente cariño. ¡Qué mal hacen los hombres que se dejan dominar de sus mujeres, especialmente acerca de la crianza o educación de sus hijos!" [my mother perverted me more; my father had to cede to her impertinent tenderness. What harm men do when they let themselves be dominated by their wives, especially when it comes to the education of their sons!] (25).

The Mysterious Ecstasies of Male Bonding

The narrator, the mature Pedro Sarmiento, has much to say about the education of his young alter ego, el Periquillo Sarniento. Of note is the value he attributes to his various homosocial learning relationships, whether they take place in schools with his teachers, at work with

his "amos" ["bosses," or literally, "masters"], on the street with his
buddies, or in the homes of his various mentors. In fact, the relationships between older or more experienced men (i.e., father figures) and
the younger Periquillo pervade the novel and create a sense of the paternal that goes beyond the familial and becomes national. As Kemy
Oyarzún puts it, "Queda configurado el paso de lo paterno (biológico,
individual y concreto) a lo patriarcal (ordenamiento social, colectivo
y abstracto)" [The move from the paternal (biological, individual, and
concrete) to the patriarchal (social, collective, and abstract order) is
thusly configured] (33).

The nexus between these masters and apprentices that lead the
young Periquillo through a wide variety of trades and social classes
and diverse regions of the country and even the world have nothing to
do with heterosexual romance. The narrator very clearly demonstrates
that he indeed experiences bonds of love, but of love between men,
love that we might label fraternal or homosocial, a noble love that
manifests itself in shared adventures, horseplay, intimacies, embraces,
devotions, and even "éxtasis misteriosos" [mysterious ecstasies] (532),
as he overzealously puts it (in a burst of enthusiasm upon a chance
meeting with an admired acquaintance), without worrying about the
contagion of perverse homosexuality that was to arrive in Mexico by
the turn of the century.

Love first comes to el Periquillo at school. While his bad teachers appear only briefly and exist mainly through their attitudes and
actions, the first good teacher is the only one who is embodied as a
physical figure with a body ("un cuerpo delgado" [a thin body]), aesthetic taste ("vestía decente, al uso del día y con mucha limpieza" [he
dressed decently, according to the style of the day, and very cleanly"]),
a face ("su cara manifestaba la dulzura de su corazón" [his face manifested the sweetness of his heart]), and the appearance of having
been "nacido para dirigir la juventud en sus primeros años" [born to
instruct youngsters in their early years] (35). In 1816, when Schopenhauer's aforementioned essay proposing Greek-style intergenerational
homosexual pedagogy had not yet appeared, we see how the lack of
a discourse on homosexuality permits the following on the part of
young Pedro's tutor:

"Conque si unas avecitas no necesitan azote para aprender, un niño como tú, ¿cómo lo habrá menester...? ¡Jesús...!, ni pensarlo. ¿Qué dices? ¿Me engaño? ¿Me amarás? ¿Harás lo que te mande?"

—Sí, señor— le dije todo enternecido y le besé la mano, enamorado de su dulce genio. Él entonces me abrazó, me llevó a su recámara, me dio unos bizcochos, me sentó en su cama y me dijo que me estuviera allí.

Es increíble lo que domina el corazón humano un carácter dulce y afable, y más en un superior. El de mi maestro me docilitó tanto con su primera lección, que siempre lo quise y veneré entrañablemente, y por lo mismo le obedecía con gusto.

So if little birds don't need a spanking to learn, a boy like you, why would he need one...? Jesus...!, we wouldn't even think of it. What do you say? Am I fooling myself? Will you love me? Will you do as I say?

"Yes, sir," I told him, feeling touched, and kissed his hand, enamored with his sweet disposition. He then hugged me, took me to his bedroom, gave me some biscuits, sat me down on his bed, and told me to stay there.

It is incredible how a sweet and affable character, especially that of a superior, can dominate the human heart. My teacher's temperament made me so docile with his first lesson that from then on I loved and venerated him dearly, and for the same reason obeyed him eagerly. (36–37)

The expression *venerar entrañablemente* might be translated as above ("venerated dearly"), but the words' roots are troubling. *Venerar,* like "venereal" and "venom," comes from the Latin *venus,* "physical desire," while *entrañablemente* comes from the Latin *interanea,* or "guts." Thus, the docile young boy sits upon his teacher's bed venerating him dearly or, perhaps, desiring him from his entrails. This teacher is only one of many of el Periquillo's mentors and is not characterized much beyond this scene; it is therefore not possible to imagine what Lizardi really meant his readers to understand here. However, perhaps this is one of those "filthy" and "disgusting" scenes that critic Luis Urbina was so appalled by, and it is not surprising that, along with most of what I will cite from the novel, critics never refer to this scene.

Nor are they comfortable dealing with the scenes from the *arrastraderito* [dive] where we encounter the *bribones* [scoundrels] who play cards, betting their clothes, "quedándose algunos como sus madres los parieron sin más que un *maxtle,* como le llaman, que es un trapo con que cubren sus vergüenzas, y habiendo pícaro de éstos que se enredaba con una frazada en compañía de otro, a quién le llamaban su *valedor"* [some of them being left the way their mothers bore them without so much as a *maxtle,* as they call it, which is a scrap of cloth that covers their shame, and there being these rascals who would wrap themselves up in a blanket in the company of another guy, who they would call their *protector*] (186). Funny that these rogues he meets in the gambling dive use the term *valedor* to refer to the men who they sleep naked with; while el Periquillo never uses that precise term, it certainly would apply to any of his teachers, masters, or older male friends, several of whom he actually does admit to sleeping with on occasion, as we shall see.

This rare nineteenth-century reference to same-sex sexual relations is of particular note in that these *bribones* who curl up naked together are never referred to as effeminate—just as numerous references to effeminacy in men in novels such as *El Periquillo, Astucia,* or *El fistol del diablo* never seem to have homosexual implications. The term *valedor* is used only once more in the novel to refer to a female lover (*valedora*) with whom el Periquillo has an illicit affair (344). This particular (homo)sexualized definition does not appear in Porrúa's dictionary of Mexicanisms, which merely defines *valedor* as a vulgar term used by criminals to refer to a friend or comrade. Interestingly, it gives a series of examples from nineteenth-century novels (*Astucia, El fistol del diablo, Los bandidos del Río Frío*) including as its final reference this precise scene from *El Periquillo Sarniento* (Santamaría 1104).

Another rather queer scene of fraternal love transpires not between teacher and student, but between another authority/father figure, a lieutenant, and his new pal, el Periquillo, who recounts the following: "Me convidó con su cuarto; yo admití y me fui a dormir con él. Luego que vio mis pistolas se enamoró de ellas y trató de comprármelas. Con el credo en la boca se las vendí en veinticinco pesos" [He invited me to share his room; I accepted and went to sleep with him. As soon as he saw my pistols he fell in love with them and tried to buy them from me. With a silent prayer in my mouth, I sold them to him for twenty-five pesos] (504). While he worries briefly that he is selling the guns of his partners in crime, he expresses no remorse for his one-night stand with the enemy, a policeman in search of the band of highway robbers into which el Periquillo has been recently recruited.

This strange scene in which discussion of sharing a room and sleeping together abruptly turns to pistols (not to mention the scene in *Astucia* examined earlier in which as an initiation ritual Astucia's colleagues try to strip him of his pistols but end up only stripping off his clothes) calls to mind Paz's invocation of pistols as a phallic symbol that links machismo to homosexuality. Whether it's the *valedor* huddling naked with his accomplice under the blanket in the gambling dive or the military man admiring the pistols of the vagabond he's invited in to sleep with him, these intimate male spaces are fraught with homoerotic innuendo.

Locura de los Hombres: Heterosexual Romance

Meanwhile, the role of male-female relations in *El Periquillo*, following in the tradition of the picaresque coming of age novel,[24] seems to be much less essential in the personal development of the hero or in the concurrent symbolic process of forging *patria*. Heterosexuality in general is presented more as a hindrance to the advancement of men. For example, the young Pedro becomes more and more perverse and *vicioso* [licentious] because his father is too much in love with his mother. Later, the wise Antonio, the errant Periquillo's mentor, describes marriage as "locura de los hombres" [men's folly] (203), and in Antonio's case, it is his wife's beauty that leads him to an unjust imprisonment.

Pedro Sarmiento, for his part, marries twice, although neither of his wives is a major character in the novel. The first time, he meets a girl who "estaba resuelta a casarse con el primer hombre de bien que encontrara, por pobre que fuera, antes que servir de diversión a ningún rico" [was resolved to marry the first good man who she found, no matter how poor he was, rather than be some rich man's plaything] (346). She acknowledges no sexual desire on her part and plans to marry any man who happens to be virtuous and, despite what she says, rich. Mariana married Pedro (about the most unvirtuous guy she could have found, not to mention poor, little does she know) and, happily, does not become a mere plaything to her husband. Instead they end up, as Pedro puts it, "aborreciéndonos de muerte" [abhorring each other to death] (354)—and he speaks literally because Mariana dies shortly thereafter.

One of the major problems for married men is that their wives get uglier with age—"los años arrancan los dientes, les emblanquecen el pelo, les pliegan y manchan el cutis y las desfiguran de modo que ni ellas mismas se conocen al verse en el espejo. Sólo una muerte temprana las libra de caer en la fealdad" [the years yank out their teeth, whiten their hair, wrinkle them and blotch up their skin, and disfigure them in such a way that not even they recognize themselves in the mirror. Only an early death will free them from their fall into ugliness] (*La Quijotita* 168)—resulting in "casi siempre...un aborrecimiento eterno" [almost always...an eternal loathing] (*La Quijotita* 169). Therefore, although heterosexual desire of a man for a woman is inevitable ("basta ser hombre, porque todo hombre se inclina a la mujer" [it's enough to be a man, because all men are inclined toward women]) (*La Quijotita* 132), it is insufficient to maintain the institution of matrimony.

Thus, Lizardi instructs us in his other major novel, *La Quijotita y su prima*, with regard to the ideal (female) lover with an example:

> reconociendo al mismo tiempo la superioridad de su marido y la dependencia necesaria que le constituía su inferior;...así jamás le preguntaba a dónde iba, ni de dónde venía; tampoco investigaba sus secretos ni le tomaba cuenta del dinero que adquiría con sus arbitrios; mucho menos se oponía a su gusto para nada, ni disipaba en lujo ni en modas el sudor de su rostro; se contentaba con la decencia a que estaba acostumbrada en su casa.

> recognizing both the superiority of her husband and the necessary dependence that constituted her as inferior,...she therefore never asked him about where he was going nor where he was coming from; nor did she investigate his secrets, nor take any account of the amount of money required for his whims; nor did she ever oppose his tastes, nor dissipate in luxury or fashion the sweat on her face; she contented herself with the decency to which she was accustomed in his house. (253)

The ideal heterosexual love is found in a woman who is an expert in decency and dissimulation and a man who can forget the eternal loathing of marriage with a secret life somewhere away from his house.

Is there such a thing as long-term happiness in heterosexual love for Lizardi? In *El Periquillo,* heterosexual bliss finally turns up not in a matrimony of love between man and woman, but in a marriage between a man and a woman who happens to be the daughter of his fraternal friend. *El Periquillo* gets married for a second time to the daughter of his old mentor, Don Antonio, and the marriage seems to be more an expression of Pedro's love for Antonio and a way of inserting himself into his good family than a desire to be with his adolescent daughter. So the functional marriage of Pedro Sarmiento and his new wife, Margarita, is defined in a way that conforms more to the paradigm that Gayle Rubin has called "the traffic in women" than to any romantic model of heterosexuality.

After more than five hundred pages and twenty years of adventures, Pedro Sarmiento has had relations, all of them brief, with a handful of women, but he has loved dozens of men. So when the mature Periquillo resolves to reform, confesses to his friend the priest, Martín Pelayo, and vows that, "me quitaré de las malas ocasiones; y adiós tertulias; adiós paseos, alameda,... adiós, Pepitas, Tulitas y Mariquitas" [I'll rid myself of bad habits; goodbye to hanging out; farewell to strolls, avenues,... *adiós,* Pepitas, Tulitas, and Mariquitas] (474) one wonders just who are his Mariquitas? Never on any occasion has he spoken about other affairs or encounters with women, nor even of having an interest in such activities. Is he just making up women to impress Pelayo? In fact, the word (not the name) *marica* has antecedents in the novel, such as in the discussion of Hercules who, when berated for letting Omphale dominate him, is called "abatido" [humbled], "sinverguenza" [shameless] and "marica" [effeminate] (46). I do not mean to suggest that el Periquillo indeed carried out clandestine homoerotic affairs that he left out of his life story, but I do argue that any reading of the novel that takes for granted an overarching heterosexuality is naïve.

Foundational Masks

In a book in which disguise is so central a theme, the reader is prod-
ded to read between the lines. The life of Pedro Sarmiento, once again
following the archetype of the *pícaro,* is a performance, an endless
putting on and taking off of masks. He wears, for example, masks of
vocation, performing as beggar, doctor, politician, barber. Such performances are carried out with a particular attitude of self-assurance
that allows most anyone to be fooled by them. El Periquillo goes so
far as to feign a noble lineage and has great success at it because, as
he says, "el mundo las más veces aprecia a los hombres no por sus
títulos reales sino por los que dicen que tienen" [most of the time the
world appreciates men not for their real titles, but for those that they
say they have] (448). Likewise, he often makes use of costume, dressing his exterior to suit his immediate needs. El Periquillo is aware
that appearances can be deceiving but learns from an early age to
manipulate his own appearance to his advantage; as a wise *trapiento*
[ragamuffin] advises him, "advierta que no son los hombres lo que
parecen por su exterior. Hombres verá usted en el mundo vestidos
de sabios, y son unos ignorantes; hombres vestidos de caballeros, y
a lo menos en sus acciones, son unos plebeyos ordinarios; hombres
vestidos de virtuosos, o que aparentan virtud, y son unos criminales
encubiertos" [note that men are not what they appear to be on the
outside. You will see men in the world dressed as wise men who are
ignorant; men dressed as gentlemen who, at least according to their
actions, are ordinary plebians; men dressed as virtuous citizens, or
who feign virtue, who are criminals in disguise] (332). In fact, on
various occasions, el Periquillo simulates being virtuous, acts out, in
his words, "el papel de hombre de bien" [the role of an honest man]
(121). And, interestingly enough, sometimes he has to play the role
of a man.

His friend, the highwayman el Aguilucho, wants el Periquillo to
participate in some holdups, but first he must explain to him what it
is to be a man: to be brave. Cowards, according to el Aguilucho, are
effeminate; men are brave and those who expose themselves to risks
are "muy hombres" [very manly] (500). El Periquillo sees masculinity

somewhat differently: "aunque no todos los hombres sean valientes, a lo menos todos quieren parecerlo cuando llega la ocasión, y tan lejos están de conocer y confesar su cobardía que el más tímido suele ser el que más bravea cuando no tiene delante al enemigo" [though not all men are valiant, all men at least want to appear so on occasion, and so far are they from recognizing and confessing their cowardice that the most timid of them tends to be the one with the biggest swagger as long as the enemy's not around] (493). Thus, since the very beginning of Mexican literary history, masculinity has been presented practically in accordance with the thesis of Samuel Ramos, published more than a century later, which states that Mexican masculinity is the neurosis of Adlerian masculine protest.[25]

El Periquillo admits his fear because, as he claims, he doesn't know how to lie (which is nonsense considering that he has confessed that most of his life was spent simulating and dissimulating). But for his fear, he is accused of being a "collonote" [big coward], "amujerado" [effeminate man], and "maricón" [big sissy] (496, 500).

On the other hand, when el Periquillo's Chinese mentor decides to put an end to his travels and return to his country because "según las observaciones que había hecho, no podía menos el mundo que ser igual en todas partes, con muy poca diferencia, pues en todas partes los hombres eran hombres" [according to the observations he had made, the world couldn't be anything other than the same everywhere, with very little difference, since everywhere men were men] (547), one might wonder just what are *hombres* in *El Periquillo Sarniento;* how would el Pensador Mexicano define the term?

We recall that his hero's masculinity has been compromised since his early youth when horror stories, as he tells it, "me formó un espíritu cobarde y afeminado" [formed in me a cowardly and effeminate spirit] (24). And in *El Periquillo*, Hercules, a figure who often appears in the Mexican literature of the century as an icon of masculinity, is mentioned only in a warning to men not to allow their women to henpeck them:

> no os afeminéis como aquel valentísimo Hércules, que después que venció leones, jabalíes, hidras y cuanto se le puso por delante, se dejó avasallar tanto del amor de Omfale que ésta lo desnudó de la piel del

león Neneo, lo vistió de mujer, lo puso a hilar, y aun le reñía y castigaba cuando quebraba algún huso o no cumplía la tarea que le daba. ¡Qué vergonzosa es semejante afeminación aun en la fábula!

don't become effeminate like that super-valiant Hercules who, after vanquishing lions, wild boars, hydras, and whatever was put in front of him, let himself be subjugated so much by his love for Omphale that she stripped him of the skin of the lion of Neneus, dressed him up like a woman, set him up at a spinning wheel, and even chided and rebuked him when a spindle would break or if he didn't manage to complete the tasks she gave him. How shameful is such feminization even in fables! (46)

Masculinity, then, has more to do with behavior than with the body.

And even if one believes that the male body is essential to the study of masculinity, *El Periquillo* is an ideal resource because it likely features more nude male exhibitionism than any other book of the time, save for those of the Marquis de Sade. A few examples: el Periquillo enters a corral where a bull knocks him down, after which he recounts the following: "me levanté...sin advertir que al golpe se me habían reventado los botones y las cintas de los calzones, y así habiéndose bajado a los talones quedé...sin poder dar un paso y en la más vergonzosa figura" [I got up...without noticing that the blow had torn off the buttons and waistband of my breeches, and with them dropped around my ankles I was left...without the ability to take a step and in an utterly shameful position] (76–77); when he and his buddy Januario go to hang out at the gambling dive, they find a large number of guys "encuerados" [naked], and when it is time to go to bed, he can't sleep because of "el miedo que me infundieron aquellos encuerados, a quienes piadosamente juzgué ladrones" [the fear instilled in me by those naked guys, whom I sympathetically judged to be thieves] (167); la Aguilita [Little Eagle] (who would later become the hypermasculine robber el Aguilucho [Eaglet], in the process changing gender) appears for the first time as "un mulatillo gordo, aplastado, chato, cabezón, encuerado y demasiadamente vivo y atrevido" [a little chubby mulatto, flat-faced, flat-nosed, big-headed, naked, and too lively and bold] (239); etc.

Homosocial Spaces and God's Will

What goes on in these homosocial spaces inhabited by naked men? Today such scenes might be qualified as homoerotic. And by the turn of the century, as shown in a recent study by Rob Buffington, there was a great deal of sex between men going on in male homosocial spaces such as the prisons of México. In the gambling den where "entre todos no se veía una cara blanca ni uno medio vestido. Todos eran lobos y mulatos encuerados" [among all of them not one white face or half-dressed body could be found. They were all naked half-breeds[26] and mulattos], el Periquillo confesses: "En fin, nos acostamos como pudimos los que nos quedamos allí, y yo pasé la noche como Dios quiso" [Finally, those of us who remained lay down however we could, and I spent the night as God willed] (186–87). The obvious question is, just what did God will that night? Or when el Periquillo spends his first night in jail and wakes up soaked with the urine that his cellmates have thrown on him with the intention of making him spend the night naked,[27] the question no critic has ever dared to ask is, just what are we to understand to have gone on in the jails of Mexico in those days?

The rites performed in such male homosocial spaces, particularly in the forgotten past, are often mysterious and erotic to us today— if Lizardi was not "queer," he certainly did have an interesting erotic bent to his imagination. A striking scene from a few decades later—reminiscent somehow of *El Periquillo*—is recounted by the ever curious Frances Calderón de la Barca, who somehow found a way to sneak into a nocturnal religious service open only to men. Such homo-social spaces, forbidden to her, naturally attracted her. She comments, for example, on monasteries where "not only no woman can enter, but it is said, with what truth I know not, that a vice-queen hav-ing insisted on the privilege of her vice-royalty to enter, the gallery and every place which her footsteps desecrated were unpaved" (288). But the scene she paints of the all-male night ritual sizzles. She is se-cretly let into a gallery overlooking the church floor where she views "about one hundred and fifty men, enveloped in cloaks and *sarapes,* their faces entirely concealed." A particularly dramatic discourse ("a rude but very forcible and eloquent description of the torments prepared in hell for impenitent sinners") is followed by the shutting off of all lights. Then:

> Suddenly, we heard the sound of hundreds of scourges descending upon the bare flesh.... Before ten minutes had passed, the sound became splashing, from the blood that was flowing.... At the end of half an hour a little bell was rung, and the voice of the monk was heard, calling upon them to desist; but such was their enthusiasm, that the horrible lashing continued louder and fiercer than ever. In vain he entreated them not to kill themselves.... No answer, but the loud sound of the scourges, which are many of them of iron, with sharp points that enter the flesh. (275–76)

It would be silly to conclude that church services simply served as the gay S&M clubs of the 1840s. On the other hand, to deny the frequently erotic nature of such male homosocial spaces would be naïve, or more probably indicative of another kind of dissimulation, that which ignores that which is discomforting.

In one of the final chapters of the novel, the narrator informs us: "Si todos los hombres tuvieran valor y sinceridad para escribir los trabajos que han padecido moralizando y confesando ingenuamente su conducta, veríais, sin duda, una porción de *Periquillos descubiertos,* que ahora están solapados y disimulados, o por vergüenza o por hipocresía" [If all men had the courage and sincerity to write of the travails they suffered, ingenuously moralizing and confessing their conduct, you would see, without a doubt, a number of Periquillos uncovered, who now are concealed and disguised, whether for shame or hypocrisy] (489). Later he says: "Yo os he escrito mi vida sin disfraz; os he manifestado mis errores y los motivos de ellos sin disimulo" [I have written my life for you without disguises; I have displayed for you my errors and the reasons for them without misleading] (549). All this talk of masks, disguises, dissimulation: a contemporary analogy comes to mind here, that of the homosexual's closet. And while such contemporary signifiers clearly have little use in times when the world was not conceptualized as it is today, this particular analogy is actually appropriate, in its way. However, here we do not find homosexuals hidden in closets, but instead find homoeroticism hidden in a culture that had no concept of such a thing and therefore virtually no vocabulary to express it.

Altamirano and National Literature

Altamirano's Studs

A discussion of nineteenth-century nation-building literature would not be complete without taking a look at its most energetic promoter, Ignacio Altamirano. Altamirano's use of male homosocial bonding in the allegorical forging of *patria* is more complex than that of Payno, Cuéllar, or even Lizardi for two reasons. First, his novels are normally read as heterosexual romances—certainly Sommer's reading of *El Zarco* convincingly fits Mexico into her broad continental arguments (220–32). Second, questions of race are brought to the forefront by an author "from an indigenous family."[28]

Altamirano's interest in race issues unfortunately does not imply that he strives to reach the masses in the way that Lizardi did. Altamirano was an elitist who prided himself on being cultured.[29] José Joaquín Blanco, in an acerbically ironic article ("Altamirano: Las letras mesiánicas," *Crónica literaria* 41–51) takes Altamirano to task for attempting to somehow link his idealizing mission with the miserable reality of poverty, illiteracy, illness, and brutality that characterized the life of most Mexicans. Altamirano's self-appointed Messianic mission was:

> el forjar una nación a partir de una literatura...crear una literatura nacional en un país que no tenía sino una minúscula población alfabetizada, y entre ella, una microscópica porción de literatos empeñados en moldear, según sus inspiraciones europeas o norteamericanas, a millones de peones, indios o "plebe," carentes no sólo de la civilización moderna, sino aun muchas veces de la antigua, y brutalizados por le hambre y el trabajo expoliador, la diferencia de lenguas y la dispersión geográfica, las epidemias y la dura mano de los caciques y gobernantes, liberales o no, ilustrados o no.

> the forging a nation out of a literature...to create a national literature in a country that had but a miniscule literate population, and within

it, a microscopic portion of literates committed to molding, according to their European or North American inspirations, millions of peons, Indians, or plebs, lacking not only in terms of modern civilization, but many times in terms of ancient civilization, and brutalized by hunger and ravaging labor, the difference in languages and geographical dispersion, epidemics, and the heavy hand of the *caciques* and government officials, liberal or not, enlightened or not. (42)

On the other hand, if dark-skinned Altamirano could become a member of the cultured elite, why shouldn't it have been possible to convert the masses?

Issues of race were paramount to Altamirano's national allegories. He even refers to his generation as "la nueva raza literaria" [the new literary race].[30] Sex, too, was clearly on his mind as is made clear in references to "literatura hermafrodita" [hermaphrodite literature], this time referring to writing that mixed European and American qualities.[31] On the other hand, his own definitions of Mexicanness were often slippery: "¿Qué es lo mexicano? Altamirano se contradice: condena como antinacional el can-can, degeneración 'exótica,' pero no el ferrocarril ni el barco de vapor. Su clasificación nacionalista frecuentemente se vuelve una mera calificación moral: lo mexico es lo bueno... lo antimexicano es lo malo" [What is Mexican? Altamirano contradicts himself: he condemns can-can as an antinational, 'exotic' degeneration, but not the railroad nor the steamship. His nationalist classifications frequently turn into mere moral qualifications: Mexican is good... anti-Mexican is bad] (Blanco, *Crónica literaria* 43). Race and sex, in fact, were key to Altamirano's tricky national allegories. But in addition to traditional readings of his work as heterosexual romance, his treatment of homosocial bonding is also worth examining.

Feminists have correctly pointed out that historically, in modern Western cultures, it has been women who have felt obligated to attain idealized levels of beauty, while men have been socialized to compete to possess, control, and take pleasure in this beauty contained in women. Laura Mulvey, for example, in her well-known exploration of women in film, notes that "pleasure in looking has been split between active/male and passive/female. The determining male gaze projects its fantasy onto the female figure, which is styled accordingly" (19). Meanwhile, "the male figure cannot bear the burden of sexual objectification.... Hence the split between spectacle and narrative supports the man's role as the active one of advancing the story, making things happen" (20). Generally speaking, this schema is regularly found in literature as well. However, contemporary queer theory alerts us to be suspicious of such a heterosexist view. The protagonist who advances the action, the writer, and the reader are all presumably male while the beautiful and passive object of their desire is female. Already we've seen that desire was not so invariably simple in nineteenth-century Mexico, and even less so in the nation-building works of Altamirano.

Teresa de Lauretis argues that the desire that drives narrative fiction is traditionally Oedipal in nature; it is a "movement... which specifies and even produces the masculine position as that of mythical subject, and the feminine position as mythical obstacle" (*Alice Doesn't* 143). Once again, narrative itself is shown to be masculine, and heterosexual. Yet Freud himself reveals a variety of mechanisms in which the Oedipus complex ends up producing homosexual desire (Silverman 362–73). Altamirano, one of nineteenth-century Mexico's most avid literary patriarchs, most definitely wrote within a traditional patriarchal narrative framework. The question is: Did such a framework in nineteenth-century Mexico preclude homosexual desire?

I do not dispute the worth of conventional allegorical readings of Altamirano's novels; the heterosexual romance across ethnic and class lines that Sommer investigates in her reading of *El Zarco* clearly does symbolically forge a multidimensional nation, which is not to say a nation without racial or class conflict, but one in which racial or class conflicts occur in the realm of the national, not at its frontiers.[32] Indigenous, mestizo or white, rich, middle class, or poor, all of Altamirano's protagonists are Mexican, and Altamirano's Mexico is constructed of a diverse range of social classes and ethnicities.

La Navidad en las Montañas

Altamirano, in fact, goes beyond ethnic dividing lines to address religious ones. In a century in which Catholicism had come in conflict with national self-determination and the church had aligned itself aggressively with Mexico's political conservativism, Altamirano posited an allegorical fusion of the rural Catholic and the metropolitan progressive in *La Navidad en las montañas* (1871), as symbolized in the novella's affectionate ending. The liberal soldier narrator leaves a small-town parish priest after spending a pleasant Christmas in the town "que abandoné el veintiséis, no sin estrechar contra mi corazón a aquel virtuosísimo cura a quien la fortuna me había hecho encontrar, y cuya amistad fue para mí de gran valía desde entonces" [that I left on the twenty-sixth, but not without embracing against my heart that very virtuous priest whom fortune had led me to meet and whose friendship has been of great value to me ever since] (125). The novella reveals a blind spot in the above mentioned criticism, a blind spot perhaps impossible to fully and accurately fill in: the romantic novels of the nineteenth century did not always include beautiful females as the objects of male desire that helped forge a notion of multicultural Mexicanness.

It would be unthinkable to imagine heroic figures such as Fray José de San Gregorio of *La Navidad en las montañas* to be homosexual. In fact, there is nothing to indicate that there ever was any queer hanky panky between Fray José and Altamirano's noble narrator—even in the bizarre scene in which, while traveling on horseback along a mountain path, the narrator is so moved by the priest's ramblings that he suddenly insists that both men dismount so that he can throw himself upon him in a tearful embrace (99). Oddly, while such a passionate embrace between men is not to be taken as indicative of homosexual desire, the much more controlled interactions between the male and female protagonists of Altamirano's other novels are unquestionably and invariably read as heterosexual.

What is especially telling, however, is the physical beauty of Fray José, a physical beauty described in a degree of detail traditionally reserved to create the visual spectacle of the lovely but passive heroine. The priest is first introduced as "Spanish" (representative of the old colonial aristocracy) and "todo un hombre" [a real man] (96). Only after they have met, bonded, and cried in each other's arms does the narrator pause to describe the "belleza varonil" [manly beauty] (105) of the "robust" and "muscular" priest, in loving detail.

The ardent and enchanting Clemencia and her tragically heroic lover Fernando Valle (of Altamirano's 1869 novel *Clemencia*) never do more than dance of couple of waltzes, and "off stage" at that—the dance scene consists of one line: "Se bailó un poco" (94). Meanwhile, Nicolás and Pilar, the heroic leads of *El Zarco* (published posthumously 1901, written 1888) end up marrying, but are never described as so much as touching. However, as noted earlier, physical beauty and the power to attract are generally assumed to belong exclusively to the female sex. And no doubt Pilar and Clemencia are gorgeous babes. Why wouldn't the feelings of Nicolás (for Pilar) and Fernando (for Clemencia) go beyond platonic admiration into the realm of physical desire? On the other hand, if a man such as Fray José is beautiful, might he not also be an object of sexual attraction?

Of course, the fact that the narrator-protagonist took notice of the priest's outstanding physical beauty and took to spontaneously embracing him does not prove that any homosexual desire existed between the two men (any more than the romantic exchange of a flower between Clemencia and Fernando proves heterosexual desire between them). However, what is particularly noteworthy in all three of Altamirano's major prose works is the central role of male beauty. Male beauty, if not always an ideal for Altamirano, is certainly a major catalyst in plot action.

El Zarco

Male beauty is more problematic in *El Zarco*. Both male protagonists are initially described in lofty terms. Nicolás is indigenous looking, but tall, svelte, strong, manly, well proportioned, and of Herculean forms (11). The bandit el Zarco's physique coincides in being svelte, tall, well proportioned and with a Herculean back (16, 25). El Zarco, part of the *plateado* gang, unlike Nicolás, is known to accessorize with all kinds of showy silver adornments. Nonetheless, only el Zarco's beauty is well known. The main female character at the beginning of the novel, Manuela, is madly in love with el Zarco, but finds Nicolás repugnant and unattractive. In fact, Nicolás, despite the initial description, is repeatedly described as ugly, and his redeeming value seems to be that he is reliable, thrifty, and honorable, traits recognized and admired not by libidinous Manuela, but by her nervous mother, Doña Antonia. Even by the novel's end, when Doña Antonia's goddaughter Pilar declares her love for and eventually marries Nicolás, she never demonstrates any physical desire, and readers are left to assume that she loves him only because he is noble.

Meanwhile, Manuela impetuously runs off with el Zarco to live among his bandit army, where it becomes clear that she is no more than another item in his booty. "Iba a poseer a la linda doncella para satisfacer una necesidad de su organización, ávida de sensaciones vanidosas, ya que había saboreado el placer inferior de poseer magníficos caballos y de amontonar onzas de oro y riquísimas alhajas. ...Una querida como ella sí era un triunfo entre sus compañeros" [He was going to possess the lovely maiden to satisfy a need of his organization, avid for vain sensations since it had already tasted the inferior pleasure of possessing magnificent horses and amassing ounces of gold and the richest of jewels.... A mistress like her was a great triumph among his men] (27). This is not to say that he did not feel any desire for her—his was, in fact, "un deseo sensual y salvaje, excitado hasta el frenesí por el encanto de la hermosura física y por los incentivos de la soberbia vencedora y de la vanidad vulgar" [a sensual and savage desire, excited to frenzy by the charm of physical beauty and by the incentives of triumphal haughtiness and vulgar vanity] (27). On the other hand, despite his early enthusiasm, he was not known for his steadfastness, and the fact that he thought of his colleagues not as friends, but as "compañeros de placer y de vicio" [companions of pleasure and vice] (24) soon led him to share Manuela with other members of the gang, most notably el Tigre, whom Manuela describes as "el mulato colosal y horroroso" [the colossal and horrific mulatto] (73) and "aquel monstruo de fealdad y de insolencia" [that monster of ugliness and insolence] (74).

Nevertheless, Manuela remains loyal, viewing el Zarco in "las proporciones de un héroe legendario" [the proportions of a legendary hero] (57). Even as she faces reality and sees that she has been mis-treated, even as she realizes that Nicolás was the more sensible catch, even as the bandits are arrested and el Zarco put to death, she remains at the side of her beautiful lover. It is quite clear, then, that if the re-lationship between Manuela and el Zarco is based on sexual desire, that desire is mutual. El Zarco is as much the desirer as the desired.

Moreover, it is his male beauty that drives the novel. It is his beauty that inspires Manuela to run away, which in turn spurs the town (es-pecially Nicolás) into action and leads to the eventual downfall of el Zarco and his *plateados,* which allows Nicolás to forget Manuela and turn his attentions to the more sensible Pilar. Nicolás may be the novel's hero, but it is el Zarco who drives its action. Doña Antonia makes a fatal error in judgment early in the novel, the same error made by many critics in their examination of this novel: she ignores the power of male beauty. She obsesses about hiding beautiful young Manuela from the *plateados,* while failing to understand that it was el Zarco whom she should have found a way to keep hidden from Manuela, failing to realize that this gallant horseman did not neces-sarily resemble a "demonio vomitado del infierno" [demon vomited out of hell] (10) to a young woman with an active libido.

Clemencia

The role of male beauty is even more complex in Altamirano's most critically successful novel, *Clemencia.* The narration opens in the first-person plural voice of the guests of a certain Doctor L., who soon becomes the narrator of the story at hand. The only point in estab-lishing this extra level of intermediation would seem to be to provide an opportunity to describe the narrator himself, Dr. L., who turns out to be "un guapo joven de treinta años y soltero" [a handsome thirty-year-old single man] (12). Moreover, the doctor does not write himself, but "estimula a sus amigos" [stimulates his friends] (12) as a sort of benevolent muse.

The introduction of this extra narrator establishes male beauty as an important theme of the novel even before the principal action starts. However, Dr. L. is not the principal male beauty in question. Nor is the novel's hero, Fernando Valle, who is described as weak and rachitic, pale, sickly, repugnant, unpleasant, dry, fastidious, and repulsive, especially to women (20–24). It is his fellow junior military officer, Enrique Flores, who represents a degree of male beauty even beyond that of hunks Fray José and el Zarco. Flores is gallant, handsome, distinguished, likeable, irresistible, manly, Herculean, well formed, elegant, cheerful, graceful, witty, and generous. Not only does he attract women wherever he goes, but he is idolized by his soldiers and is a favorite of the colonel, who "no tenía otra voluntad que la de Enrique" [had no other will than that of Enrique] (18). While Flores has so many superficially good qualities relating both to his well-formed, manly body and his pleasant personality, there is no reason to assume that women are attracted to the former and men to the latter, i.e., that the desire directed toward him must necessarily be hetero*sexual* and homo*social*.

The sickly Valle is constantly compared to the virile Flores. Despite their being presented as nearly polar opposites, sharing only their military rank, the two were friends, more or less: "se había entablado entre ambos jóvenes, si no una amistad, al menos una relación que no era la del odio" [there had formed between the two young men if not a friendship, then at least a relationship that was not one of hatred] (26), which is apparently as close to friendship as Valle got with anyone. In fact, Fernando "no parecía querer a nadie en el cuerpo, más que a Enrique" [did not appear to like anyone in the corps besides Enrique] (26). So while for Flores Valle is just one of so many male admirers, Flores is really uniquely attractive for Valle, who shows his regard for his colleague by offering him gifts such as wine and flowers—as Dr. L. discreetly puts it, "algunas veces se propasó hasta regalarle alguna botella de exquisito vino, o un ramillete para que obsequiase a sus queridas" [on several occasions he went a little too far, to the point of presenting him with a bottle of exquisite wine, or a bouquet to give to one of his girlfriends] (26). The fact that the narrator is not omniscient and must speculate about Valle's intentions leads us to wonder whether Valle's gifts were really intended for Flores's paramours (which is queer in its own way), or whether Valle intended them as expressions of his queer affection for Flores.

Flores's interest in Valle increases not due to seductions through wine and flowers, but when he discovers that Fernando has a pretty young cousin. Valle dutifully invites Flores to meet her, and when the meeting occurs, cousin Isabel is accompanied by her seductive and conniving friend Clemencia, both of whom, of course, are beguiled by the handsome and charming Flores, while Valle is left to chat with his Aunt Mariana: "El triste Valle continuó su conversación con la tía y le habló de plantas y árboles frutales. Era algo botánico, y como estaba poco habituado a las conversaciones de sociedad, procuraba mezclar siempre sus pequeños conocimientos para no quedarse callado" [The sad Valle continued his conversation with the aunt, and he spoke to her of plants and fruit-bearing trees. He had a botanical bent, and as he was hardly used to the conversations of society, he managed to always mix in his little bits of knowledge so as not to remain silent] (45).

The story that then develops is clearly one of heterosexual desire. Flores initially courts Isabel, but then falls out of favor when the subject of marriage comes up, and he suggests she just run off with him instead. With Isabel out of the way, Clemencia, who has been leading Valle on until this point, moves in, and Valle, in turn, is heartbroken when he catches his best friend and the woman he loves seeing each other behind his back. The plot complicates itself further when the popular Flores is promoted and becomes Valle's superior. When Flores tries to implicate Valle in a crime, it comes out that Flores has betrayed military secrets to French invaders and is sentenced to death.

Meanwhile Clemencia believes that Valle has made up accusations against Flores only out of jealousy. Valle, feeling guilty, exchanges places with Flores on death row. Flores escapes and Valle is sent to the firing squad. At this point, sickly, ugly Valle suddenly becomes "heroicamente hermoso" [heroically handsome] (185). While Valle is presented as having been in love with Clemenca, it is not totally clear whether he feels more betrayed by her or by Flores. Valle has only one lady love, but also has only one male companion. And if Clemencia's gift to him of a flower is meant to symbolize (albeit falsely given that she is only toying with him) her affections toward him, is his similar gesture to Flores to be seen differently? It is impossible to tell. While Valle's relationship with Clemencia is presented colorfully and dramatically, his precise relationship with Flores is only hinted at.

Most interesting is the fact that in both *El Zarco* and *Clemencia,* the swarthy but ugly Nicolás and Fernando take the place of the blond and beautiful romantic heroes of the early parts of the novels. Neither Nicolás nor Fernando appears destined to become a romantic protagonist. Not only do they come to assume that role, however, but they do it by replacing their rivals. Manuel eventually realizes that she has erred and would have been better off with Nicolás. Valle goes so far as to exchange identities with Flores, and in doing so becomes "handsome" for the first time. The national integration through literature desired by Altamirano is achieved not so much through heterosexual bonding as through racial and political fusion. Blond Zarco fuses with indigenous-looking Nicolás; liberal Valle fuses with royalist Flores.

And while political fusion is important, racial integration is Altamirano's passion. Race is not easy to define in nineteenth-century Mexico. Strict colonial definitions were too complicated to apply and what ultimately mattered was not so much actual as perceived race.[33] Moreover, enlightenment discourse promoted equality among all men (not women), no matter what their race. While on the one hand, new hierarchies had clearly developed that "replaced the old distinction between Indian and non-Indian with a new division between rich and poor" (González Navarro, *"Mestizaje"* 147), on the other hand, the many nineteenth-century indigenous revolts in Mexico showed that race was important and that racial difference was an obstacle to full citizenship: the indigenous insurgents were the enemies within Mexico's borders. Altamirano does not force heterosexual miscegenation on a readership that most likely read the term "mestizo" as a synonym of "bastard" (González Navarro, *"Mestizaje"* 145), but instead promotes racial integration through homosocial bonding in a way that resembles less Paz's conception of Mexicanness as the product of interracial rape than Vasconcelos's cosmic vision of racial integration crossed with the distinctively Mexican queer vision of Villaurrutia. While never overtly homosexual, the nationalist homosocial bonding of Altamirano is a clear precursor to the Mexican queer literature that would begin to erupt around the turn of the century and would develop its own voice by the 1920s.

Valle, after all, is a queer sort. Friendless, taciturn, dull, he operates outside of the mainstream. And yet he turns out to be the novel's handsome hero. Just before his death he confesses the root of his otherness to the handsome Dr. L.: at a young age he had entered into a passionate friendship with a male classmate, "el único cariño profundo de mi vida solitaria!" [the sole profound affection in my lonely life] (178). This friendship with a youth of a less fortunate economic background and liberal ideals forever transforms him. Although only a child, he became devoted to his young mate and his ideas to the point that his family, particularly his father, came to look down on him. His father went so far as to remove him from school and never again treated him with sympathy. Of course, Valle's fanatical devotion to this boy at the cost of his relationship to his family is not necessarily evidence of his homosexuality. Still, it is odd that his "only profound affection" prior to Clemencia had been with another male, and that in the military he ended up drawn to, of all people, the physically irresistible Flores.

Once again, it is Flores (and not Clemencia, as the title of the novel would suggest) who is the catalyst of the story's action. Flores persuades Valle to set up the meeting with Isabel, whom Valle would never have bothered to contact on his own. It is due to Flores's beauty that Clemencia seduces and later betrays Valle and because of these complicated tangled relations that Valle ultimately sacrifices himself for the man who has become his enemy. Due to Flores's physical attractiveness and the way he makes use of it to manipulate others, these three characters meet their fate: Valle dies before a firing squad, lovely Clemencia ends up locked away in a convent, and Flores manages to resume his life as if nothing had happened. At the novel's end, Dr. L. watches a parade go by and observes: "Llegaba frente a nosotros un cuerpo de caballería, y a su frente venía un gallardo coronel que caracoleaba un soberbio caballo, y veía al balcón con ese aire de don Juan que acostumbraban usar los militares buenos mozos. Era Enrique Flores, el miserable autor de la muerte de Fernando" [A corps of calvary passed before us, and at its head rode a gallant colonel who pranced by on his haughty steed, and looked up to the balcony with the air of a Don Juan that good-looking military men are accustomed to exhibiting. It was Enrique Flores, the miserable author of the death of Fernando] (187).

In *Clemencia,* not only does male beauty drive the plot, but in contrast with the case of *El Zarco,* here, male beauty also triumphs. Of course, this is not Altamirano's message. He wanted to make clear that superficial beauty is less important than the inner nobility of characters like Nicolás and Fernando. Some critics have gone so far as to identify these ugly, indigenous-looking heroes with Altamirano himself (J. L. Martínez 153). Nonetheless, the ending of *Clemencia* makes clear that while male beauty may allow men to become objects of desire (whether masculine or feminine), the fact that they remain active subjects with access to power differentiates their beauty from that of females. Clemencia cannot control the outcome of the drama, but Enrique is able to. Manuela's beauty gives her certain options that the less radiant Pilar does not have, but she never removes herself from el Zarco's control.

Mexicanness: A View from the Border

Altamirano succeeds in establishing and reinforcing a lasting notion of Mexicanness in terms of gender, race, and politics through a literature that defines this Mexicanness internally. Even his villains such as el Zarco and Flores are Mexican, and Spanish-born immigrant Fray José has renounced his birthland and is committed to Mexico. Less famous than the work of Altamirano in its day was a nascent class of literature that was also concerned with defining Mexicanness, but this time by contrasting it with a non-Mexican other. The literature *de la frontera,* of Texas, of California, Mexican territories that fell into possession of the United States mid-century, concerned itself from its late nineteenth-century origins with defining Mexicanness, although not so much in order to found notions of nation in Mexico as to advocate political views regarding conflictive race relations along the border.

Nationality was a key theme of border literature. In *The Squatter and the Don* by María Amparo Ruiz de Burton, the novel's "Spano-Americans" are likely as white as the *gringo* squatters, but only the latter have access to all the privileges of U.S. citizens. *The Squatter and*

the Don's recent republication has given the text greater importance
than it managed to earn in its day. Its unique role as an early border
text written in English by a native Mexican woman to argue the cause
of former Mexicans now living in U.S.-controlled California makes
it of particular interest to scholars of U.S. culture, Mexican culture,
border culture, and ethnic studies today.

The extraordinary Ruiz de Burton was born in Baja California in
1832 to a prominent creole family. During the occupation of Baja
California in the Mexican-American war, she and her mother along
with several hundred other Mexicans renounced their citizenship and
became U.S. subjects. Living later in Alta California, she married
U.S. Navy captain Henry Burton of New York. This marriage itself
symbolized national integration in the United States as the "Anglo"
Protestant from the East wed the "Spano" Catholic from the West.
The 1885 publication of the novel under the pseudonym C. Leal
pointed to the author's position as a loyal citizen of Mexico, but its
publication in English in the United States shows her urgency to reach
a non-Mexican U.S. readership.[34]

The Squatter and the Don in fact is a romance of the type described
by Sommer in *Foundational Fictions* and despite being written in English belongs alongside *Amalia, Sab,* and *Iracema* in Latin American
literary histories. Unlike the romances of Cooper with their construction of nation based on racial purity and racial difference, Ruiz de
Burton proposes national integration through interracial heterosexual
romance.[35] The American Mechlin and Darrell families unite with the
Mexican[36] Alamar family through a series of marriages. In those marriages, the Mexicans gain a degree of legitimacy in U.S. society that
they could never attain by marrying other Mexicans, while the Americans, who were squatters on the Alamar property, attain something
of the aristocratic social standing of the Alamars.

The only trouble is that the squatters, most of whom are enemies
of the Alamars and whose children do not aspire to marry into the
family, and the U.S. government are little by little driving the once rich
Mexicans into bankruptcy. Their loss of social standing is illustrated
by gender allegory. The once strong and virile Alamar men become
sick, injured, and debilitated in their struggles to maintain their land.

Don Mariano Alamar, the Don of the title, catches pneumonia trying to protect his livestock from the marauding squatters. In the same way, his son Victoriano loses the use of his legs after a severe frostbite. Brother Gabriel is reduced to working as a stonemason and is severely injured on the job. Even the political connections of George Mechlin, husband of the former Elvira Alamar, are of little use. In the end it is only the money of stock market wizard and entrepreneur Clarence Darrell that saves the day. The Alamars, even when married to Americans, are not accepted by other Americans and cannot enter their society except if they happen to be rich.

In fact, it is not so much the heterosexual romance, then, that achieves the allegorical "racial" integration in the new Southwest, as the homosocial bonding that occurs between rich Clarence Darrell, well connected George Mechlin, and the handsome Alamar brothers, Gabriel and Victoriano. While it is Mercedes Alamar who eventually weds Clarence, his friendship with Victoriano at times recalls the homosocial bonding of Mexican literature that so often borders on the homoerotic: "As for Victoriano, his attachment to Clarence was now an acknowledged and accepted fact...and certainly fully and sincerely reciprocated by Clarence. Both found great pleasure in each other's society, and saw each other every day" (100). While passages like the one above do not indicate an overt erotic attachment, they are no less erotic than those describing the romantic relationship between Clarence and Mercedes, naturally assumed to be hetero*sexual*.

On the other hand, the fall of the Mexican family implies a nostalgia that does not connect with Mexican literary history. The feminization of the Mexican protagonists is most strongly represented in the physical decline and eventual death of the great patriarch, Don Mariano. The figure of the patriarch would seem to represent Mexican patriarchy and its fall to landgrabbing Yankee conquerers. The squatters bring to mind the other side of this trope, representing the unjust occupation of Mexican territory by greedy, lazy, but powerful Yankees.

The defeat of Mexico to the United States is clearly seen in the fall of the patriarch to the mangy squatters. However, this noble patriarch figure is not one with significant antecedents in Mexican literature. *El*

Periquillo Sarniento is all about a quest for father figures—the protagonist is a perpetual son. Likewise, while it is not unusual to find strong mother figures (often single mothers or widows) in nineteenth-century Mexican literature, the heroes of *Astucia,* the novels of Payno along with those of Altamirano, Cuéllar, and Castillo are most often young men, portrayed as suitors, lovers, buddies, and often sons, but almost never fathers, let alone wise and powerful patriarchs. The virility of Mexico's major nineteenth-century heroes remains boyish; the mature virility of Don Mariano indicates a false nostalgia for a national image of a noble and powerful father who cannot be found.[37]

"Los Hijos de la Chingada" Meet "la Hija del Bandido"

A final novel presents an interesting twist to the male homosocial bonding model of national integration described above. The role of women, I have argued, tends to be relatively insignificant in nineteenth-century Mexican literature. Even when heterosexual romance appears to form the national allegory, it is often more a case of one or another variation of traffic in women in which the love object is an object of trade, symbolic or literal, between men. She is a means to link families; she is also a means for one man to attain the status of a rival—by obtaining what belongs or belonged to a rival, one man can take the place of another man, become him.

La hija del bandido by Refugio Barragán de Toscano presents in its characters a series of relations that never fully succeed in allegorizing national integration. Its homosocial relations at times appear to resemble those of other Mexican texts of the age, but the role of women, particularly that of the protagonist María Natividad Colombo, is not quite conventional, and things do not turn out quite as they do in canonical novels written by men.

The story opens with an allusion to the thin line that separates the honorable national military from bands of highway robbers. The famed *plateados,* who also inspired novels such as *Los bandidos del Río Frío* and *El Zarco,* in fact, straddled just such a line. The government's need to enlist their aid in wartime facilitated certain institutional connections that would permit the *bandidos* to flourish later as criminals.[38] Here, *bandido* Vicente Colombo wishes to exchange identities with a certain Colonel Miranda since the two of them "tenían la misma estatura, el mismo color y una, casi idéntica fisonomía" [were of the same height, the same coloring and a nearly identical physiognomy] (17). His plan is to kidnap the colonel's daughter and use her to convince the colonel to allow him to usurp his place in society.

Meanwhile, one of ringleader Colombo's subordinate bandits, Andrés Patiño, desires (and tries to kidnap) María, his rather brutal affection for her likely symbolizing his craving the status of Colombo which he could achieve by possessing what is his. But Patiño is not her only admirer. A young suitor, Rafael, who describes himself as "mexicano de sangre pura y honrado, aunque pobre" [a pure-blooded Mexican, honorable but poor] (132), pursues her, knowing that her hand has been promised to a corrupt viscount. The latter match is naturally the doing of her father, who knows that the viscount aspires to viceroy, and he would not mind being the father of a vicereine. María understands that her marriage to the viscount would allow her father to retire from banditry, and she accepts on the condition that the colonel and his daughter, Cecilia, her dearest friend, be set free.

All these "love" transactions seem to have other issues behind them, except in the case of Rafael, and perhaps that of Martín, an Indian childhood playmate of María's now described as her "perro fiel" [faithful dog] (20). Martín would selflessly do anything for María, and although his love is sincere, one can't help wondering whether race is at issue. As in *Black Skin, White Masks,* Martín perhaps aspires not to be a white man, which he can never be, but to have what a white man has, a beautiful white wife.[39] Nonetheless, the presence of an indigenous character, portrayed as an individual (if stereotypically humble) and not one of an undifferentiated mass that one author would sarcastically refer to as "los Joseses," is quite unusual for the period.[40]

Martín and María eventually conspire to free the colonel and Rafael, who has been captured by his rival, Andrés. Cecilia, unbeknownst to anyone, had already been saved by María's long lost maternal grandfather. Andrés Patiño drugs and nearly kidnaps María, but Martín kills him and rescues her. Meanwhile, Colombo himself is killed in a battle with authorities, and the viscount also dies in a fight with a criminal conspirator.

One after another version of traffic in women is put down by María herself or her faithful servant Martín until finally the smoke clears and Rafael proposes to María. In a traditional "foundational fiction" such a marriage would resolve differences and allegorize a comfortingly peaceful national unity. The lawless *bandido* element would unite with civilized law-abiding society as represented by the honest law student, Rafael Ordóñez. An alternative traditional ending for this novel, though a bit less likely, would call for a marriage between María and Martín. Some benefactor, perhaps the colonel, would have to intercede and provide a place for them in civilized society, but it certainly would be exquisite to see white and indigenous Mexico lovingly joined as the bandits are wiped out. However, no such romantic climax is to occur. As María informs a disappointed Rafael: "un juramento sagrado me separa de tí [*sic*]; y hoy será la última vez que nos veamos sobre la tierra" [a sacred vow separates me from you; and today will be the last time that we see each other on earth] (227). She decides to become a nun, leaving Rafael to die in the war of independence and Martín to his own devices.

Neither heterosexual romance nor male homosocial bonding manages to achieve much of anything resembling national integration. The men end up pretty much killing each other, and all for naught because whatever might be achieved depends on María, who has her own plans. Interestingly, unlike *Clemencia,* whose male narrator both disguises and intensifies the novel's male homoerotic subtext, given the likely expectations of nineteenth-century readers, the narrator of *La hija del bandido* must take some kind of sadistic pleasure in frustrating male desire for romantic closure time and time again. The narrator, the undisguised voice of the author herself, is merely repeating, she claims, what has been elaborated to her by her Aunt Mariana. This singular female voice reminds readers that national integration may be the project of men but often depends on women who may have wills of their own. Traffic in women can be achieved only with women who are helpless and stupid enough to allow it. A woman with brains, guts, and an independent spirit, like María, needs to be reckoned with. Homosocial bonding among virile men is not enough.

Conclusions

The nineteenth century, then, despite widespread illiteracy, was a time of nation formation through literature. Mexicanness was explored and defined through novels such as *El Periquillo Sarniento, Astucia, El fistol del diablo,* and *El Zarco.* These texts focused on male characters as virility was a key concept in laying a foundational framework of national identity. And despite the popularity of romantic novels and an almost paranoiac concern about heterosexual relations, it is relations between men that most often allegorize the literary national integration so vociferously promoted by Mexico's leading cultural figures. This ubiquitous homosocial (and often homoerotic) bonding between men is *the* foundational trope in nineteenth-century Mexican literature.

Masculinity at the time was presented in a variety of ways. More often than not the *machismo* that informs twentieth-century stereotypes is criticized as false or vulgar. It is more often the *hombre de bien,* the honest and loyal friend, the social do-gooder that presents a model of Mexican masculinity. Interestingly, the *hombre de bien* figure is not the wise and generous father figure. Instead, it is a more youthful man, more committed to friendships and love affairs than to marriage and family, who most often protagonizes the literature of the era.

This trope is altered in border literature, where the benevolent and protective patriarch who appears so rarely in Mexican literature (a rare exception: the colonel in *La Quijotita y su prima*) becomes prominent, suggesting a false nostalgia for an institution that in fact did not play a major role in the construction of the Mexican national imaginery, but which was useful in constructing a Mexican culture worthy of incorporation into U.S. society. However, the physical deterioration of the patriarch, the emasculation of the manly Mexican under U.S. rule, allegorizes the new social position of Mexicans—even rich, white cultured ones—in racist U.S. society.

The figure of the woman, clearly inferior to man for nineteenth-century Mexican authors, does play an important role in many foundational texts. The figure of the strong mother (Doña Antonia of *El Zarco*), the idyllic and innocent beauty (Rafaelita of *Hermana de los ángeles*), the frivolous girl (Pomposita of *La Quijotita y su prima*), the arrogant seductress (Aurora of *El fistol del diablo*), the manipulating fiancée (Rebeca of *Los mariditos*) all play important roles in the novels of the age. However, even in novels that conform most clearly to the genre of romance tend to devalue the woman and point to a stronger reading of national allegory through the interactions of male characters who either themselves bond, or become rivals and use a woman as an intermediary to obtain the symbolic status of the other man.

Since fatherhood is so rarely attained (even couples who marry very seldom procreate in these novels), nineteenth-century Mexican novels do not unite different races or ethnicities through heterosexual union. More often it is through traffic in women that, for example, darker men are able to take the place of or attain the status of lighter skinned men (as is the case in the novels of Altamirano). The guiding principle is less often *mestizaje* than egalitarianism.

This male-centered national literature is challenged in the writings of women such as Refugio Barragán de Toscano. In *La hija del bandido* conventions of national romance are thwarted by a strong-willed, intelligent, independent thinking protagonist who does not permit her father or her many admirers to use her. She manages to put a stop to all sinister machinations as well as all apparently noble ones, and escapes the androcentric society of corrupt politicians, marauding bandits, and jealous lovers by entering the female homosocial space of the convent. *La hija del bandido* shows that women are necessary to national integration, and their passive complicity should not be taken for granted.

Gender and sexuality in nineteenth-century Mexico remained hidden in the *habitus*. Men were assumed to naturally have certain characteristics. At the same time they needed to learn them. And some men might not learn them and end up effeminate. Also, gender was represented in an absolute binary model of masculine or feminine with no other options; yet expressions like "ser muy hombre" imply the simultaneous belief in a contradictory model of gender as a continuum of masculinities and femininities. Contradictions like these went unnoticed. Likewise, since heterosexuality was seen as the only natural form of sexual relations, the erotics of relations between men, even when conspicuously visible, were ignored. However, a growing interest in issues of gender and sexuality in the late nineteenth century would change all that. During the *porfiriato,* gender and sexuality would be explored and questioned in scandalous depth; and notions of masculinity and male sexuality would fall into major crisis.

Chapter 2

Criminal Male Sexuality
The Turn of the Century

Gender, Sexuality, and Crime in the *Porfiriato*

Nineteenth-Century Masculinities

The previous chapter showed that in an era when the meaning of masculinity was never questioned, when it was deeply embedded in the Mexican *habitus,* there were nonetheless numerous contradictions about just what the term meant. By the turn of the century, however, that was all to change. Thanks to increasing sexual frankness in literature, a growing scientific and juridic discourse on sexual issues, along with a few celebrated scandals that popularized a new archetype of male homosexuality, notions of gender were to become even murkier. In Mexico as elsewhere in Latin America, both the elite poets of *modernismo* and the earnest positivist *científicos* of the *porfiriato* addressed gender with a heightened level of curiosity and intensity.[1]

However, the most significant event of the epoch for the history of Mexican masculinity played itself out not in *Revista Moderna,* nor in the eminent conferences of Mexico's new breed of criminologists, psychiatrists, and sociologists, but in the popular press. And it is with the quotidian scandals and polemics of turn-of-the-century Mexico City that we will begin our look at this key turning point in Mexican gender discourse.

"Otra Mujer Que Hiere"

As Alberto del Castillo points out, sex crimes and scandals were events of major interest to the bourgeois readers of turn-of-the-century Mexican newspapers. The most scandalous events, particularly murders involving sexual transgressions (adultery, rape, incest, prostitution, etc.), were of special interest, often extending from the pages of daily newspapers to more literary or scientific vehicles such as Carlos Roumagnac's criminological text, *Matadores de mujeres* (1910) and Ángel de Campo's novella *La Rumba* (1890). These heterosexual sex crimes played out late nineteenth-century phobias about male-female relations. Lizardi's colonel of *La Quijotita*, would cry "I told you so" to all those women who subverted customs designed to protect them from ravenous male libidos, and to all those fathers and other male authority figures who neglected to safeguard their women from dangerous types of heterosexual desire occurring outside the traditional institution of marriage. Even worse is when not even marriage can protect women from men's abuses, as is the case of la Rumba and her tragic marriage to the abusive *barcelonete*.[2]

Gender is a major issue in Campo's novella from the first. His heroine, la Rumba—really Remedios; her nickname is the same as that of her *barrio*—is introduced in her early youth with an aspect hardly fitting of feminine stereotypes: "Prometía ser una mujer de aspecto varonil; rasgaban casi su estrecho vestido las formas precozmente desarrolladas, con enérgicas curvas" [She promised to become a woman with a masculine look; her precociously developed forms practically tore through her tight dress with their energetic curves] (193). The description is oddly contradictory. It is clear that she is unusually strong and daring, "hosca, feroz, intratable" [surly, ferocious, intractable] (194); she even once beat up "el valiente" [the bully] of the neighborhood. On the other hand, "había crecido ... bajo la suave ternura de su pecho la poesía de la virgen, pero con la cabeza poblada por los caprichos de la mujer" [under the soft tenderness of her breast, a virginal poetry had grown, but her head was full of womanly caprices] (193–94). Her masculine "curves" coexist with a feminine beauty.

On the other hand, her attitude toward outward feminine beauty is ambivalent. While "odiaba a las elegantes, a las *rotas* que visten de seda; sentía una inmensa rabia de ser *una cualquiera*" [she hated elegant girls, *rotas*[3] who dress in silk; she felt an immense fury at the idea of being common] (194–95), she also envied elegant women and strove to become one by marrying a foreigner. "Yo he de ser como las *rotas*" [I have got to be like those *rotas*] (195), she swears early on, and is reproved as a golddigger when she marries out of her social class. As one neighbor comments, "Mire usted... a Remedios, esa va a acabar mal... apenas habla, está hecha una catrina; contesta con puros *gringos*, y... esa acaba mal. De que se ven bonitas ya quieren salir de su clase, y no, hombre; si semos [sic] pobres así tenemos que quedarnos" [Look... at Remedios, that one is going to turn out bad... practically from the time she could first speak she became pretentiously elegant;[4] she answers with foreign expressions, and... that one will turn out bad. Whenever they look pretty, they want to move out of their class, and no sir; if we are poor, we ought to stay that way] (215).

While it might be argued that it was more the inappropriate, if apparently innocent, attentions of her ex-suitor, Don Mauricio, that triggered the row that was the central event of the novella, in fact, the blow-up between la Rumba and el Cornichón (her husband) was the culmination of months of insensitive behavior on his part—insensitive, but not out of the ordinary. The male, with his *vida callejera* [street life] who leaves his wife closed up in the female social space of the home, albeit an ugly little apartment; the man who brings home the bacon and controls the family budget; the husband who expects his wife to serve him and fulfill his every caprice: these might be seen today as abusive types, and they may have seemed unfair to Campo's readers, but in fact they reflected commonly held notions of spousal relations. Perhaps it is the fact that Campo, while not fully redeeming his heroine, develops her and her circumstance in a sympathetic manner that implicitly questions these traditional conjugal relations that makes la Rumba sympathetic. While such abusive marital relations are not new to Mexican literature—another prominent example: Evaristo, the brutal wife murderer of Payno's *Los bandidos del Río Frío*—what is radical about *La Rumba* is its ending in which, remarkably, the murderess (Remedios) is pardoned and escapes judicial punishment.[5] If she returns to her *barrio* in disgrace, the very fact that she is allowed back is of major significance in Mexican literary history. The subjugated wife overcomes what appeared to be fatal circumstances.

Campo's story is reflective then of turn-of-the-century attitudes toward crime (a sexualization of and a fascination with it) and gender (a curiosity about, at times a preoccupation with, gender stereotypes and challenges to them) in Mexico, if not precisely representative of factual circumstances. After all, while the headline in *El Noticioso*, the novella's fictional newspaper, announces "Otra mujer que hiere" [Another woman who wounds] (276), it was rarely women who wounded, let alone killed men. It was, in fact, almost always the reverse. On the other hand, as Pablo Piccato notes, "En una situación marcada por la desigualdad de los contendientes, las mujeres eran las vícitmas más frecuentes de los crímenes pasionales. Los casos en que la mujer empuñaba las armas contra un hombre o contra otra mujer, resultaban particularmente atractivos porque invertían la supuesta debilidad y pasividad que debía caracterizar a su género" [In a situation marked by the inequality of the contenders, women were the most frequent victims of crimes of passion. The cases in which a woman drew arms against a man or against another woman appeared especially attractive because these women inverted the weakness and passivity that were supposed to characterize their gender] (" 'No es posible' " 107).[6] As the exceptions to the rule began to multiply in the public consciousness, gender discourse began to slip out of Mexico's *habitus* and a real interrogation of gender stereotypes began to emerge both in literature and in the press.

Masculinity as Perversion, Vice, and Flatulence

Typical of the age were cases such as that of Jesús Negrete, "The Tiger of Santa Julia," the serial murderer of women who took pride in his misogyny. He is quoted as remarking, "Las mujeres, ¿quién puede darles crédito? Las mujeres, ¿de qué no son capaces?" [Women, who can believe them? Women, of what are they not capable?]. Accused of the minor crime of robbery, he goes on to demonstrate an essential link between masculinity and murder as he defends his honor: "De acuerdo soy hombre, he matado, pero no soy ningún ratero" [In accordance with being a man, I have killed, but I am no thief] (quoted in A. del Castillo 46).[7]

Class difference becomes apparent here. El Tigre seems to see murder as a socially acceptable behavior for men, while the *científicos* who write about crime and sexuality in turn-of-the-century Mexico are clearly of another opinion. Miguel Macedo, in his landmark study *La criminalidad en México: Medios para combatirla* (1897), the positivist allays the fears of his middle- and upper-class readers by noting that "los delitos de sangre, son cometidos casi en la totalidad de los casos por individuos de la clase baja contra individuos de la propia clase" [bloody crimes are committed almost in the entirety of cases by lower-class individuals against individuals of their own class] (6). Likewise, for another positivist criminologist, Julio Guerrero, the middle and upper classes are "morally superior" to other Mexicans, while the lowest classes "viven en la promiscuidad sexual, se embriagan cotidianamente..., riñen y son los promotadores principales de los escándalos..., son encubridores oficiosos de crímenes muy importantes" [live in sexual promiscuity, get drunk daily..., fight and are the principal promoters of scandal..., they are officious collaborators in major crimes] (159).

In this class-based discourse, machismo, the bane of mid-twentieth-century explorations of *lo mexicano,* had already surfaced as a major social disorder in Mexico. Much of the violent crime—those crimes of passion that so fascinated Roumagnac, turn-of-the-century journalists, and their respective readers—arose out of a need in Mexican men to defend their "masculine honor," and while questions of honor might have been considered as attenuating circumstances in many of those crimes (Piccato, " 'No es posible' " 107), there was also a growing distaste for or even rancor toward belligerent, exaggerated manifestations of (heterosexual) masculinity.

Complaining of turn-of-the-century Mexico's frequent barroom brawls and rampant prostitution, José Juan Tablada writes, "La perversión moral creada por aquel estado de cosas llegaba al grado de identificar la hombría y la esfuerza masculina con la práctica de todos los vicios" [The moral perversion created by these circumstances reached the point at which manliness and masculine strength came to be identified with the practice of any and all vices] (74). Men were not only expected to defend their honor, but also coerced into participating in all kinds of immoral behaviors (drinking, disobedience, sexual exploits, fights) in the name of masculinity: "el amigo corruptor...decía invariablemente:—Si no haces esto, ¡no eres hombre!" [the corrupting friend...would invariably say: "If you don't do this, you're no man!"] (Tablada 74).

Likewise, Macedo, who blames much violent crime on intemperance, associates both excessive drinking and crimes of passion with the "valor salvaje...de *ser muy hombre*" [savage value...of *being very manly*] (11, emphasis in original). Luis Urbina is similarly worried that with Mexican male behavior and the violence that it implies, "tendremos muchos valientes, pero no mucha civilización" [we'll have many brave men, but not much civilization] (*Crónicas* 85).[8] This linking of masculine behavior with the barbarous, and condemnation of hypermasculinity plainly challenge binary models of gender that view gendered behaviors as being innate to the sexes. Clearly it was not just a matter of being effeminate or masculine. Between *maricón* and *muy hombre,* there was a range of possible degrees of masculinity. Furthermore, the brand of masculinity that was being prescribed by bourgeois intellectuals evidently required a certain measure of acculturation to get beyond the savage.

For example, Guerrero groups all foreigners among the "morally superior" classes in Mexico (172). Macedo, forever comparing Mexico to more "civilized" European countries, remarks that, "Tal vez en otros países, entre individuos de otra raza, de otro temperamento y de otras costumbres, sean extirpables tales vicios; mas entre nosotros su extirpación parece una utopía" [Perhaps in other countries, among individuals of another race, of another temperament, and of other customs, such vices might be eradicable; but among ourselves their eradication seems utopian] (32).

Guerrero proposes that violent crime can be found in all social classes because its etiology lay in Mexico's climate, for example, in evaporation rates (37). Also problematic for Guerrero is flatulence:

El mal humor o flato...es generalísimo en todas las edades y en todas las clases de la sociedad, ocasionando la mayor parte de los disgustos domésticos...Aparece en los niños desde su más tierna edad....Ya de hombres, y cuando no tienen algún freno moral restrictivo, no es raro sino muy frecuente que sin razón ni pretexto agredan al primer transeúnte que encuentran. Hay artesanos y colegiales que, presos de él, salen de sus casas con el único objeto de reñir para descargar sus nervios.

Bad odor or *flatulence*...is a general condition at all ages and in all classes of society, causing the majority of domestic disputes....It appears in children from the most tender age....Once they have become men, and when they have no restrictive moral restraint, it is not rare but very frequent that without reason or pretext, they attack the first passerby they encounter. There are artisans and students who, prisoners to it, go out with the sole intention of fighting to discharge their nerves. (38)

While Guerrero's ideas may seem amusing today, they were taken quite seriously at the time.

On the other hand, *modernista* Amado Nervo repeatedly pokes fun at Mexico's brand of hypermasculinity. He ridicules the expression so frequently used to excuse violence in the name of virility in an 1895 article entitled "¡Yo soy muy hombre!" [I am very manly] (*Fuegos fatuos* 4–6). He marvels that his title phrase is used, often hand in hand with accusations of "¡Marica!" [Nelly] or "¡Pareces mujer!" [You seem like a woman] by Mexicans "de todas clases, de todas edades y ¡cosa extraordinaria! de los dos sexos" [of all classes, all ages, and, extraordinarily, of both sexes] (*Fuegos fatuos* 5). He gives a colorful example:

Dos mujeres, por un ello, se agarran a mordiscos en pleno arroyo, y después de arrancarse los cabellos entre una y otra interjección que tiembla el mundo, llega el gendarme de la esquina y trata de separar a los energúmenos femeniles. Ellas se resisten y oponen todas sus fuerzas a la autoridad de que está investido el guardián aquél; hacen causa común contra él, se le echan encima pretendiendo aniquilarlo y le gritan detempladamente: ¡que le importa! nos peleamos porque ¡somos muy hombres!

Two women, because of a *he,* go at each other tooth and nail in the middle of the street, and after yanking at each other's hair, between interjections loud enough to shake the world, the local gendarme arrives and tries to separate the female energumens. They resist and oppose all forces of authority vested in that sentinel; they then gang up on him, throwing themselves at him in an attempt to annihilate him while shouting riotously: "What do you care!" "We're fighting because we're very manly!" (*Fuegos fatuos* 6)

Nervo, anticipating Octavio Paz by fifty-odd years in his 1896 article "Cavallería rusticana" (*Fuegos fatuos* 333–35), views the fact that "[l]os mexicanos somos muy hombres" [Mexicans are very manly] as "una de las bases fundamentales de nuestra bizarría" [one of the fundamental bases of our bizarreness] (333), and then goes on to elaborate on Mexican manliness as something more specific than merely an exaggerated expression of valor. "¡Los hombres no *se rajan* ni en la orilla de la eternidad!" [Men don't *give in* even on the cusp of eternity!] (334, emphasis Nervo's). *Rajarse* is translated idiomatically as "to give in," but literally means to be rent or split open. Here we recall Paz's much later notion of the Mexican macho who strives to avoid being penetrated at all costs.

In another early essay entitled "El aumento de la criminalidad" [The increase in criminality] (*Fuegos fatuos* 210–13), Nervo mocks positivist discourse on criminality and degeneration, although it should be noted that Nervo's essay is published prior to the most serious and rigorous Mexican studies in this field, namely, those by Macedo, Guerrero, and Roumagnac. Nervo jokingly assembles a list of signs of degeneration including such items as premature baldness, nearsightedness, and feminine attitudes. This posture, while not an open defense of male effeminacy, is consistent with Nervo's mocking of hypermasculinity. And yet Nervo's attitudes toward gender roles are by no means so simple, as will be made clear when we look at his prose fiction. Nor is turn-of-the-century Mexico merely worried about extremist gendered behaviors. By the middle of the *porfiriato*, Mexico has become generally ill at ease about gender and sexuality, and once again, it is the anxiety about masculinity and male sexuality that needs addressing.

The Barbaric Impudicity of Underdrawerism: Sheathing the Penises of the Indians

The nascent discourse on sexuality spurred both an industry of soft-core pornography[9] and a paranoia regarding sexuality in general. The fear of female sexuality is well documented. The archetypes of the pure sexless virgin and the profane sexualized whore that dominated the literature of the day have been studied fruitfully elsewhere.[10] However, the fear of male sexuality that also arose in this age is less often discussed, and dangerous masculinity was not only present in the unruly and self-destructive criminal classes, but also among a class of Mexicans described by Guerrero as "humilde hasta las lágrimas" [humble to the point of inspiring tears] (161). Specifically, one of the most rampant anxieties of the age was caused by the clothing worn by certain indigenous males. The Spaniard Julio Sesto, in his study of Mexico during the *porfiriato,* was noticeably alarmed by the fact that "[e]l indio anda en calzoncillos por las ciudades como anda en el campo, 'como se anda en casa,' y siquiera esos calzoncillos fueran limpios y...sin ventanas" [the Indian goes around the city in underdrawers[11] just as he goes around in the country, or 'as one goes around his house,' and if only those underdrawers were clean and...without any peepholes...] (231). He goes on to elaborate on these peepholes: "al ceñirse en sus ondulaciones flexibles á las flacideces masculinas, denuncia relieves o muestra por sus agujeros impudicias de cafrería" [worn tightly in flexible undulations against masculine flaccidities, they reveal outlines or, through their holes, show barbaric impudicities] (232). Historian Moisés González Navarro records the broad move, well documented in the popular press, to "empantalonar a los indios" [to trouser the Indians] in order to combat "calzonismo" [underdrawerism] ("El porfiriato" 396).

Macedo, too, notes that the sexual danger of underdrawerism has spread even to the urban mestizo class whose perversity is even more marked since these men seem not only to have sexual organs, but to blatantly use them:

> su traje se reduce a la camisa y al calzón de manta, insuficientes como abrigo e insuficientes también para cubrir decentemente sus carnes, llegando cuando más a tener una frazada que funciona alternativamente como cobertor de lecho y como abrigo personal, a guisa de capa, bien para protegerse del frío o para que bajo él se oculten, por cierto de modo muy deficiente, aventuras amorosas que se desarrollan en plena calle.

their clothing is limited to cotton shirt and underdrawers, insufficient as protection from the cold and insufficient as well to decently cover their flesh, some of them even going so far as to have a blanket that functions alternatively as a bed cover and as an overcoat, in the form of a cape, either to protect from the cold or to conceal beneath it, clearly in a most deficient manner, amorous adventures that are carried out openly in the street. (15)

Macedo is particularly preoccupied with questions of clothing. He finds not only that social and economic class is closely linked with one's clothing, but also that, given the pronounced tendency toward crime in the lower classes, "basta dirigir una mirada al aspecto de una persona, para comprender inmediatamente...su grado de moralidad" [it is enough to take a look at a person's appearance to understand immediately...his degree of morality]. Macedo divides men into economic and moral classes based on items of clothing, outlining "la clasificación usual que tenemos hecha de personas de *levita,* de *chaqueta* y de *camisa"* [the usual classification that we have made up of people who wear *frock-coats, suit jackets,* and *shirts*] (16, emphasis in original).

Probably uncomfortable with Macedo's blatant classism, Guerrero rebuts him directly:

La distinción vulgar de pueblo, clase media y aristocracia no corresponde, sin embargo, a caracteres diferenciales importantes de los grupos, y menos la que se ha pretendido fundar en la diferencia del traje: hombres de camisa, de chaqueta y de levita...propongo en su lugar la...clasificación de los habitantes de la ciudad de México, basada en la vida privada de los individuos.

The vulgar distinction of lower, middle, and upper classes does not correspond, however, to major differencial characteristics of the groups, and even less applicable is the attempted basing of class distinction on clothing: shirts, suit jackets, and frock-coats....I propose in their place the...classification of the inhabitants of Mexico City based upon individuals' private life. (131)

Guerrero's analysis is more complex, and includes numerous categories of people: *léperos* [street beggars], Indians, soldiers and *soldaderas,* factory workers, servants, artisans, scribes, gendarmes, bureaucrats, foreigners, and professionals. His focus on heterosexual promiscuity as the key factor in defining class difference, however, in the end yields a result not much different from Macedo's. The lower classes are more primitive and are a threat to the "order and progress" promoted by the Porfirian government.

Particularly troublesome for those who wish to classify men by their apparel was the trend, however mild, to challenge notions of gender difference. Feminism had many worried; although feminist rhetoric in Mexico was insubstantial compared to what was being pronounced and published in some other countries.[12] Even more vexatious were certain men's fashions that blurred gender boundaries; after all, the threat of effeminacy among men had been a major concern in Mexico throughout the nineteenth century. González Navarro notes, citing turn-of-the-century newspaper fashion commentaries:

> De un lado, se anunciaba tímidamente el uso por parte de la mujer de prendas tradicionalmente masculinas; y de otro, se criticaba la indumentaria de los "pollos," empeñados en imitar "de manera tan perfecta a las mujeres que casi lo han conseguido. . . . Lo que a las mujeres les han quitado en el vestido, a los hombres se los han cedido en los pantalones angostos."

> On the one hand, women's tendency to wear traditionally masculine clothes was timidly announcing itself; on the other, the style of dress of the "dandies," who were bent on imitating "women in such a perfect way that they have nearly succeeded . . . ," was being criticized. "What women have lost by not wearing dresses has been ceded to men in their wide pants." ("El porfiriato" 395)

Civilization and Effeminacy

This brings us to an interesting quandary for turn-of-the-century Mexicans preoccupied with gender. Lower-class masculinity was being marked as sexually dangerous and roughly masculine. However, the bourgeois identified *pollos* who were dressing effeminately as threatening to a whole gendered system of values. Barbarous lower-class men exhibited truculent aggressiveness and menacing sexuality. Civilized upper-class men were not committing violent crimes, but it seemed their soft, cultured style was leading them into dreaded effeminacy. Such discourse was not, of course, unique to Mexico at the time. As gender was becoming a major issue in cultures in which civilization and barbarity had been prominent topics of national discourse for decades, it is not surprising that the two themes would eventually cross.[13]

Urbina, as we have seen earlier, addresses the problem directly in his essay "Los valientes y la civilización" [Valiant men and civilization] (*Crónicas* 83–85), in which Mexican manly valor is contrasted with European civilized refinement, linking a key trait of Mexican masculinity (as seen in so many nineteenth-century novels) with an undesirable, backward barbarity. His *crónicas* of crimes associate masculine violence with savageness. The child murderer Timoteo Andrade is compared to "esos ogros devoradores de carne cruda, recién salidos de la selva primitiva, insaciables y furiosos.... Tiene la crueldad de su sexo; es un macho bravo" [those ogres who devour raw meat, having recently emerged from the primitive jungle, insatiable and furious.... He possesses the cruelty of his sex; he is a ferocious male animal] (*Crónicas* 4).

Victoriano Salado Álvarez, a minor turn-of-the-century writer, not usually associated with *modernismo*—Nervo called him "enemigo acre de las escuelas modernas" [acrimonious enemy of the modern schools] ("Victoriano Salado Álvarez" 162),[14] but known as a great defender of the *porfiriato,* published a short story in 1900 that also dealt with the issue of masculinity and civilization, "El eunuco" [the eunuch]. Here, greedy landowner Prudencio Rubalcaba finds himself confronted by a band of robbers renowned for their barbaric violence. The leader, Antonio Rojas, demands Rubalcaba's money and there is a standoff, a very masculine battle of wills. However, Rubalcaba is alone, everyone else from the ranch having fled in fear, while Rojas has his band of brigands to back him up. As the evil Juan Diente sharpens his machete, Rubalcaba must decide between his hard-earned money (the spoils of civilization) and the punishment that awaits him: "y pudieron más la avaricia y el afán de atesorar, que el amor a la vida, y a más que eso, a la virilidad, al amor, a los senos ebúrneos, a los semblantes delicados, a los talles cimbradores" [and avarice and eagerness for material possessions held sway over love of life, and more than that, love of virility, love for ivory breasts, delicate demeanors, supple waists] (19). He allows Juan Diente to castrate him and thereby gives up his masculinity for the sake of his money, ending up a "residuo de hombre" [remnant of a man] (19), "un viejecillo rechoncho, lampiño, de carne fofa, de busto corto, de largas piernas y de regordetes y desmesurados brazos" [a chubby little old man, beardless, flabby-skinned, short-busted, with long legs and pudgy and disproportionate arms] (14), a eunuch.

A more representative modernist tale addressing the same theme is Ciro Ceballos's bizarre 1903 short story, "Un adulterio" [an adultery]. Rogelio Villamil, like Prudencio Rubalcaba, is a mere vestige of a man. Rich Rogelio had, as a "doncel,"[15] to use the author's term, suffered from "satyriasis" (the male version of nymphomania), which led him to have excessive sexual adventures, or as the narrator puts it with an ever so slight misogynistic sentiment: "Sucumbió en absoluto a la inmundicia bíblica de la varona condenada que ofrece siempre al idealismo sideral del hombre enamorado, la llaga incurable que sangra, la llaga que apesta, la llaga que pudre, que contamina, que mata, la llaga maldita, la llaga" [He succumbed absolutely to the biblical filth of the accursed woman[16] who, to the sidereal idealism of the man in love, offers up the incurable bleeding wound, the stinking wound, the rotting, contaminating, killing wound, the cursed wound, the wound] (22).

Ceballos's view of male sexuality is clear. It is a dirty impulse, but clearly the fault of the foul female sex who inspire it. The "sidereal idealism" of young Rogelio's refined masculinity eventually gives way to more guttural expressions of lust that nearly destroy him. His primary ailment is apparently tuberculosis, although references are made to less tangible afflictions including hysteria. Just as young Rogelio had achieved manhood by having sex for the first time with a servant girl who worked in his house, his later sexual escapades put him in danger of losing his manhood. He goes so far as to imagine his "agilidades" [agilities]—his health, his masculine vigor—threatened by "la pesantez urania" [uranic gravity] (29) during his illness.[17]

So his doctor sends him out to the country for the familiar modernist scene of convalescence. There he falls nobly in love with a neighbor who is, bizarrely, a virgin widow whose husband died in a horseback riding accident before having the chance to consummate their marriage. There are two complications, however, with the woman, Geraldina: first, she likes Rogelio but does not actually love him back; second, she does exhibit affections, but they are all for her pet, who happens to be a gorilla. So Rogelio ends up competing with a gorilla for Geraldina's attention.

Eventually Rogelio wins out and they marry. However, on the wedding night, Rogelio discovers that the virgin widow is not actually a virgin. This knowledge nearly destroys him, bringing on a relapse of the illness that had been wearing him down when he met her. She confesses nothing and reacts to Rogelio's jealousy with indifference. Finally, one day from his sickbed, Rogelio hears "un rumor de lamentos espasmódicos" [the sound of spasmodic moans] (46) and sneaks into his wife's room to investigate only to find that "[e]n la alfombra su esposa completamente desnuda se copulaba con horrible rijo con el cuadrumano" [on the carpet his wife, completely naked, was copulating with horrible lust with the quadrumane] (46). Thus, the competition—between the man who for reasons of health is forced to behave in a civilized manner with women, and the savage ape—is won by the ape. Civilized masculinity, we might conclude, is a major contributing factor to society's decadence.

Civilized masculinity, in fact, presents mortal dangers, as the *modernistas* were to learn the hard way. According to Rubén Campos, a leading *modernista,* the "civilized" institution of the bar became center of social life for turn-of-the-century Mexican poets. The bar, a more refined drinking establishment than the more traditional *cantina* or utterly lower-class *pulquería,* was a totally masculine space, with entrance forbidden to women (*El bar* 34).[18] It was a major locus of male homosocial bonding ("Todo era fraternidad" [Everything was fraternity] [32]), but in a most refined and civilized style ("Todo en el bar era cortesía, caballerosidad, reciprocidad y camaradería" [Everything in the bar was courtesy, chivalry, reciprocity, and camaraderie] [33]). This civilized masculinity was still masculine; barflies Salvador Díaz Mirón—"Cuando se estaba ante Díaz Mirón teníase la convicción de estar frente a un hombre" [When you met up with Díaz Mirón, you would have the conviction of being in the presence of a man] (145)—and Manuel José Othón—with "un pecho rudo y rauco, ancho y recio, busto magnífico de una cabeza segada al rape, sólida y salvaje" [a rude and husky breast, broad and robust, a magnificent bust, with a buzzcut, solid and savage] (155)—for example, were known as pillars of turn-of-the-century masculinity.[19] However, what became increasingly clear with the passing of years was that civilization in excess was not healthy. While criminologists such as Macedo and Roumagnac complained to no end about the alcoholism of the lower classes and its links to violent crime,[20] alcoholism was also quietly taking its toll on the upper classes. No less than five of the chapters of Campos's *El bar: La vida literaria de México en 1900,* treat untimely deaths of modernist poets with drinking problems.[21] Institutions of civilized masculinity such as the bar escaped the violence and the sexual debauchery of barbarous lower-class masculinity but did not solve Mexico's gender crisis.

Lower-class versions of masculinity, then, reflected degeneration into barbarous historical patterns[22] while upper-class versions reflected the decadence of modern civilization.[23] Effeminacy itself was another key issue of the time, and Mexican society's neurosis regarding male effeminacy became especially acute as it came to be linked with a new social ill that was to fascinate turn-of-the-century Mexico: homosexuality.

A Case of Literary Pathology

The first important discussion of homosexuality in Mexico occurred through a series of brief cable blurbs and rather timid newspaper articles—written mainly by correspondents in Paris who covered the story second hand via French newspaper accounts—on the subject of the Oscar Wilde trials.[24] Early reports (reprints of wire service summaries) mentioned only that Wilde was incarcerated after being found guilty of libel.[25] However, later reports were more detailed, even going so far as to link the Wilde trials with cultural anxieties prominent in Mexico.

An anonymous article in *El Universal* (April 21, 1895) took up the link of masculinity with civilization and barbarity as it played effeminate Wilde against the famous Marquess of Queensberry, the great "sportsman" and sponsor of boxers: "en este litigio en que han salido a luz tantas inmoralidades, el hombre refinado, el estético, el espiritualista, aparece con el carácter de una grosera bestia humana; y el amigo de la gente de bronce, el patrono de las riñas de hombres, aparece como el defensor y guardián de la moral por el otro conculcada" [in this litigation in which so many immoralities have been brought to light, the refined man, the aesthete, the spiritualist, appears with the character of a gross human beast; and the friend of the people of bronze, the patron of fights between men, appears as the defender and guardian of morals violated by the other] (5).

Wilde's crime is at first described still rather vaguely as "corruption of youth," but by May 3, *El Nacional,* also in an anonymous article, was willing to be more explicit, mentioning Wilde's "íntimos lazos de amistad" [intimate bonds of friendship] with "Queensbury's" [*sic*] son and "delitos contra la honestidad" [crimes against decency]. Five days later, a front-page article written by E. Gómez de Baquero, correspondent in Paris, began to exhibit greater expansiveness and literary extravagance. It opens: "Hay todo un capítulo de psicología, y de psicología femenina, en la fruición con que los periódicos franceses comentan el proceso escandaloso de Londres" [There is a whole chapter of psychology, and of feminine psychology at that, in the delight with which the French newspapers comment on the scandalous trial of London]. Gómez opines:

> Tal vez no hay tanta distancia como se piensa entre las observaciones mentales y las depravaciones físicas. El afán de buscar estimulantes intelectuales en lo monstruoso, en lo anormal, en lo extraordinario, puede pasar de la teoría a la práctica. El caso de Oscar Wilde es quizá un caso de patología literaria.... Es posible que haya en este asunto tan repugnante un aviso a los partidores de las escuelas decadentes que no quieran llegar, en su decadencia, hasta el amor griego.

> Maybe there is not so much distance as one thinks between mental observations and physical depravations. The zeal for seeking intellectual stimulants in the monstrous, the abnormal, the extraordinary, may pass from theory into practice. The case of Oscar Wilde is perhaps a case of literary pathology.... It is possible that there is in this very repugnant subject a warning to members of decadent schools who do not wish, in their decadence, to sink to the level of Greek love.

El Nacional goes on to follow Wilde's trials on a regular basis through late June, when a final article, penned by "Manrique de Lara"[26] appears outlining the specifics of the forced labor that Wilde is to undergo in prison.

Here the coverage ends, but not the appetites of newspaper readers on the subject of crimes against decency. If sex crimes such as those of the *matadores de mujeres* studied by Roumagnac were exciting, and the more unusual sex crimes committed by women were thrilling, a new type of sex crime was just coming into existence in the public sphere that would top both. But it wasn't until 1901 that discourse on male homosexuality came into its own in Mexico. In fact, to date it is still difficult to imagine any historical discussion of male homosexuality in Mexico that does not make mention of the events of November 17, 1901 at number 4, calle de la Paz.

The Famous 41 and
the Birth of Modern Homosexuality in Mexico

El Baile Nefando

The case began timidly with brief newspaper reports[27] stating the facts (or what were to be taken as such) of the case: that a private party had been raided by the police who subsequently arrested forty-one (or forty-two—according to rumor the forty-second, the son-in-law of then president Porfirio Díaz, was quietly released and quickly forgotten in the press)[28] men, half of them dressed as women. At first, the newspapers were reluctant to give any more information. One early report apologizes, "No damos a nuestros lectores más detalles, por ser en sumo asquerosos" [We won't give our readers any more details because they are supremely disgusting] (*El Popular,* November 20, 1901).[29]

However, the news quickly became the talk of the town, and as newspapers began to sell because of it, stories grew. The very same journal three days later was no longer apologizing about its coverage: "Nosotros ofrecemos publicar...todos los pormenores que se relacionen con este asunto . . . , pues es tiempo de impedir que escenas tan indecentes se repitan" [We offer to publish . . . all details related to this subject . . . , because it is time to prevent such indecent scenes from recurring] (*El Popular*, November 23, 1901).[30] Ironically, in a very Foucauldian manner, the discourse that emanated from these newspaper accounts and that would spread to popular legend and literature (the 1906 novel *Los 41*, by Eduardo Castrejón) would come to make the number 41 a symbol of Mexican male homosexuality, and in doing so make homosexuality an undeniable part of national culture.

In summary, the raid[31] was carried out because the party was being held "without proper permission" and the participants were locked up in the Cárcel de Belén "for attacks on morality." From the very first, *El Popular*, albeit timidly the first day, celebrated the transvestism: "Esos vestían trajes elegantísimos de señora, llevaba pelucas, pechos postizos, aretes, choclos bordados y en la cara tenían pintadas grandes ojeras y chapas de color" [They dressed in very elegant ladies' dresses, wore wigs, false breasts, earrings, embroidered low-heeled shoes, and had make-up painted heavily around their eyes and their cheeks rouged]; at the same time, the reports were always careful to condemn the events reported: "se censura la conducta de dichos individuos" [the conduct of these individuales is censured] (*El Popular*, November 20, 1901). This contradiction in attitudes (enjoyment, condemnation) was to endure through the entire public discourse on the event, as if the Mexicans could not help relishing this particular sexual and gender transgression, but always while remaining conscious of the fact that they should not be doing so.

The popular story also became a way to attract readers to broader political arguments. While the Catholic *El País* also began covering the story rather timidly, the event began to mushroom on November 22 when *El País* moved the story from the second to the front page with its article "El baile nefando" [The nefarious ball]. *El País* used the event to criticize "the state of immorality" in Mexico (evils of "sensuality," "degeneration"), which it attributes to "libertinage—fundamental abysm of liberalism," but can't resist recounting how the "chinos" [curly-haired boys] are mocked by soldiers upon their departure: "Nos dicen que les cantaban el '¿A dónde vas con mantón de Manila' y otros el '¡Ay! qué facha!' " [We are told that they sang "Where are you going in your embroidered silk shawl?" and "Oh! What a look!"].

Likewise, the more rebellious and cantankerous weekly, *El Hijo del Ahuizote,* used the story of the 41 to raise issues of censorship in the press ("¿Por qué se permite al libro lo que no se consiente á la prensa?" [Why is it that what is permitted in books is not admissible in the press?] [November 24, 1901]), the custom of sending criminals to serve time in the Mexican army (November 24, 1901), and even the right to privacy (December 1, 1901).

By the November 23, the fun had only started, but *El Imparcial* had already had enough (particularly after the jabs at liberalism made in *El País*) as is seen in "El baile escandaloso":

> La curiosidad pública y las embozadas referencias de la prensa, han dado motivo a que circulen versiones más o menos fantásticas. Hay quienes aseguran que entre los individuos aprehendidos había capitalistas y otras personas de posición encumbrada pertenecientes á familias muy distinguidas. También se ha dicho que los presos fueron consignados al servicio de armas.
>
> Creemos necesario rectificar esas opiniones. La verdad es que en la referida reunión, excesivamente inmoral y escandalosa, sólo se encontraba un grupo de más de 40 hombres, muy conocidos por sus costumbres depravadas, y que más de una vez han figurado en escándalos por el estilo....
>
> Todos los presos han sido enviados á Yucatán, pero no—como se ha dicho—a formar en las filas de los valientes soldados que hacen la campaña; sino que se les empleará en trabajos de zapa, como abrir brechas, rellenar bajos, abrir fosos y [l]evantar fortificaciones pasajeras.

> Public curiosity and the veiled references of the press have incited the circulation of more or less fantastic versions of the story. There are those who assert that included among the individuals apprehended are businessmen and other persons of noble position or from very distinguished families. It has also been said that the prisoners were consigned into the armed services.
>
> We believe it necessary to rectify these opinions. The truth is that in the above mentioned excessively immoral and scandalous party, the only ones in attendance were a group of more than 40 men, well known

for their depraved customs, who have figured more than once in similar scandals. . . .

All the prisoners have been sent to Yucatán but not—as it has been rumored—to join the rank and file of the valiant soldiers who are undertaking the campaign; but to be given employment in the trenches, such as opening breaches, filling in holes, digging ditches, and raising temporary fortifications.

El Imparcial finds it necessary to report on the crime to quell the scandal and to demonstrate that the liberal government is not being foolhardy in sending the perpetrators to Yucatán. An editorial two days later entitled "La inmoralidad y el liberalismo" [immorality and liberalism] defends the liberals from the Catholic conservatives. This is all that *El Imparcial* has to say about the subject.[32]

Of Decency and Stripteases

Meanwhile, the Catholic conservatives of *El País*—who advertise: "En este diario no se insertará ningún anuncio que ofenda a lo más mínimo a la moral o la decencia cristianas" [In this newspaper we will not publish any ad that offends Christian morality or decency in the slightest]—unleash a series of clamorous articles with the repeating title, "El Baile de sólo hombres" [The men-only ball] (November 23, 24, and 27, 1901), a poem by Khit[33] entitled "El fusil y no las faldas" [Rifles, not skirts] (November 23, 1901), and an editorial by the same author criticizing "Desertores del sexo" [Deserters of their sex] (November 24, 1901). Once again, as is demonstrated in the first of the above articles, the writer is unable to avoid humor in reporting the "facts":

A las 5:30 de la mañana, hora en que se pasa la lista del 24° Batallón de los remitidos al puerto de Veracruz, fueron llamados primero los doce individuos que estaban en el celebre baile y después al tocarle su turno al número 13 era un pelado, contestó al oír su nombre: "Presente mi Capitán; pero hago constar que yo voy consignado por ratero; pero no soy de esos," y señaló el grupo de los bailadores.

Esto provocó la risa de cuantos estaban presentes, porque ni el ratero quiso confundirse con los perjumaos [*sic*], como los dicen los soldados en el cuartel.

At 5:30 in the morning, the time when attendance is taken in the 24th Battalion for those being sent to the port of Veracruz, the first ones called were the twelve individuals who had been in the celebrated ball, and at number 13's turn, a *pelado*[34] answered upon hearing his name: "Present, Captain, Sir; but let me emphasize that I'm being sent away for being a thief; but I'm not one of them," and he pointed to the group of dancers.

This provoked laughs from those present because not even the thief wanted to be confused with the perfumed boys, as the soldiers call them in the barracks.

The writer then gets carried away, eroticizing the scene, while ridiculing the situation further:

El Capitán de reemplazos hizo que todos se desnudaron a la mayor brevedad y les fue repartiendo las toscas pero honrosas prendas de ropa que se les da a los reclutas.

Con las lágrimas en los ojos, fueron despojándose de todas sus prendas, suplicando algunos, que se les dejase siquiera sus ropas interiores de fina seda, a lo cual se opuso el Capitán, pues les dijo que allí eran iguales a los demás. Ni los calcetines les permitió y todos comenzaron a llorar cuando se calzaron los zapatos que iban a reemplazar a los monos choclos de glace pasia y charol.

The Captain of the reinforcements made them strip immediately and handed out the rough but honorable clothes that they give to the recruits.

With tears in their eyes, they stripped off all their clothes, some of them begging to be allowed to keep at least their undergarments of fine silk, which the Captain refused since, he said, there they were the same as everyone else. He wouldn't even let them keep their socks, and all of them began to cry when they put on men's shoes in place of their pretty patent leather ladies' shoes.

Are we to imagine that the convicts were forced to strip publicly? If not, why has the author of this "decent" and "moral" Catholic newspaper chosen to invent and feature this particular scene? *El País* has, in fact, made a few things clear: first that the dancers are not "the same as everyone else" as the Captain insists (the army would like to make them conform to norms of masculinity, but the process is painful and anything but natural for them); and second that the Catholic press is not aiming to fight what they portray as immorality, but, in fact, they are happy to celebrate such events, and even exaggerate them in order to animate and keep alive a discourse on a subject that allows them to maintain the public's attention to their constant criticism of the government's social policies.[35] For example, *El País* complains, as we saw above, that only twelve of the 41 were sent to Yucatán, but that some others were released after having their heads shaved of their curls and being fined: "esperamos que todos ellos sean eliminados de la capital.... Esa es la democracia: la igualdad de responsables ante la ley" [we hope that all of them will be eliminated from the capital.... That is democracy: equality of responsibility before the law].

Now, it would seem, the perpetrators are gone and there is nothing left to say. But this is only the beginning for *El País,* which continues with "El fusil y no las faldas," its first opportunity to really develop and celebrate the theme of transvestism ("... lucían / espléndido cuerpos, / enaguas planchadas, / pomada en el pelo," [they showed off / splendid bodies, / ironed petticoats, / pomade in their hair]). Finally, Khit turns out not to be against transvestism at all: "¡Vayan enhoramala a Yucatán estos desertores del sexo! pero no a vestir el honroso uniforme del soldado a la Patria; en mi concepto, estarían mejor en la cocina del regimiento, y les rendría muy ancho el mandil del ranchero" [Let these sex deserters go to Yucatán and good riddance to them! But not dressed in the honorable soldier's uniform of the Fatherland; in my opinion, they would be better off in the regiment's mess hall, and I'd issue each of them a big kitchen apron] ("Desertores de sexo," November 24, 1998). After all, several of them were returned to Mexico City "por inútiles" [for being useless] ("El baile de sólo hombres," November 24, 1901). It would seem that these effeminate men, in fact, would do better if allowed to continue in their feminine roles.

"Los Chismes del Día" and Other Front-Page News

Meanwhile, *El Popular,* a more bawdy scandal sheet, offered the most coverage (and the most entertaining coverage), including two articles entitled "El baile de los 41" [The ball of the 41] (November 23 and 24, 1901). They also published a number of gossip pieces, "El baile de los 41, El bautizo de un rorro y la rifa de un Pepito, Una vieja entre los pollos, Bigotitos rizados—'¡Mírame, marchando voy!'" [The ball of the 41, The baptism of a babe and the raffle of a dandy, An old lady among the boys, Curly-beards—"Look at me as I go marching off!"] (November 24, 1901), and "Los 41 de marras nacieron de nuevo" [The former 41 are born again] (November 25, 1901), a song "¡Cuarenta y un maricones!" [41 pansies] (November 25, 1901) and two pieces of comic fiction, "El viaje de los 41: Diario colectivo" [The voyage of the 41: A collective diary] (November 29, 1901) and "Las cartas de los 41" [The letters of the 41] (December 1, 1901). What had begun as serious reporting with a touch of giddiness quickly slipped into pure ridiculization and carnivalization of the subject. *El Popular* demonstrated much less pretension of moral defense and much more delight with piquant subject matter.

Through November 24, *El Popular*'s stories continued to take the form of news reports, although there was not really much new information to report. They contradicted *El País* on November 23, claiming that nineteen (not twelve) men were sent to Yucatán.[36] Also in opposition to *El País*'s claims, *El Popular* reported on the same day that pleas from the influential families of some of the men arrested for less severe punishments had gone ignored by the "inflexible" authorities, and *La Patria* (November 28, 1901), in fact, reported that two more men were sent to Yucatán a week after the first group left and that more would be sent along later.

Another new piece of data is reported in *El Popular* on the November 24; in this report, the author demonstrates that there were, in fact, two groups of men arrested, one half of them dressed up with "el disfraz tan bien hecho, que era difícil al primer golpe de vista, saber si aquellos individuos eran hombres" [their disguises so well done that it was difficult at first glance to tell whether those individuals were men], and the other half "víctimas de un verdadero chasco pues que, en las primeras horas de la noche del domingo se repartieron en varias cantinas unas tarjetas firmadas por una Sra. Vinchi en las que se invitaba a un baile en la casa citada esa mismo [*sic*] noche" [victims of a real trick since in the early hours of Sunday night, cards signed by a Mrs. Vinchi were handed out in various cantinas inviting recipients to a ball in the referenced house that same night]. *El Popular* goes on to forgive the latter group: "Conste, pues, que los comentarios severos que hacemos y hemos hecho van dirigidos a aquellos que perdiendo todo vergüenza han descendido hasta vestirse de mujer y bailar con otros tantos desvergonzados, muchos de los cuales están retratados como afeminados conocidos en la Inspección General de Policía" [We affirm, then, that the severe commentaries that we make and have made are directed toward those who, losing all sense of shame, have stooped to dressing as women and dancing with other shameless fellows, many of whom are portrayed as effeminate men well known at the Police Inspector General's office]. Here it is implied that not all of the men arrested are effeminate, and perhaps, then, not all are criminals. However, it is not clear whether only the transvestites should be punished, or if there were other effeminate men (and effeminacy seems to be the key issue) who did not dress up.

The dancing is also a key issue. Dances and parties, a central part of Mexican culture according to Octavio Paz, are troubling to hegemonic structures and hierarchies because they invite carnivalesque inversions of social norms (*El laberinto* 42–48). Dances have had a bad name among moralists in Mexico ever since *El Periquillo Sarniento,* whose narrator claims, "Los que hacen bailes . . . son unos alcahuetes y solapadores de mil indecencias escandalosas" [Those who throw dance parties . . . are pimps and sneaks of a thousand scandalous indecencies] (133).[37] He goes on, "Bailar no es malo, lo malo es el modo con que se baila" [Dancing isn't bad, what's bad is the way that one dances] (135); "Ordinariamente estos mozos bailadores, o como les dicen, *útiles,* son unos pícaros de buen tamaño; no llevan a un baile más que dos objetos: divertirse y *chonguear* (es su voz). Este *chongueo* no es más que sus seducciones o llanezas. Si pueden, pervierten a la doncella y hacen prevaricar a la casada, y todo esto sin amor, sino por un mero vicio o pasatiempo" [Ordinarily these dancing guys, or as they are called, *usefuls,* are great rogues; they bring just two objectives to a dance: to have fun and to *flatter* (as they put it). This *flattery* is nothing more than their seductions or intimacies. If they can, they pervert a maiden and corrupt a married woman, and all this without any love, but merely due to vice or in order to pass the time]

(134). Dancing seems to imply all kinds of sexual risks to women emanating from unbridled male sexuality; social controls of sexual conduct break down. Dancing, according to Lizardi, is inherently sexual.

The fact that the forty-one men were dancing together, then, would seem to imply that they were more than effeminate men, but also homosexuals. Moreover, *El Popular* implies that only some of the men were homosexuals, only those who knew what was going on. The others were victims, not because they were dancing in a more innocent or less sexual way than the others, but because, due to the perfection of the costumes, they did not know they were dancing with other men. It is ironic that the transvestites are ridiculed and made to seem like clowns at times, and at the same time are portrayed as masters of disguise capable of fooling the "real" men whom they seduced.

Once this last news story is published, *El Popular* keeps the story of the 41 alive not by adding any new information in an official manner, but—unlike *El Hijo del Ahuizote,* which linked the story for several weeks to other political issues—by publishing gossip and humor pieces on the topic. On the front page of the November 24th issue, it publishes a discussion between two *comadritas*[38] divulging more details about the case, but without any pretense of presenting hard facts.[39] The *comadres* sexualize the event from the start, comparing it to Sodom and Gomorrah ("cosas que...dejan a uno convertido en 'estuata' [*sic*] de sal" [things that...end up with one turned into a statue of salt]). They gossip about the mock baptism (of a child who apparently belonged to one of the *afeminados*) and the raffle of the curly-bearded gallant:

> —¡Por eso era la rifa de elefante! ¿Qué haría con él quién se lo sacara?
> —¡Pues hay [*sic*] está el cuento, mi alma! Pero hay cosas que no son para contadas. Pues para no cansar a usté, hicieron su bailecito a puerta cerrada, en una casa vacía que alquilaron, como los monederos falsos. Pero como era baile de hombres solos, y de máscaras, la mitá de ellos se vistieron de mujer.
> —¡Ave María Purísima!
> —Sin pecado concebida.
> —¡Qué afeminados!

"That's quite a white elephant raffle! What would the winner do with him?"

"Well, there's the story, my dear! But there are things that should not be told. Well, not to bore you, they had their little dance behind closed doors, in an empty house that they rented, like counterfeiters. But as it was a dance of men alone, and a masked ball, half of them dressed as women."

"Purest holy Mary!"

"Conceived without sin."

"What pansies!"

The *comadritas* reveal details about the dance that the newspaper reports never addressed, in the form of gossip. Gossip, like a newspaper report, reveals the news, but does not have any pretense of neutrality. Gossips revel in scandal; they moralize, but they savor every tidbit of what is said, whether it is strictly true or not. Here the newspaper is able to publish unconfirmed details and to employ a popular dialect (and in this case the vulgar terms are perhaps the most descriptive). The *comadritas* go on, describing the arrest:

—¡Los maricas tiraron la careta!

    —¡Almas mías!

    —"¡Yo tengo corazón!" gritaba uno.—"¡Pues con corazón y todo van sinvergüenzas!"

    Y así como estaban...¡a Belén presuroso, marchemos, tapándose la carabina y las lagrimitas!

    —¿Lloraban como jotos?

    —O lo fingían comadre. Pero lo mero bueno fue cuando los consignaron al Gobernador...

    —¿Qué dijo?

    —¡Yo no tengo que ver nada con esos maricones! ¡...Yucatán!

    —Dios de mi vida...¡Pero los Mayas se van a enojar! ¡Ellos no pelean con maricas!

    —¿Pues, quién les manda? ¡Que se enseñen a hombres!

"The fairies threw off their masks!"

"Dear me!"

" 'I have heart!' shouted one of them. 'Well, with heart and everything else you go, shameless ones!' "

And just as they were...to Belén quickly, let's march, covering the carbines and your little tears!

"They cried like sissies?"

"Or pretended to, *comadre*. But the best was when they sent them to see the Governor. . . . "

"What did he say?"

"I'll have nothing to do with these pansies! To Yucatán with them!"

"God of my life. . . . But the Mayas are going to get mad! They don't fight with pansies!"

"Well, who's making them? May they learn to be men!"

In this way, it is clear that a variety of terms, synonymous with "effeminate," used interchangeably here in this conversation charged with sexual innuendo, come also to be synonymous with "homosexual," e.g., "marica" and "joto."

The last reports to appear are pure comedy. On the November 29, *El Popular* publishes a "collective diary" presumably written at sea on the voyage from Veracruz to Yucatán. A few excerpts reveal the tone of the report: "Sin consideración a nuestro sexo y al estado interesante de varias de las señoritas, que somos víctimas de una barbaridad masculina nos metieron, hechas bola, en un carro de tercera clase de ferrocarril mexicano, revueltas con esos mecos soldados que, a cada rato, insultaban nuestro pudor con palabrotas muy cochinas" [Without any consideration for our sex and the interesting state of some of the young ladies, victims of a masculine barbarity, they threw us, all in a big jumble, in a third-class Mexican rail car, mixed in with those coarse soldiers who, every couple of minutes, insulted our modesty with obscene and filthy words]. This comic piece, of course, does not attempt to resolve any issues, but it does point out a certain anxiety about masculinity. Masculinity, in fact, is portrayed as vulgar and barbaric; civilization is clearly feminine. This will remain an issue of great import for decades.

The comic pieces also allowed *El Popular* to bring much more blatant sexual innuendo into the discussion. The new archetype of the Mexican transvestite was thus being constructed as a sexualized being, a person exuding an aggressive feminine sexuality clearly directed toward other men (i.e., an aggressive effeminate homosexuality). A few examples:

Beatrizito se quejaba de que el asiento era muy duro, por ser pura tabla, y le lastimaba la sección más encantadora de su personalidad.

Beatrizito complained that the seat was very hard, made of pure wood, and that it hurt the most enchanting section of his personality.

Pepita comenzó a abortar...malas palabras.

Pepita began to abort...bad words.

Probablemente Lucrecio está muy embarazado con lo que le pasa.

Probably Lucrecio is very embarrassed[40] about what has happened.

Lo malo es que esta travesía durará tres días, de aquí a Progreso, y no sabemos a lo que se atreverán esos marineros, al saber que somos mujeres y solas, y con la seguridad de que no tenemos madre.

The bad thing is that this voyage will last three days, from here to Progreso, and we don't know what these sailors will dare, knowing that we are women traveling alone, and with the assurance that we don't have a mother.[41]

The *double entendres,* the use of feminine names in masculine form (Beatrizito, Lucrecio) or masculine names in feminine form (Pepita), the thinly veiled references to anal sex, pregnancy, abortion, and rape firmly feminize and sexualize these figures.

The final installment (December 1, 1901) published in *El Popular* is a comic piece ("re")producing letters theoretically written by the 41. The authors once again are sexually undecided, at least according to their names (Concho, Lolito, Carolino). And the contents of the letters, of course are very racy:

Alfredo de mis intestinos:
    ¡Ay! No hay en el mundo mujer más desgraciada ¡Uy! ¡Como me duele el corazón y los hemisferios posteriores!
    ...ya no puedo andar espiándote de noche en la Alameda y en el Zócalo como antes lo hacía, bebiéndome mis respectivas lágrimas....A propósito...haz por mandarme los dos pesos que me debes.

Alfredo of my intestines:
    Oh! There is no woman in the world more disgraced than I, Uy! How my heart and my posterior hemispheres ache!
    I can no longer go spying on you by night in the Alameda park and in the town square like I did before, drinking my respective tears....By the way...make sure you send me the two pesos you owe me.

Mea dorado Luiz
   ...Procura mandarme mis calsones de piquitos y encajes que dejé en la cómoda.

My golden Luiz[42]
   ...Try to send me my piqué and lace underwear that I left in the bureau.

Señor Licienciado Triquiñuelas:
   ...suplico que haga lo que pueda porque me regresen a México. No puedo estar sin mi hijo. Por señas que me costó diez pesos y lo compré, con muchos sacrificios, en la juguetería de la Palma. Usted no sabe to da vía [sic] lo que es ser madre.

Mr. Subterfuge:
   ...I beg you to do what you can so that they will return me to Mexico. I can't be without my son. By token of the ten pesos I spent to buy him, with many sacrifices, in the Palma toystore. You still don't know what it is to be a mother.

These letters continue building on the stereotypes of feminine tastes, and even the desires to be actual women, i.e., mothers. Most interesting here (and this will be taken up further when we look at Castrejón's novel) are the variety of different kinds of relationships constructed among the lovers. There seems to be a live-in relationship with Luiz and Lolito, a specific kind of sexual relationship between Alfredo and Concho that is not monogamous at least on Alfredo's part, and a domestic fantasy that Carolino has involving Mr. Subterfuge. Meanwhile these relationships transcend social class with some transvestites (e.g., Lolito) or their boyfriends (Concho's Mr. Subterfuge) clearly lower class, and others (Carolino and her lover) clearly bourgeois.

José Guadalupe Posada

Aquí están los maricones
Muy chulos y coquetones....
Cuarenta y un lagartijos
Disfrazados la mitad
De simpáticas muchachas
Bailaban el que más.
La otra mitad con su traje,
Es decir de masculinos,

Gozaban al extrechar
A los famosos jotitos.

Here are the pansies
Very cute and coquettish....
Forty-one dandies
Half of them dressed up
As delightful girls
They tripped the night fantastic.
The other half in their suits,
That is masculine style,
They enjoyed themselves in getting intimate
With the *famous fairies*.

So began the *corrido* accompanying the first of a series of etchings by the popular cartoonist José Guadalupe Posada. The Posada leaflets, which borrow heavily from *El Popular* "reports"[43]—for example, Posada's line, "Al pobrecito Sofío/ Le dieron muchos desmayos" [Poor Sofío / Was afflicted with many fainting spells], is taken directly from *El Popular*'s "El viaje de los 41" article: "Sofío sufrió algunos desmayos" [Sofío suffered several fainting spells]—further popularize, and Mexicanize, the legend of the 41 by caricaturing it in Posada's celebrated Mexican style.

Posada, in the vein of the comic pieces in *El Popular*, continues with the sexual innuendo, fortifying the symbolic link between effeminacy and homosexuality, by using words such as "extrechar" (i.e., "estrechar") meaning "get close to" or "press up against," and by implying sexual harassment of the 41 *maricones* on the part of the soldiers with whom they were forced to travel. The very fact that Posada, now a Mexican icon himself, saw fit to produce no less than four etchings of the 41 in 1901 (not to mention another representation of the 41 in an etching mocking the rise of feminism in 1907) is a major contributing factor to the Mexicanization of male homosexuality in the wake of the scandal.

The vision of male homosexuality conjured up in the Posada engravings and texts is one of an effeminacy made ridiculous by the fact that the men in drag all have moustaches. Posada's ridiculing of the 41 is done, however, with affection. They are "jotones" and "jotitos," "maricones" or "maricazos" and "mariquitos,"[44] "chulos" [cute], "simpáticas" [nice girls], contributing to the general acceptance, or even welcoming, of the effeminate male homosexual as an immoral, ridiculous, frivolous, but most visibly Mexican figure. In fact, it was undoubtedly less the moral outrage than the enduring popularity of the case that inspired Eduardo Castrejón to publish a novel about it.[45]

Los 41: Novela Crítico-Social

"The publishers" of Los 41[46] justify the publication of a novel rehashing the five-year-old scandal by stating as its goals: "la corrección de las costumbres, la condenación de los vicios sociales, el anatema a todas las corrupciones, la exaltación de la moral y el anatema a la perversión del sentimiento humano" [the correction of customs, the condemnation of social vices, the damnation of all corruptions, the exaltation of morality, and the censure of the perversion of human sentiment] (iv). They compare Los 41 to El Periquillo Sarniento, which "puso sobre la plancha a la sociedad antigua, hizo la autopsia y descubrió toda la gangrena que devoraba aquel cuerpo aniquilado" [laid out bygone society on the examining table, did the autopsy, and uncovered all the gangrene that was devouring that annihilated corpse] (v). The extravagant language of the publisher's note serves both to indicate the moral indignity that supposedly motivated the publication of the novel and to whet the appetites of readers who hope for further sensationalistic flamboyance and excess in the novel to follow.

The publishers, ironically, seem little upset that the story remains alive in the public imagination five years after the fact—"un hecho que produjo el escándalo y que ha dejado en las llamas de la sátira una memoria que durará por muchos años" [an act that produced scandal and that has left in the flames of satire a memory that will endure for many years] (vi). After all this allows them to publish their novel so that they may "flagela[r] de una manera terrible un vicio execrable, sobre el cual escupe la misma sociedad, como el corruptor de las generaciones" [flagellate in a terrible way an execrable vice on which society itself spits as the corruptor of generations] (vi). But these flagellations would not serve so much to devour an annihilated corpse as to further enliven a newly acknowledged element of Mexican society, male homosexuality.

The cast of characters provides an interesting variety of personalities: the main organizer of the *baile nefando*, Mimí, exquisitely elegant, blond; his handsome blue-eyed teenaged servant "con mirada voluptuosa y melancólica" [with a voluptuous and melancholic countenance] (2); Pudor and Carolina, two effeminate lovebirds, the former particularly notorious for his hedonism, the latter noted for his ridiculously exaggerated imitation of feminine voice and gestures; Ninón, more vigorous, athletic, strong, handsome, misogynistic, apparently in the process of becoming more effeminate, the lover of Mimí; Virtud, pale, courtly, and refined; Blanca, darker, awkward, like a "female gorilla"; Margarita, well-dressed, but excessively made-up, like a third-rate "circus clown"; and Estrella, younger, "spiritual," and brand new to these activities and therefore the most attractive, like a virgin (43–45).

In brief, the story goes as follows. The big ball is being organized by Mimí and his above mentioned friends. However, the official girlfriends of homosexual lovers Mimí and Ninón—a pair of best friends named Estela and Judith—suspect the young men of committing undetermined perfidies. These two young ladies hire a private detective ("Mano de Alacrán" [Scorpion Claw]) to spy on their boyfriends. In the meantime, the dance goes ahead. Invitations are circulated to a group of men including transvestites and a more general class of libertines (among them one notorious Don Pedro de Marruecos), as well as to the patrons of certain *cantinas* who are assumed to be straight, masculine men looking for a good time. The party, described as a wild "bacchanal," goes on. There is the famous baptism of a child, and Estrella is raffled off by Don Pedro. Meanwhile, hurt and angry when they discover that their boyfriends are in fact homosexual lovers involved in a transvestite underworld, Estela and Judith see to it that the police raid the party. Everyone is arrested except for Don Pedro and his entourage, who miraculously escape via the roof. The next part of the story is well known. The transvestites are forced to sweep the streets in their feminine attire and then are sent to join the army in Yucatán. The second part of the book concentrates more on Estela (who marries a laborer in a brief story narrated in heavy-handed fashion) and Judith (who falls to even lower depths than the 41, ending up abandoning her fatherless son in order to marry rich) as well as on the ultimate reform of Ninón (who eventually marries into a middle-class family). The rest of the 41, including Mimí, who seemed to be the main character at the beginning of the book, are completely forgotten.[47]

The plot itself, in fact, is not so interesting in that it adds very little of substance to what has become, thanks to the newspapers and Posada, the legend of the 41. What is interesting about the novel is how the story is recounted, and how male homosexuality is envisioned.

La Insaciable Vorágine de Placeres Brutales

The language used to describe the activities of the *afeminados* is puzzling throughout the first part of the novel. At times, it seems as if the author not only condones their lifestyle, but admires it excessively. Constantly referring to "aquel inmenso bacanal" [that immense bacchanal] (6), "grandiosa dicha" [grandiose bliss] (9), "[e]l país de la eterna felicidad" [the land of eternal happiness] (9), "tan soberano placer" [such supreme pleasure] (9), "goces inefables y sensaciones excelsas" [ineffable enjoyments and lofty sensations] (39), "el paraíso del amor" [paradise of love] (60), etc., it seems that transvestite life is idyllic. It is not just pleasurable, but superlatively so. Castrejón's language is habitually hyperbolic, over the top, and on numerous occasions, it appears as if he idealizes (perhaps against his will) the joys of transvestism.

For example, when the transvestites' accomplice, a *modiste,* delivers their dresses, and the boys try them on, Castrejón apparently cannot contain himself:

> ¡El entusiasmo fue indescriptible entonces!
>
> Se sentían alegres, satisfechos, emocionados, pletóricos de felicidad mirándose vestidos de mujer.
>
> ¡Oh! y qué de transportes eróticos, qué de venturas, qué de embriagueces . . . . al trocar el traje de hombre para convertirse

en deliciosas niñas (?), en huríes encantadoras de suaves contornos y ondulantes líneas seductoras.

The enthusiasm was indescribable then!
    They felt joyous, satisfied, excited, plethoric with happiness seeing themselves dressed up as women.
    Oh! and what erotic transports, what joys, what intoxications . . . . in trading in their men's suits to convert themselves into delicious girls (?), into enchanting houris with soft contours and seductive undulating lines. (5–6)

Just as Castrejón feels obligated to use fourteen ellipses instead of the usual three (and at the end of the paragraph, he inserts forty-two of them!), every expression, every description requires extravagant embellishment. Moreover, his use of terms such as "paradise" and "heaven" ("los goces excelsos y venerandos [sic] del Cielo" [the supreme and venerated enjoyments of heaven] [11]) almost makes it seem as if he condones the pleasures felt by the 41.

This is not to say he is of a single mind on the subject. Castrejón also feels obliged to moralize and criticize, and his condemnations of the activities of the transvestites are equally excessive. The lavishness of language is astounding at times. A few examples:

[la] bastardía inmunda . . . de aquellos jóvenes inflamables, repudiados, odiosos para el porvenir y por todas las generaciones, escoria de la sociedad y mengua de los hombres honrados amantísimos de las bellezas fecundas de la mujer.

the filthy bastardy . . . of those young men, inflammable, repudiated, odious for the future and for all generations, scoria of society and disgrace of honorable men, ardent lovers of the fecund beauties of women; (13)

(Judith to Ninón): "te has prostituido hasta el grado de caer en el pantano donde los cerdos se avergonzarían de tocarlo por miedo de mancharse."

you have prostituted yourself to the extent of falling into the morass where pigs are ashamed to touch ground for fear of soiling themselves (32);

La desbordante alegría originada por la posesión de los trajes femeninos en sus cuerpos, las posturas mujeriles . . . representaban cuadros degradantes de aquellas escenas de Sodoma y Gomorra, de los festines orgiásticos de Tiberio, de Cómmodo y Calígula, donde el fuego explosivo de la pasión salvaje devoraba la carne consumiéndola en deseos de la más desenfrenada prostitución.

Y en esa insaciable vorágine de placeres brutales han caído, para no levantarse nunca, jóvenes que, en el colmo de la torpeza y de la degradación prostituida, contribuyen a bastardear la raza humana injuriando gravemente a la Naturaleza.

The abounding joy originating out of the possession of the feminine garments on their bodies, the womanly posturing . . . represented degrading pictures of those scenes of Sodom and Gomorrah, of the orgiastic feasts of Tiberius, of Commodus and Caligula, where the explosive fire of savage passion devoured the flesh, consuming it in desires of the most unbridled prostitution.

And into that insatiable vortex of brutal pleasures have fallen, to never rise again, youths who, at the height of torpidness and prostituted degradation, are contributing to the bastardization of the human race, gravely injuring Nature. (6)

The extravagance of Castrejón's vituperations is as outrageous as that of his descriptions of the delights of transvestism. At times he goes linguistically delirious, allowing all kinds of sexualized words to blur together connotations of pleasure and vice.

Part of the problem is that the book is relentless in sexualizing transvestism. If the newspapers hinted at links between transvestism and homosexuality, Castrejón plays them out, in his characteristic style, to the fullest. For example, when the various dandies arrive at Mimí's house to try on their new outfits, "[a]brazaron a *Mimí*[48] con efusión, se cambiaron algunos eróticos besos" [they embraced Mimí with effusion, exchanged erotic kisses] (2). The only couples in the group are Mimí and Ninón, and Carolina and Pudor; why, then, would they all be kissing each other erotically? Later, after they have tried on their dresses, once again the narrator writes of "los abrazos, los besos sonoros y febriles" [the hugs, the sonorous and feverish kisses] (6).

The link is made very clear when the situation of the *lacayitos* [footmen] of the transvestites is explained: "El lacayito [de Mimí], por su parte, entusiasta también y relacionado con toda la servidumbre de aquellos jóvenes, entre la cual había muchos iniciados en el amor secreto, había formado también su escuadrón de seres afeminados" [Mimí's footman, for his part, also an enthusiast, and well connected to the servants of the others, among whom there were many initiates into the secret love, had formed his squadron of effeminate beings, as well] (53). The servant squadron of effeminate beings is made up of initiates into the "secret love"; by 1906, there is never any doubt that effeminacy is synonymous with male homosexuality.

Castrejón's Queer Visions of Homosexuality

Castrejón's homosexuality is almost synonymous with libertinage. The vocabulary he uses to refer to the goings on among the transvestites of Los 41: "bacchanal," "savage passion," "orgy" is indicative of an unrestrained sexuality. Moreover, the fact that the consummate libertine, Don Pedro, is attracted to the group further fortifies the link. In fact, male homosexuality in Los 41 seems to be so excessive and extravagant as to be almost indefinable, a sort of polymorphous perversity.

It is true that there is a link between effeminacy and male homosexuality in Castrejón's version of the story. But it is not only the effeminate men who are homosexual. First of all Don Pedro de Marruecos, who is not portrayed as effeminate, has become disillusioned (to say the least) with women: "Veía a las mujeres como un ser inútil y despreciable, incapaz de crear nuevos placeres para él, y maldecía a la Naturaleza porque las delicias femeniles fueran tan cortas e insaciables" [He saw women as useless and despicable, incapable of creating new pleasures for him, and he cursed Nature because feminine delights were so short and insatiable] (48–49); but he becomes quickly enchanted by the nubile and effeminate beauty of Estrella (57–59).

Another particularly troublesome group for everyone writing about the event to deal with is the men from the cantinas who received invitations to the party without, as they claimed, knowing exactly what they were in for. Castrejón allows them simply to leave once they find out what the ball is about: "los que habían concurrido procedentes de las cantinas ávidos de novedad, se iban retirando la mayor parte contrariados, quedando de los mismos uno que otro rezagado, incoherente y beodo, con más ganas de beber vinos, que divertirse con los apócrifos palmitos" [of those who had gathered after coming from the cantinas, eager for novelty, the majority were gradually leaving, mortified, only a couple of stragglers remaining, incoherent and drunk, with more desire to drink wine than to enjoy themselves with the apocryphal ladies] (57). These poor victims, after much protest, were the only ones to be set free by the police.

This raises an important question about the sexualized *afeminados*. What kinds of lovers or sexual pleasures did they desire? Did they invite the guys from the *cantinas* just for a lark, or did they hope to seduce them? Or were they perfectly happy with each other? Did they want to be treated like women? Did they want to be penetrated as if they were women? Because if they were as orgiastic among themselves as Castrejón seems to imply, it would seem that either they would have to be versatile enough to penetrate as well as to be penetrated, or they would be able to get pleasure from other kinds of sexual activities. Castrejón's hyperbole in describing the transvestites' interactions aside, the fact that Pudor and Carolina were lovers needs to be explained. Castrejón's ambience of polymorphous perversity would seem to permit all kinds of couplings and desires.

The issue of class is also important here. In the newspapers, the 41 were identified as dandies, implying that they belonged to upper classes (although, as any Mexican knows from reading Lizardi's *Don Catrín de la Fachenda*, appearances can be deceiving, especially when it comes to indolent fops);[49] several were also identified as professionals (a dentist and a lawyer, for example: *El Imparcial,* November 23, 1901; or reporters, businessmen, bankers, lawyers, office clerks: *El Diario del Hogar,* November 24, 1901; or even priests: *El Universal,* November 23, 1901).[50] However, in the novel, the servants also join in the fun: "varios cocheros, lacayos y, en especialidad, camaristas y meseros...iban a compartir democráticamente con sus amos los goces venerandos [*sic*] de su cielo forjado con venturas del nuevo paraíso terrenal" [various coachmen, footmen and, especially, valets and waiters...were going to share democratically with their masters the venerable enjoyments of their heaven forged with pleasures from the new earthly paradise] (53). While the no-holds-barred at-mosphere would indicate an absolutely democratic ambience of free love, this was not always the case. For example, at one point when Mimí loosens his blouse, "provocando deseos en los ojos lánguidos del lacayito" [provoking desires in the languid eyes of the footman] (12), it is clear that they will not be acted upon. For all the talk of democracy, there is no concrete mention of any erotic or romantic homosexual relations across class lines in *Los 41*. However, there is no doubt that Mexican male homosexuality is not just an affliction of the upper classes. On the other hand, it is an affliction that belongs first to them, and men of lower classes who participate in it do so only as employees or at the invitation of these bourgeois dandies.[51]

A final problematic character is Mimí's lover, Ninón. Ninón is first introduced as "un hércules, de rostro seductor y varonil" [a Hercules, with a seductive and manly face] (2). Judith exhibits "una pasión volcánica" [a volcanic passion] for him; she tells Estela, "mis deseos buscan un ideal perfecto, un ideal sublime, [y] lo encontré en *Ninón*" [my desires seek a perfect ideal, a sublime ideal, and I found it in Ninón] (15). She goes on, "su talle gentil y hercúleo llena por com-pleto las ansias de las vírgenes que soñamos con el matrimonio" [his graceful and Herculean form completely fulfills the yearnings of vir-gins who dream of matrimony] (15). Ninón is very attractive and physically strong. He is the only one of Mimí's friends who does not dress in drag, although he does consent to perfuming his hair and moustache (40).

Ninón, however, is not at all shy about his homosexual desire. He claims to love Mimí "como se ama a una vírgen ante un cielo sonri-ente, infinito, lleno de inexplicables placeres" [as one loves a virgin under a smiling, infinite sky, full of inexplicable pleasures] (41). More-over, he is the book's greatest misogynist. He snarls, "Las mujeres son malas, vanidosas, egoístas; por una sonrisa piden un cielo; por un beso un tesoro; y luego, cuando nos aprisionan en sus redes, ya somos los esclavos que inclinamos la testuz perdiendo nuestra libertad, ¡y tro-camos nuestro amor en odio!" [Women are evil, vain, egoists; for a smile, they ask for the sky; for a kiss, a treasure; and later, when they imprison us in their nets, we become their bowing slaves, losing our liberty. And we trade our love for hate!] (42). It is only the shame of arrest and public ridicule that cause him to change his opinion (and retreat back into the closet).

Judith's opinion of him is not very generous. All it takes is one report from her spy, who claims that Ninón and Mimí "se abrazan, se besan, se tienen un afecto demasiado fraternal que traspasa todos los límites de la amistad" [hug, kiss, have an affection that is too fraternal and that transcends all limits of friendship] (19) for her to make all kinds of assumptions about his sex life. She never once doubts her spy's report. She calls Ninón an imposter, as Estela does to Mimí (30, 22). She even imagines on her own exactly what goes on between Ninón and Mimí and other men. She pictures him with "no sé cuántos más hombres" [I don't know how many more men] (30), specifically: "te sirven de instrumentos pasivos" [they serve as passive instruments for you] (30). Ninón is the only character whose specific sexual tastes are ever even implied in the novel. He is a homosexual who, as Judith imagines, plays the man's role in bed—he describes himself to Mimí as "tu maridito" [your little husband] (40)—and as the only one of the 41 resistant to transvestism, he is the most masculine of the group. And he is, as far as we know, the only one to reform and become heterosexual.

Scorpion Claw tells Judith that both Mimí and Ninón are innately homosexual: "se lo aseguro afirmativamente, que el Sr. *Ninón* y el Sr. *Mimí* no nacieron para adorar á Ud. y á la Srita. Estela" [I assure you positively that Master Ninón and Master Mimí were not born to adore you and Miss Estela] (19). Nonetheless, it would seem that Castrejón wishes to imply that Ninón was not innately homosexual, that he might be one of those men who is merely seduced into homosexuality, a discrete category of homosexual, according to sexological discourse.[52] The masculine homosexual ends up not being a real homosexual—unless, of course, his reform and marriage are merely subterfuge, as was his love affair with Judith.

A Few Observations

What is most interesting to note is that in all of the discourse about "el baile nefando," the effeminacy and homosexuality of the men involved, while treated with disdain and contempt, is also treated with affection, even celebration. At the very least it is accepted as something that exists as a part of Mexican society.[53] The subject, so taboo that it was not even discussed in the nineteenth century, is never challenged, as it was, for example, during the same years in Argentina, where, as Sylvia Molloy has pointed out in "The Politics of Posing," local homosexuality was denied. It was merely a pose, an imitation of European fashions, but not an authentic trait of Argentine men.[54] In Mexico, as we saw in Judith and Estela's reactions regarding their boyfriends, there is no hesitation; they immediately assume that Ninón and Mimí's heterosexuality was a pose, just as the newspapers assume that the dandies of Plateros Street (many of whom were thought to be among the 41) were merely posing in their flirtations with the fine young girls of city society.

In addition, a certain paradox emerges that will remain as such in Mexico for decades. In 1901, gender becomes inextricably linked with male sexuality to the point that, as Monsiváis puts it, "Desde entonces y hasta fechas recientes en la cultura popular el *gay* es el travesti; y sólo hay una especie de homosexual: el afeminado" [From then until only recently in popular culture gays are transvestites; and there is only one sort of homosexual: the effeminate man] ("Ortodoxia" 199). What is paradoxical is not the stereotype itself, but the fact that it emerged from the 41 controversy.

Let us examine what it means to equate transvestitism or effeminacy with homosexuality. Gender traits are often visible: dress, gesture, hairstyle, etc. Sexuality, on the other hand, is not an easily observable trait; sex generally occurs privately. At the *baile de sólo hombres,* transvestitism was observed, but homosexuality was only inferred. If we are to understand men dancing with men as a probable indicator of male homosexuality, perhaps we can assume that there were homosexuals at the ball.

However, were all of the men homosexuals? Are both the transvestites and the masculine men some of them may have coupled with, such as Ninón or the guys from the *cantinas,* homosexuals? Or do we just count the transvestites as homosexuals? Is homosexuality demonstrated by men desiring men, or by men desiring to play the women's role in sexual activities? It would seem that the discourse surrounding the 41 oscillates between these two very different ways of thinking. If all of the men were sent to Yucatán, as some reports claimed, then the more masculine ones were considered as guilty as the more effeminate ones. And if only the more effeminate ones were sent, as other reports claim, then the more masculine ones were somehow less guilty, i.e., either less homosexual or maybe not really homosexual, like Ninón turned out to be. Of course we don't know what really happened, nor do we know any details at all about the actual sexual tastes of any of the men involved. What we do know is that there were inconsistencies and confusions in the views on homosexuality expressed in the numerous writings on the topic of the 41.

Carolina and Pudor, both transvestites, were lovers. Other representations of transvestites such as those of the diaries and letters of *El Popular* imply that the lovers of the transvestites were masculine. In some cases, the transvestites seem to be prostitutes, or at least spongers, taking advantage of the clandestine desires of rich men; others are themselves taken advantage of by their good-for-nothing boyfriends. Consequently, the power relations between transvestites and their lovers seem to be quite varied. Simultaneous with the emergence of the stereotype of male homosexuals as effeminate and therefore in a socially subordinate position to that of their implicitly masculine lovers, was the advent of an image of the transvestite as mother, with a rag-doll baby, defiantly challenging male privilege. The fact that men were choosing to act as women called into question institutions of patriarchy that had previously been taken for granted. Moreover, the fact that the precise manner of coupling among homosexuals was open to speculation meant that apparently masculine men, along with effeminate ones, might well be homosexuals. And male-male homosocial relations would never be seen in quite the same way again. The discourse on male homosexuality and transvestism that was initiated with the 41 scandal in Mexico raised a number of questions that would go unanswered for decades, but would not be forgotten.

Quite the contrary, the number 41 would become part of the national vocabulary and would remain vivid in the national imagination, provoking anxiety and at times a superstitious paranoia. Revolutionary general Francisco Uriquizo reports the following:

> No hay en el ejército División, Regimiento o Batallón que lleve el número 41. Llegan hasta el 40 y de allí se salta al 42. No hay nómina que tenga renglón 41. No hay en las nomenclaturas municipales casa que ostenten el número 41. Si acaso y no hay remedio, el 40 bis. No hay cuarto de hotel o de Sanatorio que tenga el número 41. Nadie cumple 41 años, de los 40 se salta hasta los 42. No hay automóvil que lleve placa 41, ni policía o agente que acepte ese guarismo.

> There is no army Division, Regiment, or Battalion that bears the number 41. They go up to 41 and from there skip to 42. There is no list with a 41st line. There are no cities that label a house number 41. In the worst case if there's no other choice, they'll use 40B. There is no hotel or hospital room with the number 41. No one celebrates a 41st birthday; from 40 they skip to 42. No automobile has a license plate numbered 41, nor will police or other government agents accept this number.[55]

More recently, the number 41 has been actively deployed by Mexico City's gay[56] community ever since it began to assert itself publicly in literature (Po's 1963 novel *41 o un muchacho que soñaba en fantasmas*) and more recently in the naming of a series of nightclubs (including the legendary "41" in the Zona Rosa circa 1980, the "42" in the 1990s near Plaza Garibaldi, and the notorious "14" also near Garibaldi).

Chaotic Masculinities:
Positivismo, Modernismo, Naturalismo

Hermaphrodism and Other Manifestations of Criminal Psychology

Male homosexuality, linked as it was to effeminacy, heightened apprehension about masculinity. To further add to the confusion, biological sex itself comes under question at about the same time. As we have seen, crime was a particular topic of concern in Mexico. However, the era's criminological studies, while drawing on up-to-the minute scientific developments from Europe, were also catering to the vulgar popular interests of the day and have been cited for their "mixture of melodrama and medical science" (Buffington 131). One of the most interesting and prolific pop criminologists of turn-of-the-century Mexico City was "sometime police inspector and self-described amateur criminologist" (Buffington 59) Carlos Roumagnac.

Roumagnac published several in-depth studies on Mexican crime and criminals, but also dabbled elsewhere, earning extra cash translating the exotic novels of Pierre Loti, for example. While his studies had every pretension of scientific rigor, he also billed himself as "un simple aficionado observador" [a simple aficionado-observer] (*Los criminales* 7) and they were marketed rather sensationalistically. *Crímenes sexuales y pasionales: Estudios de psicología morbosa* [Sex crimes and crimes of passion: Studies of morbid psychology] (1906) provided an early look at sex crimes, as did its 1910 sequel, the even more topically focused *Matadores de mujeres* [Woman-killers]. But it was his first study that really established his name both as Mexico's leading criminologist and as a major scandalmonger of his day. The extended title says it all: *Los criminales en México: Ensayo de psicología criminal, seguido de dos casos de hermafrodismo* [Criminals in Mexico: Essay on criminal psychology, followed by two cases of hermaphroditism].[57]

This series of case studies includes profiles of dozens of inmates of Mexico's prisons, with data ranging from family histories to detailed descriptions of crimes committed, including personal interviews, meticulous physical descriptions, and even photographs. Roumagnac seems obliged to report figures on length and width of head, right ear, left foot, left middle finger, and left elbow, along with analyses of the shape of the forehead, nose, right ear, and chin, but is not convinced (as Cesare Lombroso was) that the tendency to commit crime is an innate attribute linked to these physical characteristics, although he often is not surprised to find that the most vicious criminals are "simian" in appearance. Background sketches of parents are also important, along with childhood histories. Patterns of poverty, abuse, and sexual initiation are of particular interest to Roumagnac, who believes that heritage, education, and environment are key factors in the development of the criminal mind (*Los criminales* 8).

Male sexuality is of especial interest to him. *Los criminales en México* includes a long chapter on rapists, including detailed studies of personages such as Andrés D., incarcerated for raping (anally penetrating) a five-year-old boy. Roumagnac reprints a report by two legist doctors who ascribe the criminal acts of Andrés D. as follows: "Teniendo en cuenta la inmoralidad del referido D. a la cual se ha entregado desde su pubertad, sin ningún freno, no es extraño que bajo la influencia de la excitación alcohólica, su perversidad le haya sugerido lo peor y lo más repugnante de la lascivia: la pederastia" [Taking into account D's immorality to which he had been surrendering since puberty, without any restraint, it is not strange that under the influence of alcoholic excitation, his perversity would have led to the worst and most repugnant form of lasciviousness: pederasty] (*Los criminales* 299).

Andrés D. raped the son of a neighborhood shoemaker because he had been permitted, and had permitted himself, to give in to his sexual urges, mainly with prostitutes, for years. The influence of alcohol, moreover, was almost always cited as a principal cause of crime in Mexico at that time. On the other hand, physical evidence was not ignored in his case. While Roumagnac makes nothing of his nose size or elbow measurements, he somehow manages to physically prove that he is not homosexual. Again, citing the doctors' report: "Por el examen físico que hicimos de sus órganos genitales no se descubre que existan en él los caracteres físicos que deja el hábito de la pederastia activa" [By means of the physical examination that we administered of his genital organs, it was not thereby discovered that there existed the physical traits that the habit of active pederasty leaves] (299). Thus, despite genital attributes supposedly indicative of certain sexual habits, it is the psychic and sexual history that builds over time and leads men like Andrés D. to perversion. Significant factors in this case include the facts that he read pornography, had wet dreams, abused neighborhood dogs, and once stoned a cat to death (301).

Interestingly, Roumagnac's earlier works include observations of prisoners of both genders, such as the case of Angela R. de P., who was accused of having kidnapped, "traficado con [la] virginidad" [trafficked with the virginity] of, and practiced "safismo" [sapphism] on a

fifteen-year-old girl (*Los criminales* 194). However, by his final criminological project, it is only the perversities of men that interest him.
Clearly, crime rates were much higher among men and there were
many more crimes of passion committed by men against women than
vice versa. Nonetheless, Roumagnac's attraction toward the former
was not necessarily typical, as the popularity of *La Rumba* proves.
Such insurgence of women against traditional gender roles has been
the subject of much study, and deservedly so. It has also been the object of attack. In fact, Roumagnac's publisher released another book in
the same era (*Eufemia ó la mujer verdaderamente instruida* by Campe)
in defense of traditional female roles, or what the author calls "el destino de la mujer" [the destiny of women]: "Han nacido, las que no
son llamadas al estado del celibato, para ser esposas, buenas madres
y prudentes gobernadoras de sus casas" [You (women), those who do
not receive the calling of celibacy, are born to be wives, good mothers,
and prudent home administrators] (Campe 11). However, this social
affliction of male violence, so frequently directed against women, as
Roumagnac shows in *Matadores de mujeres,* and its relation to the
fascinating new topic of male sexuality is not often looked at today,
despite its growing importance during the course of Roumagnac's
work and in Mexican society as a whole at the time.

Passion, as Roumagnac explains, like pederasty or any other vice
that strays from "natural" sexuality (i.e., the instinct for the reproduction and the preservation of the species), is the result of "las
lacras dejadas en el cerebro por cualquier circunstancia congénita, o
adquirida" [the marks left on the brain by any congenital or acquired
circumstance] (*Matadores* 8). Any and all forms of male sexuality
that go beyond the clinical and Catholic procreative mandate are considered "cuando no...aberraciones,...la exageración mórbida; y de
aquí la manifestación viciosa, al delito y al crimen, la distancia es
corta" [if not aberrations, then morbid exaggerations; and from the
point of vicious manifestation to misdeed and crime, the distance is
short] (*Matadores* 8).

Desire, for Roumagnac, is related to needs and instincts and remains in the realm of the natural, but: "Exagérase tal deseo, es
decir, auméntase su intensidad, hágasele constante, dominando todo

el ser cerebral, y se llegará a la pasión" [Exaggerate this desire, i.e., augment its intensity, make it constant, dominating of one's entire cerebral being, and you will arrive at passion] (*Matadores* 10). And male heterosexual passion is no less vicious than pederasty; in fact, in Roumagnac's world, it seems that it is not the pederasts whose passions and jealousies are exaggerated to the point of inciting them to commit murder. The graver danger in turn-of-the-century Mexico (as in nineteenth-century Mexico), it would seem, is unbridled male heterosexual desire.

Effeminacy beyond Transvestism

Roumagnac, as we mentioned, topped off his first criminology study, *Los criminales en México*, with a brief investigation of two cases of hermaphrodism. Whether he wished to represent hermaphrodism itself as a crime or whether he just couldn't resist publishing something about the two fascinating cases he came across is not clear, but the inclusion of the two cases certainly fits with the scheme of the rest of the book. Although a bit of a *bricoleur* insofar as criminological theory is concerned, Roumagnac consistently attempts to link sex and crime, obsessively questioning the subjects of his research regarding their sexual histories, and even examining sexual behavior in jails.

Despite the cover hype given to the stories, Roumagnac himself apparently never met either of the two hermaphrodites. He was therefore unable to perform any of his in-depth interviews on them. What he did include was a series of photographs, including several close-ups of genitalia. The four pages of photos are accompanied by a little over a page of text, which is summarized below.

The first was a case of "hipospadias," a term that Roumagnac does not bother to define, but that refers to a condition in which there is an extended urethral opening that runs along the dorsal part of the penis, making it look something like female genitalia. This subject, as the photos show, had a very flat chest and a very small penis, but was raised as a girl "por un error en la familia" [due to an error on the part of his family] (388). The story goes as follows:

Llegóse a conocer su verdadero sexo, porque estando empleado como encuadernadora, se fue una noche con otras trabajadoras del establecimiento, de visita en casa de una de ellas. Un fuerte aguacero inundó las calles, y decidieron aceptar todas, la hospitalidad que se les ofreció. Nuestro sujeto se acostó con una de sus compañeras, con la que durante la noche intentó consumar el coito. Consignada por este hecho a la autoridad gubernativa, se descubrió el caso de que se trataba.

Her true sex was revealed because, employed as a bookbinder, she went one night with co-workers from the establishment to visit the home of one of them. A strong downpour inundated the streets, and all of them decided to accept the hospitality offered to them. Our subject went to bed with one of her co-workers with whom, during the night, she attempted intercourse. Arrested and sent before the governmental authorities for this, the case in question was discovered. (388)

This very brief story reveals less about sexual anomaly than it does about Roumagnac's discomfort and confusion with the subject. He successfully avoids using gender differentiating pronouns ("él" or "ella") to refer to this "subject" or "individual," but, even after asserting that his subject was male (his feminine aspect was "an error"), he continues to use feminine forms of nouns ("encuadernadora") and adjectives ("consignada") to refer to him.

This rare conflict with biology, clearly calling binary categories of physical sex into doubt, is not even commented upon by the author, who mentions that the case "was studied by Dr. D. Ricardo Egea" without revealing any further information from that study. Likewise, with the second hermaphrodite, a case of "criptorquidia" [cryptorchidism] (failure of one or both testes to descend into the scrotum): Roumagnac's data is scanty, and his own commentaries completely lacking. Along with several photos including close-ups of the subject's genitals, he merely recounts physical characteristics of the subject: a fifty-eight-year-old married man with three well adapted children, smooth-faced, wide-hipped, with woman-like breasts, an effeminate voice, the belly of a "mujer multípara" [multi-birth mother], the penis of a ten-year-old boy, and a scrotum that looks like a vagina (389).

The Parade of Sexual Degenerates

Just as in the case of the 41—in which writers savor the scandal, but instead of clarifying the topic, end up confusing it—Roumagnac's mention of the hermaphrodites undoubtedly draws attention to the subject, but does nothing to elucidate the issues of gender ambiguity that it raises. Not surprisingly, Roumagnac's descriptions of male homosexuality are equally unenlightening. He enjoys recounting what he calls "el desfile de . . . degenerados sexuales" [the parade of sexual degenerates] (77) that occurs in the Belem prison, in which certain prisoners who have been semi-isolated from the rest for being known as homosexuals pass "delante de los demás detenidos, sin rubor ni vergüenza, haciendo, por el contrario, alarde de voces y modales afeminados, prodigándose apodos mujeriles, y muchas veces cargando en brazos muñecas de trapo o fingiendo cargarlos, y haciendo alusiones a sus partos recientes" [in front of the other prisoners, without bashfulness or embarrassment, on the contrary, making a display of effeminate voices and mannerisms, and frequently carrying or pretending to carry rag dolls in their arms, making allusions to their recent birthings] (77). It is a scene right off the 41's boat to Progreso. It is amusing and memorable but does little to elucidate the relationship between male effeminacy and homosexuality in the Mexican belief system of the epoch.

According to Roumagnac, there are two kinds of homosexuals, the effeminate ones who play the "passive" female role in homosexual relations ("caballos" [horses]) and the masculine ones who play the "active" male role ("mayates").[58] Apparently only the former need to be isolated from the other prisoners, as if they are the only real homosexuals, while the *mayates* are only temporarily homosexual due to the absence of women in prison. While this would at first seem to support Monsiváis's assertion that effeminacy was equated with homosexuality and Paz's scheme of Mexican male homosexuality elaborated in *El laberinto de la soledad*, Roumagnac shows that in practice it was not always the case that prisoners strictly played these roles; he notes, "Tienen también otras denominaciones" [They also have other denominations] (aside from *caballo* and *mayate*), but never reveals what they are or how they relate to gender roles (if indeed they do at all). In other words, the astute reader might be left wondering whether the links made between gender roles (particularly effeminacy) and male homosexuality are indicative of quotidian sexual practices in Mexico or merely the product of the author's assumptions and prejudices.

Neuter Angels

To make a few final points regarding turn-of-the-century masculinity, let us return to the high-brow realm of literature, first of all to the writer who, in his day, in all Latin America was "the most popular modernist of all after Darío" (Martin 69). Amado Nervo was certainly one of Mexico's leading figures of *modernismo*. However, unlike many of his peers whose florid and sometimes grotesque work has been largely discredited or forgotten since the Mexican revolution, Nervo is well remembered, if not always fondly. In the middle of his career (he actively published from 1895 to his death in 1919), he reverted to a spiritualist style of poetry that has been warmly admired by Catholics, mocked by avant garde literary critics, and recited by generations of schoolchildren.

In his own day, he was also ribbed for his lack of virility as a poet. An anonymous mini-biography originally published in Venezuela and reprinted in *Revista Moderna* describes him as follows:

> Tiene la América grandes poetas—poetas inspirados y viriles—; Nervo no tiene afinidades con esa raza de batalladores y transcendentales; pertenece a la blasonada de los exquisitos, a lo que representa ... el triunfo del sistema nervioso sobre el sistema muscular, la glorificación de la emoción interior sobre la emoción exterior, la victoria de la específica conciencia del individuo sobre la conciencia genérica del tipo.

> America has great poets—inspired, virile poets; Nervo has no affinity with this race of battling, transcendental men; he belongs to the braggart class of exquisite fellows, who are represented by the triumph of the nervous system over the muscular system, the glorification of interior emotion over exterior emotion, the victory of the specific consciousness of the individual over the generic consciousness of the group.[59]

Whether or not he was as virile as Martí,[60] his writings were at least admired in his day.

However, in 1928, when the Contemporáneos published their controversial anthology of Mexican poetry, they included a few poems of Nervo's, introducing him acidly as "una víctima de la sinceridad" [a victim of sincerity] (Cuesta, *Antología* 78). More recent opinions have veered from the reverential (such as Roderick Molina's study of the influence of St. Francis of Assisi in Nervo's poetry) to the sardonic (Monsiváis features a poem dedicated to Nervo by José Emilio Pacheco to open his study of tacky sentimentality in Mexico, "México, país de los cursis" [*Escenas* 171]). All this is reversed on the rare occasions when Nervo's early, more racy works are examined. Molina finds Nervo's more youthful writing to be "overcast by the clouds of wordlines [*sic*—worldliness?] and laicism which, like a cold rainstorm, chilled the hearts and darkened the minds of the most representative writers of the 19th and early 20th centuries" (46). In fact, it is this chilling rainstorm of sexual angst that brings to light the anxieties of gender and sexuality in turn-of-the-century Mexico from a perspective no longer of the popular press, but of the lofty literary establishment of the day. Nervo, an early editor of *La Revista Moderna,* was a major figure of Mexican *modernismo* not because of his religious sentiments, which prolonged his fame in the latter part of his career, but because of the controversial writings of his earliest years, which established him as a major Mexican writer by his mid-twenties. A queer bird by all accounts, he never married but secretly sheltered an ill woman in his home for years, dedicating a volume of poems to her, *La amada inmóvil.*

His first major published work, the novella *El bachiller,* tells a strange story of masculinity, heterosexuality, and religion. Young Felipe, devoted to his mother, finds himself an orphan and is sent to be raised by his "solterón" [confirmed bachelor] uncle. He studies in a male homosocial ambience, a Catholic school, whose student body represents a national microcosm including "todos los tipos que forman en México la híbrida población" [all the types that form the hybrid population of Mexico] (87). The novella, through these young men—freckle-faced blonds, light-skinned brunettes, grave Indians, etc.—aspires to the national, but a specifically male national, a national that will not tolerate the ardent sexuality that nineteenth-century heterosexual romances elided and that turn-of-the-century *modernismo* enthusiastically scrutinized.

Felipe enters this national context as a student and once graduated as a "bachiller" chooses to remain in the closed male homosocial world as a monk. He struggles to resist thoughts of love for an (ungendered) "object," who in those fantasies with which he must constantly do battle is "perennemente joven y perennemente bello" [perennially young and perennially beautiful] (90). While the novella refers repeatedly to heterosexual desire, the choice of the word "object" is typical of Nervo, allowing him to apply masculine adjectives, but always with the neuter implication that will resurface repeatedly in his early work.

Felipe manages to repress his lustful urges and appears to take masochistic pleasure in penance, which consists of a daily *Miserere*, much like the one described by Calderón de la Barca, in which he and his cohorts would whip themselves bloody. However, despite his efforts to refrain from lust, he soon sees a vision of a woman, his boyhood playmate, the "marimacho" [tomboy], Asunción. His heterosexual angst causes him to fall ill, and his uncle insists on taking him home to recuperate. Asunción is still there, now grown up into a pretty young woman and taken to cooking and sewing (perhaps like Felipe's beloved mother). Asunción takes it upon herself to nurse Felipe back to health, and it soon becomes clear that her devotion to him is indicative of something quite strong. In fact, at one point, she can no longer resist her passion and attacks him with kisses as she begs him to renounce the clergy. Felipe, frightened out of his wits by this heterosexual display, wants to squeal, "Socorro" [help] (107), but no one is there to save him from her. Suddenly he finds the solution: with Asunción apparently on the verge of raping him, he grabs his "plegadera" [letter opener] and stabs at his groin. Terrified of this torrid sexuality, sexlessness seems the solution, and Felipe castrates himself on the spot.

Biological sex is a troubling theme for Nervo. He seems comfortable with neither heterosexuality nor homosexuality and prefers to obliterate sexual difference in any way possible. An early poem,

"Andrógino" (1896), further reflects Nervo's discomfort with gender convention, telling of a love for some ephebe-like being with "neutros encantos" [neuter charms], "senos pectorales" [pectoral breasts], "virilidades de dios mancebo" [virilities of a youthful male god], and "mustios halagos de mujer triste" [soft allurements of a rueful women] (181). However, it was a tragic love, and Nervo seems to advocate not so much bisexuality as asexuality.

An 1895 vignette, "Hermafrodita," raises the theme again, making Ovid's monster into an ideal of beauty. According to Nervo's version of the myth, Hermafrodita is "el prodigo más acabado de la belleza" [the most perfect marvel of beauty], combining "los viriles encantos del sexo masculino, idealizados por la curva sagrada, por la curva augusta y gloriosa" [the virile charms of the masculine sex idealized by the sacred curve, the august and glorious curve]. Hermafrodita, who "fecúndase él solo" [fecundates himself by himself], "es casi un dios" [is practically a god] (119). Nervo's ideal here is neither bisexuality nor asexuality, but a sexuality based on reproduction by masturbation.

An early essay addresses androgyny from yet another angle: "El ser neutro" treats the author's desire for the companionship of a nongendered person. Nervo's misogyny—"La mujer es demasiado vulgar.... En la madurez, llega a una fealdad ... sin ganar, en cambio, *alma.* ... Cuando piensa un poco, resulta por lo general de una pedantería insoportable. Felizmente, casi no piensa nunca" [Women are too vulgar.... Upon maturity, they reach a state of ugliness ... without gaining soul in exchange.... When they think a little, it ends up being an insupportable pedantry. Fortunately, they almost never think.] ("El ser neutro" 170)—leads him to reject the company of women; of course, homosexuality is not a viable option. Instead, Nervo, while not rejecting marriage for the purposes of procreation, advocates associations with neutral beings ("ángeles, sin androginismo" [angels without androgyny] ["El ser neutro" 169]).

However, it is his third novella, *El donador de almas* [The Giver of Souls], on which we will focus our attention. Written in 1899, first published in 1904, it was less shocking than *El bachiller,* but undoubtedly as disturbing, particularly with regard to issues of gender.

The Giver of Souls

El donador de almas is the story of Dr. Rafael Antiga and his "hyperaesthesia," his malaise, his yearning for affection. He does not precisely desire a woman—"a los veinte deseé que una mujer guapa me quisiera, y advertí poco después que todas las mujeres guapas lo eran más que ella" [at age twenty I wished that a beautiful woman would love me, and I noticed soon after that all beautiful women were more beautiful than she] (17)—but "un alma" [a soul]. The novel opens with the doctor sitting around his house feeling sorry for himself; however, his nervous despondency is quickly interrupted by the arrival of his friend, the poet Andrés Esteves. After exaggeratedly effusive greetings, comes the following exchange:

> —...¿crees que te quiero? [pregunta Andrés]
> —¡Absolutamente! [contesta Rafael]
> —¿Qué [*sic*] te quiero con un cariño excepcional, exclusivo?
> —Más que si lo viese....
> —¿Crees que a nadie en el mundo quiero como a ti? ¿Crees en eso?
> —Más que en la existencia de los microbios....
> —Todo lo que soy—y no soy poco—te lo debo a ti.
> —Se lo debes a tu talento.
> —Sin ti, mi talento hubiera sido como esas flores aisladas que saturan de perfumes los vientos solitarios.
> —Poesía tenemos.
> —Todo hombre necesita un hombre.
> —Y a veces una mujer.
> —Tú fuiste mi hombre.

> "...Do you believe that I love you?" asks Andrés.
> "Absolutely!" replies Rafael.
> "That I love you with an exceptional, exclusive affection?"
> "More than if I could see it...."
> "Do you believe that I love no one in the world as I love you? Do you believe that?"
> "More than the existence of microbes...."
> "Everything that I am—and I am no small thing—I owe to you."
> "You owe it to your talent."
> "Without you, my talent might have been like those isolated flowers that solitary winds saturate with perfume."
> "We have poetry."

CRIMINAL MALE SEXUALITY 103

"Every man needs a man."
"And sometimes a woman."
"You were my man." (22–23)

One might wonder right off why the doctor is so preoccupied with obtaining affection when he is already so adored by his friend. The bad news is that Andrés plans to leave the country, to travel for an unspecified length of time to unstated destinations. However, to help compensate for the loss, Andrés offers to give Rafael a soul.

Rafael is puzzled, and to his first question about the soul: "¿Masculino o femenino?" [Masculine or feminine?], Andrés responds, "Los espíritus no tienen sexo" [Spirits have no sex] (25). It seems that Dr. Rafael Antiga is to receive what Nervo himself wished for, *un ser neutro*. But, in this case, there is no *ser*, just a soul. Rafael is appropriately thrilled. So, after "un cordialísimo apretón de manos" [an extremely cordial squeezing of hands] (26), Andrés departs, and shortly thereafter, Alda, the disembodied spirit of a nun (Rafael's new soul) arrives.

Rafael is content with his new companion whom he can't see, but with whom he can chat. Rafael believes that his "cerebral matrimony" with Alda will be superior to a normal marriage because he doesn't give credence to the possession of a love object that marriage entails. Nonetheless, he quickly becomes frustrated because he wants Alda to love him, but she can't, she explains, because as a mere disembodied soul, she lacks a will. What she can do is empower Rafael with a degree of genius that brings him international fame in his profession.

He travels the world, accompanied by Alda, curing the sick, but continues to be afflicted by his longing for the love of his soul. The crisis occurs during this globetrotting. Rafael had been warned not to keep Alda with him for too long (what he didn't know was that when she vacated her body, Sor Teresa, the nun, would go into raptures). When one day he agonizes with Alda for too long about her inability to love him, she returns to the convent to find her body (that of Sor Teresa) dead. When Rafael and Alda are unable to think of an adequate body for her to inhabit, she is forced to enter Rafael's body.

Though Nervo does not refer to European discourse on "uranism" (a term that never caught on in Mexico),[61] what the author has in fact devised is for a woman's soul to inhabit a man's body. The popular turn-of-the-century trope of male homosexuality comes to life in Nervo's comic novella. The situation causes great confusion for Rafael and for Alda who argue about whether to use masculine or feminine forms of adjectives when referring to themselves. Finally Rafael concludes that theirs is a case of "intellectual hermophrodism."[62] Alda consoles him by pointing out that poets ("los seres más semejantes a los dioses" [the beings most similar to gods] [63]) are both masculine and feminine. What has happened, then, is that Andrés, already half-effeminate as a poet, has feminized his close friend through the gift of this female soul.

Rafael philosophizes that his love for Alda is the same whether she is an errant soul or a part of his own person because heterosexual love is merely a variety of narcissism:

> El hombre en realidad al amar a una mujer no ama en ella más que al que a él le da de ilusión, de belleza. . . . Se ama pues, a sí mismo amándola a ella, y deja de amarla cuando la ha desnudado de aquel atavío con la que la embelleció primero. . . . En cuanto a la mujer, *esa se enamora del amor que inspira,* esto es: de sí misma también.

> When a man loves a woman, he actually doesn't love anything in her besides what beguiles him, beauty. . . . What he loves, then, is himself loving her, and he ceases to love her when he has denuded her of that trait with which he first embellished her. . . . As for the woman, *she falls in love with the love that she inspires,* that is: with herself, as well. (64, emphasis Nervo's)

The precise love object is not as important as the act of loving, or the fact of being loved in the case of women.

After Alda enters Rafael's brain (on the left side), Nervo interrupts with a chapter called "Digresiones" [Digressions] in which he identifies Rafael's brain as his tragic flaw:

> Rafael Antiga era un filósofo, lo peor que se puede ser en este mundo.
>   La Naturaleza, que bien pudo darle una berruga [*sic*] o un lobanillo, tuvo a bien dotarle de una bien calibrada, cavidad craneana, repleta de sesos de calidad, y ahí estuvo el mal.

De otra suerte el doctor habría poseído una noción exacta de la existencia; habría sido un hombre práctico; habría esquivado las relaciones con Andrés: el desequilibrado más genial que se haya visto en México, y Alda no estaría donde estaba, ocupándole, sin pagar renta, la mitad del cerebro.

Pero Dios ordenó las cosas de distinto modo y Rafael ... desde muy temprano se engolfó en los libros, se vistió de teorías, viajó por Utopía y, cuando estaba al borde del abismo, Andrés le hundió en él, como Miguel a Satán.

Rafael Antiga was a philosopher, the worst thing in the world to be.

Nature, which might have given him a wart or a tumor, succeeded in giving him a well calibrated cranial cavity, brimming with quality brains, and there was the rub.

Otherwise the doctor would have possessed an exact notion of existence; he would have been a practical man; he would have avoided the relationship with Andrés: the greatest disequilibrium that has ever been seen in Mexico, and Alda wouldn't be where she was, occupying, without paying rent, half of his brain.

But God ordered things differently and Rafael ... from an early age engulfed himself in books, dressed himself up in theories, traveled to Utopia and, when he was on the edge of the abyss, Andrés plunged him into it, as Michael did to Satan. (68–69)

In other words, the unbalanced relationship between Andrés and Rafael is clearly to blame for this invasion of a female soul into his body. Rafael's feminine side exists only as a result of his close ties to his male friend.

Andrés era pobre y Rafael era rico.
Andrés era poeta y Rafael era filósofo.
Andrés era rubio y Rafael era moreno.
¿Sorprenderá a alguien que se hayan amado?

Andrés was poor and Rafael was rich.
Andrés was a poet and Rafael was a philosopher.
Andrés was blond and Rafael was dark.
Is it a surprise to anyone that they have loved each other? (69).

The source of Rafael's effeminacy is a homosocial friendship whose passion clearly verges on the homosexual.

At first, Alda's presence in Rafael seems utopian. He loves and possesses her within himself, and the perfect heterosexual love is realized in narcissism. He entirely avoids having to deal with a female body, such as that of the only significant physically embodied female character in the novella, his housekeeper, Doña Corpus, a woman obsessed with premonitions of apocalypse and doom. Unfortunately, Rafael's happiness is short lived. His masculine and feminine sides end up being incompatible, driving each other crazy. Nervo narrates, "el amor no es acaso más que una encantadora forma del odio entre los sexos. . . . El beso no es más que una variación de la mordida" [love is perhaps nothing more than an enchanting form of hatred between the sexes. . . . A kiss is nothing more than a variation of a bite] (90). Alda and Rafael must then go off in search of Andrés, who is the only one capable of liberating her. They finally find him in the Holy Land, and he dutifully sets Alda free into the universe. Rafael is nostalgic, but relieved.

The novella's ending is rather unsatisfying in the sense that the reader does not learn what happens to Rafael later. Does he go home alone? Is he happy or disappointed? Does her hear from Alda again? And what about Andrés? What happens once Rafael and Andrés are left alone, their masculine friendship rid once and for all of the female soul? It is perhaps telling that Nervo, rather than simply having Rafael go back to Mexico alone, does not reveal precisely what happens next, leaving open unspeakable possibilities. The open ending reflects the climate of discourse on gender and sexuality at the time: crisis and confusion. Nervo's story playfully addresses a number of issues of the moment, but finds no resolutions to them.

Santa

I might include any number of other *modernista* works in this study. There is an undeniable queerness, for example, to the short stories of Bernardo Couto Castillo, Carlos Díaz Dufoo, and Alberto Leduc as well as the prose of Rubén Campos (especially his novel *Claudio Oronoz*). However, none is as abundantly controversial as Nervo. In fact, the only writer of the time whose writings achieved greater notoriety than those of Nervo was not a *modernista* but a *naturalista:* Federico Gamboa.

The most famous tale of deflowering in Mexican history is, of course, Gamboa's best-selling 1903 novel, *Santa,* the tale of a beautiful young girl who is seduced by a junior army officer and thrown out of her home by her pious mother and unforgiving brothers. She is thus forced to enter a bordello. While she finds the life degrading and is subjected to sexual harassment from a colleague—the notorious first major lesbian character of Mexican literature, la Gaditana—she adjusts to it and learns to use her beauty to her advantage. Eventually, she is seduced by a Spanish bullfighter, el Jarameño, who rescues her from prostitution and takes her to be his mistress. Despite the fact that he adores her and treats her like a queen, her vile sexual nature soon surfaces, inducing her to seduce a friend and housemate of her lover. Naturally she gets caught and is forced to flee and take up an even baser lifestyle as a drunken streetwalker. Of course, she eventually dies, diseased by her depravity.[63]

The immense popularity of Gamboa's book[64] demonstrates Mexico's fascination with the topic of prostitution. However, as Debra Castillo points out, the book is not in fact overtly sexual. The mere topic alludes to sex to a sufficient degree that sex need not be directly described (40). Even the word "prostitute" is avoided. "Y yo . . . seré siempre una . . . " [And I will always be a . . .] (Gamboa 100), moans Santa, leaving out the obvious last word, "puta" [whore]—although Gamboa does employ the term "ramera" [harlot] on several occasions. The sexually charged underworld of prostitution ought to be a final interesting site to explore turn-of-the-century notions of masculinity and masculine sexuality.

The case of Marcelino Beltrán, Santa's fateful seducer, points to a male sexuality out of control. Beltrán is animalistic, "un macho común y corriente" [a run-of-the-mill male animal] (60), although, interestingly, it is Santa who is blamed for her own downfall. Unbridled male desire is a fact of life; female desire, on the other hand, must be controlled. Santa does not know how to resist the advances of such a handsome and sexually aggressive young man.

Her brothers, Fabián and Esteban, are also animals, relentlessly hardworking but poor, devoted sons, living out the "esclavitud mansa de bestias humanas" [docile slavery of human beasts] (57). And like Beltrán, they are hunks; Gamboa writes at one point of the brothers "en toda la hermosura de sus cuerpazos de adultos sanos y fuertes" [in all the beauty of their tremendous bodies of healthy and strong adult men] (71). While we never learn anything about the sexual activities of the brothers and their "tremendous bodies," whether in or outside of marriage, it is they more than anyone else in their revulsion for their sister (which they demonstrate when they force her to leave home for having had sexual relations with Beltrán, and again when they come to inform her of their mother's death and learn that she is living as a prostitute) who validate and enforce the social interdict forbidding any exercise of female sexual will.

Another prime specimen of manhood in the novel is not actually Mexican: the bullfighter, el Jarameño.[65] Again he is brutishly handsome, "hercúleo primitivo, bestial" [Herculean, primitive, bestial] (86). His masculinity is not unlike that of Beltrán (and, the cynical reader might imagine, probably not unlike that of Esteban and Fabián); he uses his good looks to seduce women and freely fulfill his sexual desires. Male sexuality, in *Santa*, is a natural force. While it can bring about tragedy (as in the case of Santa's army officer lover), there is never any discussion of the possibility of controlling it.

This is nothing new, of course. *La Quijotita y su prima* was a book that fretted obsessively about protecting young women from dangerous male sexual desire generations before *Santa*, as did many novels of the nineteenth century. What is new in *Santa* is the sexual beauty of the men. Since Santa herself is responsible for her transgressions (hers is a natural desire that she is expected to control), it becomes necessary to elaborate on her desire, and on the sexual desirability of certain male characters who attract her. Men, in *Santa*, are not only sexual animals, but also eroticized beings who entice women (and maybe men, as well). For unlike la Rumba before her, Santa is not interested in bettering her social position when she joins up with men; she is interested in satisfying her animal drives.

Thus, when Marcelino Beltrán appears, a detailed physical description is necessary to show what it was about his body that Santa couldn't resist:

> Era en efecto el tal, apuesto mozo; ancho de espaldas y levantado de pecho; dulce en el mirar y fácil en el reír, con lo que el castaño bozo se le encaramaba a los morenos carrillos, y la dentadura, blanca, apretada y pareja, relucíale cual si de esmalte estuviese hecha; fuerte y joven; alto a pie y airoso cuando cabalgaba en su irascible moro; siempre de uniforme y el uniforme siempre limpísimo, el kepí ligeramente hacia atrás, dándole aires de espadachín y mujeriego.

> It was in fact this handsome young man; broad shouldered and high chested; with a sweet look and a ready laugh, which would raise his shadow of a chestnut moustache to his swarthy cheeks, and his teeth, white, tight and even, which would shine as if they were made of smalt; young and strong; tall standing afoot, and airy when on the back of his irascible black stallion; always in uniform and his uniform always spotless, his kepi angled slightly back, giving him the appearance of a swordsman and womanizer. (58)

Santa herself is not introduced with such assiduous physical detail. Although it is always clear that she is a great beauty, Marcelino's beauty is made more vivid than hers. Beltrán not only exhibits physical beauty, but enhances it with adornments such as his meticulously maintained uniform. His fatal attractiveness is fully understandable.

El Jarameño is another specimen of masculine beauty, another Adonis whom Santa is unable to resist. His career is based on the spectacle of male power and beauty. The bullfighter must be handsome, gallant, and brave, and it is precisely this display that attracts the public to the *corrida*. He is not only adored by his public, but "idolized" by his manservant, loved by his Spanish housemates, and desired by Santa.

His erotic beauty is meticulously displayed to a private audience of Santa and Bruno, his doting valet, in a scene amplifying the intensity of the description of Beltrán's beauty, a protracted dressing scene that is worth quoting from at length:

> Al quedar el Jarameño casi desnudo, se puso en pie. Y Santa, aunque sin hablar, lo admiró en su belleza clásica, y viril del hombre bien conformado. Los músculos, los tendones, las durezas de acero que acusaba en los bíceps, en los pectorales, en los omóplatos, en las pantorrillas

nervudas y sólidas, en los anchos de la espalda y en lo grueso del cuello, armonizábanse, le prestaban hermoso aspecto antiguo de gla- diador o de discóbolo, de macho potente y completo, nacido y criado para las luchas varoniles, las que reclaman el arrojo, el valor y la fuerza; las luchas olímpicas en las que se muere, si se muere, de cara al sol, sonriendo a las mujeres y a los cielos, salmodiado por las valientes notas de las músicas guerreras, en gallarda apostura y espléndido lecho mortuorio.... ¡Santa lo admiró!

Sí, reconocía que estaba hecho para esas luchas.... En cambio, sabía que estaba así mismo hecho para el amor suyo, de ella, en pago, lo amaba a su manera, plásticamente, por sus juramentos gitanos, por lo asfixiante de sus brazos y lo salvaje de sus caricias de incivilizado.

El Jarameño, now practically naked, stood up. And Santa, although without speaking, admired him in his classical and virile beauty of a well-formed man. His muscles, his tendons, the firmness of steel that she noted in his biceps, in his pectorals, in his shoulder blades, in his sinewy and solid calves, in the broadness of his back and the thickness of his neck, harmonized, gave him the beautiful aspect of an ancient gladiator or discobolous, of a potent and complete male animal, born and raised for manly endeavors, those that require boldness, valor, and strength; olympic struggles in which one dies, if one dies, with face to the sun, smiling up at the women and the heavens, psalmodized by the valiant notes of musical warriors, in gallant bearing in a splendid mortuary bed.... Santa admired him!

Yes, she recognized that he was made for these endeavors.... On the other hand, she knew that he was therefore made for her love, hers; in return she loved him in her way, plastically, for his gypsy oaths, for his asphyxiating arms and the savageness of his uncivilized caresses. (193–94)

The rampant sexuality of the savage man is also irresistibly attractive. But, as in the case of Beltrán, external adornments are also of great importance:

—¡Mira, morena, mira cómo se viste un matador de toros! —le dijo el Jarameño sentándose en una silla y abandonándose a las pericias de Bruno.

Primero, el calzón de hilo, corto; luego la venda en la garganta de los pies, muy apretada, contra luxaciones y torceduras; después, las medias de algodón, y sobre éstas, las medias de seda, tirantísimas, sin asomos de una arruga; despúes, las zapatillas, de charol y con su lazo en el empeine, y ¡arriba!, ¡pararse!, vengan la taleguilla y la camisa de chorreras, finísima, de hilo puro, de cuatro ojales en su cuello almidonado.

—¡Mis botones de cadenilla, Bruno! —ordenó el Jarameño, a tiempo que introducía bajo el cuello de la camisa el corbatín de seda y que se abrochaba los especiales tirantes de brega.

Metióse la falda de la camisa dentro de la taleguilla, que cerró por delante, y pidió faja de seda y sudadero de hilo, con los que Bruno lo cinchó, duro, apartándose luego a preparar el "añadido." Iba el Jarameño a abotonarse el cuello, mirándose al espejo del lavabo, cuando reparó en su medalla bendita—la que se oxidaba con sus sudores, enzarzada en los negros y abundantes vellones de su tórax—y devotamente la llevó a su boca, la besó muy quedo.

—Anda con el "añadido," Bruno, ¡menéate! —ordenó sentándose de nuevo y destrenzando la coleta....

Bruno procedió a fijar el "añadido," trenzando el pelo postizo con el del diestro y con la moña aovada. ¡Bueno! Había quedado bien.... ¡A ver el chaleco! ¡Por supuesto, acorta el correón!.... ¡ah! ¡ah!..., ahora la chaquetilla.

"Look, dark lady, look how a bullfighter dresses!" el Jarameño told her, sitting down on a chair and abandoning himself to Bruno's expertise.

First the linen undershorts; then the band around the upper ankles, very tight, to prevent luxations and sprains; next, the cotton stockings, and over them, silk stockings, pulled very tight, without hints of a wrinkle; then, the slippers, patent leather, tied across the instep, and up!, get up!, now come the breeches and the frilly shirt, of pure linen, with four buttonholes in its starched collar.

"My button chain, Bruno!" ordered el Jarameño, as he placed, below the collar of the shirt, the silk bowtie, and fastened the special suspenders.

He tucked his shirttails into his breeches, which he fastened in front, and then asked for the silk sash and linen handkerchief with which Bruno cinched them, hard, stepping aside then to prepare the "hair switch." El Jarameño was going to button up his collar, looking at himself in the bathroom mirror, when he fixed his attention on his holy medal—the one that rusted in his sweat, tangled itself among the black, thick, and abundant hairs of his thorax—devotedly raised it to his mouth and very quietly kissed it.

"Hurry up with the 'hair switch,' Bruno, move it!" he ordered, sitting down again and unbraiding the pigtail....

> Bruno proceeded to attach the "hair switch," braiding the hairpiece
> in with the bullfighter's own hair and with the oval ribbons. Good!
> That fit nicely.... Let's see the vest! Of course, pull in the leather waist
> strap!... ah!, ah!..., now the jacket. (194–95)

The loving devotion Bruno takes in dressing his master is equaled by
the affectionate detail with which Gamboa describes his hero. His
Herculean and already exquisite body is embellished with the fineries
of linen, silk, and leather, treated as sacredly as he treats his medal.
Moreover, his unbridled, savage sexuality is not tragic, as Santa's is.
In fact, he is consistently faithful and generous to her, and to all his
friends, and by the end of the book is elevated to the status of hero.
His physical beauty only reinforces his idealized allure.

An interesting reading of this love affair is provided by Salvador
Oropesa, who sees Santa as a stepping-stone for el Jarameño. The
lower-class bullfighter falls in love with her because she is the beauty
of the bordello and is desired and adored by its wealthy, upper-class
patrons. El Jarameño in his conquest of her takes their place. His noble
heterosexual love is really one more transaction between men (631).

El Ateneo de la Juventud

The male homosocial, despite the new possibility of homosexual taint,
continued to play a major part in national discourse at the turn-of-
the-century. Julio Guerrero, who sought the essence of Mexicanness
in order to combat crime in Mexico, sees male homosocial relations
as a major organizing factor in Mexican social design and even goes
so far as to assert their superiority over heterosexual unions in this
regard. The traditional system of *compadrazgo* [system of kinship
through godparents, especially godfathers] "tiene en nuestra sociedad
una firmeza de solidaridad superior a los lazos civiles de la familia en
muchas poblaciones de los estados" [has in our society a firmness of
solidarity superior to civil family bonds in many populations of the
states] (105). Relations of godfathers and natural fathers can create
political ties that are passed on to the next generation through god-
sons. This major institution of Mexican society shows women to be of
even less importance than in the "traffic in women" model of Gayle
Rubin, which seems to apply so well in Mexican literature.

In the early years of the twentieth century, as in the nineteenth century, male homosocial bonding is at the root of much cultural production. While literary fraternities had been popular for decades, Mexico's most famous example, El Ateneo de la Juventud, was formed in 1906 and remained active (changing its name to El Ateneo de México in 1912) for eight years.[66] Mexico in fact had had a tradition of "ateneos" [cultural associations—implicitly inspired by the ancient Greeks] going back to 1840 when Spaniard Ángel Calderón de la Barca (today best known as husband of travel writer Frances) founded the Ateneo Mexicano. Vicente Riva Palacio's version of the Ateneo Mexicano was founded in 1882. President Porfirio Díaz himself inaugurated a third major Ateneo in 1902, the Ateneo Mexicano, Literario y Artístico, attracting a mixed bag of *modernistas* and *positivistas,* among them Urbina, Nervo, Ezequiel Chávez, and Salado Álvarez.[67] El Ateneo de la Juventud directly opposed the spirit of its predecessor as it took on the role of denouncing positivism. Its series of conferences on ancient Greece and its publication of José Enrique Rodó's *Ariel* in 1907 and 1908 respectively generated notable attention.

El Ateneo de la Juventud provides an interesting bridge between turn-of-the-century culture and the renaissance of cultural production that would occur following the Mexican revolution. Member Martín Luis Guzmán would write two major novels of the revolution and its aftermath in the late 1920s, *El águila y la serpiente* and *La sombra del caudillo.* Another member, José Vasconcelos, would go on to become a key player in postrevolutionary cultural politics by promoting literacy and founding the national university as secretary of education in the 1920s. Later he would unsuccessfully run for president, lose his messianic idealism, and write a series of acrid autobiographical "novels," the four-volume *Ulises criollo* in the mid-1930s, and the more outrageous *La flama* in 1959. Vasconcelos's promotion of the nationalistic muralism movement (of Diego Rivera, et al.) would seem to cast him on the "virile" side of the 1920s culture wars, while his affair with Antonieta Rivas Mercado and employment of Jaime Torres Bodet would align him more with the "effeminate" side. Likewise, the Ateneo's leader, Dominican Pedro Henríquez Ureña, would develop his own ambiguous relations with the controversial next generation of Mexican intellectuals, as we shall see. Alfonso Reyes, who would never lose his attachment to Greek culture, would have his own problems in the culture wars of the twenties and thirties as nationalist hardliners demonized the foreign along with the sexually nonconformist. While the group was of exclusively male membership, female intellectuals including María Enriqueta Camarillo Roa Bárcena de Pereyra were known to participate occasionally in their conferences. One other marginal participant of note was Colombian Ricardo Arenales, as he called himself, who would later be identified among the most sexually scandalous of the postrevolutionary intellectual elite (luckily for Mexican homophobes he was not Mexican and could eventually be expelled from the country).[68] The various intellectual and personal links between the members of the Ateneo and the protagonists of the culture wars of the twenties and thirties show them to be the forefathers of all factions of the coming generation, even though in the heat of the moment it would seem that these factions could not possibly share intellectual influences.

Conclusions

By the end of the nineteenth century, Mexican masculinity was coming into question in the fields of science, literature, and popular culture. Moreover, the sudden surge of discourse on sexuality forever linked masculinity (and male effeminacy) to masculine sexuality. Masculine sexuality was the great social peril of the day. Passionate men were murdering women, lower-class men were dressing lewdly, attractive sexualized men were despoiling young women, physically feminized men (hermaphrodites) were calling into question traditional doctrine on biological sex, and effeminate (homosexual) men were threatening the *buenas costumbres* on which Mexican society was based.

Positivist scientists, particularly criminologists, were drawn to study the problems caused by masculinity. The popular press cashed in on the public's fascination with the scandals brought on by turn-of-the-century masculinity and its accompanying untamed sexuality. Modernist and naturalist literature played out the shocking dramas of the increasingly confusing discourse on masculinity in Mexico. In the midst of all these new ideas and wild stories, there was no consensus on what should be done. There were clearly preoccupations about the savagery and destructiveness of lower-class masculinity; on the other hand there were also grave fears about upper-class refined masculinity, which, in fact, seemed at times not to be masculine at all, but now decadent, effeminate, and by implication homosexual.

Moreover, masculinity increasingly came to cross barriers of biological sex as women began to take on male characteristics in terms of dress, behavior, sexual expression, etc. Women exhibited active sexual desire both toward men and even toward other women. They were willful, bold, ambitious. They committed violent crimes and even proclaimed themselves to be "muy hombres."

Curiously, all this discourse—the positivist studies, the literature, the journalistic representations—presented these questions of gender and sexuality in a singularly Mexican context. *Santa* was a major milestone in national literature. The 41 became etched in the Mexican psyche and have remained so for a century. Studies like that of Guerrero are read today as important predecessors to treatises of national identity such as those of Ramos and Paz.[69] Masculinity and male sexuality were not the issues; Mexican masculinity and Mexican male sexuality were.

All this gender chaos would be interrupted by the Mexican revolution, which would effectively put an end to government-sanctioned positivism, conclude the era of the ornate and decadent literature of the modernists, suspend the thrust of social movements not related to class struggle (such as bourgeois feminism), and deflect attention (for a time) from issues of male sexuality. The revolution would establish a rift in Mexican cultural discourse in general, including gender discourse. The latter would resume after the revolution with a resurgence of traditional views by proponents of a fierce machismo, which would be combated by an equally ferocious range of counterdiscourses growing out of all the turn-of-the-century anxiety that was temporarily suppressed, but not at all quelled.

Chapter 3

Virile Literature and Effeminate Literature
The 1920s and 1930s

The Virile Literature of the Mexican Revolution

Cultural Revolution

The Mexican Revolution was more than a political and social revolution. In fact, some would argue that it was not much of a revolution at all in political and social terms, that the same racist class structures and corrupt bureaucracies of the late nineteenth century came to exist under different guises in the twenties and thirties. Nonetheless, the revolution certainly had its symbolic value. Whether or not rural and working-class Mexicans gained any material advantages at all from the revolution, they certainly gained status in the national imagination. White *criollo* Mexico had clearly become *mestizo,* and working class peons had come to symbolize the nation itself through the revolution's mythified heroes Emiliano Zapata and Pancho Villa.[1]

Meanwhile, notable rifts were occurring in the dominant forms and styles of Mexican cultural production. Positivism, significantly questioned by the Ateneo de la Juventud of José Vasconcelos, Pedro Henríquez Ureña, Martín Luis Guzmán, and Alfonso Reyes, all of whom were to become leading intellectual figures by the twenties, would quickly disappear from national discourse. Ornate and elitist *modernismo,* likewise, as a literary school of the *porfiriato,* was firmly rejected by the end of the revolution.

Thus, the kinds of works that were questioning masculinity at the turn of the century—positivist studies such as those by Roumagnac, modernist novellas and stories such as those by Nervo—were out of fashion and no longer significant contributors to national cultural discourse. Moreover, the symbolic class discourse produced by the revolution served to reassert a traditional notion of masculinity as if in reaction to the skeptical discourses of the *fin de siglo*. The upper-class, "civilized," "feminized" masculinity of *modernista* literature was symbolically defeated along with the government of Porfirio Díaz, and the lower-class, "savage," sexually dangerous hypermasculinity criticized by the previous generation was to be exalted. Furthermore, the effeminate male homosexuality celebrated in turn-of-the-century popular culture would be demonized in the twenties in a particularly nasty wave of homophobia. As Monsiváis puts it:

> Si la Revolución crea los espacios de desarrollo de una sensibilidad distinta, también los revolucionarios se jactan de un machismo rampante. (No uso homofobia, por ser un término correspondiente a la época que ya califica negativamente el odio irracional al homosexual. Antes, cuando todos la comparten, no tiene caso especificar.)

> If the Revolution creates spaces for the development of a distinct sensibility, the revolutionaries also boast of a rampant machismo. (I don't say homophobia because it is a term corresponding to an era that already negatively qualifies the irrational hatred of homosexuals. Before, when everyone shared this hatred, there is no point in specifying.) (*Salvador Novo* 32)

This is not to say that Mexican masculinity was no longer under question. More than that, what had emerged as a cultural crisis and discourse of confusion during the *porfiriato* was now a veritable polemic. Its protagonists now acknowledged an essential ideological link between constructions of masculinity and male sexuality and of Mexicanness in their debates over national literature and national identity.

The Great Virility Debates

The polemic nature of gender discourse in postrevolutionary Mexico can best be observed in the great virility debates initiated in the 1920s around the topic of national literature. On the surface, these debates were not about masculinity, but about literature. Virile literature was the subject of a series of newspaper articles by intellectuals (of greater or lesser prominence) summarized in Víctor Díaz Arciniega's *Querella por la cultura "revolucionaria."*[2] The notion of a virile literature was nothing new. Seneca, Erasmus, Ben Jonson, and Montaigne had all addressed the topic in their day, and in the New World there was a history of constructing national literature as a virile enterprise going back as far as Andrés Bello.[3]

Julio Jiménez Rueda's 1924 article, "El afeminamiento de la literatura mexicana" [the feminization of Mexican literature] (cited at length in Schneider, *Ruptura* 161–63), contested by another penned by Francisco Monterde, "Existe una literatura mexicana viril" [virile Mexican literature does exist] (cited at length in Schneider, *Ruptura* 163–67), initiated a debate about Mexico's first generation of post-revolutionary writers. The debate was complex, concerning itself not only with whether Mexican literature was "virile" enough, but also with topics such as social responsibility (sometimes specifically socialism) in literature, Mexico's tradition of artistic corruption brought about by institutionalized government patronage, and the status of Mexican cultural production with regard to international vanguards.

Some of the participants did concern themselves with literature itself. For example, Victoriano Salado Álvarez, author of "El eunuco," on the side of those nostalgic for the old days of the *porfiriato* (but not *modernismo*, which he is famous for chastising), complained, "no hay literatura nueva y la que hay no es mexicana...y a veces ni siquiera literatura" [there is no new literature and what there is isn't Mexican...and at times it is not even literature] (cited in Díaz Arciniega 64). For others the debate was more a question of the slippery topic of literature's gender, as can be seen in the titles of a series of articles by the "red poet," Carlos Gutiérrez Cruz: "Literatura con sexo y literatura sin sexo" [literature with a sex and literature without a sex], "El sexo en la producción" [sex in production], "Los poetas jóvenes sin sexo" [young sexless poets], "Otros rasgos del afeminamiento literario" [other features of literary feminization], "Poetas afeminados y filósofos indigestos" [effeminate poets and indigestible philosophers], etc.[4]

Despite the vocabulary utilized in Gutiérrez Cruz's titles, the biological sex of Mexican writers was not at issue; it was still a given that writers of significance were men. Mexico's most prolific *escritora* of the day, María Enriqueta, once a participant in Ateneo de la Juventud events, living in exile in Spain in the twenties, has never been taken seriously in her native country;[5] and its most provocative (if sometimes lurid) female novelist of the time, "Loreley" (pseudonym of María Luisa Garza), self-published most of her books, many of them across the border in Texas and California, and never achieved any significant recognition in Mexico.[6] "Sex" for Gutiérrez Cruz, then, refers to the more social concept of gender (to put it in contemporary terms); and it is very clear that if all writers under consideration are men, any gender problems would point to the old bugaboo of effeminacy.

However, the topic of debate was ostensibly virility of literature, not virility of literati, wasn't it? If it was, of course, an immediate question arises: What is virile literature? While Patricia Parker has provided a fascinating genealogy of literary virility in European discourse, it is by no means clear that Mexico's polemicists of the twenties draw on it at all. In fact, no one in Mexico's debate bothers to define the term. And while at times it seems that what the masculinist participants in the debate favor is a socially conscious literature that supports class struggle, or at least a gritty social realism that contests the aesthetic elegance and elitism of *modernismo*, throughout the debates virile literature remains a rather nebulous notion. The rhetorical use of the vocabulary of gender to refer to abstract concepts such as national culture are not, perhaps, so unusual, but left undefined, "virile" ends up little more than a vague normative term implying "good" (with "effeminate," implying "bad"), in terms of literary quality and/or with regard to the moral virtue of its subject matter. It is difficult, then, to address this rhetoric of virility without either tacitly accepting the given terminology or getting mired in a discussion of what the term means, which is why many leading intellectuals of the day, among them Villaurrutia, Guzmán, Reyes, and Tablada, simply ignored these debates, even when their own work was implicitly or explicitly attacked. It took a wit with the incisiveness of that of Salvador Novo to deride the debate itself in his defense of Mexican literary production in which he insisted that "existe una literatura mexicana moderna cuya buena reputación de muchacha fresca y viril han querido opacar las lenguas doloridas" [that there exists a modern Mexican literature whose good reputation as a fresh and virile young lady aching tongues have wished to opaque] (cited in Sheridan, *Los Contemporáneos* 257).

The Medullar Softening of Mexican Writers

In fact, from the very first there is a certain slippage between virile writing and virile writers, which allows the debate to make subtle unexplained and untheorized links between literary personalities and their literary production. Jiménez Rueda's article, for example, which initiates the polemic, compares not the virile writing, but the traditionally—according to him—virile writers of the nineteenth century with the effeminate ones of the twentieth. The former possessed "chispazos de genio, pasiones turbulentas, aciertos indudables y frecuentes. ...Pero hoy...hasta el tipo del hombre que piensa ha degenerado. Ya no somos gallardos, altivos, toscos...es que ahora suele encontrarse el éxito, más que en los puntos de la pluma, en las complicadas artes del tocador" [sparks of genius, turbulent passions, indubitable and frequent epiphanies.... But nowadays even the thinking man has degenerated. We are no longer gallant, lofty, tough...now [the thinking man] tends to find less success at pen-point than in the complicated arts of the dressing table] (cited in Schneider, *Ruptura* 162).

Jiménez Rueda's attack on literary feminization has less to do with literary style or even with the content of literary production than it does with the perceived effeminacy of certain writers. Díaz Arciniega attributes such attacks to professional jealousies of a generation of young writers, all struggling to achieve three goals: "la posibilidad de obtener un trabajo remunerado, la posibilidad de participar en la 'reconstrucción nacional,' y la posibilidad de alcanzar reconocimiento y poder" [the possibility of obtaining remunerated work, the possibility of participating in the "national reconstruction," and the possibility of achieving recognition and power] (100); in particular, certain critics entered into the polemic with the "propósito de criticar el aspecto más vulnerable de algunos jóvenes escritores, una personalidad con manifestaciones evidentemente homosexuales" [aim of criticizing the most vulnerable aspect of several young writers, a personality with evident homosexual manifestations] (58). If the turn-of-the-century gender crisis did not manage to resolve the many contradictions in Mexican notions of gender, it did manage to crystallize the equating of male effeminacy with homosexuality; and a postrevolutionary resurgent valorizing of the more barbarous masculinity so derided and feared at the turn of the century ensured that refined and cultured men would be labeled as effeminate and homosexual.

Thus, while a few of the emerging young writers were correctly reputed to be homosexuals—namely, Villaurrutia and the more flamboyant Novo—many others (whose sexual personae ranged from the less overtly but unequivocally homosexual, to the superficially heterosexual with latent or well-hidden homosexual tendencies, to the undeniably heterosexual) apparently were not. For example, it is often intimated that Jaime Torres Bodet, who was to end up more of a politician and diplomat than a poet, was somehow not true to himself, but no one has ever published any evidence revealing him to have been a closeted homosexual. And yet, as Vasconcelos's personal secretary during the years in which the mythic figure of Vasconcelos was transforming Mexico's cultural landscape as the minister of education, Torres Bodet was clearly one of the targets of insult of Henríquez Ureña in a letter to Reyes in which he refers to Vasconcelos's entourage as a "colección de gente afeminada y mezquina, en lo moral cuando menos" [collection of effeminate and trivial people, morally speaking to say the least] (cited in Díaz Arciniega 68). While it is not entirely clear that "morally effeminate and trivial" means homosexual, there is little doubt about Henríquez Ureña's discomfort with male homosexuality, as will become evident when we look later at his relationship with Salvador Novo.

Returning to the position of Jiménez Rueda in his "El afeminamiento de la literatura mexicana," what starts as a quest for an active and brilliant national literature that embodies a feeling which is "masculino en toda acepción de la palabra" [masculine in every sense of the word] (cited in Díaz Arciniega 55), slips subtly into an attack on the writer's more successful peers. Thus it is not surprising that when Monterde contests Jiménez's article a few days later with "Existe una literatura mexicana viril," he too focuses less on literature than on writers:

> No seamos pesimistas; el tipo de intelectual, entre nosotros, siempre ha sido de corta estatura, salvo excepciones de fácil recordación.... De don Joaquín Fernández de Lizardi al mismo licenciado Jiménez Rueda, pasando por Guillermo Prieto, Gutiérrez Nájera, Ángel de Campo, etc., para no citar sino unos cuantos, nuestros escritores nunca han sido "gallardos, altivos, toscos"... No fueron colosos de estatura ni les hizo falta. Es natural que el hombre que hace una vida de sacrificio—como es la del literato en nuestras latitudes, sin reposo en la montaña ni largos veraneos—el hombre que vive respirando el aire pobre de las bibliotecas, alejado de los deportes, sea un hombre pequeño, un hombre débil físicamente. No vamos a medir, por la estatura de un escritor, la talla de sus pensamientos.

> Let's not be pessimistic; the intellectual type, between us, has always been short in stature, except for a few easily remembered exceptions. ... From Don Joaquín Fernández de Lizardi to the Licenciado Jiménez Rueda himself, including Guillermo Prieto, Gutiérrez Nájera, Ángel de Campo, etc., to mention but a few, our writers have never been "gallant, lofty, tough...." They were not colossal in stature nor did this matter to them. It is only natural that a man who lives a life of sacrifice—as is the case with the literatus in our latitudes, without repose in the mountains nor lengthy summer vacations—the man who lives breathing poor library air, far removed from sports, be a small man, a physically weak man. We shall not measure, by the stature of a man, the magnitude of his thoughts. (cited in Schneider, *Ruptura* 167)

Likewise, Gutiérrez Cruz—who had the stylistic habit of personifying abstract terms, or more precisely "engendering" them: "el arte, hijo de la cultura" [art, son of culture], "la intelectualidad mexicana ...hija legítima de la política palaciega" [Mexican intellectuality... legitimate daughter of courtly politics] (quoted in Díaz Arciniega 87, 69)—tends to concern himself with the attributes of writers in his articles presumably on literature. For example: "Ellos [los afeminados] buscan la belleza en el arte, nosotros [los viriles revolucionarios] buscamos el sentimiento; ellos quieren divertirse y nosotros queremos unificarnos" [The effeminate ones seek beauty in art, while we the virile revolutionaries seek feeling; they want to amuse themselves and we want solidarity] (cited in Díaz Arciniega 87).

In fact, gender becomes a key rhetorical tool in postrevolutionary discourse, without ever being defined. It functions tacitly to insult by emasculating an opponent much in the way that the *albur* symbolically proves the masculinity—i.e., the power, the honor, the prestige—of the vulgar *macho* described by Paz in *El laberinto de la soledad*. If it was undesirable to be seen as effeminate in the era of Independence, it was doubly so after the revolution, when effeminacy had come to be inextricably linked with the scandal of homosexuality. Thus, terms like Jiménez Rueda's "esbeltez quebradiza" [frail slenderness] (Díaz Arciniega 58) and "reblandecimiento medular" [medullar softening] (Schneider, *Ruptura* 171), or *estridentistas* Manuel Maples Arce's "menstruaciones intelectuales" [intellectual menstruations] and Germán Lizt Arzubide's "virilidades en caída" [fallen virilities] (Sheridan, *Los Contemporáneos* 128, 132) proliferate in Mexico's cultural discourse of the twenties. Postrevolutionary Mexican society in its rejection of positivism, *modernismo* and everything that recalls the *porfiriato,* is clearly receptive to a masculinist discourse that reinforces traditional stereotypes of masculinity as sharp, powerful, active, honorable, moral, and working class. Moreover, the fact that the polemicists employ these terms without defining them reinforces patriarchal structures. The masculine/feminine dichotomy is part of Mexico's gender habitus, so deeply embedded in the national subconscious that no one questions the lack of semiotic precision in the terms' rhetorical usage.

The "Discovery" of "Los de Abajo"

The most concrete result of the great virility debates is well known. It is the inauguration of "the novel of the Mexican Revolution" as a genre. In Monterde's above mentioned article, "Existe una literatura mexicana viril," he answers Jiménez Rueda's challenge by contending that not only has Mexican literature not regressed to a more exaggerated state of effeminacy than in the past, but there are also works of exemplary virility currently being produced in Mexico as evidenced by Azuela's *Los de abajo* [the underdogs].[7] It is ironic perhaps that the most strident participants in these debates about national culture were never to become as famous as the artists whom they discussed (and more often than not criticized). Most of them were writers (novelists or poets) in their own right, but Monterde, for example, is best known for discovering the novel known today as the quintessential novel of the Mexican Revolution.[8] *Los de abajo,* originally published in Texas in 1916, was still virtually unknown in Mexico (and Texas) until Monterde held it up as an example of literary virility. Monterde succeeded in arousing such curiosity that the novel was quickly published in installments in *El Universal Ilustrado,* one of the main journals taking part in these debates, and soon after was released nationally in book form in what was to become one of dozens of editions in numerous languages.[9]

But haven't we determined that the debate was actually about writers and not writing? Yes and no: the debate did in fact frequently deal with literature itself, but would inevitably turn to personalities when the specific issue of virility was brought in. Mariano Azuela, although an outsider to Mexico City cultured society, was himself an interesting specimen of masculinity.[10] He lived, for example, in a purely masculine environment, his house physically divided into two sections, one for him and his five sons, the other for his wife and five daughters. If his living space was idyllically masculine-homosocial, so was his literary taste, albeit in a quirky way. The novel that he most admired was Inclán's *Astucia,* a book that Monsiváis describes as a veritable handbook of masculinity,[11] and, as we have seen, a sometimes utopian vision of male homosocial bonding. More curiously, his favorite book was Nervo's *El bachiller,* his shocking *modernista* tale of anti-heterosexuality and anti-masculinity.

But what of *Los de abajo?* What makes it such an outstanding example of literary virility? Even Monterde is not very specific about that. His article, "Existe una literatura mexicana viril," concerns itself more with the difficulties Mexican authors have in publishing and in finding an audience for their work than with details about *Los de abajo.* He does name Azuela "the Mexican novelist of the revolution" (quoted in Schneider, *Ruptura* 166) and, in another article published a few weeks later, "Críticos en receso y escritores desesperanzados" [receding critics and despairing writers] describes *Los de abajo* as an example of "una literatura mexicana actual, no degenerada ni afeminada" [an up-to-date Mexican literature that is not degenerate nor effeminate] (quoted in Schneider, *Ruptura* 168). Díaz Arciniega concludes that the term "virile" seems, when not referring to the writers themselves, to make reference to the content of their writing (as opposed to its form), particularly as it pertains to the revolution; the frequently applied term "revolutionary," in turn, is used as a synonym for a certain brand of realism. He calls upon Monterde again (in his article "Los jóvenes y la revolución" [youth and the revolution], published three months into the debate), to reveal how the term was most likely to be employed: "para ser poeta revolucionario hay que limitarse a escribir sobre la revolución mexicana y cantar sólo para el pueblo, para el obrero y para el campesino" [to be a revolutionary poet, one must limit oneself to writing about the Mexican Revolution and singing only for the people, for the workers, and for the peasants] (91).

Monterde, in fact, rises again and again in defense of his contemporaries, as does Salatiel Rosales, who attributes the lack of "literatura seria, viril, profunda" [serious, virile, profound literature] and the preponderance of writers who are "castrados intelectualmente" [intellectually castrated] to, following Monterde, the dearth of institutionalized publishing resources in Mexico. He suggests that once some high quality literary journals are founded in Mexico, "surgirán de debajo de las piedras los escritores de mentalidad y virilidad" [writers of mentality and virility will rise up from under the rocks] (cited in Schneider, *Ruptura* 176–77). The problem, of course, with the defenders of literature, as with Jiménez Rueda and others who attack it as effeminate, is that they insist on employing the same nebulous masculinist gender rhetoric.

The Love for Valiant Men

Turning to *Los de abajo*, we might ask: Is its content exemplary of the "virile" revolution? Are its characters somehow models of a certain vision of Mexican manliness? They certainly seem to promote a certain style of masculinity exemplified by physical strength, bravery, and male homosocial bonding. In fact, expressions of affection between the valiant soldiers who are the central personages of the novel are frequent. A few examples will suffice to illustrate the importance of male bonding to the characters:

> —Yo respeto a los valientes de veras.... Y no sólo los respeto, sino que también los quiero.

> "I respect truly valiant men.... And not only do I respect then, but I also love them." (6)

> —Compadre Demetrio, tengo el gusto de presentarle al güero Margarito.... ¡Un amigo de veras!... ¡Ah cómo quiero yo a este güero!

> "Compadre Demetrio, may I have the pleasure of introducing you to blond Margarito.... A true friend!... Ah, how I love this blond guy!" (74)

> —Eso sí, mi gusto es gastarlo todo con las amistades. Para mí es más contento ponerme una papalina con todos los amigos que mandarles un centavo a las viejas de mi casa.

> "That's right, I'd rather spend everything on my buddies. For me it's more fun to get drunk with all my friends than to send a penny to the old ladies back home." (119)

The love for valiant men in general, or Anastasio's more specific fondness for blond Margarito, or Margarito's affection for his buddies over his "old ladies" is representative of the exaltation of male-male relations that permeates the novel.

The actions of Demetrio Macías, the beloved leader of the ragged troop who are the central actors in the novel, further illustrate this attitude. Although he clearly cares for his wife and evidently enjoys himself with women, he is capable of abandoning his wife and of witnessing the murder of his lover, but not of separating himself from his buddies. At the end of the book, when it appears that there is no longer any reason to keep fighting (or rather when Demetrio realizes that there was never really any reason to begin with), Demetrio nonetheless chooses to remain with his company rather than return to his long-suffering wife and child (136–37).

Women for Demetrio are of secondary consideration; in fact the most important romance of the novel is an erotic triangle typical of those described by Sedgwick in *Between Men*. Demetrio, wounded in battle early in the text, is treated by city slicker Luis Cervantes with the help of a humble girl named Camila. An affection soon awakens between Luis and Camila. Predictably (following Sedgwick), Demetrio falls in love with her. But, instead of the expected rivalry, Luis takes advantage of the desire that Camila feels for him and the power it gives him to strengthen his friendship with Demetrio, whom he admires idealistically as leader of the peasant troop. When Demetrio confronts Luis regarding his relationship with Camila, Luis responds, "No es cierto, mi jefe; ella lo quiere a usted...pero le tiene miedo" [It's not true, Chief; she loves you...but she's afraid of you] (44). Luis takes up the role of matchmaker and soon attempts to set up a date for Demetrio with Camila at a local dance, but Camila refuses, "¡Ay, curro...si vieras qué feo siento que tú me digas eso!...Si yo a ti es al que quero...pero a ti no más" [Ay, curro...[12] if you could see how awful it makes me feel to hear you say that!...If it's you that I love...you and no one else] (46). Luis, in turn, does not go to the dance with Camila, thereby reinforcing his loyalty to Demetrio to whom he has confessed, "Mi jefe...usted me ha simpatizado desde que lo conocí, y lo quiero cada vez más, porque sé todo lo que vale" [Chief...I have taken a liking to you ever since I first met you, and I love you more all the time, because I know what you're worth] (43).

In another scene, Luis invites a young girl to accompany him on a rowdy outing with the other guys. He soon notices that Demetrio is interested in the girl, so he sits at the table positioning her directly across from Demetrio. Then, however, "Luis Cervantes notó...con gran sorpresa...que el pie que sentía entre los de la muchacha no era de Demetrio, sino el del güero Margarito. Y la indignación hirvió en su pecho" [Luis Cervantes noted...with great surprise...that the foot he felt between those of the girl was not Demetrio's but blond Margarito's. And his breast boiled in indignation] (84). The girl, who remains nameless, insignificant herself, bears value only as a means of fortifying the bonds between Luis and Demetrio. Moreover, the night nearly ends in a threesome when Demetrio follows Luis and the girl into his bedroom, except that the brazen *soldadera* la Pintada[13] jumps in and breaks it up (85–86). Meanwhile, it seems that Demetrio is attracted by any woman who has any link at all to Luis, as if by acquiring such women he might gain some of the class status that Luis, the educated city boy, possesses.

On yet another occasion, Luis decides to share a booty of jewels with his esteemed Demetrio and then flee the war (elope?) with him, but Demetrio refuses: "...siento que no es cosa de hombres....Pues yo, con que no me falte el trago y con traer una chamaquita que me cuadre, soy el hombre más feliz del mundo" [...I feel like that's not quite manly....As for me, as long as I'm not without drink and if I've got a cute girl with me, I'm the happiest man in the world] (95). And when Luis, now completely in on the key to his friend's happiness, offers to bring Camila to him (they had left her village a while earlier), Demetrio accepts, finally setting the stage for the traffic in women Luis hopes will bond him forever to Demetrio. So Luis tricks Camila, convincing her to go off with him without letting her suspect that he'll hand her over to Demetrio. Camila is, of course, enraged when she discovers what has happened, but ultimately resigns herself to her fate. But by now the role of Luis as procurer for Demetrio is clear to the other guys, who note that the only women with whom they have seen Luis have been intended as gifts for Demetrio (with one inadvertently given to Margarito). A group of the guys jokingly observe the situation, one of them remarking, "Pa mí que el tal curro no es más que un... " [For me this *curro* is nothing more than a...] (97), with the obvious epithet "maricón" censored and veiled over in ellipses. By now the Sedgwickian pattern has revealed itself all too clearly. Whether Luis is homosexual or not—and the virility debates confirm the paranoiac view that Mexico's educated upper-class men, of whom Luis was the principal representative in the novel, were likely to be homosexuals—the relation between him and Demetrio (and not that of either of them with Camila) is what really matters for both of them. When Camila's rival, la Pintada, murders her, Demetrio barely reacts; he only wanted her because Luis gave her to him.

Homoeroticism in Virile Literature

In fact, women, although clearly objects of lust for some of the soldiers, do not play a very erotic role in the novel. The women of *Los de abajo* are rarely attractive at all, and when they are sexualized it is often as strumpet, almost too animalistically brazen to be attractive (la Pintada), or homely and vulgar (Camila). La Pintada never lasts long with her lovers; she quickly has Demetrio "harto" [fed up with her] (95), and Margarito tells her the same thing to her face a little while later: "¡A todos nos tienes hartos!" [You've got us all sick of you!] (113). Demetrio's wife is nice enough, but her role is that of wife and mother, not lover, and Demetrio only seems to notice how much she ages (136). Luis's young girlfriend, blonde-haired, blue-eyed, "su piel...fresca y suave como un pétalo de rosa" [her skin...fresh and soft like a rose petal] (82) is dollishly attractive, but despite being an object of so many male gazes is never described in any more detail than this.

On the other hand, the male body, a frequent object of scopophilia, is glimpsed half-naked, eroticized, idealized, on numerous occasions. For example, the troops are first introduced as "hombres de pechos y piernas desnudos, oscuros y repulidos como viejos bronces" [men with bare breasts and legs, dark and polished like ancient bronzes] (8). The enemy is less idealized but equally eroticized when they are surprised by night and appear like "espectros de cabeza y pechos oscuros como hierro, de largos calzones blancos desgarrados" [specters with dark iron-like heads and breasts, dressed in long white ragged drawers] (57). Another group of soldiers, "los gorrudos"[14] are "hombres requemados, mugrientos y casi desnudos" [sunburnt, dirty, nearly naked men] (63). Later, General Natera's men also appear half naked, in "garras de calzones y camisas que medio cubrían sus cuerpos sucios" [in tatters of drawers and shirts half covering their dirty bodies] (67–68). If they are not statues, they are brave machos, male animals; but in every case, much attention is paid to their ever visible bodies. There are several individuals, as well, who are described erotically, most notably la Codorniz [the Quail] who first appears stark naked, challenging the federal troops to attack in a mock bullfight (12), to give but one example.

Azuela's novel goes one or two steps further than nineteenth century novels of homosocial bonding such as *El fistol del diablo* or even *Astucia* in terms of its homoeroticism. And while the women of the text are rejected (la Pintada), abandoned (Demetrio's wife), forgotten (the young girl) or murdered (Camila), the links between the men, with their eroticized bodies, persist. Sylvia Molloy has observed astutely that an enduring force of homosexual panic has led to "the near-total suppression of the male body from Latin American literature" ("Too Wilde" 49); *Los de abajo* is clearly an exception, and I contend that the important allegorical metaphor of homosocial bonding in the history of Mexican literature has made the homoerotic an inevitable feature of national literature.

Actually, this eroticization of homosocial bonding was already erupting from Mexican literature by the turn of the century. Heriberto Frías's *Tomóchic*, a novel first published in 1893–95, which bears many thematic links to *Los de abajo*, also exalted its swarthy rebel heroes as "semidioses" [demigods] (18) and featured several male homoerotic scenes, the most significant being that in which the narrator Miguel Mercado spies on fellow soldier Castorena bathing nude in a river. Miguel watches him at length: "desnudo, más bufonesco que nunca, erizado el cuerpo, rechoncho de pelos amarillos, como un orangután rubio, se bañaba impávido, cantando cual si le durase la embriaguez nocturno" [naked, more buffoonish than ever, erect body, yellow-haired and chubby, like a blond orangutan, singing as if still drunk from the night before] (33). Oddly, Miguel did not like Castorena, and instinctively mocked him, yet this did not stop him from gazing intently at his nude body; and even more oddly, immediately after this scene, Miguel suddenly sympathized with Castorena for the first time.

In any case, it is especially noteworthy that this homoeroticism does not conform precisely with any sexual inversion model that equates homosexuality with effeminacy—the atmosphere of hypermasculinity in *Los de abajo* scarcely hints of the weak, effeminate masculinity so familiar in *modernista* literature.[15] But it does support another model of homosexuality, the narcissistic one fomented by Gide in *Corydon*, a book published (at first clandestinely) in France in the same era, which would eventually become well known in Mexico.[16] Gide's narcissistic-style homosexuality was always reflective of a desire between virile men and/or athletic ephebes. The narcissist, according to Freud, might desire "what he himself is (i.e., himself), what he himself was, what he himself would like to be, [or] someone who was once part of himself" ("On Narcissism" 90). Thus, narcissism might be intergenerational but would not indicate (at least superficially) any symbolic gender difference. Male narcissistic homosexual desire does not require effeminacy on the part of anyone involved, a notion at odds with the Mexican model of homosexuality that had been popularized with the scandal of the famous 41.

The first famous novel of the Mexican Revolution, the model of national literature of the twenties, the supreme example of virile Mexican writing is, like the nationalist novels of the nineteenth century, preeminently homosocial, and, despite the rise of discourse on homosexuality and the subsequent mounting homophobia in Mexico in the early twentieth century, startlingly homoerotic. The novel of the revolution, which was to become the major literary genre in Mexico by the thirties, grew in part out of a reactionary sentiment, a desire to remasculinize Mexican literature, a wish to put an end to the numerous discourses that had erupted during the *porfiriato* that had questioned aspects of Mexican masculinity previously taken for granted. However, it was really too late; the questions had already been asked, and Mexican masculinity could no longer be taken for granted. The novel of the revolution, insofar as it presented the male world of war and politics, simply provided a different scenario in which the same unresolved issues about masculinity might get played out.

Class, of course, is an important variable here. While *modernismo* focused on the travails of the urban educated upper classes, the novel of the revolution deals mainly with rural illiterate lower classes. The nonliterary discourses of positivist social science and popular journalism, of course, did inquire into the complexities of working-class masculinities during the *porfiriato* as did *naturalista* texts like *Santa* and late *costumbrista* novels like *La Rumba* and Cuéllar's *Baile y cochino*. So while the novel of the revolution, the virile literature of the twenties and thirties, is partly a reaction against the *modernismo* of the *porfiriato*, its vision of masculinity, in fact, follows directly from the same classist assumptions that inform Porfirian visions of gender.

More Spanking

The desire to reject the gender play of the *modernistas,* however, brings novelists of the revolution back to "traditional" nineteenth-century paradigms of masculinity, paradigms whose homoeroticism may have gone unnoticed a century before, but now (decades after the 41) were unmistakably queer. For example, let us recall the queer eroticized scenes of male-on-male assertions of power of the Mexican nineteenth-century novel. Two examples from Inclán's *Astucia* went unnoticed in the 1800s when there was no discourse on homosexuality to panic Mexican readers: the initiation rite in which Astucia's pals tear his clothes to rags as they attempt to disarm him; and the scene in which the enemies of *los hermanos de la hoja* are stripped, tied to trees, and publicly spanked. Similar scenes abound in Mexico's novels of the revolution, and while they generally go uninterrogated by literary critics who are more concerned with issues of class struggle and historical accuracy, it would have been hard not to notice them in the twenties and thirties. The *habitus* of masculinity and male sexuality had been jarred visible at the turn of the century, and male homoerotics were now unavoidably noticeable and discomforting.

Heriberto Frías's *Tomóchic* in 1893 may have gotten away with a bizarre opening scene in which the *tomochiteco* rebels capture a certain General Rangel, whom they do not kill, but instead spank. They send him off saying, "Nosotros no peleamos con muchachos. Usted debe estar con su mamá" [We don't fight with kids. You should be with your mom] (10). Spanking here is an insult to the very manhood of the young general. However, by the early thirties, spanking seems to have acquired a clearly more erotic flavor.

For example, "las cintareadas de Antonio Silva" [Antonio Silva's spankings] is one of many queer and unsettling scenes of the revolution presented in Nellie Campobello's idiosyncratic novella, *Cartucho* [cartridge]. Silva, a senior officer of Pancho Villa's troops, takes fetishistic pleasure in spanking his prisoners of war. Typically, he has his victims tied to a post with their pants lowered so that he might whip them at length. Silva affirms, "mis hijos necesitan la cueriadita a nalga pelona y dada por mi santa mano" [my sons need a little bare-assed whipping, meted out by my holy hand] (933). And when Silva dies, the narrator informs her readers, "mamá lloró por él; dijo que se había acabado un hombre" [Mom cried for him; she said that it was the end of a man] (933).

If erotic spanking signified manhood, then what are we to think of a more embellished beating scene elaborated in John Reed's *Insurgent Mexico?* Don Priciliano Saucedes, a Spanish usurer who had been captured in the early years of the revolution by *maderistas,* is "strapped naked upon his horse and beaten upon his bare back with the flat of a sword" (266). It is always more humiliating to punish a naked prisoner, as happens again near La Cadena. In this case, "they made him get off his horse, and took away his rifle, clothes and shoes. Then they made him run naked through a hundred yards of chaparral and cactus, shooting at him" (76).

Another bizarre scene occurs in Francisco Uriquizo's *Tropa vieja* [old troops],[17] in which new recruits to Díaz's federal army, consigned as criminals, are humiliated and forced to strip before their commanding officer as they are issued their uniforms. In a scene recalling the send-off of the 41 when they are forced to exchange their elegant gowns for masculine army garb, he watches as they get their hair cut, commenting on the "piojerío" [licebed] in their hair, then abruptly orders:

> … ahora encuérense.
>   Teníamos un poco de vergüenza.
>   —¡Encuérense, con una chingada!
>   Quedamos en pelota.
>
> … now strip naked.
>   We were a little embarrassed.
>   —Strip naked, Goddammit!
>   We were left stark naked. (386)

Only after the men are displayed naked for their commanding officer are they given their uniforms. Such eroticized assertions of power are invariably presented as proof of an exalted masculinity. The mere positioning of one man at a higher level in a hierarchy is enough to establish his masculinity, while subordination implies emasculation;

the enforced nudity, the implied threat of rape only intensifies this symbolic gendering.

Guzmán's fascinating *La sombra del caudillo* [the shadow of the chief], more a novel of postrevolutionary Mexican bureaucracy than of the revolution itself, plays out the elaborate webs of the male homosocial relations that essentially run the country. However, these webs do not imply the dispersed and ever contested loci of power that Foucault would look for;[18] instead, "discipline," "obedience," and "submission" are key to all these relations (532). Early in the novel, before opposition presidential candidate Ignacio Aguirre is disillusioned by the brutal violence of postrevolutionary politics, he conflates "friendship" and "comradeship" with hierarchical political relations, but his friend Axkaná González serves as the voice of reason: "En el campo de las relaciones políticas la amistad no figura, no subsiste. Puede hablar, de abajo arriba, conveniencia, adhesión, fidelidad; y de arriba abajo, protección afectuosa o estimación utilitaria. Pero amistad simple, sentimiento afectivo que una de igual a igual, imposible" [In the realm of political relations, friendship does not figure, does not subsist. You might speak, top-down, of convenience, adhesion, loyalty; and bottom-up, of affectionate protection or utilitarian esteem. But simple friendship, any affectionate feeling that joins equal to equal, impossible] (533). Homosocial bonding is always arranged in a web of cynically self-interested power relations.

Male bonding takes on an equally sinister form in a vastly different setting, the battlefield, among the "elite" of the rebel troops in Rafael Muñoz's *¡Vámanos con Pancho Villa!* [let's go with Pancho Villa]. Villa personally wins over Tiburcio Maya, even after he himself has murdered Maya's wife and daughter, by proclaiming his brotherly love for him and presenting him the gift of a mule (demonstrating the value of women in Villa's world). Maya is quite complacent about the special place he occupies in General Villa's heart until another chosen member of the entourage, Miguel Contreras, explains to him the precise machinations of Villa's paranoiac web of homosocial bonding:

> —Ya ves [dice Contreras], pues eso va diciendo a cada uno. El Viejo es muy lanza. Ya no más falta que a la noche te trencen.
> —¿Qué es eso?

—Ya verás: va a venir uno del Estado Mayor; te dirá: "Tiburcio, tú tienes toda la confianza del jefe, que me manda para que te dé una comisión; aquí viene uno que tiene ganas de pelarse; te vas a juntar con él y lo vigilas para que no se escape. Si se te pela, el general se enojará contigo y quién sabe cómo te vaya."

—¿Y eso qué tiene de malo?

—Que lo mismo les ha dicho a los otros; tú los vigilas a ellos, pero ellos te vigilan a ti, y hay otra trenza que los está vigilando a ustedes tres, y así, de trenza en trenza, hasta los meros gallones de toda su confianza.

"You see, says Contreras, he goes around telling that to everybody. The old guy's very clever. The only thing missing now is for them to braid you at night."

"What's that?"

"You'll find out soon enough: somebody from the senior staff is going to show up; he'll say: 'Tiburcio, you have the full confidence of the chief, who's sent me to give you a commission; here comes a guy who wants to slip off; you are going to join up with him and watch over him so that he doesn't escape. If he gets away from you, the general will get very angry with you and who knows how it'll go for you then.' "

"And what's wrong with that?"

"That he's said the same thing to the others; you're watching them, but they're watching you, and there's another braid that's watching all three of you, and likewise, from braid to braid, going all the way up to the bigwigs whom he holds in full confidence." (734)

The ardent affection of Villa—"porque él siempre fue muy fácil de emocionarse, como esos borrachitos que no soportan una mala cara, que lloran y abrazan, jurando amor eterno" [because he always got emotional very easily, like those drunks who can't stand a negative face, who cry and embrace, vowing eternal love] (733)—combined with his lethal threats is the force that joins together all of his key men.

Muerte de Hombres

Guzmán's *La sombra del caudillo* shows these inevitable hierarchical structures to be precisely what determine the masculinity of the participants. Political life in postrevolutionary Mexico is a veritable battlefield of masculinity in which "los muy hombres" [the most manly] are assassins—for example would-be assassin Adelaido Cruz is identified in exactly these terms (616)—and in which every relationship serves to reinforce or to contest such hierarchies. The book even yields a saying that by the end of the novel is repeated sufficiently to become the novel's central lesson: "La regla . . . es una sola: en México si no le madruga usted a su contrario, su contrario le madruga a usted" [There is but a single rule: in Mexico if you don't strike down your rival, your rival will strike you down] (622). Or: "La política mexicana no conjuga más que un verbo: madrugar" [Mexican politics conjugates just one verb: to strike][19] (632).

A paradox emerges in *La sombra del caudillo*. *El caudillo* is the figure who controls everything and everyone, and thus is the novel's only complete man. Practically everyone who dares to oppose him is murdered, and even the president-to-be is a mere puppet whose every move *el caudillo* controls. Given his magnitude of power, then, *el caudillo* is anything but valiant. He has no opportunities to be brave since he can do whatever he wants. The brave one in this novel would perhaps be Aguirre, who dares to oppose *el caudillo*. Aguirre in this sense is more manly.[20] Campobello relates how Pablito López is viewed as "muy hombre" because he valiantly kills without considering the consequences or risks (946). Similarly, "el gordo" [fat man] Botello of *¡Vámanos con Pancho Villa!* considers bravery in the face of death a key characteristic of manhood: "¡Peleando con la carabina en la mano, echando muchos reatazos! Esa es muerte de hombres" [Fighting with rifle in hand, whipping lots of 'em! That is a manly death] (708). But *el caudillo* faces no such risks when he has people killed. *El caudillo,* of course, does not do the killing himself, either, while Campobello's López, being of a different social class, is a hands-on killer.

However, this type of man, the valiant man who faces risks, the real man, frequently ends up dead. Perhaps it is for this reason that Campobello's young narrator is attracted to male corpses. Rafael Galán, a handsome young man in life, loved by all the girls, now dressed up and made up in his coffin "estaba mejor de como había sido en vida" [was better than he had been in life] (962). More troubling is the dead body she discovers lying near her house, which becomes an obsession for her:

Como estuvo tres noches tirado, ya me había acostumbrado a ver el garabato de su cuerpo, caído hacia su izquierda con las manos en la cara, durmiendo allí, junto de mí. Me parecía mío aquel muerto. Había momentos que, temerosa de que se lo hubieran llevado, me levantaba corriendo y me trepaba en la ventana. Era mi obsesión en las noches, me gustaba verlo, porque me parecía que tenía mucho miedo.

Un día después de comer, me fui corriendo para contemplarlo desde la ventana; ya no estaba. El muerto tímido había sido robado por alguien, la tierra se quedó dibujada y sola. Me dormí aquel día soñando en que fusilarían otro y deseando que fuera junto a mi casa.

As he lay there for three nights, I had gotten used to seeing his bent body, dropping off to the left with his hands over his face, sleeping there by my side. I felt like that dead man was mine. There were moments when I was afraid they might have taken him away and I'd get up and run, and climb up to look out the window. He was my obsession at night; I liked to see him because he seemed very afraid.

One day after lunch I ran up to contemplate him from the window; he was no longer there. The timid dead man had been stolen by someone, the lonely earth remained marked with his outline. I went to bed that night and dreamed that they had executed another guy and wished that it had been by my house. (942)

The peaceful and timid corpse is more desirable than the bellicose and rowdy soldiers. But who is more manly?

The Revolution Castrated

In *La sombra del caudillo,* one of the very few female characters, Rosario, reflects on the mountain, Ajusco, that rises up in the southern skyline of Mexico City: "A mí me gusta el Ajusco ... porque es, de todas las cosas que conozco, la más varonil" [I like Ajusco ... because it is, of all things I know, the most manly]. Aguirre wonders, "Es decir, que para usted el Ajusco es más varonil que yo" [You mean that for you Ajusco is more manly than I am]. Rosario doesn't give him a straight answer, but merely muses, "Si usted fuera el Ajusco" [If only you were Ajusco ...] (508). Men, particularly these men of the revolution, we might infer, are incapable of being as manly as the phallic symbols used sometimes to refer to them.

In *¡Vámanos con Pancho Villa!,* the authenticity of the masculinity of Villa's troops is of such importance that it must be constantly put

to test, although the arbitrariness of the particular test applied makes
the reader wonder if there was really any possibility of authenticity.
Tiburcio Maya sees masculinity as reflective of an inborn courage:
"Creo que los hombres que son valientes vienen así desde que los
echan al mundo: ni los cobardes se pueden volver valientes por más
que quieran, ni los valientes se amiedan, aunque la vean perdida" [I
believe that men who are valiant come that way from the time they
are thrown into the world: neither can cowards turn brave no matter
how much they want to, nor do valiant men become fearful even
when they see all as lost] (713). And yet Villa's senior officers test
their manhood in a weekly ritual in which, after eating a sumptuous
dinner, they turn out the lights and throw a cocked pistol up in the air
so that when it lands on the table it will go off and perhaps kill one of
them. As the organizer of these dinners, Encarnación Martínez, puts it,
"Las gallinas se pelarán y nos iremos quedando no más los hombres"
[The hens will run away and we'll be left with only the men] (711).
This process of elimination is meant to rid the troops of the cowards
who flee or avoid the ritual, but it also regularly kills men who are
brave (or foolish) enough to stay. Theoretically, those who survive are
masculine enough, but some of them, such as Tiburcio, become so fed
up with this sort of gender play, with its utter disregard for human
life, that they choose the effeminate path and desert.

Tropa vieja proclaims an even more pessimistic truth about masculinity and revolutionary army life: "aquí no hay hombres: de la
puerta del cuartel para adentro se acabaron los hombres, todos somos
borregos atemorizados" [there are no men here: from the barracks
door on in manhood ends, we are all scared sheep] (385). Later a
wise old soldier observes to the narrator:

> Ora sí, compañero; ya eres soldado de veras, dejaste de ser recluta,
> así como antes también dejaste de ser libre. Te arrancaron, como a
> mí, la libertad; te cerraron la boca, te sacaron los sesos y ahora te
> embadurnaron el corazón también. Te atontaron a golpes y a mentadas;
> te castraron y ya estás listo, ya eres un soldado.

> Now, comrade, you are a real soldier, you moved beyond being a re-
> cruit, just as you moved beyond being free before. They took away, as
> they did with me, your freedom; they shut your mouth, removed your

brains, and now they have defiled your heart as well. They stupefied you with blows and insults; they castrated you and now you're ready, now you're a soldier. (397)

Within a few years of Monterde's stimulus for the novel of the revolution to remasculinize Mexican literature, the weak, soft, cowardly effetes of turn-of-the-century *modernismo* are replaced by the subordinated, frightened, castrated pawns of the novel of the revolution.

John Reed's Adventures

Subordinated, frightened, castrated, and often eroticized pawns. On Reed's adventure to Mexico as a reporter covering the revolution, it seems at times that even more exciting than meeting Venustiano Carranza or Pancho Villa is the intimacy he achieves with common soldiers. And while there is never any doubt that these soldiers and Reed himself are manly and heterosexual (at least in terms of their self-identification), there are many times when the degree of intimacy they reach is jarring. On one of the many occasions that Reed is invited to sleep with one or more of the soldiers, he is told: "That's right— it's good to sleep with the *hombres*—take this place, *amigo*—here's my saddle—here there is no crookedness—here a man goes straight" (62). However, sometimes this straightness appears to bend.

Soldiers sleeping together is nothing out of the ordinary. In *Tropa vieja,* the hero, Espiridión Sifuentes, being the only guy around with a blanket, quite naturally invites his two new friends Jesús and Eulalio Villegas to share it with him "como fuéramos hermanos" [as if we were brothers] (379). However, when Reed takes to sleeping with Longinos Güereca, things go a bit further:

> He sat down..., smiled his homely gentle smile, and took both my hands in his.
> "We shall be compadres,[21] eh?" said Longinos Güereca, "We shall sleep in the same blankets, and always be together. And when we get to the Cadena I shall take you to my home, and my father shall make you my brother...."
> And from that time on until the end, Longinos Güereca and I were always together. (70)

Such intimacies were frequent, which is perhaps why Reed stayed so long in Mexico covering the war despite the fact that, as he writes, "A battle is the most boring thing in the world if it lasts any length of time. It is all the same" (233). Another case is reminiscent of the queer scene in *El Periquillo Sarniento* in which el Periquillo goes to bed with a police lieutenant who falls in love with his pistols. This time it is a *gringo*-hating soldier who has drunkenly threatened Reed and who later the same evening arrives uninvited in Reed's bedroom holding a revolver. " 'I am Lieutenant Antonio Montoya, at your orders,' he said. 'I heard there was a gringo in this hotel and I have come to kill you.' " Reed then offers him his wristwatch: "Reverently, carefully, he adjusted the thing to his hairy wrist. Then he rose, beaming down upon me. The revolvers fell unnoticed to the floor. Lieutenant Antonio Montoya threw his arms around me. 'Ah, *compadre!*' he cried emotionally" (159–60). It is no surprise that *Insurgent Mexico* ends not with the end of the Mexican revolution, but with another male homosocial love scene. "Fidencio and I went home with our arms around each other's shoulders," he writes, although they might better have gone riding off into the sunset together (292).

Literature beyond the Revolution: Women's Writing and Pop Fiction

The Return of the Repressed: Amado Nervo

The novel of the revolution was not the only literature being produced in Mexico in the twenties and thirties. It was at times the only literature sanctioned by a government that, since Vasconcelos had initiated the government-supported muralist movement to retell Mexico's history, was increasingly exploiting artistic production as nationalist propaganda. There were, in this same age, authors whose writing never even hinted of the revolution, novelists who undoubtedly were not interested in the topic. One novel, like *Los de abajo*, self-published by its author in Texas, emerges as a kind of anti-novel-of-the-revolution in that it is set outside Mexico during the 1910s and mentions the revolution only once, and does so demeaningly.

María Luisa Garza's *La novia de Nervo* [Nervo's girlfriend] is the sordid story of Madeleine, a half-French, half-Mexican woman living in France. She first appears shooting up with morphine in the back of a taxi, stumbling around on the lawn of a hospital, hallucinating inspiring visions of Nervo, and finally arriving desperate at the hospital door, crying out, "La regeneración o la murte [*sic*]!" [Regeneration or death!] (7–11). Meanwhile, Nervo, in Madrid, is propositioned by young Pimienta (aka María), a homeless guttersnipe, whose advances he piously refuses, but whom he nonetheless decides to adopt, sponsoring her education in a convent.

The novel frequently goes over the top—e.g., Nervo "soñó ser Dios" [dreamed he was God] (59)—but the frenetic energy it puts into its condemnation of spousal abuse, drug addiction, and child prostitution is impressive. Garza's writing at times seems merely to follow *modernista* trends in its shock appeal, but its feminist social consciousness takes it a step beyond. Madeleine, for example, cannot escape her physically abusive husband, who intentionally gets her addicted to morphine and then has her institutionalized against her will. When World War I hits the town where the insane asylum is located, all the patients are able to escape. Madeleine characteristically faints, but is carried out by another woman who is jealous of her hair and cuts it all off before she comes to.

Once conscious, she changes clothes with a drunk and unconscious American soldier in order to safely escape. Eventually she disguises herself as a French pilot and becomes a war hero. Then, finally, she sets off for America with her servant Lola, her son, and Nervo's adopted daughter (Nervo, professional diplomat, meanwhile, has been reassigned to Uruguay, where he dies in the novel as in real life). For Lola, Mexico is "la gloria" [glory] and "la más allá" [the hereafter] (63), and for Madeleine, Mexico and the United States are somehow conflated as a feminist paradise: "todos viviremos en esa ciudad [México] o en alguna de los de Estados Unidos, donde la mujer es respetada y puede defender sus derechos" [we'll all live in that city [Mexico] or in some city of the United States where women are respected and able to defend their rights] (234). It is in this sociopolitically undifferentiated grand America where Madeleine the transvestite war hero settles, although not before her husband reappears. He promptly attempts to assassinate her, but loyal Lola intervenes, taking the bullets herself, and dies, but not before killing the husband by digging her fingernails into his neck.

The only time the Mexican revolution is alluded to is in a moment of nostalgia for the old days before the tumult of the revolution. Now Mexico is "una ingenua niña, una demente, pobre loca, inofensiva enferma" [an ingenuous girl, a poor demented crazy girl, inoffensive and ill] (111). This language of degeneration, the exaltation of the figure of Nervo, the focus on gender-related social ills, the European setting, and the transgender fantasy are all reminiscent of reviled *modernismo*. Furthermore, Garza's feminization of Mexico hardly followed the dominant trends laid out by the virile nationalists of postrevolutionary Mexican letters. And yet Garza's unabashed feminism, her sincere effort to combat drug abuse, and her truly fresh and startling portrayal of domestic violence as a sort of conjugal terrorism all show the novel to be much more than a playful modernistic jaunt, or the lurid melodrama that it at first appears to be. Still this very serious, shocking, unashamedly sensationalistic, but always fun novel is barely read, scarcely remembered, and Garza, despite having had an active writing career as a novelist and a journalist, is virtually unknown today, as is Mexico's most prolific female writer of the early part of the century, María Enriqueta.

María Enriqueta's Deficient Manhood

Enriqueta's most famous and highly acclaimed novel, *El secreto,* was published in 1922 in Madrid, where she lived for several decades until after her husband's death in the forties, when she returned to Mexico. Despite her early participation in Mexico's Ateneo de la Juventud, Enriqueta is even farther removed than Garza from Mexico and its literary trends. On the other hand, who can blame a woman for not wanting to deal with a country that insisted on its writers being "virile" and simply did not grant opportunities for women to be serious writers? In *El secreto,* set in Spain, America is presented as an exotic and unknown paradise, where the narrator's father goes

for need of money. The fact that he goes to Buenos Aires, "una ciudad completamente a la europea" [a completely European style city]
(93), would not have been missed by Mexican readers. And yet the
book was quite popular in its day, especially in Europe, where it was
quickly translated into French by Paul Valéry's daughter, Agathe, and
later to Italian and Portuguese as well. It was chosen as "la mejor
novela femenina hispanoamericana" [the best Spanish-American feminine novel] in Paris (Fiscal 199). Whether the promoters of virile
Mexican literature liked it or not, Madrid-based María Enriqueta was
the best known and most highly acclaimed Mexican woman novelist
in the first half of the century.

El secreto, however, is not perhaps such a "feminine" novel. Its two
most important characters are male, and, in fact, Enriqueta endows
her protagonist with many autobiographical characteristics. In spite of
or perhaps because of this male identification, Enriqueta's reputation
is quite anti-feminist—"ella misma no confía en la capacidad de la
mujer para salir adelante" [she herself did not trust in the ability of
women to move ahead successfully] (Fiscal 194)—and yet her position
with regard to gender is more complex. The novel concerns itself quite
a lot with masculinity, although Enriqueta's vision of masculinity is
not that of the benevolent patriarchy that she is sometimes credited
with promoting. Masculinity in El secreto is a troublesome, painful,
unstable concept, unceasingly threatened by failure.

The father of the novel's hero, Pablo, from the beginning of the
novel, is in financial ruin. He is always selling possessions, searching
in vain for work, entreating young Pablo to grow into a responsible
and successful young man to help "endulzarnos la vida" [sweeten
our lives] (14). The family looks to this benevolent patriarch to support them, to hold them together, and his role as provider is never
questioned, and yet he is clearly incapable of living up to his responsibilities by himself. He needs Pablo, he needs family friend el señor
Cañez, he needs his brother Leonardo, who owns a successful business
in Buenos Aires, where he must eventually go to work, leaving Pablo
to be the man of the house back in Spain. Besides the specter of failure
that haunts the men of El secreto, the male protagonists also bear a
particular characteristic considered at the very least unbecoming of

Mexican men, or at most fully feminizing, which is the tendency of both father and son not just to cry on occasion, but to fall into drawn-out fits of sobbing when overcome by fear, doubt, or failure—which is quite often.

Pablo himself appears at the beginning of the novel quite a problematic preadolescent child.[22] He is clearly not badly intentioned but is unable to avoid getting into trouble. He plays with "asphyxiating gases" in the henhouse, killing all the family's chickens; he nearly burns down the house; he comes within inches of dropping his younger sister head first into a well. Despite the family's financial crisis and his parents' pleas that he support them in their time of misfortune by behaving, he is unable to resist misbehaving, disobeying rules, mocking authority. He would seem to be a young incorrigible rebel, ready to grow into a man perhaps not unlike the heroes of the Mexican revolution. From the very beginning of the book, when he is confronted with his father's appeal that he come to the aid of his family in its moment of need, he feels "como investido de una nueva misión. Quizá la de proteger a mi hermana; quizá la de amparar a mi abuelita, enferma siempre y delicada; quizá la de sostener a mis padres en aquel golpe" [vested with a new mission. Maybe to protect my sister; maybe to take care of my grandmother, always sick and delicate; maybe to sustain my parents in this crisis] (12). He feels that he must assume a heroic male identity, again not unlike those assigned to Mexico's revolutionary heroes Zapata and Villa, although, of course, all of Enriqueta's cultural references are European. However, like Villa—who despite being a hero is, as Muñoz's novel is adamant about revealing, always a bandit at heart—Pablo cannot resist behaving badly, pulling his poor little sister's hair, making insulting remarks to visitors who come to purchase the ailing family's assets.

It is not until Pablo's father goes off to Buenos Aires to work for his wealthy brother, leaving Pablo as the man of the house, that Pablo seriously feels he must contribute even morally to his family. It is during this time that the secret of the novel comes into play. Although Pablo's mother says nothing, she clearly is suffering a tragedy that

Pablo concludes must be the death of his father. He keeps his knowledge secret as well, but undergoes a complete change of character. He gives up his bad behavior totally, tries to provide emotional support for his mother, and takes to sobbing fits reminiscent of those of his father before his departure. He feels "ya no como un niño que pide protección y consuelo, sino como un hombre que se dispone a dar una y otra cosa" [no longer like a child in need of protection and consolation, but like a man who disposes himself to give one thing or another] (193). And while he is aware that "no es de los hombres llorar" [it is not manly to cry] (230), his new role soon overwhelms him, and he cannot help crying all the time, growing weaker, and eventually falling into delirious illness, diagnosed as hypochondria. Poor young Pablo is not up to the task of filling his father's shoes, even emotionally.

The book ends on a note of compromised happiness, which does little to resolve the issues of manhood that are explored throughout the book. Pablo is rescued from his delirium when his father returns from Buenos Aires, alive after all. And yet the father is not a patriarchal savior. The mother's trauma, it turns out, is not without foundations; in a freak factory accident, the father has lost both his arms. His appearance, of course, shocks and saddens everyone, but he objects: "Podéis[23] congratularme ampliamente, porque no he perdido mis brazos: se los he pasado a mi hijo" [You can amply congratulate me because I have not lost my arms: I have passed them on to my son] (251).

It would seem that two failed or failing masculinities combined will finally lead to success for the family. And yet the reader is left with the feeling that for Enriqueta, masculinity is precarious, frail, and deficient. The will of individual men is not enough to sustain them in the heroic roles that society expects men to live up to. Patriarchy is not a privilege, but a frighteningly difficult burden, and men's failure to achieve its ideals is tragic not only for men themselves who lose face, but for women who, following patriarchy's rules, depend on them. While Enriqueta does not openly criticize men themselves as Garza does in *La novia de Nervo*, *El secreto* seems to be a subtle but indefatigable assault on patriarchal ideology. Moreover, by taking up the voice of a male protagonist and making Pablo the sympathetic but tragic hero of her novel, she avoids the more direct (but to some more offensive) tactic of showing women as the victims of a system favoring men, instead portraying a situation in which men and women alike suffer under patriarchy. Of course, she does not offer any solution. She does not imply that women should be given more opportunities, or that they should take charge; perhaps, then, she is not really a feminist novelist. And yet this unmasking of the patriarchal hero makes Enriqueta a precursor of the major feminist novelists such as Rosario Castellanos and Elena Garro, who were to emerge in Mexico a few decades later. Furthermore, the failures of her anti-heroes have something in common with the failed aims of the men of the revolution: the "castrated" soldiers of *Tropa vieja* or the hopeless idealists who live under *La sombra del caudillo* who end up *madrugados,* executed by a firing squad. Of course, such comparisons have never been made since Enriqueta has been all but forgotten by literary critics. Logically then, to many, Mexico's first great female novelist is Nellie Campobello, who began publishing after Garza and Enriqueta, perhaps because Campobello chose to work with the sanctioned genre of the moment. Needless to say, in a generation when "virile writing" was glorified as the future of Mexican letters, it was not easy for a woman to be successful writing about anything, in any style.

Gender Trouble and "Low" Literature

Clearly, there remained in the twenties and thirties a paranoia about gender that resulted in both the popularization of the virile literature of the revolution and also the emergence of a pop literature that explored gender anxiety, but that was ignored by Mexico's literary establishment because it did not address class issues so much as gender issues and therefore was not considered serious. Enlisting pop genres such as science fiction, this minor literature competed with the novel of the revolution, but without the benefit of sanctions from the cultural elite of the day, it never had the chance to be incorporated into Mexico's literary canons and nowadays has been forgotten.

One example of this "low" literature is Eduardo Urzaiz's *Eugenia,* a science fiction novel in the tradition of *El donador de almas.* As might be guessed from the title, it treats eugenics, itself a topic of popular discourse of the age,[24] but with a truly odd twist. In the futuristic society of the novel (not specifically Mexico, since this utopian futuristic world has eliminated national boundaries), a particular form of government-controlled eugenics has been instituted. Because women who bear children have a maternal instinct that turns them into loving mothers (as opposed to productive workers or thinkers), it is decided that women are no longer to give birth. Thus, not only are degenerates (criminals, mentally inferior people, the insane, etc.) sterilized and is conception arranged by the state, but women are freed from the burden of childbearing. Following the discourse of civilization and barbarity, the fear that humanity's mental advancements have resulted in physical degeneration (i.e., society's emasculation) leads to a new system of "scientific selection." A scientist explains: "En las sociedades de antaño, triunfaban los individuos más inteligentes, los más astutos o los más ricos, que por lo general eran los peor dotados físicamente, por lo que la especie degeneraba a pasos agigantados" [In bygone societies, those who triumphed were the most intelligent, the most astute or the richest individuals who, generally speaking, were the most poorly endowed physically, because of which the species was degenerating in huge steps] (60).

Taking advantage of the fact that men had no innate maternal instinct that would attach them unnecessarily to their children who were now to be raised by the state, the role of the "gestator" was instituted:

> Por su puesto [sic] desde pequeños han sido nulificados como reproductores activos y, antes de cada injerto, hay que aplicarles una serie de inyecciones intravenosas e intraperitoneales de extractos ováricos para modificar el dinamismo de sus secreciones internas y sus condiciones humorales. Así se hacen aptos para el desarrollo de los óvulos, se feminizan, en una palabra; todo impulso erótico desaparece en ellos durante la gestación y, con el tiempo, su efectividad y sus inclinaciones llegan a cambiar definitivamente; acaban por aficionarse a los pasatiempos y ocupaciones femeniles.

> Of course from childhood they have been nullified as active reproducers and, prior to each grafting, it is necessary to carry out a series of intravenous and intraperitoneal injections of ovarian extracts to modify the dynamic of their internal secretions and humoral conditions.

> Thus they are capacitated for the development of the ovaries, they are feminized, to put it bluntly; all erotic impulse disappears during the gestation and, over time, their effectuality and inclinations come to change definitively; they end up acquiring a taste for feminine pastimes and occupations. (74)

It is ironic perhaps that Urzaiz's 1919 version of transsexualism is entirely centered around giving birth, the act most obviously impossible for today's male-to-female transsexuals. The gestators have a recently conceived fetus grafted into their peritoneal cavity, where it incubates. The central drama of the novel plays out through what happens to the character of Ernesto, who is chosen by the state as a gestator. His resistance to a system of eugenics managed by the government, which tyrannically controls the lives of its citizens, is tragically futile.

Once again, despite the fact that the novel was published in 1919, there is no mention of the Mexican revolution anywhere in it. It seems concerned more with feminism itself and a paranoia that women's advances into the workplace will result in the annihilation of the institution of motherhood. Further, despite the fact that the eugenics of the novel is meant to invigorate the species, men (at least the most superior specimens of manhood who are chosen as gestators) are brazenly emasculated in this futuristic dystopia.

Such wildly lurid tales are not uncommon in postrevolutionary Mexico. A second example is woman writer A. Izquierdo Albiñana's *Andréïda: "El tercer sexo."* In another manifestation of the fear of an impending feminist social upheaval, the masculinized Andréïda is introduced as "un ser de porvenir que se adelantó" [a being of the future who arrived ahead of her time] (13), "el monstruoso ejemplar primero del Tercer Sexo" [the monstrous first exemplar of the third sex] (16). This third sex is not homosexual, but merely androgynous, although at one point Andréïda proclaimed that attraction among adolescent girls "era natural, sano, puro, biológico" [was natural, healthy, pure, biological] (44). It is at once a masculine woman and a superwoman, inspired by Villiers and his artificially created perfect female.[25] Andréïda explains: "yo he ido más allá de Villiers...yo he fabricado con mi propio protoplasma esa perfección por él anhelada"

[I have gone a step further than Villiers...I have fabricated this perfection that he longed for out of my own protoplasm] (65).

Moreover, Andréïda's sinister plan is to use this attraction that her perfection will inspire to win power:

> No seré yo quien haga entrega de la simbólica flor de oro al Amado...
> En cambio, seré una autómata de la vida que abandonará sus caminos trillados....He logrado liberarme de la carne maldita que desde las primeras noches del Mundo nos encadenó, en calidad de siervas, de seres inferiores, al homo sapiens...Por primera vez en la historia de los siglos, la mujer dominará al Mundo, y el hombre se arrastrará a sus pies irremediablemente vencido.

> I will not be the one to deliver over the symbolic golden flower to the Loved One....Just the opposite, I will be an automaton of life who will abandon its trite paths....I have succeeded in liberating myself from the cursed flesh which, since the first nights of the World, has chained us down, as servants, inferior beings, to homo sapiens....For the first time in the history of the centuries, woman will dominate the World, and man will drag along at her feet, irremediably conquered. (67–68)

Andréïda, despite the novel's excessive length, doesn't get very far in terms of conquering mankind, and ultimately ends up surrendering to her innate femaleness when she finds herself pregnant by one of the men she has been dragging along at her feet. Andréïda cries to her lover, "La llama de la maternidad....Tienes razón, Raúl,...¡Me has vencido!" [The flame of maternity....You're right, Raúl,...You've conquered me!] (441). Once again, the fear that feminism means the masculinization of women and the feminization of men is played out, but this time there is a happy end as maternal instincts, so successfully held in check in *Eugenia,* win out over unnatural feminism.

The issue of androgyny and sexual ambiguity was clearly a major selling point for both of these novels. *Eugenia*'s cover is a portrait of a figure of indeterminate sex, wearing a gown that leaves a muscular breast (man's or woman's?) bared; *Andréïda*'s shows merely the face of a woman with a perfectly sculpted male countenance in the background, but the subtitle "the third sex" is clearly meant to be provocative. The fact that Izquierdo Albiñana chooses to employ the popular trope for male homosexuality to combat feminist ambition suggests that the social anxiety reflected in Posada's use of the number 41 in his 1907 print "El feminismo se impone" still carried weight thirty years later.

The Novel of the Revolution for Butch Girls

While most of this literature focusing intently on gender anxieties confined itself to the realm of science fiction, in 1933 the theme was to infiltrate the virile writing of the revolution itself. Salvador Quevedo y Zubieta, a minor but respected writer of novels of social criticism since the tail end of the *porfiriato,* came out in that year with *México marimacho* [Tomboy Mexico]. Once again, the titillating notion of ambiguity of gender and sexuality is brought into play, this time in the major novelistic genre of the day, that of the Mexican revolution.

In his prologue, Quevedo y Zubieta reveals that his inspiration for the novel came while walking past a girls' school:

> Frente al portón me crucé con una joven que salía de allí en cuerpo gentil, vestida de blusa, ancho cinturón, falda corta bien ajustada y un conotier en la cabeza, sujeta a estricta tonsura. Parecía muchacho.... A pocos pasos se encuentra con otra del mismo tipo "garzón," ataviada por el mismo estilo.
>
> —¿Cómo te va, hombre? —dijo la primera abriendo los brazos a la segunda, quien correspondió al abrazo y contestó:
>
> —¡Hombre! ¿Cómo te va?

> In front of the gate I passed a young lady who was on her way out. On her graceful body, she wore a blouse, a wide belt, a rather tight short skirt and a cap on her head, which was subject to a close cropped haircut. She looked like a boy.... A couple of steps later she ran into another of these "boyish" girls, dressed in the same style.
>
> "How's it going, man?" said the first, opening her arms to the second, who returned the embrace and answered:
>
> "Man! How's it going?" (5–6)

Yet again a brand of gender trouble brought about by women who want to be like men causes sufficient anxiety to inspire a novel. Quevedo y Zubieta, who had dedicated most of his literary career to exposing political corruption, this time felt obliged to take on gender corruption in *México marimacho.*

The novel is not his best, and it takes quite a long time to get going. In fact, it is largely rather bland for a couple hundred pages, until finally a doctor becomes concerned with the mysterious ailments of Mexico's women who have been abandoned by the revolution. These women, lost *soldaderas* and deserted housewives, were feeling useless and frustrated until a certain doctor (Edgardo below) discovers a solution for them and for Mexico:

> Vírgenes, medias vírgenes y madres clandestinas fueron sometiéndose a la ablación, si no siempre total, aunque sólo fuese una especie de circuncisión interna, más efectiva que la viril judaica.
> —Hombre, Petrona, que nos quieran....
> —Sí, hombre, Rosalinda, ¡que nos castren!...
> —¡Bueno, lo has hecho, Edgardo! —clamó Guadalupe...—Tus muchachas operadas reclaman cada una, pistola y caballo.
> —¡Mejor! Irán con nosotros a la revolución. Se creará para ellas una nueva brigada sanitaria, la BRIGADA MACHORRO.

> Virgins, half-virgins, and clandestine mothers were submitting themselves to the ablation, if not always total. Even if it was only a sort of internal circumcision, it was more effective than the Jewish male version.
> "Man, Petrona, let them desire us...."
> "Yes, man, Rosalinda, let them castrate us!..."
> "Well, now you've done it, Edgardo!" cried Guadalupe...Your operated women are all demanding pistols and horses.
> "So much the better! They'll go with us to the revolution. A new sanitary brigade will be created for them, the STERILE BRIGADE." (327)

Female castration is the solution to the nebulous ailments of the lonely and confused women of the revolution. And oddest of all, just as male castration leads to effeminacy in men, female castration apparently leads to virility in women!

The book ends on a sarcastic note in which this female castration is discussed as a means of forming a cosmic race, a sort of racial eugenics through sterilization: "Se trata de fomentar el marimachismo neto en la raza méxico-sajona, que es la culminante. Las demás son razas inferiores, destinadas a las tareas groseras de la proliferación, como ganados de cría.... De mi sanatorio, de nuestro sanatorio monstruo que rascará los vientres de las nubes dispersas, va a salir el

México del porvenir, México marimacho, indio-sajón" [It's a question
of promoting the pure masculinization of women in the Mexicosaxon
race, which is the pinnacle. The others are inferior races, destined
to the gross chores of proliferation, like breeding livestock.... From
my sanatorium, from our monster sanatorium that will scrape the
wombs of the scattered clouds, the Mexico of the future is going to
arise, butch, Indiosaxon Mexico] (338–39). This final proclamation
mocks eugenics and Vasconcelos's entire discourse on racial superiority while playing out what has clearly become by 1933 a widespread
anxiety about changing notions of gender.

And while these anxieties were played out quite vividly in these
obscure novels, it was in more publicly notorious circles that vigorous challenges to gender paradigms had a more profound and
lasting influence on Mexican culture. While it is undoubtedly the
combined effect of numerous events that caused attitudes to shift
over time, clearly some have had greater impact than others. In
postrevolutionary Mexico, the cultural personages who most prob-
lematized notions of gender and sexuality on a national level were the
so-called Contemporáneos.

The Queer Nationalism of the Contemporáneos: Jorge Cuesta

Homophobia and Contemporáneos

Following the revolution, as we know, virility came to be the metonym
of Mexicanness leading to the advent of an often strident homophobia. In particular, the Contemporáneos, a cenacle of young poets,
some of whom were known to be homosexuals and others who
were presumed guilty by association, were vigorously attacked for
decades.[26] These attacks by rival writers, artists, politicians, and literary critics appeared within newspaper debates on national culture,
under the guise of literary criticism or even art, and as organized
plots to expel these poets from their bureaucratic posts in the federal
government. For example, in a 1934 petition submitted to the Public
Health Commission, a group established to rid the public sector of

"counterrevolutionaries," signed by numerous prominent intellectuals (including virile novelists such as Rafael Muñoz and Francisco
Uriquizo, polemicists such as Julio Jiménez Rueda, and numerous
others), called for the defense of "las virtudes viriles" [virile virtues]
by combating "la presencia del hermafrodita" [the presence of the
hermaphrodite] (Monsiváis, "Ortodoxia" 201). That same year, a
nasty campaign against Jorge Cuesta's journal *Examen,* including
charges of pornography, led to the forced resignation of Cuesta and
other Contemporáneos from their public posts (they were eventually
legally exonerated) (Sheridan, *Los Contemporáneos* 388–90). In a
lighter vein, Antonio Ruiz "el Corzo" painted a group of "preciosas
ridículas" [*précieuses ridicules*] under the sign of 41 including the like-
nesses of Contemporáneos Novo, Villaurrutia, and others (notably,
Lupe Marín, wife of Jorge Cuesta) ("Ortodoxia" 201).

Mexico's homophobia in the first half of the twentieth century
authorized itself in a number of ways, but since much of the most
authoritative discourse on homosexuality came out of the fields of
sexology and psyochoanalysis, it was natural that psychoanalytic discourse fueled homophobia as well. Monsiváis notes that a Mexicanized
Freudian psychoanalysis was taken up by the state as a partial replace-
ment for Roman Catholic dogma, giving a scientific basis for traditional
systems of social control. "De hecho, el machismo que conocemos es un
invento cultural, un primer producto de la 'freudianización' del país"
[In fact, machismo as we know it is a cultural construct, one of the
first products of the "Freudianization" of the country] ("Ortodoxia"
193). In other words, psychoanalysis was not innocently applied in
Mexico but rather cynically misread to rationalize existing hegemonic
structures, including patriarchal ideologies, which had been threatened
openly by male effeminacy and homosexuality since at least 1901.[27]
In the case of Cuesta's life and legend,[28] such a biased application of
Freud occurred within the realm of psychoanalysis itself.

The One and Only Lupe Marín

Cuesta himself was not specifically a homosexual. He was a close
friend of Villaurrutia and of Novo, both homosexuals, but the only
published specifics regarding Cuesta's putative homosexuality appear

in his ex-wife Lupe Marín's autobiographical novel, *La única* [the one and only], which reads like a lively, perhaps therapeutic, and acutely vitriolic maligning of both her ex-husbands (Cuesta and Diego Rivera). Lupe herself, despite her frequent representation as Mexican female beauty, particularly in the paintings of Rivera (for which Salvador Oropesa nicknames her "la encuerada nacional" [the national nude] ["Novelista de la modernidad" 217]), was gender trouble. During her young and wild years, in nocturnal adventures with Villaurrutia and Novo, in which they'd go out to "levantar soldados" [pick up soldiers], she would fail: " '¡Con este joto vestido de mujer, nunca!' contestaban a sus avances, prefiriendo a sus acompañantes que les parecían más auténticos o apetecibles" ["With this fag dressed up as a woman, never!" they would reply to her advances, preferring her companions who seemed more authentic or desirable] (Bradu, *Damas* 254). On one particular excursion to a dancehall, tall Marín was dancing with shorter Juan Soriano, the painter. A drunk approached the couple,

> intrigado por la desproporción física entre los dos bailarines. Pero en lugar de cuestionar la escasa estatura del pintor, dirigió su agresividad a Lupe: "Oiga usted, ¿qué es: hombre o mujer?" Sin dudar un solo segundo, ella le replicó: "¡Soy más hombre que tú y más mujer que tu chingada madre!"

> intrigued by the physical disproportion between the two dancers. But instead of questioning the scant stature of the painter, he directed his aggressiveness toward Lupe: "Listen, what are you: man or woman?" Without hesitating a single second, she replied, "I am more man than you and more woman than your fucking mother!" (Bradu, *Damas* 278)

Marín enjoyed hanging out with homosexuals, but this does not mean that her husband was one, although practically from the very beginning of *La única,* she claims that Cuesta had been recruited by his friend "Lorenzo"[29] to the "gremio" [guild] (Marín 8). Such rumors were undoubtedly eaten up by the Contemporáneos' enemies, who always did the most damage to the group not through intellectual debate but with scandalous accusations and name-calling. In Cuesta's case, it didn't help that he was something of an iconoclast who, unlike many of his more low-key cohorts who tried to stay out of politics, became notorious for his articulate and biting attacks on traditional institutions. For the record, Elías Nandino separates Cuesta from the homosexual Contemporáneos Novo and Villaurrutia, "los marcados por la mano de Dios" [those marked by the hand of God], classifying him as a bisexual (61).

El Más Triste de los Alquimistas Mexicanos

Besides being a poet and a critic, Cuesta was a scientist. He not only worked as a chemist and engineer throughout most of his adult life but also occupied himself constantly with his own experiments and inventions, a practice that gained him the affectionate nickname among his friends of "el alquimista" [the alchemist] (Villaurrutia, *Obras* 847–49). Cuesta's experiments are not well documented, and as with his personal life, what we know about them is perhaps as much legend as fact, but the general thrust of his interests is clear. Like his criticism, which is dominated by a recalcitrant distrust of institutions, Cuesta's "alchemy" seems directed toward undoing inevitabilities of time and nature. Preservation is a key theme in his work: preservation of art (he sought to concoct a substance that would preserve paintings), preservation of food (it is said that he had come up with a powder that would prevent fruit from rotting), preservation of life (he studied the curative properties of marijuana, sought a cure for cancer in enzymes, and is rumored to have been at work on a panacea based on his fruit preservation concoction). Perhaps this theme in his work has helped spawn the rumor that he had been in search of "the elixir of life." Furthermore, he was interested in metamorphosing substances (in a truer tradition of alchemy). For example, it is said that he could change water to wine (or at least that he had produced a concoction tasting something like wine by adding certain substances to water); it is also claimed that he was able to fabricate the scent of English lavender in his laboratory. In addition, he had supposedly invented a serum that would allow one to drink liters of alcohol without getting drunk. He was in the habit of experimenting on himself, on his own body, a deed that was to have serious ramifications for him later on. Specifically, he is known to have injected himself with the substance he was using to preserve the freshness of oranges.

Although he was a scientist, his respect for the branch of science known as psychiatry was slim. In an essay on the poet-killer Salvador Díaz Mirón, Cuesta becomes incensed at the labeling of Díaz Mirón as a pathologically antisocial being. Instead, Cuesta argues that Díaz Mirón's acts of violence are not pathological; such acts may damage society, in which case society can be viewed as becoming ill through them. However, such crimes for the criminal might have "las consecuencias fisiológicas más saludables" [the healthiest of physiological consequences] (*Poesía y crítica* 331). Cuesta further protests, "cuando un alienista define las características de un temperamento antisocial, la sociedad que toma como referencia es un ser exento de anormalidad en virtud de la misma definición" [when an alienist defines the characteristics of an antisocial temperament, the society that is taken as a reference is an entity exempt from abnormality by virtue of the same definition] (330). Cuesta's unconventional views, in fact, would appear to mirror those of French writer Antonin Artaud,[30] whom he undoubtedly knew while the latter was visiting Mexico City. However, while Paz indicates that they may have hung out in the same cafés (*Xavier Villaurrutia* 14), Nandino perceived a mutual disdain between Artaud and the Contemporáneos who did not manage to see beyond the severe drug addiction that marked his stay in Mexico City, prior to making his famous trip northward in search of peyote (Nandino 113–15).

Why was Cuesta concerned with psychiatric institutions? The question posed in January 1940 (when he published his essay on Díaz Mirón) would have been answered by most, even Cuesta's closest friends (except, of course, for his ex-wife),[31] with a shrug of their shoulders. However, a few months later, this was not to be the case. In September 1940, Jorge made an appointment to meet with the Spanish exile Dr. Gonzalo Lafora, a prominent medical doctor, specializing in sexual questions.[32] Cuesta's migraines were getting worse, and he also had a seemingly chronic hemorrhoidal condition that worried him.

The Incident with Dr. Lafora

The incident that occurred in the office of Dr. Lafora and Cuesta's response are both documented in an undelivered letter addressed

to the doctor.³³ Cuesta confesses that some of his experiments involving the ingestion of enzymes seem to have been exacerbating
his singular somatic symptoms. Specifically, "el carácter que habían
tomado unas hemorroides que me afligen desde hace diez y seis años
me habían dado el temor de que se tratara de una modificación
anatómica, que tuviera caracteres de androginismo...o de estado
intersexual" [changes in the character of some hemorrhoids that had
been afflicting me for sixteen years had made me fear that I might
have been undergoing an *anatomical* modification, with qualities of
androgyny...or of an intersexual state] (quoted in Irwin, "The Legend" 36–37). Dr. Lafora refuses to examine Cuesta's body, somehow
sure that his symptoms were "absurd" and that it was all merely a
nervous disorder, specifically, "un padecimiento *mental o nervioso,*
constituido probablemente por una obsesión sexual, originada en
una homosexualidad reprimida" [a *mental or nervous* ailment, probably constituted by a sexual obsession, originating from a repressed
homosexuality" (quoted in Irwin 37–38). Clearly, Dr. Lafora, at least
according to Cuesta's letter, had jumped to conclusions. Cuesta was
judged mentally ill based on the fact that he insisted on speaking about
intersexuality, and not on whether his statements reflected physical
realities. His body apparently made no difference to the doctor.

However, Dr. Lafora's refusal to examine Cuesta's body suggests
that it was actually of major significance. It was, after all, rumored
to be a homosexual body. Perhaps Dr. Lafora felt threatened by
this locus of putative homosexual desire, now claiming to be, even
more frighteningly, an intersexual body. If hemorrhoids did not seem
the most logical indication of androgyny, the prospect of examining Cuesta's sphincter to verify this may have been too much for
Dr. Lafora, compelling him to diagnose Cuesta's body based on his
testimony alone.

This case would seem to confirm the opinion of Monsiváis that
Freudian psychoanalysis quickly (certainly by 1940) became a mys-
tified, totalizing, normative system, an ideological structure that,
through tropes such as the Oedipal complex and penis envy, was
mobilized to calcify norms of gender and sexuality. Here, Cuesta's
references to intersexuality were immediately deemed absurd and the

result of a nervous disorder; even a physical challenge to gender could be contained through psychoanalytic authority.

Freud, Paranoia, and Homophobia

At this point, it is worthwhile to take a look at Freud's notion of paranoia. It is ironic that Freud's famous study of paranoia has undoubtedly constructed its own legend of a man whom Freud never met during his illness, but whose case Freud interpreted only by reading his autobiography: Daniel Paul Schreber. There were certain existing tropes of paranoia that Freud recognized in Schreber. (Freud, we often forget, was not the first to write on the subject and in fact did not present such a radically new position on the subject as he is sometimes given credit for.) Most pointedly, his delusions of persecution and sexual metamorphosis had been discussed decades earlier by Richard von Krafft-Ebing under the rubric of "metamorphosis sexualis paranoia" in his catalogue of the many types of "antipathic sexuality." In Krafft-Ebing's discussion of homosexual neuroses, "[t]he determining factor...is the demonstration of perverse feeling for the same sex; not the proof of sexual acts with the same sex" (247). Thus, Freud's diagnosis of Schreber's paranoia as being the result of repressed homosexual desire was not revolutionary. However, what Freud ignores in his analysis of a patient whom he had never met is the physical, an aspect that was considered by Krafft-Ebing, who recognized what he called "organic taint," or physical anomalies distorting gender and contributing to "cerebral neuroses" of the antipathic variety (294). Still, assuming that Schreber's transsexuality/ hermaphrodism was delusionary, perhaps the only clear difference between Freud and Krafft-Ebing was that the homosexuality inferred by both was seen as "moral decay" and "perversion" by the latter and was viewed more sympathetically as a universal, if not unproblematic, part of everyday life by the former, as he makes clear in his "Three Essays on the Theory of Sexuality."

The Cuesta case bears many eerie similarities to that of Schreber, similarities of which Dr. Lafora was likely aware. Cuesta, like Schreber, feared he was becoming a woman. But Lafora, unlike Freud, did not infer homosexuality from this in his patient because Lafora already knew that Cuesta was one of the publicly vilified Contemporáneos. It is not at all surprising, then, that Lafora assumed Cuesta, with or without somatic indications of intersexuality, to be homosexual.[34] And although, at least in Cuesta's letter, the term "paranoia" was not used, nor was Schreber's other major symptom, delusions of persecution, named, the case clearly recalls not Freudian persecutory paranoia so much as Guy Hocquenghem's recasting of persecutory paranoia as "a paranoia that seeks to persecute" homosexuality (56). Certainly some discourse on sexuality did deal with biological intersexuality, including Krafft-Ebing; and Spaniard Gregorio Marañón's *La evolución de la sexualidad y los estados intersexuales* [Evolution of sexuality and intersexual states] experienced fairly wide diffusion in Latin America in the 1930s. On the other hand, in a country where even literature was strictly gendered masculine or feminine, how could it be permitted that a body be recognized as intersexual?

Marañón and Intersexuality

In Marañón's book, published a decade before the Cuesta-Lafora incident, the author proclaims, "Para mí es, en efecto, seguro, que el perfeccionamiento de la humanidad, en lo que se refiere a la vida de los sexos, se hace y se ha de hacer en el sentido de la aspiración a una diferenciación sexual cada vez más precisa: que el hombre sea ... cada vez más hombre; y la mujer, cada vez más mujer" [For me it is, in fact, certain that the perfection of humanity, in what pertains to the life of the sexes, is achieved and can only be achieved through an aspiration to an ever more precise sexual differentiation in which man becomes ever more manly; and woman ever more womanly] (234–35). And yet he admits that "los estados, de confusión sexual, en una escala de infinitas gradaciones que se extiende desde el hermafroditismo escandaloso hasta aquellas formas tan atenuadas que se confunden con la normalidad misma, son tan numerosos, que apenas hay ser humano cuyo sexo no esté empañado por una duda concreta o por una sombra de duda" [the states of sexual confusion, on a scale of infinite gradations that extends from scandalous hermaphrodism to those forms that are so attenuated that they become confused with normality itself, are so numerous that there is hardly a human being whose sex is not blurred by a concrete doubt or the shadow of a doubt] (10–11).

Nonetheless, for Marañón, biological intersexuality and homosexuality are merely two related categories of inversion. And his hyperbolic text offers little clarification: "nosotros no admitimos la clásica definición de los homosexuales en congénitos y adquiridos. Para nosotros, todos son congénitos; y a la vez, todos son adquiridos" [we do not accept the classic definition of homosexuals as congenital or acquired. For us, all of them are congenital, and at the same time, all are acquired] (157). Such confusion is undoubtedly one reason why Lafora chose simply not to deal with Cuesta's case. Whether or not Cuesta was delusional, Mexico was not ready to try to understand gender ambiguity in 1940.

Perhaps Cuesta was not either. Not long after the incident with Dr. Lafora, Cuesta, like Lupe Marín before him, was institutionalized, and soon afterward, an increasingly unstable Cuesta castrated himself. In 1942, Jorge Cuesta, having recently completed his final poem, "Canto a un dios mineral" [Song to a mineral god], generally considered his master work, committed suicide.

Los Contemporáneos: Los señores Literatos "Jotos"

Jorge Cuesta was only one of the loosely organized group of intellectuals—a "grupo sin grupo" [group without a group], as Xavier Villaurrutia once put it—known as the Contemporáneos,[35] who posed a lasting challenge to stereotypes of gender and sexuality in the first half of the twentieth century in Mexico. There are many different versions of exactly which figures of the Mexican intelligentsia ought to be included among them, but some of its best known members or close associates are Cuesta, Novo, Villaurrutia, Gilberto Owen, Jaime Torres Bodet, Bernardo Ortiz de Montellano, Carlos Pellicer, Samuel Ramos, Elías Nandino, José and Celestino Gorostiza, Agustín Lazo, Antonieta Rivas Mercado, Manuel Rodríguez Lozano, and Roberto Montenegro. Many of them were active participants in the various literary journals of the age including the most memorable and the one that gives them their name, Contemporáneos. Many were likewise involved in another generation-defining activity of the group:

the *Ulises* avant-garde theater project. Monsiváis sums them up best in his description:

> Más que un grupo o generación ... los Contemporáneos son, en México, una actitud ante el arte y la cultura ..., normada por el rigor, la crítica, la creación en contrapunto de la "realidad nacional," la oposición al chovinismo, el desdén por el éxito inmediato, la voluntad de poner al día una literatura, la integración simultánea al orden ... y a la marginalidad.

> More than a group or generation ... the Contemporáneos are, in Mexico, an attitude toward art and culture ..., governed by rigor, criticism, creation in counterpoint to "national reality," opposition to chauvinism, disdain for immediate success, will to bring literature up to date, simultaneous integration to the mainstream ... and to marginality. (*Salvador Novo* 47)

On the level of identity politics, the group provided Mexico with its first openly homosexual public figures, including Villaurrutia, Montenegro, Lazo, Rodríguez Lozano, Pellicer, Nandino, and, of course, the notorious Salvador Novo (all with varying degrees of openness). In terms of cultural politics, most of them professed themselves to be apolitical, which, in fact, entailed, in the area of rampant nationalism, taking quite a firm ideological stand. Some have argued that the virility debates of the twenties were largely directed against this group of intellectuals, most of whom were too young to have participated in the revolution and who had not joined afterward in the efforts to institute a literature of the revolution or an authentically Mexican national literature. Their approach to cultural production (among them there were poets, playwrights, painters, etc.) was "universal," to use the term they used; rather than limit themselves to an ill-defined nationalistic cultural production, they openly admitted to European and North American influences (as well as Latin American and Mexican ones) and aimed to promote a version of Mexican literature (and theater, art, etc.) which was up to date in the global arena. After all, wasn't the institution of nationalism itself an import? Cuesta writes, "Las obras nacionalistas [mexicanas] no han logrado otra cosa que imitar servilmente a los nacionalismos de Europa" [Mexican nationalistic works have not achieved anything more than servile imitation of European nationalisms] (*Poesía y crítica* 109).

The Contemporáneos were not so quick to deny links to Mexican *modernismo* since they were too young to resent the *porfiriato* as their elders who had fought in the revolution did (although the spirit of the work has much more in common with the Ateneo de la Juventud, which is credited with being the intellectual impetus to the revolution and to postrevolutionary Mexico's foundational cultural programs).[36] Their work, however, was by no means retrogressive or nostalgic for past styles; on the contrary, they were very much at the forefront of the artistic vanguard of their day.[37]

In terms of gender politics, up to now we have seen the epoch immediately following the revolution to have included three general currents. The dominant one was that of the novel of the revolution, which attempted to revive nineteenth-century values of masculinity as a system of hierarchies, behaviors, personality traits, and male homosocial (and never homosexual) relations, which are full of contradictions, and yet meant to be taken as self-evident, natural, unambivalent, and indisputable. At the same time, two minor strands in literature existed. One was that of women writers who, if not taking outright militant feminist stances for the advancement of women's rights and gender equality, were critical of traditional views on masculinity. At the same time, particularly in science fiction writing, but also in other popular (if minor) texts, there was an assault on feminism, interpreted as the masculinization of women and the feminization of men, which presented not a solution to the gender anxieties of the turn of the century, but a reflection of continued angst regarding perceived feminist blows to traditional gender roles. Yet no one was promulgating any radical notions of gender. Books like *Andréïda* presented the radical only to condemn or ridicule it. Even Garza, whose censure of domestic violence appears to represent a feminist criticism of patriarchy, remains essentially a gender traditionalist; her next book after *La novia de Nervo*, *Alas y quimeras*, dedicates itself to the eternally feminine role of motherhood.

A fourth current emerges in the work of the Contemporáneos that subtly and radically brings homosexuality openly into mainstream Mexican cultural production. The Contemporáneos were firmly rejected by the cultural power brokers behind the nationalist movements in literature and the arts; yet at the same time they had enough talent and support (from both in and outside of government institutions) to gain prominence even as they came to exemplify the antithesis of nationalist cultural production.[38]

Their reputation as aesthetes, as "extranjerizantes" [foreignizers], as anti- or at least non-revolutionaries, as elitists, and as homosexuals made them, despite their position of being removed from politics, actually quite political (i.e., in terms of gender politics, national aesthetics, culture wars), and subject to relentless attack during the course of their careers. Particularly given that they gradually came to count themselves among the most important and well respected artists of their day, their vision of Mexican art and literature grew to be of importance even in their youth and had significant influence on succeeding generations of artists including such major figures as Octavio Paz, Carlos Fuentes, and Carlos Monsiváis.[39] However, their fame combined with their lack of direct involvement with political parties laid them open not just to criticism but also to more material offensives including several attempts to sweep them from governmental posts for being homosexual (whether they all were or not).

Their contributions to Mexican gender politics continue to this day. For example, much of Antonieta Rivas Mercado's writing remained unpublished or largely unread until long after her death.[40] Also, the Consejo Nacional para la Cultura y las Artes began in 1994 to publish a massive collection of Salvador Novo's newspaper chronicles (*La vida en México en el periodo presidencial de.* . . . [Life in Mexico in the presidential period of . . .] series), and only in 1998 were his long awaited sexually explicit memoirs (*La estatua de sal* [The statue of salt]) published in their entirety. Meanwhile, two excellent biographies were published in the last few years (Barrera's 1999 *Salvador Novo: Navaja de la inteligencia* and Monsiváis's 2000 *Salvador Novo: Lo marginal en el centro*). Nandino's autobiography (*Juntando mis pasos*) was finally published in 2000, seven years after his death. In addition, recent translations to English including *The War of the Fatties,* a collection of Novo's writings, and the excellent Eliot Weinberger translation of Villaurrutia's poetry, *Nostalgia for Death* and the accompanying *Hieroglyphs of Desire* by Paz (originally *Xavier*

Villaurrutia en persona y en obra), translated by Esther Allen, have attracted a renewed interest to the Contemporáneos in the United States. Some critics have even gone so far as to argue that the Contemporáneos have received undue attention in recent years, at the expense of rival personages of their day including the *estridentistas* who are sometimes better remembered for their homophobic attacks on the Contemporáneos than for their poetry.[41] *Estridentista* leader Manuel Maples Arce became a full-time politician when the movement fell apart after lasting for just a few years in the twenties and was a leading proponent of homophobic legislation in Congress in later years (Sheridan, *Los Contemporáneos* 391).

Maples Arce took the "virile literature" discourse a step further in his 1939 *Antología de la poesía mexicana moderna* when he claims that Villaurrutia "se sirve de la inversión como método poético" [makes use of inversion as a poetic method] (366). The vagaries of masculinist discourse of the twenties had, by the thirties, lost any pretense of concern with literary quality and became an unabashed homophobic assault. Similarly in 1934, Bolivian literary critic Tristán Marof, in his *México de frente y de perfil*, includes a chapter on "Literatos afeminados" [effeminate literati], in which he associates Novo and Villaurrutia with his assertion that "se sorprende en México del abuso literario de la palabra 'joto' " [one is surprised in Mexico by the literary abuse of the word "faggot"]. He nullifies any charade of seriousness in his criticism when he remarks at one point, "¡No usan vaselina!" [They don't use vaseline!] (quoted in Monsiváis, *Amor perdido* 274)—a point radically refuted by Novo, who in his memoirs describes how he and Villaurrutia were engaged in participating, in their own way, in what he calls "la resurrección estruendosa del nacionalismo decorativo" [the clamorous resurrection of decorative nationalism]:

> Sobre este estilo me consagré con entusiasmo, tijeras, aguja, martillo, a decorar nuestro "estudio." Un idolillo nalgón, a quien llamábamos San Polencho, colgaba a la cabecera del couch o "piedra de los sacrificios" a presidir las escenas. Y un nacionalismo extremado me indujo a emplear una jícara pequeña como el depósito más a tono de la vaselina necesaria para los ritos.

Concerning this style, I devoted myself with enthusiasm, scissors, needle, and hammer to decorating our "studio." A cute fat-bottomed idol, which we named San Polencho, hung at the head of the *couch* or "sacrificial slab" to preside over the scenes. And an extreme nationalism induced me to employ a small earthenware vessel as the most stylish deposit for the vaseline necessary for the rites. (*Estatua* 105)

In any case, with the Contemporáneos, in fact, it is not just their homosexuality that made them literary *jotos*. Their writing itself presents a truly radical view of gender going beyond the playfulness and uneasiness of the literature of *fin de siglo modernismo* and *naturalismo*. Theirs is a confident gender militancy, which for the first time in Mexican literary history advocates a revised masculinity and male sexuality not as a popular joke or an aesthetic pretense, but as a key element of Mexican culture. Salvador Oropesa argues that Marín's radical value is that she inserted the topic of sexuality—prominently including homosexuality—"en el discurso de la definición nacional" [in the discourse of national definition] ("Novelista de la modernidad" 222). The Contemporáneos, at times against their will, did the same, and with much more resounding repercussions.

The Queer Nationalism of the Contemporáneos: Xavier Villaurrutia, Salvador Novo

Villaurrutia, As Invisible As He Was

Villaurrutia is, in fact, not known as a gender activist; on the contrary, he is famous for writing poetry habitually devoid of apparent human presence, whether male or female.[42] "Nocturno" [Nocturne], which opens his seminal *Nostalgia de la muerte* [Nostalgia for death], is typical. It creates a fully eroticized scene that is clearly not autoerotic, and yet not inhabited by any identifiable beings. There are shadows, voices, knocks, footfalls; then there are more erotic images: "el vaho del deseo" [the vapor of desire], "el sudor de la tierra" [the sweat of earth], "la fragancia sin nombre de la piel" [the unnamed fragrance of skin], "el sabido sabor de la saliva" [the known taste of saliva]. Finally, there are more overtly sexual images: "la boca de una herida" [the mouth of a wound], "la forma de una entraña" [the form of an entrail], "la fiebre de una mano que se atreve" [the fever of a hand that dares] (*Obras* 44–45).[43]

"Nocturno" is a poem of nocturnal pleasure, vice, and desire; however, never does a tangible person appear in it. Skin is present only in its odor, kisses in the taste of saliva, human contact in dream or in the heat (not even the touch) of a hand. "Enigma" is key to Villaurrutia's poetry; it is in the contradictions, ambiguities, innuendos, and absences that Paz finds Villaurrutia's "poetic drama" (*Xavier Villaurrutia en persona* 59). Yet that enigma is also plainly a masking of a homosexual desire that Villaurrutia chose to express discreetly.

Paz, in his *Xavier Villaurrutia en persona y en obra,* a text that seems at times to be an uneasy apologia for Paz's relationship to Villaurrutia, calls the poet "discreet" (10). Xavier was an early mentor of the young Paz, and Villaurrutia's influence is apparent throughout the Nobel laureate's work. And just as one of Paz's primary goals in *Las trampas de la fe* seems to be to stamp out speculation about Sor Juana's lesbianism,[44] a key objective of his slim volume on Villaurrutia appears to be to establish that Paz's relationship with his queer mentor was strictly professional. Early on he establishes the limits of their friendship: "Durante algunos años vi a Xavier dos o tres veces por semana. ¿Fui su amigo? Jamás nos tuteamos, nunca me invitó a su casa y él estuvo en la mía apenas dos o tres veces. Hablamos mucho y nada supe de su vida íntima ni él de la mía" [For several years I saw Xavier two or three times a week. Was I his friend? We never addressed each other using the familiar "tú" form, he never invited me to his house, and he was in mine only two or three times. We spoke a lot and I never learned anything about his private life, nor did he learn about mine] (19). Later he confesses to having entered Villaurrutia's private studio, but only "para recoger un manuscrito o un libro" [to pick up a manuscript or a book] (22). What Paz imagines that his readers might suspect him of having done there is left unstated.

Salvador Novo might have agreed with Paz about Villaurrutia's discretion. In his memoirs, *La estatua de sal,* he relates how once Villaurrutia broke into a chest and stole some of Novo's autobiographical writings because they explicitly named him, associating him with a certain "crudeness" (113). Certainly, Nandino describes

Villaurrutia as "amable, educado y discreto" [kind, well mannered, and discreet] (65). Guillermo Sheridan describes an argument, years later, between Villaurrutia and Gilberto Owen over Xavier's translation of Gide's *The Return of the Prodigal Son*. Once again, it is Villaurrutia's discretion that, to Owen's annoyance, leads him to timidly translate "embrasser" as a fraternal "hug" and not a passionate "kiss" between the brothers (*Los Contemporáneos* 77n17). Villaurrutia, despite being a well-known poet, translator, playwright, avant garde actor, and critic of literature, art, and cinema, valued his privacy. This is undoubtedly why in his novella, *Dama de corazones* [Dame of hearts], he whimsically inserts himself into a monologue by his narrator. The narrator sees himself as a figure comparable to Xavier Villaurrutia, a figure "tan invisible como él...con un cuerpo inclinado cada día más a desaparecer" [as invisible as he is...with a body tending more and more every day to disappear] (*Obras* 582). Likewise, Villaurrutia's sexuality, berated and mocked by some, has for the most part been ignored in the realm of academic literary criticism, rendering it invisible in this sphere until quite recently.[45] That is why, for example, one critic, in his reading of *Nostalgia de la muerte*, conjures "a passionate love affair between the poet and his mistress" (Moretta 7/18–19). Even as recently as a few years ago when Weinberger, in his introduction to the English translation of *Nostalgia de la muerte*, named Villaurrutia a precursor to gay identity politics, such frankness was met with disdain in Mexico.[46]

Still, critic José Quiroga sees Villaurrutia's poetry differently: "Xavier Villaurrutia's poems...may...seem 'closeted' to a North American audience although I think it is better to understand them as strategic texts, as queer performances that mobilize different public actors" (18). For Quiroga, Villaurrutia, like several other "queer" figures of early and mid-twentieth century Latin American letters, is not "the subject who proclaims his or her own sexuality [but] the melancholic subject who refuses the confession, the subject who chooses to mask it, while at the same time showing us the mask" (19).

For Villaurrutia was not invisible in his own day. He was acutely aware of his public image, and he managed it consciously. In a notebook, he writes, "El juego de la personalidad es siempre nuevo

porque crea siempre nuevos espectadores y porque cada uno es autor, actor y espectador" [The game of the personality is always new
because it always creates new spectators and because everyone is an
author, actor, and spectator] (*Obras* 620). His homosexuality, in fact,
was well known, due to gossip, or often to his own subtle affirma-
tions. While there were no overtly autobiographical writings referring
to his homosexuality published during his lifetime (and even now
very little exists attesting to his private life in his own words)[47]—and
even gossipy allusions such as one made by Luis Cardoza y Aragón
to Villaurrutia dancing with a "chofer" [driver] in a foul-smelling
Mexico City dive would not appear until well after Xavier's death in
1950[48]—he was not that shy about hinting at his sexuality.

One of his boldest writings is a brief dialogue published in the
short-lived journal *Cima* in 1942 entitled "Debate en torno de Walt
Whitman" [Debate on the subject of Walt Whitman] (*Obras* 945–48).
Here a group of intellectuals argue about Gide's reproach of a timid
translation of Whitman by Bazalgette. The erudite reader would have
recognized that this critique was made precisely in Gide's scandalous
homosexual manifesto, *Corydon*. The dialogue goes on to criticize
Spanish translations of Whitman, which insist on using the feminine
gender for adjectives and nouns of undecidable gender in English so
as to mask possible homosexual connotations. This is the only case
in all Villaurrutia's published work in which the word "homosexual"
appears. More typical for Villaurrutia is the provocative mention of
major literary figures reputed to be homosexual. Whitman, Proust,
Wilde, especially Gide, and even Langston Hughes are often employed
to evoke homosexuality both by Villaurrutia (and by homophobic
critics such as Maples Arce and Vasconcelos).[49]

Villaurrutia, in fact, evoked such writers constantly. Gide was well
known to be a big favorite to the point that in a newspaper interview,
when Villaurrutia was asked in a very general way about "influences,"
he assumed that the question referred to Gide. While Villaurrutia's
writings are stylistically quite dissimilar to Gide's, Villaurrutia admits
Gide as an influence, the influence being not "aesthetic," but "moral"
(quoted in Sheridan, *México en 1932* 154). Meanwhile, the influence of
Gide's morality was precisely what homophobes criticized Villaurrutia

for. In 1932, in *El Nacional,* Héctor Pérez Martínez chastises "esta generación equívoca, sabia en el truco unanimista y descastada en la promulgación de las todavía más equívocas enseñanzas morales de André Gide. A la literatura mexicana le está faltando una lección de virilidad en el más completo sentido humano" [this mistaken generation, wise in the tricks of unanimity and outstanding in their promulgation of the even more mistaken moral teachings of André Gide. Mexican literature is in need of a lesson in virility in the most complete human meaning of the word] (quoted in Capistrán 29).

In another interview, accused of being an egoist, Villaurrutia responded,

> ¿Egoísta? Tal vez, pero a la manera del héroe de una novela inglesa que me ruborizaría tener que nombrar. Egoísta desinteresado. Me ocupo de los demás por el placer de sorprender un día súbitamente, en un gesto, en una palabra, en una reacción moral, algo que yo dejé caer en ellos conscientemente.
>
> Egoist? Maybe, but in the manner of the hero of an English novel whose name I blush to mention. A disinterested egoist. I occupy myself with others for the pleasure of surprising them one day, suddenly, with a gesture, with a word, with a moral reaction, something that I consciously let slip. (Rojas 278)

Villaurrutia, then, was discreet, but not exactly secretive. He was never ostentatious about his sexuality as his friend Novo was. Novo's plucked eyebrows, eye makeup, and effete mannerisms made his sexuality boldly "obvious" to most and earned him the nickname "Nalgador Sobo" (which roughly translates as "Pawing Assman") (Monsiváis, *Amor perdido* 277). And yet his homosexuality, even when it was not an overt theme, was key to his poetry.

Gender in Villaurrutia

A poetry devoid of people would also, it would seem, by consequence be devoid of gender. However, this is not the case here. Villaurrutia is able to put forth an implicit critique of the "virile literature" movement, and not just in his translations of such texts as Gide's *L'école des femmes* [School for women], a collaboration with Rivas Mercado, but also in his poetry. His most interesting poem with regards to gender issues is one of the most often studied of the *Nostalgia de la muerte* collection, "Nocturno de la estatua" [Nocturne of the statue] (*Obras* 46–47).

Like "Nocturno," "Nocturno de la estatua" has no human protagonists, only a statue, although there is an implied narrator. It would seem that the statue, given that it appears as the mirror image of the narrator, is male. Yet Villaurrutia's statue abruptly becomes "an unexpected sister." Then, its mirror image, the narrator, too, must be gendered feminine. The statue is not made a "sister" to make the narrator's caress seem an expression of heterosexual desire; on the contrary, the mirror reveals a narcissistic and gender-bending homosexual desire.

Desire is central to the poem. The homosexual narrator, in fact, is absent. Grammatically, the poem utilizes infinitive verb forms and therefore leaves out any human subject. Of course it is implied that someone pursues the statue and later finds his or her reflection in a mirror. The infinitive form, however, not only conceals subjectivity, but also embodies desire. Desire (to dream, to run, to touch, to seize) itself is the grammatical subject (technically speaking, it is the verb, not the subject, that is missing); the human subject who ought to be present is overwhelmed and rendered invisible by this desire.

More importantly, the desire erases gender difference. Villaurrutia, instead of reinforcing the gender difference essentialized in Mexican culture even in its views on homosexuality, obliterates it, eroticizing gender likeness. Homosexuality by definition requires sexual sameness but does not proscribe gender difference; in fact, in the case of Mexican discourse on male homosexuality (following Paz), homosexuality normally implies gender difference. Someone must play the male role while the effeminate homosexual plays the female role. Villaurrutia's narcissism initiates a new and radical discourse on male homosexuality—Quiroga refers to Villaurrutia's "versatile universe" in which "flows of desire" negate stereotypes and fixed sexual identities of any kind (62)—whose implications go beyond gender issues, as we shall see.

La Homosexualidad Cósmica

Before expanding this investigation of narcissism in Villaurrutia's poetry, let us look at a very important discourse initiated in the early years of postrevolutionary Mexico, which at the time remained unmired by gender polemics: Vasconcelos's formulation of the "cosmic race." In 1925, Vasconcelos gained renown throughout the hemisphere with the publication of *La raza cósmica,* a treatise positing the superiority of the hybrid *mestizo* race.[50] For Vasconcelos, *mestizaje* was not the result of the rape of unfortunate or traitorous indigenous women by sexually sadistic or desperate Spanish *conquistadores;* instead it was a result of a process of natural selection by aesthetics. In *La raza cósmica,* Vasconcelos envisions the best (most beautiful, most intelligent) specimens of each race (particularly the white and red races) naturally falling together and mating, leading eventually to the creation of a race superior to all pure races individually.

While Vasconcelos clearly occupies himself with issues of heterosexual procreation, there is nothing to indicate that he does not believe his theory to apply to homosexuality, as well. Although he may not have approved of homosexuality, he certainly recognized its existence, and one might conclude that if asked how homosexual attraction functions, he would have extrapolated his theory of heterosexual racial mixing in response. Beauty, particularly a beauty of racial difference, would be a key factor in explaining heterosexual or homosexual attraction. The important difference between homosexuality and heterosexuality for Vasconcelos would be that the former, not involving reproduction, does not result in *mestizaje,* does not actually promote the cosmic race.

Vasconcelos's position is actually quite radical. Its appeal to postrevolutionary Mexico was its exaltation of *lo mestizo,* symbolic representation of the new Mexico that had superseded the liberal, but white, creole culture of the *porfiriato.*[51] It built on the idealism of José Enrique Rodó's writings, which used Greek iconography to pit U.S. Anglo-Saxon mores against Latin American ethics.[52] Vasconcelos betters Rodó by not depending on European icons to promote Latin American greatness in the global arena. He also goes against previous Mexican nationalist discourses, which inevitably assumed white Mexican culture to be superior to the cultures of indigenous or *mestizo* Mexicans (not to mention racial minorities: Asians, blacks, for example).[53] Interracial heterosexual bonding has a long, problematic history in Mexico.[54]

Oddly, since the inception of discourse on homosexuality in modern Mexico, racial difference was never depicted as a taboo within that subculture. At the famous 41 ball, attending were high-class dandies, their servants, and invitees from downtown *cantinas*. These men were clearly from a variety of social classes, and undoubtedly a combination of racial types. Of course, in 1901, the scandal of homosexuality itself was such that no one noticed whether there was any transgressing class or racial boundaries. Now that racial mixing was being idealized in Vasconcelos, it might be interesting to see how racial difference played out in the queer poetic vision of Villaurrutia, who wrote his most important poems roughly within the decade or so following the publication of *La raza cósmica*. Villaurrutia, one of the first prominent homosexual poets in Mexican literary history, helped to establish the theme of homosexual desire in the national literary canon. Whether or not Villaurrutia's sexuality was representative of any generalized Mexican homosexuality of his generation or social class, it offers one of only a few reliable clues toward an understanding of homosexuality in Mexico in the first half of the century.

Villaurrutia attached a curious importance to racial themes, which has gone unnoticed by literary critics, in his writing. His two versions of the legend of the *Mulata de Córdoba* (a film script and an opera libretto)[55] are among only a handful of visions of black identity and sexuality in Mexico of the era. While it might be said that Villaurrutia used the archetype of the heterosexual *mulata* to explore a forbidden sexuality without having to directly bring in the extremely contentious issue of homosexuality,[56] it is in the more opaque medium of Villaurrutia's poetry that the themes of race and sexuality are most interestingly played out, without skirting the issue of homosexual desire.

Nocturno de los Ángeles

The most audacious, most erotic of Villaurrutia's poems—his poem "con asunto" [with a subject], as he once commented ironically (quoted in Sheridan, "Villaurrutia habla" 222)—is his "Nocturno de los ángeles" [Nocturne of the angels, or of Los Angeles] (*Obras* 55–57). He wrote it in Los Angeles in 1936 during his only voyage abroad and dedicated it to Agustín Fink.[57] The poem portrays a city which is "maravillosa de noche" [marvelous by night]; according to a letter from Villaurrutia to Novo, "Ni en New York fluye, como aquí, el deseo y la satisfación del deseo" [Not even in New York do desire and the satisfaction of desire flow as they do here] (*Cartas* 75). In the poem, celestial beings, beautiful "angels," drop from the heavens to form "imprevistas parejas" [haphazard couples] with mortals. As they loiter under the dim city lights, the "secret" that all of them are in on remains unrevealed, as "es tan dulce guardarlo y compartirlo sólo con la persona elegida" [it is so sweet to keep it and share it only with the chosen person].

There is little doubt as to what the secret is. In 1936 when the poem was originally published, there might have been some uncertainty for some readers, but following the publication of Villaurrutia's letters to Novo and the even more eye-opening 1987 release of Villaurrutia's original illustrated manuscript with its drawings of sailors reminiscent of the figures that illustrate Cocteau's controversial *Livre blanc* [White book], which first came out in 1928, there can be no doubt that homosexual cruising is the secret in question. The desire—"las cinco letras del DESEO formarían una enorme cicatriz luminosa...y esa constelación sería como un ardiente sexo" [the six letters of DESIRE would form an enormous luminous scar...and this constellation would be like an ardent sex]—of these men who come and go on the flowing streets of Los Angeles, the desire of these men—"sedientos seres" [thirsty beings] who "caminan, se detienen, prosiguen" [walk, pause, proceed], "cambian miradas, atreven sonrisas" [exchange glances, venture smiles] and "forman imprevistas parejas" [form haphazard couples]—is quite plainly the little *asunto* of the poem.

While at first it seems that this is a straightforward vision of a narcissistic, promiscuous homosexuality in which the haphazard couples might be comprised of any men at all among those who wander Los Angeles's streets, later in the poem it becomes clear that there are men ("the men who come and go"), but that there is another entirely different set of beings involved as well: "¡Son los ángeles! Han bajado a la tierra por invisibles escalas. Vienen del mar . . . a fundirse y confundirse con los mortales" [They are angels! They have dropped down to earth on invisible ladders. They come from the sea . . . to fuse and confuse themselves with the mortals]. Now there are mortals and angels, the angels being sailors ("They come from the sea") of the United States Navy ("Se llaman Dick o John, o Marvin o Louis" [They're named Dick or John, or Marvin or Louis]). The narcissism expressed in the imagery of the twins—"los Gemelos que por primera vez en la vida se miraran de frente, a los ojos, y se abrazaran ya para siempre" [the Twins who for the first time in their lives look at each other face to face, eye to eye, and embrace forever]—indicates an identification between the mortals and the angels that is unrelated to race, unless we take into account the original manuscript—which Villaurrutia had given to Carlos Pellicer, unpublished until after the latter's death—in which the angels are depicted, embracing and kissing, as blond sailors.

The fantasy complicates itself if we try to locate where Villaurrutia or his Mexican readers might identify in the scene. It might be read as a voyeuristic fantasy of spying on the erotic games of homosexual sailors in the United States on the part of a Mexican observer who remains aloof from the action. It might also be a case of narcissism in which the Mexican identifies with the blond not because he is also blond, but because he wants to be blond. Villaurrutia's narcissism, read thusly, would recall that of the novels of the revolution in which an eroticization of the male body of another social class (recall Miguel Mercado's narcissistic gaze at his comrade in arms, Castorena in *Tomóchic*) plays out a narcissism of desiring what one would like to be but is not, one's ego ideal. Here, darker Mexicans might want to be blond sailors, and Villaurrutia might have identified with blonds from the United States, seen as a rich country with an enviable degree of sexual freedom. Another possible explanation would relate the poem to the work of Gide. After all, Gide's sexual escapades outside his native France could be compared to Villaurrutia's adventures in California.[58] However, neither the interracial eroticism and sexual tourism found in *L'immoraliste* and *Si le grain ne meurt,* nor the economy of desire and institutionalized pederasty so notoriously fomented in *Corydon* can completely explain Villaurrutia's brand of narcissism in which the angels "fuse," as "twins," with their mortal lovers.

None of these explanations fully satisfies. In no other moment of Villaurrutia's erotic poetry are there elements of voyeurism. Nor did Villaurrutia envy the United States its sexual freedom; in fact, there are no indications that he was at all discontent with the lively homosexual underground world of Mexico City. Moreover, the moral influence of Gide played out not so much in particular sexual tastes as in Gide's "gay pride," i.e., his valor in expressing his inclinations and passions without worrying about his reputation. To understand how racial difference figured in the eroticism of Villaurrutia's poetry, it is necessary to look at one more poem.

North Carolina Blues

"North Carolina Blues" (*Obras* 65–66), the poem Villaurrutia dedicated to Langston Hughes,[59] has not often been studied. Nor is anything known about whether the two were acquainted. Hughes, whose father spent most of his life in Mexico, traveled there several times; it is also possible that Hughes and Villaurrutia may have met during the latter's visit to the United States in 1935–36.[60] Whether they knew each other or Villaurrutia merely admired Hughes is a matter of speculation. In any case, the dedication itself does not signify an influence. "North Carolina Blues," despite its English title (reminiscent of the titles of many of Hughes's poems) and its topic (race in the United States), is actually more representative of two stylistic traits typical of Villaurrutia's poetic work than of anything Hughes ever wrote.

First, there are his vanguardist linguistic games. In another poem, he plays with whiteness: "¿Qué nombre dar a la blancura sobre lo blanco?" [What name to give whiteness on white] he writes in "Cementerio en la nieve" [Cemetery in the snow] (*Obras* 64–65). In "North Carolina Blues" he plays with blackness: "Cómo decir que la cara de un negro se ensombrece?" [How to say that the face of a black man darkens]; or later: "Habla un negro:— Nadie me entendería si dijera que hay sombras blancas en pleno día" [No one would understand me if I said that there were white shadows in broad daylight]. In one case, Villaurrutia's ironies appear to have an uncharacteristic political edge: "En diversas salas de espera aguardan la misma muerte los pasajeros de color y los blancos, de primera" [In different waiting rooms, the passengers of color and the whites of first class await the same death]. Later on, the familiar image of the fragmentary body appears: "Una mano sin cuerpo escribe y borra negros nombres en la pizarra" [A disembodied hand writes and erases black names on the blackboard]. Here the black body fits nicely into Villaurrutia's poetic language of shadows, the nocturnal ("En North Carolina el aire nocturno es de piel humana" [In North Carolina the nocturnal air is made of human skin]), and death, mysterious but intimate, disquieting but sensual.

This eroticism is the second familiar element in "North Carolina Blues." The poem's black bodies are abstract, expressed in metaphors ("Meciendo el tronco vertical, desde las plantas de los pies hasta las palmas de las manos el hombre es árbol otra vez" [Upright trunk swaying, from the soles of his feet to the palms of his hands, man is tree once more]), treated with irony at certain moments, but very much eroticized at others. The first strophe contains a gesture most unusual for Villaurrutia in this era: the narrator himself participates actively in the erotic encounters of the poem. Unlike the poet's removed stance in "Nocturno de la estatua," here, referring to the night air ("made of human skin"), he writes: "Cuando lo acaricio, me deja, de pronto, en los dedos, el sudor de una gota de agua" [When I caress it, it quickly leaves a drop of sweat on my fingertips]. Intertwined into his familiar uninhabited nocturnal scene, this time we find the palpable image of the poet, caressing sweating black skin.

At another moment, there is a curious parallel between "North Carolina Blues" and "Nocturno de los ángeles." In the latter poem, the haphazard couples of mortals and angels "[s]onríen maliciosamente al subir en los ascensores de los hoteles donde aún se practica el vuelo lento y vertical" [smile maliciously as they ascend in the elevators of hotels where slow vertical flight is still practiced]. In "North

Carolina Blues," we find the following nocturnal hotel scene: "lle-gan parejas invisibles, las escaleras suben solas, fluyen los corredores, retroceden las puertas, cierren los ojos de las ventanas" [invisible cou-ples arrive, the stairways ascend by themselves, the corridors flow, the doors back up, the windows close their eyes]. The similarity of the two poems here (the nocturnal hotels, the mysterious couples going up to the rooms) indicate a link between the vague eroticism of "North Car-olina Blues" and the unabashed homoeroticism of "Nocturno de los ángeles." Moreover, the image of the windows closing their eyes re-calls several other erotic nocturnal scenes in *Nostalgia de la muerte*[61] and points to relations that cannot be seen, that may not be described, that must remain veiled.

More interestingly, the final strophe of the poem also recalls "Noc-turno de los ángeles": "Confundidos cuerpos y labios, yo no me atrevería a decir en la sombra: Esta boca es la mía" [Tangled to-gether bodies and lips, I would not dare to say in the shadows: This mouth is mine]. Once again, bodies become confused into one, lips join absolutely, forming either a single mouth or remaining as two mouths that have become indistinguishable from each other. Fusion ("They come from the sea . . . to fuse and confuse themselves with the mortals") is a key concept in Villaurrutia's erotic imagery. However, the racialized eroticism of both poems yields a very particular image. In the sensual act, the poet fuses together with his lover; his identity and, significantly, his race are lost.

It is quite interesting to note that sex as a force that fuses identities presents itself only in these two poems, the only poems in Villau-rrutia's *oeuvre* that mark racial difference. Taking into account the fact that in the majority of his erotic poems it is not possible to identify bodies—only shadows, loose voices, corporeal fragments—the pres-ence of white and black bodies indicates that racial difference has an evident value in both poems. Villaurrutia's narcissism, then, does not follow a simple Freudian language of seeking a version (present, past, or future) of oneself in the other. Here, it is the other, not oneself, who dominates. In another moment, Villaurrutia paints a singular image: "el juego angustioso de un espejo frente a otro" [the anguishing game of one mirror in front of another] ("Nocturno en que nada se oye"

[Nocturne in which nothing is heard] [*Obras* 47–48]). As mirror of one's lover, the poet loses himself in the other, fusing himself with his lover. If the poetic protagonist does not actually become the other, nor does the other entirely disappear; what happens is that they both give of themselves to the point that the difference between the two of them evaporates.

Here, in an odd and unexpected way, Villaurrutia's homoeroticism coincides with Vasconcelos's model of the cosmic race. The Mexican homosexual desire of Xavier Villaurrutia permits racial difference and, in fact, difference of any kind. But what occurs in Villaurrutia is that any kind of difference is annulled through erotic contact. The shared enigma of the homosexuals requires that they all hide themselves from view, but that they also share the fact that they must live with the difference of their sexuality. Difference is not as threatening for them as it might be for others who do not live difference perpetually through their desires. Villaurrutia's narcissism might be read as the desire for oneself as encountered in the other, in the mutual reflection of marked difference in beings different not only from each other, but from everyone else.

Villaurrutia's queer vision of male homosexuality, then, diverges from the stereotypical Mexican view in which a difference in gender identification is key between homosexual partners, and in which the true homosexual partner must be effeminate. For Villaurrutia, while difference may be an important part of sexual attraction and inflamer of desire, it might just as well be a difference marked by race; in fact, it would seem that racial difference is much more interesting to Villaurrutia than any difference of gender identification. Villaurrutia's *raza cósmica* is formed, if only momentarily, through a sexual union between two men of different races, undoubtedly not what Vasconcelos had in mind when he coined the term, but not too remote from his utopian racial symbolism. Curiously, this paradigm is not new in Villaurrutia, although his overtly homosexual references are. The reader will recall that racial difference was dealt with quite similarly on an allegorical level in Altamirano. In his novels heterosexual rivalry permitted one man to take the place of another man of another race; when *Clemencia*'s Fernando Valle assumed Enrique

Flores's identity, he assumed not only the image of romantic hero that Flores had always cultivated in himself, but also Flores's physical beauty. Villaurrutia's is just another variation on the very Mexican theme of male homosocial *mestizaje.*

Yet another configuration of Mexican male homosexuality, also at odds with stereotypes, is presented by Villaurrutia's friend and cohort Salvador Novo in his posthumously published memoirs, *La estatua de sal.*

La Pedo Embotellado: The Spirit of Play

La Pedo Embotellado, the bottled fart, gendered feminine because, of course, the person with this nickname was a man, is one of a whole troupe of amusing personages who appear in Salvador Novo's racy memoir. Aside from *la Pedo Embotellado,* the many acquaintances Novo mentions include: Clarita Vidal, *la Cotorra con Pujos* [the constipated chatterbox], Chucha Cojines, *la India Bonita, la Perra Collie, la Madre Meza, la Golondrina* [the swallow], *Sor Diablo* (a priest), *la Virgen de Estambul, la Nalga que Aprieta* [the squeezing ass cheek], *la Diosa de Agua* [the goddess of water], *Nelly Fernández y su Chingada Madre,* and, of course, *las Chicas de Donceles* (Xavier Villaurrutia and Salvador Novo). Meeting in such notorious dives as the flophouse nicknamed "el Vaticano," these entertaining characters capture the spirit of play with which the queer underworld of Mexico City circa 1920 named and so defined itself. By examining such few textual clues that we have of how queer Mexicans have expressed same-sex desires, what Sylvia Molloy has called "queer traces" ("Speaking/Reading Silence") we can further challenge the rigidity of some of the well-known stereotypes. Novo, more audacious than Villaurrutia, is of particular interest in this regard. While he was not adverse to compromising himself politically for the sake of his career, he boldly maintained an effete and effeminate public persona throughout a most colorful life.

The primary source for interesting data regarding Novo's personal life is his slim memoir, *La estatua de sal.* Written in the forties, and chronicling Novo's childhood and early adult life in the early twenties, these memoirs are a coming of age narrative and a fascinating record of Mexico City's literary scene in the first years after the revolution. They are also full of gossipy anecdotes recounted in Novo's unique saucy and acerbic style, including graphic accounts of his often wild sexual adventures. This latter element makes *La estatua de sal* a uniquely brazen exposure of Mexico's homosexual underworld four decades before it meekly began to take form in the public imagination with the publication of Mexico's first novels with homosexuality as a central theme.[62] Fragments of these memoirs had been published both in Mexico and the United States in the late seventies, but it was not until 1998 that the entire document appeared in bookstores.[63]

The Queer Pedagogy of Pedro Henríquez Ureña

One of the most interesting of Novo's recollections is that of his relationship in the early twenties with the great Dominican educator and literary critic Pedro Henríquez Ureña, who had become something of a mentor to the young Novo during the Dominican's years teaching at Mexico's national university at the request of another great Latin American educator, José Vasconcelos. The pedagogical relationship between Henríquez Ureña, former founder and intellectual leader of the Ateneo de la Juventud, and Novo was sexually charged from the first fleeting glance, which left the young Novo "intrigued" (113).

Novo, sexually marked by his plucked eyebrows and elegant mode of dress,[64] quickly became a favorite of his *maestro,* rousing the suspicions of his peers, among them the Nicaraguan poet Salomón de la Selva. De la Selva was Novo's first friend among the group, although the friendship was predicated upon a test of sexuality. This test apparently convinced de la Selva of Novo's "orthodoxy," as Novo put it; however, it merely proves the difficulty in defining with any certainty that which occurs in the realm of the private. The fact that Novo agreed to hole up in a *hotelucho,* or seedy hotel, with a Czechoslovakian whore who, according to Novo, "no logró conmover mi frigidez" [did not succeed in stirring my frigidity] (114) did not make him a heterosexual, although it implied as much to his colleagues.

Around the time of Novo's rite of passage into this clique of disciples and hangers on, Henríquez Ureña went off to South America on what Novo termed "el Arca de Noé intelectual y artística con que Vasconcelos materializaba su fogoso iberoamericanismo" [the intellectual and artistic Noah's Ark with which Vasconcelos materialized his ardent Iberoamericanism] (114). In the absence of his mentor, Novo was free to go on a spree of sexual adventures: "Una insaciable sed de carne y una audacia...me arrojaban a la caza del género de muchachos que me electrizaba descubrir, tentar, exprimir: los choferes que en el México pequeño de entonces eran la joven generación lanzada a manejar las máquinas, a vivir velozmente" [An audacity and an insatiable thirst for meat...thrust me into a hunt for the kind of guys who it electrified me to discover, tempt, and take advantage of: taxi and bus drivers who in *el México pequeño* of those days headed up the brazen young generation of fast cars and fast living] (115). Specifically, in order to facilitate such liaisons, he got involved in the production of a journal for these drivers called *El Chafirete* [the reckless driver] in which he published parodic pieces such as "Madregal, sonetos lubricantes de Sor Juana Inés del Cabuz."⁶⁵ Apparently the director and other collaborators of the journal had more of a taste for the newsboys who sold it or for the young fare collectors on the buses, while Novo went after the most solidly built of the drivers themselves.

This atmosphere of sexual conquest inspired young Novo to embark on the competitive endeavor of conquering an object of colossal size: "me atreví a lo que era fama que sólo su amante Nacho Moctezuma toleraba: la verga de Agustín Fink, positivamente igual en diámetro a una lata de salmón" [I dared to attempt to take on what only his lover Nacho Moctezuma was known to tolerate: the dick of Agustín Fink, positively equal in diameter to a can of salmon] (115). This was not the first time Novo took on a sexual partner more as a challenge than out of a physical desire. His friend *la Golondrina* once set him up with an anarchist who had set off a bomb at the U.S. Embassy. The agitator was "feo, pero dueño de una herramienta tan descomunal, que no era fácil hallarle acomodo. La Golondrina me retó, y acepté su desafío" [ugly, but armed with a tool of such remarkable size that its accommodation was a forbidding task. La Golondrina dared me, and I accepted the challenge] (107). The venture required that the anarchist penetrate Novo before a group of "curious witnesses" who would verify that Novo was capable of taking "the whole thing." Of course, he succeeded. Novo describes his encounter with Fink with even greater candor: "Consciente de su gigantismo, la introducía cautelosamente dormida y bien forrada del lubricante entonces conocido antes del benemérito advenimiento del KY: *la vaselina*. Pero una vez adentro, se abría como un paraguas, estrellaba la estrechez de su cautiverio" [Conscious of its gigantic size, he would introduce it cautiously limp and well coated with the lubricant of choice in those days before the meritorious advent of KY jelly: namely, vaseline. But once inside, it would open up like an umbrella, bursting the bounds of its captivity] (115). Novo ended up seriously injured, forced to undergo a treatment that involved carrying a specially treated cotton wad in his anal cavity all day long on a daily basis.

Upon his return, Henríquez Ureña got wind of certain rumors regarding Novo's nocturnal escapades and called his young pupil into his office. When Novo arrived, his professor began nervously talking in circles, "Parpadeaban sus ojos negrísimos y pequeños, aclaraba su garganta, movía los dedos de los pies dentro del calzado. Por fin: '¿Lo haría conmigo?' Y se me acercó, como si esperara un beso" [He fluttered his very black and small eyes, cleared his throat, scrunched up his toes in his shoe. Finally: 'Would you do it with me?' And he came up close to me as if he were waiting for a kiss] (116). When Novo reluctantly decided he'd better kiss him, the Dominican had an attack of homosexual panic: " 'Pues, eso está muy mal' —replicó apartándose, conteniéndose, volviendo a su gran escritorio de cortina. 'Es un acto sucio e indebido.' " ['Well that is very bad,' he replied, backing off, containing himself, retreating to his large curtained off desk. 'It's a filthy, improper act.'] (116). He then went on to recount a similar scene of pedagogical desire between himself and a handsome young student he'd taught in the United States whom he'd allowed to kiss him: " 'me besó aquí, en la mejilla. Pero está mal. No debe ser.' " ["He kissed me here, on the cheek. But it is bad. It shouldn't be."] (116). At this moment, the awkward scene was interrupted when the notorious medicated cotton wad, which had slipped out of Novo's posterior cavern rolled out of his pant leg onto the floor.

Rumor has it (Novo denies it, but relates it nonetheless) that one final melodramatic scene completed the romantic tragedy. During Henríquez Ureña's wedding, which occurred soon after the aforementioned events, Novo, in the middle of the religious ceremony, spread open his arms and fell dramatically to his knees in a pose of desperate entreaty and cried out, "Señor, cuídamelo, Señor, protégelo; Señor, ¿qué va a hacer con una mujer?" [Lord keep him for me, Lord protect him, Lord, what is he going to do with a woman?] (117).

Play in Novo

The richness of Novo's comic narrative might lead the reader to overlook the document's historical importance. It is a rare first-person narrative by an admitted homosexual about Mexican homosexuality decades prior to the so-called gay rights movement. While Novo's description of the Mexican homosexual underworld of 1920 does not explicitly contradict the stereotypes reductively equating homosexuality with effeminacy in men—in fact, at first glance, the feminized nicknames of his cohorts would seem to support such stereotypes—they do offer some interesting insights that have gone largely unprobed by scholars. For Novo's queers, the feminine plays an important role, as does anal penetration. However, the spirit of play seen in their names does not reflect any rigid schema of roles. Quite the contrary, it ridicules such intractable rules.[66]

Novo's flamboyant acquaintance Clarita Vidal illustrates. Vidal enjoyed the activity of *putear,* of playing up her queer persona, in public. She would flirt boisterously—"a veces, con inmediata eficacia" [sometimes with immediate efficacy] (94)—with passersby. If they confronted her, "él afrontaba con una súbitamente recuperada virilidad, para preguntarse si traían aretes, y si se habían creído dignos de semejante invitación" [he countered with a suddenly recuperated virility, asking them if they wore earrings, and if they believed themselves worthy of such an invitation] (94). Clarita's ability to turn on or off his/her virility at will recalls the playfulness that Roger Lancaster finds in some examples of gender performance ("Guto's Performance" 23–29). While transgender performance is by no means necessarily

subversive, someone like Clarita is capable of strategically performing a variety of scripts of gender, or merely playing around with
existing ones. Such play exposes the performative aspect of gender,
disrupts norms that are assumed to be natural, and challenges the
rigidity of stereotypes.[67] Such disruptions dislodge definitions traditionally viewed in clear and certain terms; as Lancaster states: "The
whole point of such fun and games is that a final meaning evades
us" (11).

Novo, on the other hand, takes this playfulness a step further by
recasting the role of the penetratee. Novo demonstrates a very active
strategy of "passive" sex. The term *maricón activo* is not an oxy-
moron. Instead, it debunks the stereotype. Both the penetrator and
the penetratee can experience pleasure; both can be sexually aggressive; both can demonstrate "virility." There is even a popular belief
that there are macho men who play the "passive" role in anal intercourse in order to prove their manhood by showing that they can
take it.[68] In the case of the seduction of Fink, it is clearly the penetratee, Novo, who is the active, aggressive partner. Furthermore, the
colossal size of Fink's member shows Novo to be the one with the
balls. Novo's motivation of sexual competition and his willingness to
endure physical pain for the sake of sexual pleasure show him to be
the "manlier" partner in the transaction. Perhaps this is part of the
reason why biographer Reyna Barrera refers to him as "el más macho
de los poetas jotos" [the most macho of the fag poets] ("Novo en la
memoria" 40).

In *La estatua de sal*, Novo presents a vast variety of homosexual
configurations. He mentions his own experiences of oral sex; for example, "la primera, instintiva vez, que mi boca cumplió gustosa y
súbitamente experta una caricia que me llenó de gozo" [the first,
instinctive occasion, that my mouth delightfully and precipitately delivered an expert caress that filled me with pleasure] (102). Some
characters, namely Villaurrutia, shift roles (120). He cites couples
in which both partners are *locas* [effeminate men], such as Clara
Vidal and Carlos Luquín (118). Another type of relation joins men
across generations, the most prominent example being that of Antonio Adalid and his young lover Antonio (107–10). All these variations

would appear as "queer" literature emerged in Mexico beginning in the sixties.[69] But most important is the spirit of play with respect to gender and sexual stereotypes that characterizes Novo's writings.

Still, while the Contemporáneos did exert some influence on the debates over Mexicanness that were to follow from the publication of their colleague Samuel Ramos's *El perfil del hombre y la cultura en México* in 1934, the questions of male sexuality raised in their works are only now being brought into constructive dialogue with discourse of national identity. And as we have seen, even the most macho visions of *lo mexicano* have their queer elements. The Contemporáneos are not at all an aberration, but in fact fit as neatly into a genealogy of national literature as Lizardi, Altamirano, and Azuela, as well as Paz and Rulfo, as we shall see.

Conclusions

The great virility debates of the 1920s occurred around the two major literary trends of the time. The first was the novel of the revolution, which was promoted by the debates themselves. Canonical novels— the best known of which was Azuela's *Los de abajo*—promoted Mexicanness and virility as synonymous. This literary virility, in terms of representation, is a vindication of turn-of-the-century notions of barbarous lower-class masculinity. However, the focus on manliness within the male homosocial environment of the military inflects a homoeroticism on virility itself. By the 1920s it is no longer an option to ignore the perpetual latent possibility of a sexual aspect, i.e., a homosexual aspect, of any homosocial environment. Homosexuality entered the national consciousness at the turn of the century, and the attempts to remasculinize Mexican literature only seem to make it queerer.

The second was a more avant garde trend of a consciously universal and not national literature whose motivations are at least apparently more aesthetic than social in nature. The macho *vanguardismo* of the *estridentistas* died out quickly while the effete poetry of the Contemporáneos gradually emerged, despite homophobic assaults of their rivals, as a major force in postrevolutionary Mexican literary history. While the group ostensibly focused on formal issues, the homosexuality of some of them (and general queerness of many of them and their associates) necessarily made their visions of Mexican masculinity different from those of the macho novels of the revolution. This is not to say that their literature was somehow effeminate. In fact, the complexity of the notions of male sexuality and homo-eroticism that can be teased out of the writings of Xavier Villaurrutia and Salvador Novo indicate that the stereotypes of homosexuality propagated by heterosexuals with regard to Mexican homosexuality are usually false.

Chapter 4

Homosexual Panic
The 1940s and 1950s

Nationalism, Masculinity, and Homosexuality:
Samuel Ramos, Octavio Paz

Nationalism and the Search for Lo Mexicano

The postrevolutionary debates on virile writing emerged from a nationalist discourse that reflected an impetus to establish a particular kind of image to represent Mexico and Mexicanness. Roger Bartra notes that Mexico's cultural elite had been in significant pursuit of *lo mexicano* since the *porfiriato,* with positivists such as Julio Guerrero among the first to make the theme central to their work. While the positivists' foremost concerns had been solving social problems and treating (often fortifying) class difference, much of the debate of the thirties concerned issues of foreign influences on national culture and of masculinity.

The brand of nationalism that had fomented the novel of the revolution tended toward a xenophobia that sought to ensure that Mexican cultural production not be a mere imitation of French, Spanish, or U.S. models. While such figures as Altamirano had in prior decades been strong advocates of establishing a national literature, the *costumbrismo* and *modernismo* that had dominated literary production in Mexico through the early twentieth century drew openly from popular traditions abroad. The novel of the revolution (along with the muralist movement) pretended to create an autochthonous image of Mexico, free from foreign influence. The employment of gender rhetoric in these debates, as discussed earlier, was often a cheap shot of homophobia but would come to occupy a more and more central place in discourse on *lo mexicano* in the decades to come.

El Perfil del Hombre y la Cultura en México

Samuel Ramos's *El perfil del hombre y la cultura en México* (1934) is widely considered to be the first major study of the Mexican psyche and the first of what would come to be an abundance of large-scale attempts to apply psychoanalytic theory to *lo mexicano*. Paz's 1950 essay *El laberinto de la soledad,* of course, would become the most famous such study, but many of Paz's ideas were already on the table in Ramos. Paz does indeed recognize Ramos's influence on his work, and it is particularly when it comes to the intersection of the national and the masculine that Ramos's *El perfil* is seminal.

Ramos famously claims that Mexicanness is marked by an inferiority complex, a consequence of the Spanish conquest of Mexico, of colonial and postcolonial culture that has subordinated Mexico to Europe in the world cultural arena. Mexicans, following Ramos's thesis, never feeling themselves in a position to assert their native culture as equal to that of more wealthy and powerful countries, have resorted to imitating "superior" cultures, or to pumping themselves up and calling themselves more inherently virile than their European counterparts. Invoking Adler's notion of masculine protest, Ramos argues that Mexicans need to assert a superficial hypermasculinity to mask their inner feelings of weakness.

Ramos's vision of Mexicanness does not make it very clear whether he believes Mexican women to be superficially hypermasculine along with Mexican men, or whether the former are simply not worthy of his consideration. In a few years, Paz would more than make up for this omission (to the chagrin of many Mexican women) by addressing female Mexicanness at length. On the other hand, while Paz merely recounts traditional feminine stereotypes, in Mexican literature of the forties and fifties explorations of masculine women would begin to appear as more than expressions of anxiety about feminism in such novels as Francisco Rojas González's *La negra Angustias* and Rosario Castellanos's *Balún Canán,* as if to demonstrate that masculinity in women were somehow a cultural possibility or even probability in Mexico.

Aside from Paz, Ramos is the most renowned author of discourse on *lo mexicano*. Moreover, Ramos's move for Mexico to give up imitating Europe linked him ideologically with his generation's nationalists. And yet, as Bartra points out:

> During the thirties a reaction against revolutionary nationalism arose which, paradoxically, was to bear the principal responsibility for the codification and institutionalization of the myth of the Mexican character. In fact, curiously, the group of writers emerging from the journal *Contemporáneos* (1928–31), with the philosopher Samuel Ramos as spokesman, contributed most to the devising of the profile of *Homo mexicanus*. (4)

The irony is clear. The very same intellectuals who had been criticized for not being Mexican enough were responsible for the mythopoesis of the Mexican man. The irony, in fact, goes beyond what Bartra indicates; these intellectuals were not only challenged for not being Mexican enough, but for not being man enough. Yet through Ramos, masculinity became the central issue in discourse on *lo mexicano*.

Given that Ramos was not one of the "revolutionary nationalists," it is perhaps not surprising that his interpretation of Mexicanness harks back to the work of the positivists of the *porfiriato*. *Científicos* such as Macedo had dichotomized Mexican masculinity along class lines, associating vulgar, barbarous machismo with the lower classes, and a more civilized (European) style of masculinity with bourgeois and upper classes. Such a view had perhaps gained even more legitimacy by mid-century, by which time what Monsiváis has called the "Freudianization" of the country was well in force. In *Civilization and Its Discontents*, Freud defines civilized societies as "collections of men [who] are...libidinally bound to one another" (82). Similarly, civilized man is "estrange[d]...from his duties as a husband and father. Thus the woman finds herself forced into the background" (59). Meanwhile the libidinally charged male homosocial space of civilization is "perpetually threatened with disintegration" due to man's barbarous "inclination to aggression" (69).

Freud thus proposes a paradox in which a move toward civilization creates and fortifies a culture based upon and conducive to male homosocial bonding. At the same time, the dominance of male homosocial bonding in a given culture heightens an innate masculine barbarity. Masculinity, libidinous and savage, while belonging specifically to neither civilization nor barbarity, destabilizes both conditions. This same tension was of course in play at the turn of the century as the civilized masculinity of the *porfiriato* seemed to promote a sort of male homosocial bonding constantly on the verge of slipping into barbarous homosexuality. Although Ramos was more an Adlerian or at times a Jungian than a Freudian, similar tensions are clearly at work in Ramos's vision of Mexicanness.

He centers his discussion of *lo mexicano* on a lower-class archetype, *el pelado*. Like Macedo's lower-class criminals, Ramos's *pelado* "busca riña" [seeks out fights], and evokes his virility at every turn:

> Es como un náufrago que se agita en la nada y descubre de improviso una tabla de salvación: la virilidad. La terminología del "pelado" abunda en alusiones sexuales que revelan una obsesión fálica, nacida para considerar el órgano sexual como símbolo de la fuerza masculina. En sus combates verbales atribuye al adversario una femineidad imaginaria, reservando para sí el papel masculino. Con esta actitud pretende afirmar su superioridad sobre el contrincante.

> He's like a man in a shipwreck who swashes about in nothingness and then discovers a raft of salvation: virility. The terminology of the *pelado* abounds in sexual allusions that reveal a phallic obsession, designed to take the sexual organ as a symbol of masculine force. In his verbal combats, he attributes an imaginary femininity to his adversary reserving the masculine role for himself. With this attitude, he attempts to affirm his superiority over his opponent. (Ramos 52–53)

In competitive circumstances, then, a victor emerges who is masculine, while the loser becomes feminine. Discursive power assertions are fully gendered.

The Mexican in this way is able to take on European "civilization":

> Cuando [el pelado] se compara con el hombre civilizado extranjero y resalta su nulidad, se consuela del siguiente modo: "Un europeo—dice—tiene la ciencia, el arte, la técnica, etc., etc.; aquí no tenemos

nada de esto, pero...somos muy hombres." Hombres en la acepción zoológica de la palabra, es decir, un macho que disfruta de toda la potencia animal.

When *el pelado* compares himself with civilized foreign man and his insignificance stands out, he consoles himself as follows: "A European," he says, "has science, art, technical expertise, etc., etc.; here we've got none of that, but...we are very male." Male in the zoological acceptation of the word, i.e., a male who enjoys a full animal potential. (55–56)

Once again, civilized culture is feminized as the lower-class *pelado* exemplifies a symbolic hypermasculinity. It is the discourse of masculinity that permits a nationalist challenge to an imported discourse of civilization. Moreover, to the extent that gender remains embedded in the national habitus (i.e., it is taken for granted to be natural and not an ideological construct), its discursive deployment is quite effective—until Ramos interrogates and critiques it. Nonetheless, although Ramos's intent is clearly to critique the *pelado* stereotype, his articulation of it in a book that was to achieve great renown, in fact, serves to establish the stereotype as the basis for any discussion of national identity.[1] *Lo mexicano* would, despite Ramos's Adlerian proto-feminist grounding, from 1934 on be synonymous with the overstated masculinity of masculine protest.

The Politics of Posing

Sylvia Molloy, we have mentioned, has made interesting observations about rhetorical attempts to deny homosexuality's existence in turn-of-the-century Argentina by identifying it as a mere pose, an imitation of a European fashion. We have already pointed out that, oddly enough, homosexuality, through the scandal of the 41, was never denied in Mexico, but instead embraced with great humor and affection, and an often hyperbolic disapproval as a Mexican debauchery, an aspect of the carnivalesque lurking below the surface of everyday convention.

Certainly, "the politics of posing," as Molloy names the phenomenon, follow a moralistic logic in Argentina. Homosexuality perhaps can best be kept in check by denying its existence, foreclosing it as an option. Moreover, national culture can claim a sort of moral superiority by labeling homosexuality foreign. Jorge Salessi writes of "la amenaza de una infección homosexual que desde Europa y Estados Unidos podía hacer tambalear el proyecto de modernización y creación de una nueva raza argentina" [the threat of a homosexual infection that from Europe and the United States might cause the project of modernization and creation of a new Argentine race to falter] (207). Mexico's acceptance of homosexuality as Mexican follows its own moralistic logic as homosexuality becomes a rhetorical weapon employed to denigrate enemies vulnerable to homophobic rancor in public discourse within the national sphere, as occurred in the attacks on the Contemporáneos—although at the same time, as Monsiváis points out, Novo's strategy of "posar como lo que se es" [posing as what one is] (*Salvador Novo* 81) served to increasingly humanize the homosexual in Mexico's public sphere. However, with Ramos, the politics of posing enters Mexican discourse, but in an utterly unexpected fashion.

Herculean Ninón, the gallant nontransvestite homosexual in *Los 41,* as we have mentioned, was accused by his girlfriend not of faking homosexuality, but of having faked virile heterosexuality with her. Ramos shows Ninón to be representative of Mexican men:

> No debemos, pues, dejarnos engañar por las apariencias. El "pelado" no es ni un hombre fuerte ni un hombre valiente. La fisonomía que nos muestra es falsa. Se trata de un "camouflage" para despistar a él y a todos que lo tratan. Puede establecerse que, mientras las manifestaciones de valentía y de fuerza son mayores, mayor es la debilidad que se quiere cubrir.

> We shouldn't, then, let ourselves be fooled by appearances. The *pelado* is not a strong man, nor a brave man. The physiognomy that he shows us is false. It concerns a "camouflage" to throw off both himself and those who deal with him. It can be established that the greater the manifestation of bravery and force, the greater the weakness that he wishes to conceal. (56)

Mexicans do not pose as homosexuals; they pose as virile men. This is not really a new idea: recall that this was a major lesson of *El Periquillo Sarniento* over a century earlier.

Years later, social psychologists Erich Fromm and Michael Maccoby would confirm this idea in a study of family relations in a Mexican village.

> The results show that approximately two-thirds of the husbands (66 percent) are dominant. But this figure has to be taken with a good deal of skepticism. In some instances it includes men whose wives allow them to appear dominant, but who privately dominate or even sabotage their husbands.... These data also support the finding that the patriarchal role is different from sadistic machismo, which is usually a compulsive compensation for feelings of weakness and dependence on women. This is confirmed by the striking fact that only 59 percent of the husbands who scored high on machismo dominate their wives compared to 77 percent who scored low on machismo. Aside from this, we assume that a large percentage of wives of the macho-type man pretend that he dominates the family, because they know that he needs this conviction in order to function well. (150–51)

Men and women both conspire (although not necessarily together) to promote the notion of male strength and superiority,[2] but Mexican shows of masculinity conceal feelings of weakness.

Ramos is careful to say that the Mexican inferiority complex demonstrates feelings of inferiority, but not necessarily an actual inferiority. Mexican men identify with idealized archetypes of masculinity that are not authentically part of their personae because they believe themselves incapable of really achieving those ideals, which is not to say that this pose of exemplary virility signifies an utter lack of virility. Thus, Ramos fails to get at the root of *lo mexicano*. On the other hand, the impulse to pose at masculinity, the proclivity to assert one's masculinity at the expense of a rival's, and the assumption of one's own defective masculinity do emerge as components of an essentially Mexican masculinity, explicitly delineated for the first time.

La Chingada

Octavio Paz expands on many of Ramos's ideas in *El laberinto de la soledad,* first published in 1950. Mexicans, according to Paz, engage in a constant defensive struggle to keep themselves closed, to avoid vulnerability.[3] He uses the term "rajarse" [to split, to crack, to back down] to express this essential Mexican behavior: "el ideal de la 'hombría' consiste en no 'rajarse' nunca. Los que se 'abren' son co-bardes" [the ideal of "manliness" consists in never "cracking." Those who "open up" are cowards] (26). On the subject of "rajarse," Paz concludes, "Las mujeres son seres inferiores porque, al entregarse, se abren. Su inferioridad es constitucional y radica en su sexo, en su 'rajada,' herida que jamás cicatriza" [Women are inferior beings because, in giving of themselves, they open up. Their inferiority is constitutional and lies in their sex, in their "crack," the wound which never heals] (27).[4]

Paz later introduces the term "chingar" [to fuck, to fuck over] and describes the commonly held view of the Mexican woman as *la Chingada*, one who has been fucked, penetrated, cracked. Mexi-can woman is "passive," inferior, and sexualized to the point where all women must either be the "bitch-goddess" prostitute examined in Debra Castillo's *Easy Women* or the good version of femininity that moves from pure virginity to saintly motherhood that Lilia Granillo Vázquez examines in "La abnegación maternal." Mexican men, of course, aspire to be the *chingón*, the big fucker, a figure who domi-nates others, penetrates their being. Paz's "chingar" is not unlike the term "madrugar," which Guzmán had used to represent the Mexican revolution in *La sombra del caudillo*, except that for Paz, this mascu-line display of force is always sexualized. Heterosexual sex is always rape, a reenactment of the conquest of Mexico with the male *conquis-tadores* invading, penetrating, and violating Mexico, now represented as the traitorous indigenous woman, la Malinche. Indigenous Mexi-cans are identified with her, passive and effeminate, regardless of their biological sex.

The difficulty for Mexican men under Paz's scheme is that they are not the Spanish *conquistadores*, but the *mestizo* "hijos de la Malinche" [sons of la Malinche]. There are no fathers in this sym-bolic world (the Spanish *conquistadores* are no longer around), only mothers and sons. And "los hijos de la Malinche" must continually overcome the conquest of Mexico by asserting their masculinity and proving themselves to be *grandes chingones*.

In relations between men and women, roles are clear cut. Women are symbolically *chingadas, rajadas,* and men their penetrators.

However, between men, things are more complex. *El pelado* means "the peeled one"; *el pelado* is *rajado* and vulnerable from the start. However, between men, a *pelado* can attain an image of superiority by symbolically cracking his cohort; he can *chingar* his rival and make himself *el gran chingón,* and his rival *el chingado.* His rival, then, is symbolically penetrated and feminized in this losing encounter.

Such a rivalry is frequently played out, according to Paz, through the popular institution of the *albur,* a kind of obscene word game in which the quick witted *pelado* symbolically fucks his opponent by using *double entendres.* Encounters between men then take on a sexual charge, a homosexual charge. If female inferiority is rooted in a woman's sexual organ, which is fucked, men's superiority is more ambiguous and can be sustained only so long as he is fucking, and not being fucked. In heterosexual relations, there is no apparent problem: the man fucks, the woman is fucked; however, in homosexual relations, one man fucks another. The fact that a man can be fucked means that his masculinity is not essentially sacrosanct and is open to constant challenge from other men:

> el vencido es el que no puede contestar, el que se traga las palabras del enemigo. Y esas palabras están teñidas de alusiones sexualmente agresivas; el perdidoso es poseído, violado, por el otro. Sobre él caen las burlas y escarnios de los espectadores. Así pues, el homosexualismo masculino es tolerado, a condición de que se trate de una violación del agente pasivo. Como en el caso de las relaciones heterosexuales, lo importante es "no abrirse" y, simultáneamente, rajar, herir al contrario.

> the loser is the one who can't answer back, the one who swallows the words of his enemy. And those words are tainted with sexually aggressive allusions; the loser is possessed, raped by the other. On him fall the mockery and jeers of the spectators. Thus, male homosexuality is tolerated, as long as it concerns the violation of a passive agent. As in the case of heterosexual relations, what is important is to not open oneself up and, simultaneously, to crack, to wound the adversary. (35)

Competitive masculine relations in Mexico, then, take on homosexual overtones. The macho's need to prove his masculinity by asserting his superiority over other men invariably implies a homosexual relation of *chingar* in which only the penetrated man, the loser in the competitive encounter, actually becomes symbolically homosexual and effeminate.

This is undoubtedly why Paz finds homosexual tendencies to be inherent in machismo, as we have seen previously: "No sería difícil percibir...ciertas inclinaciones homosexuales [en el macho], como el uso y abuso de la pistola,...el gusto por las cofradías cerradamente masculinas, etc." [It would not be difficult to perceive...certain homosexual inclinations in the macho, such as the use and abuse of the pistol,...the taste for closed masculine brotherhoods, etc.] (74).[5]

Homosexual Shit Eaters

This growing discourse that defined homosexuality not as the opposite of hypermasculinity, but as an attribute latent in the most masculine of men, caused an increase in anxiety about male homosexuality in Mexico beginning in the fifties. According to Clark Taylor, "[b]eginning in 1959, there was a general crackdown on pleasure in Mexico. It was first to hit homosexuals" (199). Establishments in Mexico City known to be frequented by homosexuals were raided and shut down following the triple murder of a bisexual hustler and his two lovers (one male, one female). Sergio González Rodríguez dates the crackdown earlier in the decade with campaigns against underground nightlife and pornography (42). Even in the realm of literature, in 1956 the Institute of Mexican-Cuban Cultural Relations had difficulty in publishing Adela Palacios's novel *El hombre* because it presented "la homosexualidad, la lujuria y la vida bohemia en forma contraria 'a las buenas costumbres'" [homosexuality, lust, and bohemian life contrary to "good customs"] (González Rodríguez 42).

In 1959, F. Ferrer Torrents and Joan D'Oc published *Sodoma pide fuero: ¿Es respetable un país con veinte millones de homosexuales?* [Sodom demands privilege: Is a country with twenty million homosexuals respectable?] in reaction to the scandalous publication of the Spanish translation of Donald Webster Cory's *The Homosexual in America* in Mexico. The latter book was a very early attempt to promote homosexuality as a vibrant part of world culture through history, and to argue for gay rights; it is quite amazing that such a text got translated into Spanish and published in Mexico. On the other hand, homosexuality had been a titillating topic for Mexican readers since the turn of the century. *Sodoma pide fuero,* cowritten by a hypnotist and a psychiatrist, the latter claiming to be well experienced in "curing" homosexuals and other sexual deviants, denies that homosexuality is a major problem in the Americas outside of the United States: "lo que dicen ser posible en Norteamérica es imposible en cualquier país de la América Latina y en Canadá" [what is said to be possible in the United States is impossible in any country of Latin America and Canada] (11). They attribute its apparent prominence in the United States to a national immaturity: "Los 'gringos' no han sabido hacerse simpáticos porque no han llegado a la madurez humana: actúan como neuróticos molestos e inseguros de sí mismos" [The gringos haven't figured out how to make themselves likable because they have not reached human maturity: they act like bothersome, insecure neurotics] (49).

Their psychoanalytic perspective ignores the cultural specificities that Paz presents and attributes universal homosexuality to a whole range of possible causes, fourteen in all, including intense love for the mother, intense love for the father, hatred of the mother, and hatred of the father (the only ones safe would then be those who are indifferent to both parents, that is, assuming that they don't fall into any of the other ten risk categories) (88–91). While *Sodoma pide fuero* does not dialogue with *El laberinto de la soledad,* it does reflect a growing paranoia in Mexico regarding homosexuality in the years immediately following Paz's groundbreaking introduction of the topic into Mexican high cultural discourse. I have argued that the specifically Mexican cultural constructions of masculinity have been implicated with homosexual overtones dating back to *El Periquillo Sarniento,* although this subtlety has gone largely overlooked; but now that Paz has articulated it so prominently, a new homosexual paranoia is appearing in texts like *Sodoma pide fuero.*

The volume's most bizarre eccentricity is to repeatedly compare homosexuals to coprophagists (shit eaters):

> Un coprófago no tiene la culpa de serlo—y que se nos perdone la coprofagia, pero creemos que hay bastante similitud . . . —y nadie debería

sentirse molesto porque un caballero ingiriera una torta de excrementos, pero la humanidad ... sentirá asco y rechazará al señor que tal
cosa haga.

A coprophagist is not to blame for being one—and forgive us for bringing up coprophagia, but we believe there is a lot of similarity ... —and
no one ought to feel annoyed because a gentleman ingests an excrement
sandwich, but humanity ... will feel disgusted and will reject the man
who does such a thing. (110)

Later, in a chapter whose goal is to find a "rationalization" for
homophobia, the authors point out:

En efecto, no hay motivo racional para sentir aversión hacia un caballero que coma excrementos. A nadie obliga a compartir con él este
manjar ni a nadie perjudica. Si éste es su gusto ¿por qué no los va
a comer?

In effect, there is no rational motive to feel aversion toward a gentleman
who eats excrement. No one is obliged to share this dish with him nor
does he harm anyone. If this is his taste, why shouldn't he eat it? (117)

The answer of course is that coprophagia, like homosexuality, is
unnatural and disgusting to society, so both perversions should be
controlled on moral grounds, a view supported in an appendix that
quotes at length from sections of the Roman Catholic Code of Canon
Law concerned with (unnamable) "nefarious," "dishonest," or "execrable" crimes (204–6). In the book's final chapter on common sexual
aberrations (aside from homosexuality), in the inevitable section on
coprophagia, they explain why they continually make this link: "El
coito anal, práctica común en los homosexuales masculinos, tiene
algo, por no decir mucho, de coprophagia" [Anal intercourse, a common practice among male homosexuals, has some, if not a lot, of
coprophagia in it] (195).

La Región Más Queer

Thus, in the years when William Burroughs was hiding out in Mexico,
enjoying what he saw as a sort of homosexual paradise—full of gay
bars, available young boys, drunken cops who his narrator picks up
and shows "how the cow ate the cabbage" (Queer 34), cliques of

"screaming fags" with picturesque names like the "Green Lantern boys"—and writing his novel *Queer,* male homosexuality in Mexico was such a cause of anxiety that Mexicans could not write about the topic except to try to wipe it off the national landscape, as was the case with *Sodoma pide fuero.* Interestingly, the rich queer underworld Burroughs describes both in *Queer* and in his letters would cast doubt on the success of the crackdowns to which Taylor alludes.

On the other hand, it is no surprise that the manifestations of homosexual themes that began to emerge in Mexican literature with a certain frequency beginning in the early sixties were fraught and anxious. Miguel Barbachano Ponce's fascinating *Diario de José Toledo* ends with the suicide of the protagonist. The queer dwarf in José Revueltas's *Los errores* is a hopelessly tragic and grotesque figure, an outcast who is marginal even in the criminal underworld where he is forced to dwell. The queerness permeating the pages of Vicente Leñero's *Los albañiles* reflects a sexual repression that, in the ambience of poverty or what José Joaquín Blanco calls "la miseria" ("Ojos" 185), pushes its characters constantly to the edge of despair. Paolo Po's *41, o un muchacho que soñaba en fantasmas,* perhaps Mexico's first real "queer novel,"[6] reveals an immensely vast subculture, but one fraught with violence, anxiety, empty promiscuity, and solitude. The even earlier appearance of Gus, a frivolous party boy (along with caricatures of the Contemporáneos), in Carlos Fuentes's *La región más transparente* in 1958 shows Mexican homosexuality to be decadent, vacuous.

The male homosexual personages of the early sixties in Mexico were a pretty ill adjusted bunch, but it is truly remarkable how common they had become. Suddenly, in the sixties, male homosexuality was coming to pervade Mexican narrative fiction. The crass sensationalism of Castrejón and the coy allusions of Villaurrutia were now becoming a visible part of the everyday landscape of Mexican culture. Confirming the assertion that the famous 41 were "bailarines estilo 'nuevo siglo' " [dancers in the style of the new century] (*El Popular,* November 25, 2001), Tomás Mediana (Fuentes's fictionalization of Villaurrutia in *La región más transparente*) refers to the literature of Rimbaud, Gide, and Proust as indicative of "una nueva sensibilidad que es de veras la nuestra, la de nuestro siglo" [a new sensibility that is truly ours, that of our century] (*La región* 147); only it appears that in Mexico, this new century was to really launch itself in the sixties.

Whether or not this new visibility can be attributed to Paz's portrayal of homosexuality as a concealed potential of Mexican machismo is arguable. What is clear is that what had been unmentionable in the nineteenth century, scandalous at the turn of the century, and un-Mexican and anti-revolutionary in the twenties and thirties, was now as an essential (if undesirable) part of Mexicanness as *la casa chica*. And while early literary representations were not necessarily positive, authors like Po and Barbachano Ponce were clearly sympathetic, opening the way for the queer literature inspired and informed by gay rights discourse that would emerge in Mexico by the late seventies in such authors as Luis Zapata, José Joaquín Blanco, and José Rafael Calva. If an increased openness about male homosexuality was an unexpected consequence of the upsurge in discourse on *lo mexicano*, Ramos and Paz had a less direct effect on the cause of feminism.

Ramos and Paz clearly did not promote misogyny and homophobia; they merely described a mentality, an ideology that they found to be preeminent in Mexico and central to popularly held notions of Mexicanness. They described what many Mexicans took for granted, laying the groundwork for the deep interrogation that literary feminists would begin to initiate with bravado by the fifties.

Postrevolutionary Masculinities:
Francisco Rojas González, José Revueltas,
Rosario Castellanos

Algo Horroroso

Discourse on femininity—femininity in women, that is, not effeminacy in men—was pretty limited in Mexican literature prior to Rosario Castellanos. Most of it confined itself to exploring and exploiting minor variations on two themes, that of the bad woman (the prostitute) and that of the good woman (the virgin, the mother). One

alternative that had begun to appear here and there was the masculine woman, the woman who was able somehow to take advantage of
male privilege by assuming its guise. In *Los de abajo*, La Pintada was
more than a *soldadera;* she was one of the guys, rough and aggressive
as any of them. Madeleine, protagonist of *La novia de Nervo*, went a
step further by disguising herself as a man and becoming a war hero.
Unforgettable as well are the "castrated" soldier women of *México
marimacho* and the superwoman/supermonster, Andréïda.

The Masculinity in women was to play out further, although with troubling ambivalence, in Rojas González's *La negra Angustias* (1944).
Referring to María Félix movies such as *Enamorada* (1947) in which
the *grande dame* of Mexican cinema plays strong, masculine women,
challenging patriarchal structures, ridiculing gendered hierarchies, se-
ducing Mexican viewers into a subversive world of female domination
over hapless men, only to be inevitably thwarted at the end of each
ultimately moralistic film, Jean Franco muses, "we have no means of
knowing how women spectators saw *Enamorada*. Did they simply
enjoy the spectacle of powerful María Félix without bothering about
the ending?" (*Plotting Women* 159). Rojas González presents his readers with a similar scenario: a plot that challenges notions of male
superiority, the violence of male heterosexuality, and essentialized gender difference, but that totally reverses itself in the end as if to say he
was only kidding.

The story traces the life of Angustias Farrera, a simple *campesina*
with a special characteristic: she is black. She is introduced singing
as she washes clothes and waiting on her aging father, who has an
illustrious past as a fearless highwayman. From the first, comparisons arise between *la negra* Angustias and Villaurrutia's *mulata de
Córdoba*. Like *la mulata*, Angustias is associated with witchcraft: her
mother having died in childbirth, Angustias is raised by her father
with significant help from the local *bruja* [witch or female shaman],
Señora Crescencia. The other distinguishing characteristic of *la mulata de Córdoba* is her sexuality, raw and primitive, unconstrained
by social convention. Angustias is not a loose woman; however she
is clearly a sexualized persona and before long is stalked by a local
oxherd, Laureano, who soon attempts to rape her. Here Angustias

remains a pure virgin, and it is Laureano whose sexuality is raw and primitive. Angustias, upon returning home from the attack, tells her father not that someone tried to rape her but that she was pounced upon by a coyote. Angustias presents herself as asexual. When a local boy from a rich family is fixed up to be Angustias's husband, she refuses, seeing him as "uno de tantos machos hinchados de vanidad y empecinados de repugnante lujuria" [one of so many male animals, swollen up with vanity and obstinate with repugnant lust] (27).

Her rejection of such a desirable young man spurs on a latent racism in the local community. Whispers begin: " 'Algo horroroso debe pasar al otro lado de las paredes de la casa de los negros. . . . ¡Algo horroroso! . . . ¡Algo horroroso!,' repitieron las voces sin precisar nada, sin señalar en qué consistía aquello que llevaba de pavor a las mujeres y repugnaba hasta las náuseas a los hombres" ["Something horrid must be happening on the other side of the walls of the black people's house. . . . Something horrid! . . . Something horrid!" repeated the voices without being in any way specific, without indicating what constituted that which inspired dread in women and repugnance, to the point of nausea, in men] (30). They speculate that if there are not incestuous relations going on between father and daughter, then she must be a lesbian. There is even a rumor that she is a pedophile and that she kidnapped a young girl.

Eventually, the villagers attempt to stone her to death, and if that is not enough, Laureano reappears to get his revenge. He thinks to himself, "tú, Angustias, tienes que ser mía, te me antojas por machota y despreciadora. . . . ¡Oíste! Me revolcaré contigo como un verraco y destrozaré tus entrañas igual que tu padre lo hizo con tantas mujeres" [you, Angustias, have to be mine, you whet my appetite with your manliness and contempt. . . . You hear! I will trample you like a boar and then destroy your entrails just like your father did with so many women] (44). When the "bestial" Laureano attempts to rape her again, she knifes him to death, then runs off until, exhausted, she falls unconscious in a field somewhere.

Angustias is soon awakened by three lusty *charros* who consider raping her, but instead take her captive and deliver her to their boss, Efrén el Picado, at his ranch, where she is enslaved as his mistress.

Luckily, another of his mistresses helps her escape, along with a sympathetic underling of Efrén known as el Güitlacoche. With him, she goes to Real de Animas, her father's old stomping ground, where she is treated as royalty because she is "la hija de Antón el negro, al que cantan los corridos de esta tierra; al que le alzan pelo todavía los mineros y los comerciantes ricos, pero al que quieren los probes [*sic*]" [the daughter of black Anton, who is the subject of so many local ballads, who still raises the hair of rich miners and businessmen, but who is loved by the poor] (80). Following in her father's footsteps, Angustias decides to become a hero of the poor by transforming herself into a leader in the revolutionary war. Unlike Garza's Madeleine, who must disguise herself as a man to become a World War I hero, Angustias is already practically a hero, and the community makes her a colonel in the revolutionary army.

One of her first acts is to capture her own captors, particularly Efrén el Picado. She has him brought before her and then declares, "Yo voy a juzgarlo a nombre de las mujeres, de ésas de las que usté [*sic*] se ha burlado, ésas que ha estropeado con su brusquedad y su estúpido orgullo de macho.... Las viejas, señor don Efrén, hablan ahoy [*sic*] por mi boca, y aquí mi boca manda" [I am going to judge you in the name of women, those whom you have mocked, those whom you've spoiled with your roughness and your stupid male pride.... The old ladies, Don Efrén sir, speak today through my mouth, and here my mouth is in charge] (91). As a punishment, she has her men castrate him. Afterward, Angustias expresses her joy, "¡... sólo así son menos malos los machos! ... ¡Si machos pueden llamarse el buey o el cerdo de engorda!" [... only like this are machos not so bad! ... If you can call oxen or castrated pigs machos!] (93). The civilization/barbarity discourse plays out clearly here. The barbarous men are too masculine, too heterosexual, in need of civilizing feminization.

Angustias not only despises men, she despises heterosexuality in general, at least the typically Mexican brand of heterosexuality in which women are subordinated to men and sexual intercourse is little more than rape. When a woman in love appeals to Angustias to spare her lover, *lo coronela* lashes out

Pos es otro caso más que veo en que una hembra busca y sigue así al macho. ¡Otra cabrita amarilla!.... Vergüenza había de darle, ofrecida cínica. ¡Asco de las mujeres! ¡Yo no entiendo eso, verdá [*sic*] de Dios! Yo no entiendo eso, pero sí siento repugnancia por usté [*sic*].... ¡Fuera de aquí, perra, a lamber [*sic*] otra cazuela!

Well this is one more case in which I see a female animal seeking out and following the male. Another yellow goat!... She should be ashamed, the brazen hussy. Scum of womankind! I swear to God I don't understand! I don't understand it, but I do feel repugnance for you.... Get out of here, dog, to lick some other pot! (114)

When the woman insists on protesting further and confesses that she is pregnant, Angustias rages on:

usté me sigue provocando vómitos y eso debo castigarlo a nombre de las mujeres. Usté, inmunda, que llama amor a su brama y que para calmarla sigue al macho con el celo de una verraca, tiene que llevar el castigo que merece.

you go on making me vomit and that should be punished in the name of womankind. You filthy thing, you call your animal heat love and then to calm it you follow the male animal with the fervor of a sow, you've got what's coming to you. (115)

Angustias then personally strips her naked, orders el Güitlacoche to whip her, and then lets her and her fiancé go. Such actions, although carried out "in the name of womankind" reflect a brutality associated only with men. As one observer of Angustias's troops notes, "Lástima que el más hombre de todos sea mujer" [What a shame that the most manly of all is a woman] (129).

A bit later, a "curro" [fancy city slicker], not unlike Luis Cervantes of *Los de abajo,* shows up with the idea, as he puts it, to "hacer de la de ustedes una revolución...decente, digna de merecer un juicio relevante de la opinión europea" [make of yours a decent revolution, worthy of a judgment relevant to European opinion] (153). In his mission to Europeanize, i.e., to civilize, the Mexican revolution, he takes it upon himself, among other things, to hire a tutor to teach the illiterate colonel to read. The effete tutor, Manuel de la Reguera y Pérez Cacho, mysteriously (and quite against his will) charms Angustias, but when she offers to marry him, her blond, upper-crust tutor refuses to compromise his social standing: "mi unión con usted sería considerada por la gente más que como un matrimonio como una cruzada absurda" [my union with you would be considered by people not so much a marriage as an absurd miscegenation] (176).

Hot-headed Angustias promptly kidnaps him, explaining:

> No, hijo, nada de cruzas absurdas. Es necesario que sepas que yo siento un asco terrible por los hombres; que los detesto y los odio por crueles y ordinarios, pero que me siento cabal para ser amiga de algunos y de soportarlos cerca de mí; no para que me empreñen, sino de esos que sepan enseñarme algo de lo mucho que tú sabes de letras y de geografía.... Por eso resolví cargar contigo y con tus melindres de señorita.

> No, son, nothing of absurd miscegenation. You need to know that I feel terrible disgust for men; that I detest them and hate them for being cruel and ordinary, but that it feels great to be a friend of some and to bear having them near me; not so that they'll impregnate me, I mean those who can teach me something out of all that you know of literature and geography.... That's why I resolved to burden myself with you and your girlish finickiness. (190)

The only possibility of heterosexuality for Angustias is one not based on the convention of procreation, but one in which it is the man who is girlish and the woman, of course, dominant and manly.

Rumors soon circulate that she has castrated Manolo just as she had Don Efrén. It is perhaps appropriate that Rojas González has chosen the genre of the novel of the revolution to interrogate Mexico's gender habitus more profoundly than the novels of Enriqueta or Garza, or the novellas and short stories of Nervo and the *modernistas* ever did. However, all subversiveness is lost in the last thirty or so pages, from the time that the previously asexual Angustias decides to seduce her Manolo in the same bushes where she previously killed Laureano. She then reverts to the role of the feminine and obedient housewife, while Manolo takes advantage of her war hero's pension and even goes so far as to install her in a *vecindad* [rudimentary tenement-like multifamily dwelling] where she spends her time washing clothes and singing as she had at the beginning of the story.[7]

The heroic rise of *La negra* Angustias, like that of Andréida, inevitably has to fail. Rojas González does not link Angustias's masculinity to an organized feminist threat; instead her masculinity is a single female's reaction to male violence. She is content doing laundry until she is sexually assaulted by an oxherd. The masculinity of Angustias is an indictment of Mexican masculinity and the spirit of *chingar.* Of course, the novel does not alter the stereotype so much as malign it. Angustias is Mexican, but every bit an outsider. She is not a *mestiza,* nor even an *india,* but a black woman. In reality, Mexico is not without an African immigrant population, but it is not a population in any way visible in Mexican high cultural production, and is completely absent from explorations of *lo mexicano.* Angustias not only is black but also comes from a background of witchcraft and crime. And to top it off, until she makes the very unconvincing shift from heroic and powerful *coronela* to humble housewife, she is a sexual outsider, either asexual or maybe lesbian, as *las malas lenguas* would have it.

Thus, the great virago is never quite Mexican, a point highlighted in her fade to obscurity after the war, and the fact that the war for her is not about Mexico and Mexicans so much as it is about women and men. She never makes a move in the name of *la patria,* but instead does so in the name of womankind. It is not, as we shall see, until Cousin Francisca of *Balún Canán* that Mexican literature sees a virago who does not meet a tragic downfall, although once again she must resort to witchcraft to survive.

Still, even in her fall from glory, Angustias lives out a critique of Mexican machismo. She castrates machos (although some might argue that Mexican masculinity is castrated to begin with);[8] she chooses the effeminate aristocrat over the *pelados* who surround her, then becomes living proof that it is not Mexican masculinity itself that results in the abuse of women by men. After all, her husband is "finicky" and "girlish," hardly worthy of being *el gran chingón,* and yet he is as abusive of her as Efrén el Picado or Laureano the oxherd. The deviations in behavior of Angustias and Manolo do not cancel out patriarchy. Angustias's giving in to heterosexual desire forces her to buy into patriarchy. In fact, in the late versions of the novel of the revolution, the complex network of male homosocial relations that constitute patriarchy take a new shape, and Mexican masculinity comes under fire like never before.

El Luto Masculino

In Guzmán's *La sombra del caudillo,* friendship existed only through hierarchical relations, hierarchical relations ensconced in violence. Recall the novel's bleak dictum: "en México si no le madruga usted a su contrario, su contrario le madruga a usted" [in Mexico if you don't strike down your rival, your rival will strike you down] (622). The verb "madrugar" reappears as key to male-male relations in José Revueltas's *El luto humano* [human mourning], a novel that deals not with the revolution itself but with the agrarian conflicts that followed it.

The first contact between men in the novel occurs when Úrsulo arrives in a rainstorm at the house of Adán, whom he rouses to help him cross the river in search of a priest to bless his infant daughter who has just died. Úrsulo shouts through the door that he wishes to cross the river and that his daughter has died. Adán cannot conceive of Úrsulo coming for help: "Miente —pensó... —es Úrsulo que viene a madrugarme" ["He's lying," he thought.... "it's Úrsulo and he's come to strike me down"]. Then, when asked again what he wants, "Úrsulo no dijo nada. Ahora pensaba, a su vez, que lo iban a matar" [Úrsulo didn't say anything. Now he too thought that he would be killed] (16).

The relations between men in *El luto humano* are never more cordial than this. Adán, in fact, does agree to take Úrsulo across the river in his boat to get the priest. While Adán turns out to be an exceptionally notorious character, famous for having killed and savagely tortured several rebel leaders, the relationships between other men in Revueltas's novel are not much nicer. Úrsulo's neighbor Calixto, even with his own wife nearby, openly flirts with Úrsulo's wife, Cecilia, at the wake for the dead infant. And when Jerónimo, intoxicated, passes out, even as flood waters are rising all around, neither Úrsulo nor Calixto will help their neighbor, forcing Jerónimo's wife to carry his body as they wade through the rising waters in search of higher ground.

Even Natividad, a heroic figure who had organized a strike against a government irrigation program and who does not participate in the main plot of the novel but is only remembered as a past protagonist in the other characters' lives, seems only to relate to other men through rivalries and antagonisms, and it is only through these rivalries that he is able to attain heroic stature. Tellingly, the only time when the term *hermano* is applied between men is in a scene in which Natividad challenges the treacherous Adán, an assassin for hire, to kill him, knowing that he doesn't have the strength of will to do so:

> —Nunca podrás matarme —dijo [Natividad] rotundo y sin abandonar su sonrisa, pues conocía ya los propósitos de Adán.
>
> Apretó éste los dientes, sin voluntad ni fuerza para agredir. Aun disparando, las balas no podrían tocar a este hombre, e incluso tocándolo no le causarían daño alguno, potente como era y confiado.

> "You'll never kill me," Natividad said bluntly without ceasing to smile, since he already knew Adán's purposes.
>
> The latter gritted his teeth, with neither the will nor the strength to attack. Even if he fired, the bullets couldn't touch this man, and even if they did touch him, they wouldn't cause him any harm, as potent and confident as he was.

Adán, then, backs off: "Otra vez será, hermano" [It'll have to be some other time, brother] (114). Friendship between men does not exist in *El luto humano,* with violent conflict, like that of Cain and Abel— an analogy made by Revueltas himself (179)—being the only way of relating and the closest anyone gets to brotherhood.

Adán finally does fulfill his charge from the government to kill Natividad on another occasion and is then assigned the murder of Úrsulo. Such cruel acts make Adán feel "poderoso, dueño del dolor y de la vida" [powerful, master of pain and of life] (174), although they ultimately reflect his powerlessness, his impotence. Like the mask of masculinity worn by *el pelado,* Adán's performative acts of aggression are mere strident manifestations of masculine protest, as he demonstrates in a scene with his wife: "Cuando propusieron la muerte de Úrsulo ... Adán aceptó, sintiéndose, cuando menos por algunos instantes, fuerte otra vez" [When they proposed that he kill Úrsulo ... Adán accepted, feeling, at least for a couple of moments, strong again]. When his wife, la Borrada, warns him against taking on another peasant hero, he slaps her across the face, sending her, lips bleeding, in meek retreat into a corner. It is then that his true inner weakness becomes apparent to him:

> Ahora reconocíase vencido. Aquel bofetón sobre el rostro de la Borrada no era otra cosa que un medio para afirmar su endeble poder. No era más que una demostración de su incapacidad y su falta de fuerzas. "Ya no soy el mismo," díjose.

> Now he recognized his defeat. That slap across the face of la Borrada was nothing but a means of affirming his frail power. It was nothing more than a demonstration of his inadequacy and lack of strength. "I'm no longer the same," he said to himself. (180)

To *madrugar* a fellow man is a means of asserting one's manhood, albeit falsely, because the need to flagrantly assert manhood is masculine protest. This does not mean that such acts fail in their superficial goals. Úrsulo clearly still fears Adán, regardless of the fact that Adán has come face to face with his impotence. Adán has killed the heroic Natividad and appears to be, in a sense, the local *gran chingón*.

However, to *madrugar* a woman, although a routine manifestation of Mexican masculinity, is even stronger proof of a man's inherent weakness. Women are beaten left and right in *El luto humano*. Calixto's wife, Calixta, is happy to leave the hotel where she works (as a prostitute) to marry Calixto because she believes that Calixto will beat her less often than her boss: "Estaba acostumbrada a los golpes y no podía concebir que los hombres dejasen de pegarle a sus mujeres. ... Tan sólo pedía un poco de menos rigor, de menos brutalidad" [She was used to the beatings and couldn't imagine that men might stop beating their women. ... She only asked for a little less force, less brutality] (104–5).

Even Úrsulo, who seems more sensitive than Adán or Calixto, has the desire to beat his wife because he believes that "dañándola, hiriéndola, la sentiría suya" [hurting her, injuring her, he would feel

like she was his] (49); physical violence will put on a show of the possession, a performance of his power over her, a power that he does not
in fact hold. Úrsulo feels a "cólera impotente" [impotent rage] upon
realizing that "Cecilia era dueña de una fuerza ante la cual Úrsulo se
daba cuenta de la derrota" [Cecilia possessed a force before which
Úrsulo realized his defeat] (44). His desire to beat her rises out his
feelings of impotence. Likewise, sex is neither erotic nor productive
for Úrsulo: it is an act of possession, a performance once again that
fails, a mere pose of masculine supremacy:

> Úrsulo no había fecundado a Cecilia por impluso de procreación,
> sino tan sólo para poseerla sin límites; para adueñarse de su alma.
> Este propietario descomunal no aspiraba al cuerpo, sino al señorío de
> espíritu, y había ultrajado los rincones más inalienables de Cecilia.

> Úrsulo hadn't fecundated Cecilia on an impulse of procreation, but only
> in order to possess her without limits; to take ownership of her soul.
> This extraordinary proprietor did not aspire to the body, but to the
> dominion of the spirit, and had outraged the most inalienable corners
> of Cecilia's being. (84–85)

Here, the term *madrugar* gives way to its near synonym *chingar,* with
the sexual symbolism of Úrsulo's relations with Cecilia now apparent.
Úrsulo would assert his power to possess Cecilia by beating her or
by penetrating her. Heterosexual relations, which in *El luto humano*
include little more than domestic violence and rape, are just another
manifestation of masculine protest.

This nasty masculinity in which friendship and homosocial bonding seem no longer possible comes to be commonplace in Mexican
literature by the forties. The old days of duels turning into lifelong
friendships (*El fistol del diablo*), merry bands of brigands who become blood brothers (*Astucia*), and fraternal love between men as the
major metaphor of cultural cohesion (*El Periquillo Sarniento*) that
we saw in the nineteenth century are gone. Now the threat of homosexuality is so strong and so feared that men can no longer relate
except to *madrugar* or *chingar*. Other major male protagonists of the
age including Pedro Páramo, Artemio Cruz (*La muerte de Artemio
Cruz* by Carlos Fuentes) and his predecessor Federico Robles of *La*

región más transparente, César Argüellos of *Balún Canán,* and General Francisco Rosas of Elena Garro's *Recuerdos del porvenir* behave similarly.[9] All of them make shows of asserting their power over other men, often violently, and all of them abuse women (by beating, raping, humiliating, deceiving, and/or confining them).

Los Hijos de la Malinche

Paz famously uses the phrase "los hijos de la Malinche" to designate Mexican men as *mestizo* sons born of white fathers and indigenous mothers. Following Paz's scheme, Mexicans are "hijos," sons, and not fathers, while mother imagery in Mexico is so strong that it is said that "la familia mexicana sufre de exceso de madre y falta de padre" [the Mexican family suffers from an excess of mother and a lack of father].[10] Daughters and fathers are absent from the symbolic family of Mexico, which is reduced to a mother-son dyad. In terms of deities, Mexicans worship the mother, the Virgin of Guadalupe, but not the father: "no existe una veneración especial por el Dios padre de la Trinidad, figura más bien borrosa. En cambio, es muy frecuente y constante la devoción a Cristo, el Dios hijo, el Dios joven, sobre todo como víctima redentadora" [there is no special veneration for the Trinity's God the father, a rather sketchy figure. On the other hand, devotion to Christ, the son of God, is frequent and constant, especially in his incarnation as redemptive victim] (*El laberinto* 75).

Paz traces the tradition of son worship to pre-Hispanic cultures in which son-Gods such as Huitzilopochtli and Xipe Totec predominated in the pantheon. Meanwhile, modern father images are weak. Paz writes, "Hidalgo, el 'padre de la patria,' como es costumbre de llamarlo en la jerga ritual de la República, es un anciano inerme, más encarnación del pueblo desvalido frente a la fuerza que imagen del poder y la cólera del padre terrible" [Hidalgo, the "father of the fatherland," as he is customarily known in the ritual jargon of the Republic, is a harmless old man, more an incarnation of the populace crippled in the face of power than an image of the strength and rage of the almighty father] (74).

Paternity, in fact, becomes a particular problem in the literature of postrevolutionary Mexico. In Mexico's early canonical novels such as *El Periquillo Sarniento* and *Astucia,* fathers do play a role but disappear quickly from the narrative. More often they are missing entirely, as in the case of the families of Julia (Riva Palacio's *Los piratas del Golfo*), Manuela (Altamirano's *El Zarco*), Teresa (Payno's *El fistol del diablo*), or Gamboa's Santa—which is not to say they are not missed. In the case of Cuéllar's Chucho el Ninfo, the protagonist's chief character flaws are due to his mother's overprotectiveness and the absence of a male role model—not to mention her impulse to dress her young son up as a girl (9). Fathers, although rarely appearing in major roles in early Mexican literature, are of central importance in Mexican society, as authors like Lizardi make clear again and again when they urge that fathers take an active role in educating their male children in order to keep them from turning out effeminate.

However, by the 1940s, fathers seem to have lost much of their good name in Mexico. In *La negra Angustias,* the father is, like *el padre* Hidalgo, old and impotent. In *El luto humano,* even young fathers are inferior beings. Cecilia's maternity is of such force that her husband becomes her son, or worse, is feminized into a daughterlike role: "Cecilia volvió su rostro maternal (tan maternal que ya de pronto él, Úrsulo, era como su propio hijo, como su propia hija)" [Cecilia turned her maternal face (so maternal that suddenly he, Úrusulo, was like her own son, like her own daughter)] (14). Úrsulo, himself, recalls his mother, whom he never even knew, as a goddess:

> Su madre murió al darlo la luz y una antigua leyenda del país contaba de la diosa indígena que pariera desde el cielo un cuchillo de obsidiana. Al estrellarse, de las astillas negras y relucientes del cuchillo había nacido la primera pareja humana.... Úrsulo era hijo del cuchillo de obsidiana, y su madre la diosa misma, una joven diosa.

> His mother died giving birth to him and an ancient legend of the country tells of the indigenous goddess who gave birth from the heavens to an obsidian knife. With a crash, from the knife's shiny black splinters the first human couple was born.... Úrsulo was a child of the obsidian knife, and his mother the goddess herself, the young goddess. (61–62)

His father, of course, was "todo un señor español, como sus antiguos abuelos" [fully a Spanish lord, like his ancient grandfathers] (63) and Úrsulo (*el hijo de la chingada*) had been conceived by rape.

Balún Canán

The theme of the centrality of the son in Mexican culture is played out once again (as it is bitingly criticized) in Rosario Castellanos's 1957 novel, *Balún Canán*. Castellanos, Mexico's first feminist to achieve major success as a writer, in a later essay sarcastically lauds Lázaro Cárdenas, who was president during the time in which the novel is set for his land reform campaigns, which attempted to materially aid the indigenous peoples of places like Chiapas. These campaigns resulted in the impoverishment of some old white families such as her own, forcing her to break tradition and, rather than learn to be a lady and the mistress of a house, go off to Mexico City to get a formal education.[11] University education was not necessary for daughters who needed only to get married off to a rich husband. The future of the family lay in the person of the son.

In *Balún Canán*, the father of the Argüellos family, César, does wield a certain power. He is a wealthy landowner and as such is respected by the peasants of his land. Ernesto, bastard son of César's brother (and therefore never fully a member of the family), sees "fuerza" [power] and "invulnerabilidad" [invulnerability] in César (77). Their relationship is a static one in which Ernesto constantly tries to prove himself to César, and César constantly asserts his superiority over Ernesto by evoking his status as landowner and patriarch. César also holds a certain power over the women of his plantation. Indian women, it is said, want to be impregnated by him so that their sons will have some of his blood, and he is known by everyone including his wife as the "semental mayor de la finca" [greatest stud of the ranch] (81). And yet, as with so many other male characters of the literature of the age (Adán from *El luto humano,* Pedro Páramo, Artemio Cruz, to name just a few), his power is all a pose. It exists only so long as everyone else believes that it does.

Cousin Francisca, for example, eventually shows herself to be more "manly" than César by better protecting her land, by remaining stubbornly impenetrable. As she herself asserts:

> Pero yo soy la que se queda y ustedes los que se van, los que huyen. No era Chactajal nada para defenderlo. Eso tú lo sabrás, César, cuando

tan fácilmente lo abandonas. Somos de distintos linajes. Yo no cedo
nunca lo mío. Ni muerta soltaré lo que me pertenece. Y así pueden
venir todos y quebrarme las manos. Que no las abriré para soltar el
puñado de tierra que me llevaré conmigo.

But I'm the one who's staying and you are the ones who are going, who
are fleeing. Chactajal was nothing worth defending. You should know
that, César, since you are abandoning it so easily. We are from distinct
lineages. I never cede what's mine. Not even in death will I let go of
what belongs to me. So let them all come and break my hands. But I
will not open them and let go of the fistful of land that I will take with
me. (218–19)

It would seem not that the two cousins are of distinct lineages, but of
distinct genders. Francisca, woman "de zalea y machete" [of rough
sheepskin and machete] (114), acts the macho by not giving in, while
César is forced into retreat. The problem is that the peasants no longer
believe in his power. Once they had been docile, but now they no
longer respond to his orders except at gunpoint. By the end of the
novel, it is clear that César's power was only a flimsy lie.

Still, masculinity retains its *cachet* in *Balún Canán*. Even as the
family is forced to recognize its downfall, which is César's downfall,
they continue to believe in a future imagined through the life of their
son. Of course, it is their daughter who narrates the novel, a daughter
who is clearly of secondary importance to both parents. Early in the
novel, Zoraida, the mother, reflects, "Gracias a Dios tengo mis dos
hijos. Y uno es varón" [Thank God that I have my two children. And
that one of them is male] (92). In fact, there is a struggle between César
and Zoraida over their son, Mario. César believes that as a young man
he should learn the manly skills of a cowboy, while Zoraida protects
him from physically challenging activities in hopes of cultivating his
brain and sending him off to study in Mexico City to become rich and
successful. No one worries about the daughter's future.

The importance of the male child to the family does not go unnoticed by the revolting peasants who unleash sorcerers on him,
causing him to fall ill. Zoraida becomes frantic as she sees her young
son begin to waste away, pleading at one point with a female shaman
for help, "Es el único varón. Y es necesario que se logre. Es necesario"

[He's the only male child. And it is necessary that he come of age. It is necessary] (242). But neither she nor a priest can help. When the latter tries to comfort Zoraida by asking her to have faith and to accept God's will, she becomes hysterical, "Si Dios quiere cebarse en mis hijos. . . . ¡Pero no en el varón! ¡No en el varón!" [If God wishes to vent his fury on my children. . . . But not on the male child! Not on the male child!] (250). The ultimate destruction of the family comes not from César's loss of face, but from the death of the son, the symbolic core of the family.

Although Castellanos is not as concerned with national allegory as Rulfo or Revueltas appears to be, her focus on the figure of the son is consistent with national discourse of masculinity. Paternity is almost an animalistic function. Men breed with all classes of women: wives, employees, townsfolk, etc. César is the father of many children with many different women. Sex is one more way of asserting power; it is always a kind of rape: to procreate is to *chingar*. However, fathering children is not the same as being a father. Santiago Ramírez finds "la psicopatía del mexicano" [the psychopathy of the Mexican male] to lie in a machismo that refuses to recognize authority because Mexican men have no father figures with which to identify. In other words, Mexicans, especially Mexican *machos,* are perpetual sons, never evolving into fathers (83). *Pedro Páramo* is not really a tale of patricide because Páramo never assumes his role of father anyway.[12] His *machismo* is not a reflection of his fatherly strength, but of a youthful rebelliousness against authority, a rebelliousness that never matures. In Castellanos, the shamans who target Mario attack the Mexican family in its most vulnerable spot, the point of greatest symbolic consequence. The death of the landlord's son, attributed as it is to the witchcraft of local peasants (with the complicity of his own sister), allegorizes the demise of the wealthy, white, or even *mestizo* landowning class in Chiapas, and perhaps the demise of patriarchy. *Lo mexicano* is no longer just white male landowners; the indigenous peasants (and women) who kill Mario are a force to be reckoned with, and part of the nation as well. Castellanos's vision is not, of course, one of a unified *mestizo* Mexico, but one of a racially factionalized Mexico, a Mexico with unresolved cultural rifts and gender discord, a national identity fragmented and conflictive. An old version of Mexicanness is dead, although no single persona steps in to replace *el hijo de la chingada*.

Border Masculinities

Pocho

It is not only in the south that the Mexican son is a synecdoche for Mexicanness. In the north, Mexican immigrants bring their notions of Mexicanness to the southwest of the United States through a literature centered on sons. The struggles of the sons of immigrant families to understand their heritage, to assert their Mexicanness, and to assimilate into U.S. society carve out the plots to early Chicano novels including Américo Paredes's *George Washington Gómez* (written in 1940, finally published in 1990), John Rechy's *City of Night* (1963), and José Antonio Villarreal's *Pocho* (1959).

Paternity is a key issue in all of these texts, particularly as it pertains to the personal development of the young sons who are their protagonists. Both Guálinto Gómez, the main character of Paredes's novel, and the hustler who narrates *City of Night* are fatherless. Gómez is raised by his mother and an uncle, his lost father's identity and reputed heroism of crucial importance to young Guálinto. The Rulfian theme of patricide (without paternity) arises unexpectedly near the end of the novel, along with a very Mexican assault on the character of the absentee father. Guálinto's murder, in self-defense, of the roguish criminal who turns out to be his long lost father, becomes an act of involuntary heroism.

Rechy's protagonist speaks of his father only in the past tense. He remembers his father as "a defeated old man" who had been a renowned orchestra conductor in Mexico, but was reduced to being a hospital janitor in the United States (13). The narrator detests him for his savage fits of anger and recalls that his fearful mother refused to share a bed with him. He calls him "a failure—as a man, as a father!" (17), a fact that the narrator links to his own rebellion against God. When his father dies, he declares, "I know that now Forever I will have no father, that he had been unfound" (19).

Richard Rubio, the protagonist of *Pocho,* does have a father, although the latter is once again of problematic but most significant influence on the character of his son. Juan Rubio is a character right out of any novel of the Mexican revolution; Luis Leal, in fact, finds him quite similar to Demetrio Macías of *Los de abajo* (*Aztlán* 39). Juan is both a distant cousin of Emiliano Zapata and a devoted officer in the troops of Pancho Villa. His devotion to Villa is such that at one point he comments, "He [Villa] was telling me to go die for him and it might help him win his battle and I knew it, but at that moment if he had asked me to turn my backside and submit to him, I would have done it without a qualm. So I rode toward the enemy" [11]. The male homosocial relations marked by images of anal penetration and the sexual symbolism of manliness mark Juan Rubio as distinctly Mexican. A remark he makes about Villa ("How can they kill a man like that—a man with such balls" [11]), and another remark made to Rubio ("I will tell you about courage. I left my gonads in Torreón, I left them in Zacatecas . . . and I finally lost them at Celaya" [14]) make this well-known Mexican link between manliness and male genitals. Recall what Ramos wrote: "Para el 'pelado,' un hombre que triunfa en cualquier actividad y en cualquier parte, es porque tiene 'muchos huevos' " [For the *pelado,* when a man triumphs anywhere in any activity, it is because he has "a lot of balls"] (55) and "[l]a terminología del 'pelado' abunda en alusiones sexuales que revelan una obsesión fálica, nacida para considerar el órgano sexual como símbolo de la fuerza masculina" [the terminology of the *pelado* abounds in sexual allusions that reveal a phallic obsession that views the sexual organ as a symbol of masculine force] (54).

Such imagery continues to be important in *Pocho,* even after Juan Rubio flees north as "part of the great exodus that came of the Mexican Revolution" (15). When Richard is born, one of the first things Juan Rubio notes about him is that his "genitalia seemed enormous in proportion to [his] little body" (31). "Enormous" was, of course, the only word used to give any idea of the physical attributes of the best known literary symbol of national masculinity of mid-century, Pedro Páramo. The adjective was applied by his servant and procuress Damiana Cisneros when she observed him going to rape a young servant girl in the middle of the night (Rulfo 154). Later, at age twelve, *Pocho* protagonist Richard Rubio feels that his mother loves him too much and that this might make him into a hermaphrodite; but when he wakes up with "a hardon, and it was a real good one," he is reassured of his manhood and dreams of becoming a cowboy (96).

Pocho is a story of assimilation, of culture clash, of the struggles of a family of Mexican immigrants to make a life for themselves in the United States. Among the most important issues that they must confront is that of gender relations and gender difference. In Mexican heterosexual relations, of course, a woman's selfless submission to her husband is a given. Richard's mother is counseled on her wedding day "that she should submit to anything intimate [her husband] should want to do. It would be unpleasant all her life...but it was the lot of all women to satisfy the desires of their man" (127) and married life in Mexico turns out to be quite tough. But once in the United States, Richard's mother quite logically welcomes assimilation with regard to gender attitudes: " 'We have certain rights in this country,' she said. 'It is not the primitive way here that it is in Mexico' " (93). Yet even as her own shifts in attitude break up her marriage, she advises Richard "to marry a Mexican woman, because only a Mexican woman can appreciate the fact that her husband is a man" (94). Ironically, adolescent Richard selects neighborhood tomboy Zelda (an "Anglo") as his steady girlfriend and adolescent sex partner, the narrator remarking, "They never tired of each other's young virility" (144).

Richard's sexuality seems always to be in question, even after he realizes that he is not becoming a hermaphrodite. Juan Rubio confesses to his son that he has worried about Richard's sexuality: "for a long time I thought you would become like that. Because you had the bad lot to live with a houseful of girls, and your mother protected you so much" (168). When an intellectual mentor of Richard's turns out to be a pedophile, Richard has to reassure his father, "And you must not worry about me....I have a feeling for girls already" (90). Early adolescent Richard also makes the mistake of declaring his love for his young buddy, Ricky, who reacts, "Hey, you're not going queer, are you?" Richard is forced to defend his position: "Jesus...You said you love your father—you thinking of sticking him or blowing him?" (112). Years later, suspicion falls on Richard again when he is seen "in San Jose with a couple of guys that looked queer as hell." Richard defends them, while maintaining his own heterosexuality, of course:

> And those two guys you were talking about—they're queer, and they have a bunch of friends that are the same way, but they're real intelligent and good people. They just happen to be like that, that's all. Like a guy with only one leg, or a deaf-and-dumb guy, or a guy with the con. They can't help it, but they make the most of their life. And, another thing—they like being that way, and they never fool with me, because they know I'm straight, and I respect them for that. Those two guys live together, and they really love each other. You ought to see them, how nice they talk to each other and the way they take care of one another. Hell, even married people don't act that good. (177–78)

If Villarreal elaborates gender difference in the United States as something less crucial than it is in Mexico, he does not, as it might appear here, locate homosexuality as a phenomenon exclusive to the United States. Juan Rubio had in fact immigrated to the United States in the company of a reporter who he suspects of having been "one of 'those others'" (168). René is a character comparable to Azuela's possibly queer Luis Cervantes and just as Cervantes strives to cultivate a close relationship with Demetrio Macías, René prides himself on his former role as the right hand of a revolutionary general.

Gender conflict eventually drives Juan Rubio from the house, leaving Richard to fill his shoes. However, like Demetrio Macías before him, Richard is uneasy in the role of man of the house and decides to enlist in the armed forces as a means of escape. The Mexican army is a male homosocial institution in which hierarchies are established and reinforced through an imagery of anal penetration, but it is really more of a place where men attempt to reinforce their masculinity than one in which they go to live out homosexual fantasies. The U.S. Army, on the other hand, has a troublesome image in Mexican literature dating back to Villaurrutia's "Nocturno de los ángeles" in which sailors, presumably members of the U.S. armed forces, engage in homosexual promiscuity in Los Angeles (it should be noted that Richard chooses specifically to join the navy). One of *Sodoma pide fuero*'s fiercest indictments is that "[m]iles y miles de homosexuales se hallan incorporados al Ejército de los Estados Unidos" [thousands upon thousands of homosexuals can be found incorporated in the Army of the United States] (Ferrer Torrents and D'Oc 41), giving the example of "aquellas orgías homosexuales de los marineros de la base de San Diego" [those homosexual orgies of the sailors of the San Diego base] (13). Is Richard following in the footsteps of Demetrio Macías, fortifying his manhood among the men of the armed forces, or in those of Luis Cervantes, collocating himself among men out of a desire for homosocial companionship quite possibly indicating a repressed homosexuality?

Meanwhile Juan Rubio is "fanatical about masculinity" (90). As he tells Richard, "you are a man, and it is good because to a Mexican being *that* is the most important thing. If you are a man, your life is half lived; what follows does not really matter" (131). Interestingly, it is at the same moment that Richard renounces male privilege that he also renounces Mexicanness itself: "And he knew that he could never again be wholly Mexican, and furthermore he could never use the right he had as a male to tell his mother that she was wrong" (95).

Yet is Mexican masculinity feminized by assimilation into a more "civilized" culture, or is it forced into a "feminine" position by relations of political power at large? Mexico is economically weaker than its northern neighbor and has lost important military battles to *yanqui* imperialism. Rogelio Díaz-Guerrero psychoanalyzes quite a different stereotype, that of the lazy, abnegating, obedient, self-sacrificing, submissive, dependent, polite and courteous, "passive" Mexican (120–21) versus the more aggressive, competitive, independent, contentious, "active" style common to men of the United States (129), attributing psychological difference to historical political relations. Perhaps this explains the attitudes of the *pachucos* whom Richard joins up with at one point:

> They had a burning contempt for people of a different ancestry, whom they called Americans, and a marked hauteur toward México and toward their parents for their old-country ways. The former feeling came from a sense of inferiority that is a prominent characteristic in any

Mexican reared in southern California, and the latter was an inexplicable compensation for that feeling. They needed to feel superior to something, which is a natural thing. The result is that they attempted to segregate themselves from both their cultures, and became a truly lost race. (149)

Villarreal points out the specificity of Mexicanness in the United States. The sense of inferiority with regard to the United States is particularly pronounced for "any Mexican reared in southern California" (149).

The ultimate contestation to this cultural war of masculinities comes not from Villarreal but from John Rechy in *City of Night*, a novel that barely touches upon the Mexican background of its protagonist, but that etches out a vision of American masculinity that practically plagiarizes Ramos's vision of *lo mexicano*. The term "American" is Rechy's, as his novel tours the great cities of his semi-mythical "America." And yet Rechy's America is perhaps born as much out of Xavier Villaurrutia and Samuel Ramos as it is out of Walt Whitman.

Although when he lists the favorite writers of his youth, Rechy counts no Mexicans among the thirty-odd names (with Lorca as the only Spanish-language writer in the list) (x–xi), there are several strikingly Villaurrutian moments in *City of Night*. In "Nocturno de los ángeles," Villaurrutia describes a scene of nocturnal cruising in Los Angeles in which "las cinco letras del DESEO formarían una enorme cicatriz luminosa" [the six letters of DESIRE would form a huge luminous scar] (*Obras* 55) as if there were a great neon sign overlooking the action. In Rechy's Times Square: "Giant signs—Bigger! Than! Life!—blink off and on. And a great hungry sign groping luridly at the darkness screams: F*A*S*C*I*N*A*T*I*O*N" (30), once again overlooking the queer street cruising that goes on below. Villaurrutia introduces his street cruisers: "¡Son los ángeles! Han bajado a la tierra por invisibles escalas. Vienen del mar, que es el espejo del cielo, en barcos de humo y sombra, a fundirse y confundirse con los mortales" [They are the angels! They have dropped down to earth on invisible ladders. They come from the sea, which is the mirror of the heavens, on ships of smoke and shadow, to fuse and confuse themselves with the mortals] (*Obras* 56). Rechy's eccentric Tante Goulu moves the scene to San Diego, where he is explicit that there is a category of "angels" who are sailors. "I suppose perhaps they are the original angels. I would watch them . . . as they invaded our streets, descending, all white, as if they just arrived from Heaven, scattering themselves among the rest of us, unworthy mortals!" (63).[13]

Villaurrutia's angels never come to take a very specific form; his poetry was rarely populated by anything more tangible than shadows or echoes. Rechy too has shadows: "By now, of course, I have met several of the shadows along Times Square" (33). However, Rechy's do become quite well developed, particularly through his characterizations of street hustlers. His narrator learns to be a hustler by cruising Times Square, where he "would discover that to many of the street people a hustler became more attractive in direct relation to his seeming insensitivity—his 'toughness.' I would wear that mask" (32–33). Yet these same street people, the "scores" of the hustlers, were perfectly conscious of the masks their fantasy hustlers wore:

> I became aware of overtones of defensive derision aimed by some scores at those youngmen they picked up for the very masculinity they would later disparage—as if convinced, or needfully proclaiming their conviction, that the more masculine a hustler, the more his masculinity is a subterfuge. (54)

The masks of toughness that the hustlers wear do not appear to be much different from the Adlerian masks of masculinity worn by Ramos's *pelados*. This conclusion is born out by what lies beneath the masks. One particularly attractive Hollywood hustler, Lance, "valiantly dropped the mask: He desired young males like himself, and he admitted it openly" (185).

Here Rechy goes a step beyond Ramos. Hypermasculinity in Rechy masks effeminacy and homosexuality. For this reason, the hypermasculine male hustlers are even greater a threat than drag queens. In a police raid, the narrator notes that "theyre [*sic*] avoiding questioning the queens; concentrating on the malehustlers as if the hustlers' presence somehow threatens them personally" (295). If the hustlers are really queer under their virile façades, any man might be.

Moreover, as Mexican masculinity, according to Paz, is proved through male homosocial competitions that turn symbolically homosexual as the winner metaphorically fucks the loser, in *City of Night*, the hustlers' masculinity is proved by the fact that other men desire them as men. Sylvia, wise observer of the queer scene in New Orleans, describes the representative scenario of a young man "hustling a score, trying to prove with another man . . . that he *is* a man . . . even if he has to prove it by finding another man who will pay him for his . . . masculinity" (314). In Rechy's queer underworld, *albures* play out quite literally, for the same gendered stakes. The setting is the United States, but the cultural connections with Mexico, intentional or not, are clear. The queer masculinity of early Mexican American writers such as Villarreal and Rechy continue to play out the conflicts of Mexican masculinities, but now in the geographical context of the United States.

Conclusions

Mexican masculinity, then, from the forties became an even more troublesome topic than it had been in the past. The growing consciousness of the inability to make a pure and distinct separation between virility and effeminacy, between homosocial and homosexual relations, particularly in a national context was kindled by the psychoanalysis of the national character initiated in Ramos and made world famous by Paz. Masculinity came to be intrinsically linked with notions like Guzmán's *madrugar* and Paz's more sexualized version of the same idea, *chingar*. Increased paranoia about and repression of homosexuality in the national forum in the fifties led to the emergence of the male homosexual as a commonplace in Mexico's cultural production of the sixties. Meanwhile, fatherhood was demonized as the son became more the focus of the literature of nation than ever: Mexicans are *los hijos de la Chingada*. Finally, as Mexican literature increasingly made its way north, crossing geographic and linguistic borders, Mexican notions of Mexican masculinity dueled with Mexican notions of U.S. masculinity, these battles playing themselves out most interestingly in the novels of Mexican-American authors.

I return a last time to Villarreal's *Pocho* for a symbolic closing gesture. In this novel, Juan Rubio's Mexican masculinity is tested as he attempts to make a life in the unwelcoming environment of the United States; likewise, his son Richard must learn to be masculine living between two cultures whose ideas of masculinity often conflict. The antagonisms between the two men finally culminate in a physical battle in which Richard is knocked unconscious. The scene ends with a teary reconciliation in which Juan urges his son, "Do not ever forget that you are Mexican," to which Richard responds, "I could never forget that!" Finally, as they part, Richard asks his father for "un abrazo" [a hug], which results in a rather shocking display: "They put their arms around each other in the Mexican way. Then Juan Rubio kissed his son on the mouth" (169). This kiss, overstepping the limits of masculine decorum, indicates the queer edge that commonly held notions of masculinity cannot shake off in either culture, a queer edge that can be dissimulated, contested, manipulated, or accepted. For a moment, the Rubio men let down their guard and act out this inevitable queerness, performing the paradox of masculinity that depends on homosocial bonding while vainly denying homosexual desire.

Conclusion

The Trials and Tribulations of los Hijos de la Chingada

Pedro Páramo

Pedro Páramo is Mexico's best known and most highly acclaimed novel of mid-century, and as it focuses attention on many of the same issues that have guided this study, I have chosen it to outline my summary of how notions of masculinity and male sexuality have shifted in the national context from independence to the mid-twentieth century. *Pedro Páramo* is yet another Mexican novel whose main protagonist is a son. Like his now nearly ancient ancestor el Periquillo Sarniento, Juan Preciado is on a quest in search of his father, in this case his biological father (as opposed to the father figures sought in Lizardi's novel). However, this biological father, Pedro Páramo, has been entirely absent from his son's life, and like so many Mexican literary families (protagonists of Altamirano's *El Zarco*, Cuéllar's *Chucho el Ninfo*, Riva Palacio's *Los piratas del Golfo*, Gamboa's *Santa*, Urzaiz's *Eugenia*, etc.), Juan's is without a father figure of any kind. He is his mother's son and uses her last name; early in the novel, he states why he has come to Comala, to find "aquel señor llamado Pedro Páramo, el marido de mi madre" [that man named Pedro Páramo, the husband of my mother] (8).

Once again, it is the mother, as Granillo argued so convincingly ("La abnegación"), who holds together and rules the Mexican family. Preciado never has the chance to confront his father, experiencing him only through rumors and echoes, but manages to meet a series of substitute mother figures including one who nearly bore him ("yo estuve a punto de ser tu madre" [I was on the verge of becoming your mother] [25]) and another who had taken care of him as an infant ("Te conozco desde que abriste los ojos" [I've known you ever since you first opened your eyes] [50]). And while Páramo goes ballistic when his father is killed, his intimate memories feature dialogues with his *amada* Susana, his mother, and his grandmother, but never with Don Lucas. Franco argues that Páramo represents a paternalistic feudal order that no longer exists, even though the belief in it still might exist (*Critical Passions* 429–46). The *cacique* Pedro Páramo for Franco is "an anachronism" (442), and for Bastos and Molloy, "an illusion" (267); they argue that "lo femenino circunscribe y signa la novela a pesar de que un hombre parezca ser el eje de su argumento" [the feminine circumscribes and marks the novel despite the fact that a man appears to be the axis of its argument] (247).

And yet the patriarchy that Páramo represents does carry with it a visible show of power. The "enormous" figure of Pedro Páramo literally rules the town. He never takes on the responsibilities of a father, except arguably with his rapacious son Miguel, yet he is the biological father of nearly everyone in town. No authority is greater than his in Comala, not the law—at one point, he decides to usurp some of his neighbor's land, commenting to his right hand, Fulgor Sedano, "¿Cuáles leyes, Fulgor? La ley de ahora en adelante la vamos a hacer nosotros" [What laws, Fulgor? From now on we are going to be the law] (60)—nor religion—his control of the church, which he buys, makes him godlike, or better put, diabolical; Bartolomé San Juan calls him "la pura maldad" [pure evil] (123). When the revolutionary army arrives at his ranch to rob and plunder, he bribes them and tricks them into submitting to his control. Later, when they ask for the money he's promised them, he retorts to their leader, "¿Para qué crees que andas en la revolución? Si vas a pedir limosna estás atrasado. Valía más que mejor te fueras con tu mujer a cuidar gallinas. ¡Échate sobre algún pueblo!" [What do you think you're doing in the revolution? If you're going to ask for alms you're backward. You'd have been better off going back to your wife to raise chickens. Go throw yourself on some town!] (157). Páramo, the small-town cacique, is more powerful than the revolution itself. Or so it would seem.

Before long it becomes clear—as it did in Lizardi, in Azuela, in Ramos, in Castellanos, etc.—that his masculine power is by no means inherent, and is in fact quite superficial. Women who are afraid of him will submit to whatever he wants, but the woman he loves most, Susana San Juan, pays him no mind whatsoever and remains outside of his control. When one of his illegitimate sons, Abundio Martínez, finally murders him, he "se fue desmoronando como si fuera un montón de piedras" [crumbled as if he were a pile of stones] (181). His masculine power was a mask that served him well as long as everyone believed in it. Preciado's mother sends her son to extract revenge, urging him, "cóbraselo caro" [make him pay dearly] (8), as if hoping to get him to pay cash for years of neglect. But what Juan reveals in his journey among the phantasms of Comala is perhaps of greater value for Mexican sons and mothers who have endured the cult of machismo: it's all show. Of course the often ingenuous *pícaro*, Pedro Sarmiento, could have told them that a century and a half before.

The State of Male Homosocial Bonding: ¿Sodoma Pide Fuero?

However, not all has remained the same. Most striking is the role of male homosocial bonding in allegorical constructions of nation. The male bonding so central to nineteenth-century literature was contaminated by the emerging discourse on homosexuality at the turn of the century. However, homosexuality was quickly made safe by equating it with effeminacy in men. If only effeminate men were homosexuals, male bonding among *machos* remained kosher. Homosocial relations among men remained key to literary Mexicanness in novels of the revolution. But by the fifties, Paz had cast suspicion on male-male relations of all kinds by implying that all Mexican men engaged in symbolic *chingar* battles, homosexualizing half of them in every instance. The queer side of hypermasculinity was revealed and a veritable paranoia of male bonding in mid-century novels such as *Pedro Páramo* is the result. The loyalty among friends that had been paramount in Inclán's *Astucia* and Campos's *Claudio Oronoz* was no longer possible. Lawyer Gerardo Trujillo, who had been a loyal associate of Pedro's father and who had aided Pedro in countless shady dealings for decades and hoped to be compensated when he retired, practically has to beg to get a small pittance from Pedro.

This apparent impossibility of male-male relations that are not caged in violence, that are not one form or another of *chingar,* is part of what gives *Pedro Páramo* its feeling of vacuity. In Comala there is no possibility of fraternity among citizens and neighbors; Comala is a space of suspicion inhabited by voices, shadows, and echoes. In this way, *Pedro Páramo* is oddly reminiscent of the poetry of Villaurrutia.[1] And yet Villaurrutia's empty spaces reflect, at least in part, his circumspection about depicting homosexual desire in an open way. Rulfo's emptiness would seem to reflect not so much circumspection as paranoia about male homosexual desire. I would argue that both homosexual desire and homophobic paranoia of homosexual desire are crucial aspects of Mexicanness by mid-century. Oddly enough, Salvador Reyes Nevárez's study of Mexicanness, *El amor y la amistad en el mexicano,* which predates *Pedro Páramo* by several years and is the only such text that emphasizes the importance of love and male bonding in the Mexican character (as opposed to aggression, rivalry, destructiveness, etc.), cites Villaurrutia's poetry at length.

Novels of the sixties will play out some of these questions, most particularly *Los albañiles* by Leñero, which explores the very macho arena of the construction site, the ambiguous sexuality of the *pelados,* and the sexually charged atmosphere of working-class male homosocial space. However, the forties and fifties are clearly a time when the anxieties of the *fin de siglo* and the culture wars of the early years following the revolution undergo a nervous and tense evolution. Male homosexuality is almost entirely absent from Mexican narrative fiction, at least superficially speaking, and yet it lurks beneath the surface in the shadows and echoes of texts such as *Pedro Páramo.*

Fin de siglo discourse had associated effeminacy with upper-class masculinity, implying that lower-class men were more barbarous, but also more virile. As long as the equation of homosexuality and effeminacy stood up, it remained a foible of the elites, like the Contemporáneos. However, the same studies of Mexicanness that served, according to their critics, to reify gender stereotypes, also launched a new interrogation into those gender stereotypes that for the first time included a serious (although sometimes still convoluted) interrogation of how notions of masculinity and male homosexuality interrelated.

In 1964, Paolo Po would publish *41, o el muchacho que soñaba en fantasmas,* and Miguel Barbachano Ponce, *El diario de José Toledo,* Mexico's first pair of "gay" novels. Both would portray a world in which homosexuality might be found anywhere. Both would bring to life characters who came from all kinds of backgrounds and had all kinds of personalities. Both revealed a vast world of homosexuals, barely hidden beneath the surface of everyday life. In the same year, Leñero's *Los albañiles,* which located homosexuality among Mexico's most macho of working-class men, construction workers, opened up discourse on homosexuality as never before.

I have argued here, then, that Mexican literary history, from *El Periquillo Sarniento* in 1816—with its roguish *valedores* curling up naked under a blanket and its bizarre male bonding scenes in which beds are shared and pistols exchanged—to the 1964 novels of Po, Barbachano Ponce, and Leñero, is a genealogy of Mexicanness as constructed through notions of masculinity, male homosocial bonding, and male sexuality. It is nothing less than the trials and tribulations of *los hijos de la Chingada.*

Notes

Introduction

1. Unless otherwise noted, all translations from the Spanish are my own.

2. For a definitive study of the 41, see the essays collected in Irwin, Mc-Caughan, and Nasser, a volume that also includes a new bilingual edition of Castrejón's novel.

3. See Bonfil.

4. See Franco, *Plotting Women* (175–87) on the growing importance women's writing in the 1960s in Mexico.

5. See Franco, *Plotting Women;* also Debra Castillo; Ramos Escandón, et al.; Macías; Domenella and Pasternac; and Valdés to name but a few well-known book-length studies.

6. See Monges Nicolau regarding Wright de Kleinhans's major historical project, *Mujeres notables mexicanas,* published posthumously in 1910.

7. Licia Fiol-Matta's work on Mistral touches on many of the same issues (gender, race, nation) explored here (see bibliography).

8. On masculinity, see Gutmann, Huerta, and Mirandé; regarding sexuality, see Monsiváis's essays "Ortodoxia," "Los que tenemos unas manos," and "El mundo soslayado"; also books by Lumsden, Prieur, Carrier, Guillén, Núñez Noriega, and Schaefer.

9. See *History of Sexuality,* vol. 1, 92–102.

10. Ramón Saldívar defines Chicano literature in cultural terms. I apply this Chicano studies perspective to Mexico. See also Bruce-Novoa.

11. My use of the term "culture" follows Edward Said, who sees it as aesthetic practices that promote shared identity (xii–xiv).

12. Julio Ramos, "The Buena Vista Social Club," lecture at Tulane University, April 13, 2000.

13. Questions of nation are given attention, for example in Martínez and Bartra, but such studies do not address gender issues; nor do broad-based feminist studies such as Franco's *Plotting Women* focus specifically on nation building.

14. On "imagined communities" and nineteenth-century nation building, see Anderson; on "national brotherhoods" and the relentless "androcentrism of the modern national imaginings," see Pratt (50).

15. For an excellent summary of the many ways in which masculinity has been defined, see Connell (1–86).

16. "The *habitus* is [an] immanent law ... laid down in each agent by his earliest upbringing, which is the precondition not only for the co-ordination of practices but also for practices of co-ordination" (Bourdieu, *Outline* 81).

17. Bourdieu writes: "The constancy of habitus ... is ... one of the most important factors in the relative constancy of the structure of the sexual division of labour: from body to body, below the level of consciousness and discourse, to a large extent they are beyond the grip of conscious control and therefore not amenable to transformations or corrections ... ; moreover, being objectively orchestrated, they confirm and reinforce one another" (*Masculine Domination* 95).

18. As Mexican feminist Marta Lamas puts it, "se construye el *género* ... como una especie de 'filtro' cultural con el que interpretamos el mundo, y también como una especie de armadura con la que constreñimos nuestra vida" [*gender* is constructed as a sort of cultural "filter" through which we interpret the world, and also as a sort of framework with which we constrain our life] (3).

19. Nancy Chodorow writes: "People are born with ambiguous genitalia or abnormal chromosomal patterns, yet we always label them as one or the other sex. We define people as male or female according to reproductive organs and capacities, but a woman who has a radical mastectomy, or total hysterectomy, or who is sterile, is still unambiguously female. A castrated or sterile man, or one whose genitals are amputated or mutilated in anything other than an intended sex-change operation, is still male. On several statistical variables, there may be more difference within each sex than between the sexes. Moreover, the extent of between-sex variation varies among societies, and variation among cultures is often greater than that between the sexes of any particular culture (people of both sexes in one culture may be taller on average, or have more body hair, or higher muscle to fat ratio than people of both sexes in another)" (15).

20. Regarding Mexico, see also González Méndez.

21. Bourdieu argues that "the perceived body is socially ... determined" and that "bodily properties are apprehended through schemes of perceptions whose use in acts of evaluation depends on the position occupied in social space" (*Masculine Domination* 64).

22. See Sandra Bem's often cited research, which models masculinity and femininity as independent variables. This model is adapted by Alfredo Mirandé in his study of Chicano masculinity. While he correctly notes that Bem's research is mistaken in assuming masculinity and femininity to be "fixed across time and social context" (14), his own research ignores cultural difference among U.S. Latino groups by conflating Latino with Chicano, and yet using Mexican history (and not Latin American history) as its background.

23. For example, Butler has only recently come out in Mexico in Spanish translation (see "Actos performativos" in *Debate Feminista* of October 1998),

although *Gender Trouble* began appearing in bibliographies as early as 1994 (see Lamas's "Cuerpo: diferencia sexual y género").

24. David Gilmore's cross-cultural analysis in *Manhood in the Making* demonstrates convincingly that "people in so many places regard the state of being a 'real man' or 'true man' as uncertain or precarious, a prize to be won or wrested through struggle, and...many societies build up an elusive or exclusionary image of manhood through cultural sanctions, ritual, or trials of skill and endurance" (1). His structuralist cross-cultural analysis is, however, problematic in that it assumes certain structures to exist everywhere and then finds them. James Clifford, assessing the impact of poststructuralism on the field (Gilmore's) of anthropology notes: "Much of our knowledge about other cultures must now be seen as contingent, the problematic outcome of intersubjective dialogue, translation, and projection. This poses fundamental problems for any science that moves predominantly from the particular to the general" (109). Had Gilmore taken into account such contingencies, his cross-cultural arguments would have been more convincing; as they are they might easily be seen as a false rendering of the other as "just like us."

25. See, for example, Lancaster, "Guto's Performance."

26. Carlos Monsiváis writes, "Si en el virreinato se condena a los sodomitas a la hoguera porque 'mudan de orden natural,' en el siglo XIX jamás se les menciona por escrito" [If during the viceroyalty sodomites were condemned to be burnt at the stake for 'changing natural orders,' in the nineteenth century they are never mentioned in writing] ("Ortodoxia" 197). For more on homosexuality during colonial times, see Olivier, Gruzinski.

27. See also Palaversich.

28. "Mayate" is a Mexicanism of Nahuatl origin referring to a masculine appearing man who plays the "active" role in anal intercourse with a homosexual man.

29. Prieur argues, "I would hold that part of what gives spice to the homosexual encounters is exactly that it [*sic*] implies transgression of a prohibition" (223).

30. See Schneider's "El tema homosexual" (republished with revisions in *La novela mexicana entre el petróleo, la homosexualidad y la política*); see also Schaefer, Mario Muñoz. My arguments are mirrored in Palaversich, although she works with texts from various countries and from a later period.

31. My analysis of civilization/barbarism and masculinity in Mexican culture owes much to Gail Bederman's similar analysis of U.S. culture.

32. For an interesting reinterpretation of homosexuality and patriarchy in Whitman, see Yingling.

33. On the general separation of politics from aesthetics in Latin American literature beginning in the late nineteenth century, see Julio Ramos, *Desencuentros*.

34. See, for example, Ludmer, Leland.

1. Early Paradoxes of Masculinity and Male Homosocial Bonding

1. I borrow the term "expresión nacional" from José Luis Martínez's book with this title on nineteenth- and early twentieth-century literature in Mexico, which formed the basis of a notion of national culture.

2. See Murray and Carrier. Tomás Almaguer takes for granted that this tautology is true for Mexican sexuality when he attempts to theorize a Chicano male sexuality. Annick Prieur's *Mema's House* also takes such assumptions as a starting point for her investigation of transvestites in Ciudad Nezahualcóyotl; however, she is careful not to overgeneralize. See pages 198–207, along with her "Concluding Notes," pages 271–75.

3. For a thorough summary of early colonial discourse on sexuality, see Olivier. It is particularly interesting to note that Spanish chroniclers typically confused effeminacy and sodomy; see Trexler, particularly pages 38–101.

4. Regarding historical changes in views on sexuality, including terminology, see Foucault. As to the lack of discourse on homosexuality in nineteenth-century Mexico, see Monsiváis, "Ortodoxia" (197). Alan Sinfield writes that in Europe, "[u]ntil the Wilde trials, effeminacy and homosexuality did not correlate in the way they have done subsequently" (4). See his mapping of a British genealogy of effeminacy in *The Wilde Century*, especially pages 1–83.

5. Looking at Latin America as a whole, it appears that sodomy continued to be a major issue in the nineteenth century only in Brazil (see Beattie). While in-depth research is clearly lacking, it appears that the situation in Argentina is comparable to that in Mexico as evidenced by a comment in a letter from Tulio Halperín Donghi that Doris Sommer quotes in *Foundational Fictions*: "[Juan Bautista] Alberdi didn't hesitate to declare his entirely feminine character in letters to friends; this self-portrait didn't suppose a confession of sexual ambiguity. On the contrary he and his friends never pardoned [José] Rivera Indarte's homosexuality, so extreme an infarction [*sic*] that they refer to it only vaguely" (351n20).

6. See Barajas 110, 344–45. I am not so sure that the kiss implied "una relación homosexual, lo que entonces debe haber resultado sumamente escandaloso" [a homosexual relation, which then must have proven to be supremely scandalous] (344) to a public unaccustomed to the concept of illicit sexual relations between men.

7. See Martínez, Benítez-Rojo; also in Blanco's *Crónica de la poesía mexicana,* he writes, referring to nineteenth-century Mexican literature's authoritative influence on identity, "No somos mexicanos por esencia, sino por decreto; no somos como somos sino como se ha impuesto que debemos ser" [We are not Mexicans by essence, but by decree; we are not as we are, but as we should be according to what has been imposed on us] (26).

8. See Ludmer's *El género gauchesco*. Also, see Ria Lemaire's reading of Brazilian José de Alencar's *Iracema* ("Relendo *Iracema*") and Francine Masiello's take on José Mármol's *Amalia* (*Between Civilization and Barbarism* 28–34), these texts being major foundational fictions in Brazil and Argentina, respectively.

9. On Lizardi and the new notion of a marketplace for writing and the need to address a broad public, see Franco, *Critical Passions* 479–80. On the female reading public during this period, see Staples 105–7. On the role of mothers, see Franco, *Plotting Women* 81–92.

10. According to Teresa Lozano Armendares, early nineteenth-century "delitos sexuales" [sex crimes] included rape, prostitution, adultery, corruption of minors, and cohabitation, all of which were viewed exclusively as heterosexual crimes. Her study makes no mention of sodomy or pederasty.

11. For a fascinating reading of *Chucho el Ninfo*, in which the critic Carlos Monsiváis sees the protagonist as "un gay evidente" [an obvious gay], see *Los iguales* (without pagination).

12. In Mexico, as in much of Latin America, women are frequently classified either as self-sacrificing saintlike mothers and virgins, or as lascivious whores. *La Quijotita y su prima* begins to lay out this scheme in the earliest years of independent Mexico. See also Debra Castillo's recent *Easy Women* on prostitute archetypes and Brianda Domecq's "La virginidad en la literatura mexicana" on female virginity in Mexican literature.

13. A peculiarity that José Martí repeats, years later, perhaps less ingenuously, as Sylvia Molloy suggests in "His America" (88). See also Joan DeJean's study concerning the historical interpretations and misinterpretations of Sappho as poetess and protagonist in sexual history.

14. Cultural fraternities were clearly male institutions, although Jean Franco points to the occasional participation of women such as the extraordinary Laureana Wright de Kleinhans (*Plotting Women* 93, and 212n31).

15. "A la fraternidad," poem presented by Ramírez at the Fraternal Banquet of the Gregorian Association in 1867, *Obras*, vol. 1 (3–6).

16. While the novel is essentially a historical novel based in colonial Mexico, it wanders throughout the Caribbean, and the role of the pirate protagonists, some of whom are European while others are Mexican or from other parts of the Americas, make national allegorical readings troublesome.

17. The use of female pseudonyms by male writers insidiously permitted men to "assert control over the private... sphere" and the everyday lives of women (Franco, *Plotting Women* 82). On the ways in which such social control was carried out in the nineteenth century, see *Plotting Women* 79–101. See also Carner.

18. It should be noted, however, that despite (or perhaps more because of) its popularity, *Astucia* would not be taken seriously until 1904, nearly forty

years after its publication and thirty years after the author's death (Glantz "*Astucia*" 89).

19. This brotherhood is in fact a band of tobacco smugglers who, apart from their criminal livelihood, are noble citizens and loyal friends.

20. While I am not convinced by Gilmore's methodology nor his conclusions, his view of manhood as a state achieved by rites of passage certainly resounds in Mexico, although as we have noted in Paz, it is not a single rite of passage, but a continual proving and re-proving that establishes manhood in Mexican culture. His primary example of a sexualized rite is among the Sambia of New Guinea in which boys ingest semen of men in order to stimulate masculinization. He then worries that this rite of institutionalized homosexual oral sex might seem "bizarre to some of us" and goes on to assuage the fears (of "some of us") by listing numerous other cultural contexts in which institutionalized homosexuality has contributed to cultural ideals of masculinity (154–55). It is just this obsession with establishing masculinity as a concept nearly uniform across cultures that is troubling.

21. See Benedict Anderson's discussion of *El Periquillo* in *Imagined Communities* (29–30). On the novel's foundational role as Mexico's and Latin America's first novel, see Benítez-Rojo. For the most complete analysis of Lizardi and his novels to date, see Vogeley, *Lizardi and the Birth of the Novel in Spanish America*.

22. On the relationship between journalism and literature in this era in Latin America, see Aníbal González. He claims that while *El Periquillo* "mimics" a novel, it is really a mere extension of his lifelong journalistic endeavors, or as González puts it (a bit less elegantly), his relentless "pampleteering" (21).

23. Wet nurses are pretty generally and extravagantly abhorred by Mexican writers of the century. Cuéllar, in *Los mariditos,* in calculating the costs of having children lists "ese monstruo que se llama *nodriza* que consume litros de pulque y kilogramos de carne; y que, representante del precioso don de la maternidad, se impone, se erige en potencia, domina, abusa y consume lo que diez niños juntos" [that monster known as a wet nurse who consumes liters of pulque and kilograms of meat; and who, as representative of the precious gift of motherhood, imposes herself, erects herself in power, dominates, abuses, and consumes the food of ten children put together] (110).

24. See, for example, B. Sifuentes Jáuregui's analysis of *Lazarillo de Tormes.*

25. According to Adler, "All neurotics have a childhood behind them in which they were moved by doubt regarding the achievement of full masculinity.... The structure of the neuroses ... shows the often ramified feminine traits carefully hidden by hypertrophied masculine wishes and efforts. This is the masculine protest. It follows necessarily as overcompensation, because the feminine tendency is evaluated negatively" (47–48). From this, Ramos concludes that the hypermasculinity of the Mexican *pelado* is not an authentic or

natural behavior, but a mask, a lie (Ramos 50–65). Note that according to Agustín Yáñez, the original representation of Mexican *peladaje* is none other than Lizardi's Periquillo (xxii).

26. The term "lobo" is a synonym of "zambo" which in colonial times was used to refer specifically to a racial mix of half black and half "indian." See Barjau (4–5).

27. The descriptions are quite graphic: "comienzan a disparar sobre mi uno jarritos con orines; pero tantos, tan llenos y con tan buen tino, que en menos que lo cuento, ya estaba yo hecho una sopa de meados, descalabrado y dado a Judas . . . y yo me quedé en cuclillas, junto a la puerta, desnudo y sin poder acostarme porque mi sarape estaba empapado, y mi camisa también" [they begin to fire jars of urine at me; so many, so full, and with such good aim that in less time than it takes me to tell the story, I was already soaked in piss, wounded in the head and given over to Judas . . . and I was left squatting by the door, naked, and unable to go to bed because my sarape was soaked, and my shirt as well] (218). El Periquillo makes it clear that they wanted to make sure that he stripped off even his underdrawers, "porque mis amados compañeros, creyendo que los botones eran de plata, no se descuidaron en quitárselos" [because my beloved buddies, believing that the buttons were silver, did not neglect to pull them off] (219).

28. Jean Franco refers to him in these terms (*Plotting Women* 93), although most simply classify him as "indigenous." Federico Gamboa, for example, writes, "el maestro por ser indio . . . era doblemente mexicano" [the master because he was an Indian . . . was doubly Mexican] (*La novela mexicana* 19). However, biographer Juan Campuzano reveals that he was not purely indigenous, but was born to an indigenous father and a *mestiza* mother with white skin and light eyes (12).

29. When he met Sara Bernhardt and later was told she thought "que no eres indio, sino el helenista más sabio que ha nacido en México, y que no eres feo . . . sino que por el francés que hablas, por tu cultura teatral y por tu amor al teatro francés . . . , eres el hombre más hermoso que ha conocido" [that you aren't an Indian, but the wisest Hellenist ever born in Mexico, and that you aren't ugly . . . but because of the French you speak, your theatrical refinement, and your love of French theater . . . , you are the most handsome man she's ever met], his response was: "Vaya, eso demuestra, que he logrado algo de lo que me he propuesto ser en la vida" [Well, that shows that I've achieved something of what I've proposed to be in life] (16).

30. He aligns himself in a patrilineage not only of Latin American luminaries such as José María Heredia, José Joaquín Olmedo, and Andrés Bello, but also with North Americans William Prescott and Washington Irving (*La literatura nacional* 7).

31. For example, he criticizes the writing of Argentines Esteban Echevarría and José Mármol for being hermaphrodite (*La literatura nacional* 14). Eighty

years later, Mariano Azuela would claim that *El Zarco,* unlike *Astucia* or *Los bandidos del Río Frío,* "carece de lo auténticamente nacional" [lacks an authentic national quality] (*Cien años* 117); Azuela adds: "Doble error, creer que escribía novela para el pueblo y leerla en los salones literarios" [Double error: to believe that he was writing a novel of the people and then to read it in literary salons] (121).

32. Another interesting allegorical reading sees Manuela as la Malinche and Pilar as the Virgin of Guadalupe. See Cruz.

33. For a discussion of the contradictory trends in race discourse in nineteenth- and early twentieth-century Mexico, see González Navarro, "*Mestizaje* in Mexico during the National Period."

34. See José David Saldívar 154–71.

35. For Sommer's positioning of Latin American romances in relation to the U.S. tradition whose most influential practitioner was Cooper, see Sommer 52–62. On the *The Squatter* as a "foundational fiction" see José David Saldívar 168–82.

36. The whiteness of the Alamars is stressed in their identification not as Mexican but as Spanish. While on the one hand they may feel rejected by a motherland that did not protect them and in fact delivered them into the hands of foreign invaders with the Treaty of Guadalupe Hidalgo, on the other they most likely would use their identification as Spanish to assert their superior social class and racial pedigree to *mestizo* Mexicans.

37. Interestingly, Leslie Fiedler finds a similar paradigm of national masculinity in the United States (and also notes a certain queerness in the prominence of homosocial bonding in major novels of U.S. literature of the nineteenth and early twentieth centuries).

38. Paul Vanderwood in his study of Mexican bandits describes the *plateados* as representative of the masculine national archetype of the *charro,* a type he describes as "best of all cowboys, possessed of a carefree, masculine arrogance that emphasizes their qualities as horsemen and lovers" (7). But he goes on to add a caveat to their masculinity by calling them dandies: "The Plateados had class and they dressed the part" (8). Lamberto Popoca y Palacios recounts the romantic legend of Salomé Placencia (and not his real-life colleague Felipe "El Zarco") and Homobona Merelo, which inspired Altamirano's novel (12–33) and judges Placencia "noble" (99). For Popoca y Palacios, unlike the Zapatistas ("salvajes" [savages]) of the Mexican revolution, the *plateados* ("charros bien montados" [well-mounted *charros*] [92]) were national heroes for having fought in the war against France (62).

39. See Fanon 63–82 on "this desire to be suddenly *white*" (emphasis in original): "I wish to be acknowledged not as *black* but as *white*. Now . . . who but a white woman can do this for me? By loving me she proves that I am worthy of white love. I am loved like a white man. I am a white man" (63).

40. See Illades and Sandoval's critique of Payno's treatment of indigenous Mexicans (43–72).

2. Criminal Male Sexuality

1. For studies on Argentina, see Salessi, Molloy (especially "The Politics of Posing" and "Too Wilde for Comfort"), and the various articles of Masiello and Nouzeilles; on Cuba, see Montero, "Julián del Casal"; on Brazil, see Beattie's study of the Brazilian military.

2. "Barcelonete" refers to one who comes from Barcelonette, a region of Provence, France.

3. "Rota" is a nineteenth-century slang term for the female version of a "petimetre," or fop, particularly referring to lower-class girls who try to dress up and live like rich girls.

4. "Catrina" is roughly a synonym for "rota."

5. Perhaps it is not so remarkable. Josefina Ludmer finds a range of similar texts in Argentine literary history, texts in which a heroine challenges social norms, is provoked to murder a man, and escapes unpunished. Such a heroine twists tropes of femininity such as the "mujer honesta" [honest woman] (795). Ludmer concludes: "Mujeres que matan: los elementos claves y violentos de esta figura lingüística, cultural y literaria: eliminar el poder en su raíz y marcar un avance en la independencia femenina, la hacen especialmente apta para la criminalización, para la fundación y al mismo tiempo para la alegoria de la justicia" [Women who kill: the crucial and violent elements of this linguistic, cultural, and literary figure: to eliminate power at its root and mark an advance in women's independence; these elements make this figure especially apt for the criminalization, for the foundation, and at the same time for the allegory of justice] ("Mujeres que matan" 796).

6. A notable exception was the notorious case of María Villa aka "La Chiquita," who murdered notorious rival prostitute "La Malagueña." See Buffington and Piccato, Sagredo. Buffington and Piccato cite additional cases (397–98) including one of "a knife duel to end a protracted dispute over some chickens" (397n20).

7. For an interesting look at honor and violent crime, see Piccato, *City of Suspects.*

8. The essay is taken from his collection of commentaries on turn-of-the-century crime, originally written for journals and later gathered for publication in his book, *Psiquis enfermo* of 1922.

9. See González Rodríguez.

10. See, for example Chaves, D. Castillo, and Ramos Escandón.

11. "Calzoncillos" are underdrawers, but this, of course, was the interpretation of white bourgeois writers. For the indigenous men themselves, these were their pants, albeit light cotton pants worn without underdrawers beneath them, and to these men there was nothing indecent about them.

12. On feminism during the Porfiriato, see, for example, Ramos Escandón and Macías.

13. Such was the case, for example, in the United States; see Bederman.

14. Nonetheless, Salado Álvarez contributed frequently to Mexico's modernist vehicle, *Revista Moderna*. See Martínez Peñalosa. For details on his polemics with the modernists, see Schneider, *Ruptura* 120–58.

15. Literally "young man," usually of the noble class; however, the word is rarely used in its masculine form, while its female counterpart, "doncella" [virgin] is more common. Thus, it would seem that Ceballos is both playing with gender and calling attention to the etymological implications associating youth with virginity only for women.

16. The term "varona" comes from "varón" [male] and often refers to a masculine woman. Again it would seem that Ceballos is deliberately provocative here.

17. Whereas the term "uranio" might translate as "celestial," the more literal translation, "uranic," might allude to "uranism," which in Europe at the time was a popular term for homosexuality. See Oosterhuis and Kennedy.

18. *El bar* was not published until 1991, although Campos's manuscript is dated 1935.

19. Which is not to say that they were necessarily "civilized"; Othón's savage style was perhaps not as outrageous as Díaz Mirón's temper, which landed him in jail on two different occasions—for murder. See José Luis Martínez 253–57.

20. See Piccato, " 'No es posible,' " for a detailed examination of the perceived links between alcohol and crime during the Porfiriato.

21. These chapters bear titles such as "El primer víctima del bar" and discuss the lives and deaths of figures such as poet Bernardo Couto Castillo, who died in 1901 at age twenty-one, and illustrator Julio Ruelas who managed to survive to age thirty-six, as well as key literary figures of the day such as Jesús Valenzuela and Alberto Leduc.

22. Cristina Rivera-Garza summarizes Guerrero's vision of social Darwinism in Mexico as being "an inverted evolutionary process in which primitive forms of life (atavisms), at both physiological and psychological levels, appeared in a more advanced milieu, threatening the basis of progress and civilization" ("Dangerous Minds" 26).

23. On European decadence, see Spackman.

24. Monsiváis is incorrect in stating that Wilde's trials were not covered until Julio Torri concerned himself with the subject some decades later ("Ortodoxia" 197). In fact, the trials were covered in *El Universal,* and even more thoroughly in *El Nacional* in 1895.

25. *El Universal* and *El Nacional,* April 9, 1895. Note that most newspaper stories during this era are not attributed to any writer. Any stories cited without mention of their author are anonymous.

26. Undoubtedly using a pen name, María Luisa Manrique de Lara, also known as the Condesa de Paredes, was the woman to whom Sor Juana Inés de la Cruz had addressed many of her love poems, frequently read today as indicative of lesbian affection and desire.

27. Many of these newspaper stories are reprinted in bilingual form in Irwin, McCaughan, and Nasser.

28. The earliest reports on November 19 and 20 noted that forty-two men had been apprehended, but beginning on the 21st, the figure mysteriously changed to forty-one, in all papers. Monsiváis divulges "el nunca desmentido rumor popular" [the never contradicted popular rumor] about Díaz's son-in-law, Ignacio de la Torre, in "El mundo soslayado" (14).

29. This report was repeated the same day in *La Patria,* a paper that often borrowed stories from *El Popular* or *El Universal.*

30. Also repeated the same day in *La Patria.*

31. While there was undoubtedly a raid, *La Patria* reports a strange fact on the November 22. It claims that the scandalous dance had been discovered by a passing policeman hours before the raid and that several officers had entered "undercover" and remained there for several hours until the raid was actually carried out. Since no newspaper ever mentions interviewing a witness (whether one of the 41, or any of the police, or the old woman who was rumored to have been present), we can only wonder what those policemen did for those hours they spent undercover.

32. *El Imparcial*—also known as a scandal sheet, although it seems to have decided to leave this scandal to its competitors—was subsidized by the government and served as its mouthpiece, although to its credit, the journal is considered to have pioneered visually oriented investigative reporting in Mexico. *El País,* on the other hand, was run by conservatives who basically supported the *porfiriato,* but criticized its "social" policies as being too "atheistic" and tended to report popular scandals with a moral rhetoric designed to combat the "de-Catholicization of the nation" (A. del Castillo 32–38).

33. Pseudonym of Benito Muñoz Serrano.

34. "Pelado" refers to the kind of lower-class man who Samuel Ramos would find emblematic of Mexicanness in the 1930s.

35. It should be noted that, in contrast, *El Tiempo,* another newspaper that advertised itself as "Catholic," very briefly covered the initial arrests on November 19, and thereafter offered no further coverage.

36. Most other papers concur with *El Popular* on this issue. See *El Diario del Hogar* (November 22, 2001), *La Patria* (November 22, 2001), *La Voz de México* (November 23, 2001), for example.

37. See also Cuéllar's *Baile y cochino* on the vulgarities of popular *bailes* (*La linterna mágica* 1–146).

38. "Comadre" is the term of address used between mothers and godmothers; however, it is also used to portray the stereotype of the middle aged female gossip in Mexico.

39. The article was signed by "Diablo Rojo," pen name of José Peón y Contreras.

40. Of course, the more common acceptation of "embarazado" in Spanish would be translated as "pregnant"; thus, the *double entendre.*

41. The expression "no tener madre" usually means "to have no shame."

42. Here the *double entendre* refers to piss ("mear").

43. Posada was known to have published in a "sensationalist paper" called *El Diablito Rojo* (recall that El Diablo Rojo aka José Peón y Contreras was the author of many of the pieces on the 41 published in *El Popular*).

44. The augmentative forms "-ón" and "-azo," as well as the diminutive form "-ito" are used commonly with nouns identifying persons in Mexico, and while they can be depreciatory, they are frequently affectionate.

45. The novel has been published in an abridged, bilingual form in Irwin, McCaughan, and Nasser.

46. The circumstances of the publication of Castrejón's novel, *Los 41,* are quite mysterious. The author is not included in any Mexican literary history, and the book had never even been mentioned in any literary or historiographic study prior to 1995 (Monsiváis, "Ortodoxia" 199–200). Moreover, most books published in Mexico at the time, and particularly those published at printing shops (such as Tipografía Popular, which published *Los 41*), were self-financed, according to Pedro Ángel Palou (*La casa* 48–49), so one wonders who "the publishers" might have been. Judging from their tendency for hyperbole, I would venture that Castrejón served as his own publisher.

47. The cover promises a sequel, but there is no evidence of its having been published.

48. Castrejón always italicizes the nicknames of the transvestites.

49. Lizardi's *Don Catrín* presents Mexican literature's first icon of the *catrín,* a very Mexican dandy and social climber who is able to deceive people as to his true social and economic status by dressing up in expensive looking clothing.

50. *El Universal*'s articles might have been written by Castrejón himself. In this long, raging article, after accusing the priests, the anonymous writer goes on, "En [esa clase] se encuentran viejos satiriacos pervertidos por la impotencia y por el abuso del deleite carnal y jóvenes, púberes apenas, roídos y muertos en plena juventud por la ponzoña asquerosa de la más terrible de las crápulas" [In that class can be found old "satyriacs" (male nymphomaniacs) perverted by impotency and by the abuse of carnal delight, and youths, barely pubescent, gnawed away and killed in the glory of their youth by the revolting poison of the most terrible of debaucheries].

51. Roumagnac comments: "Recuérdanse casos sensacionales de individuos, pertenecientes algunas veces a clases no de las más bajas de nuestra sociedad, sorprendidos mientras se entregaban a su vicio favorito; y no está tan lejano el escandaloso caso de aquellos cuarenta y un jóvenes, y no jóvenes, que fueron encontrados por la pollicía, en un baile compuesto todo de elemento masculino" [Remember sensational cases of individuals, belonging sometimes not to the lowest classes of our society, caught giving themselves over to their favorite vice; and not so long ago was the case of those forty-one young and not so young men who were found by the police at a dance composed only of masculine elements] (*Crímenes sexuales y pasionales* 151).

52. See, for example, Krafft-Ebing on congenital vs. acquired homosexuality and seduction theory (247–94).

53. For an excellent historical analysis of the 41 that also explores the event's lasting impact on Mexican culture, see Monsiváis, *Los iguales*. See also Irwin, McCaughan, and Nasser.

54. Discourse on homosexuality erupted simultaneously in different parts of Latin America, but in distinct styles in each place. For example, Ingenieros's theories of simulation would not arrive to Mexico until 1911 (see Rivera-Garza, "Dangerous Minds" 43n88).

55. From Francisco Uriquizo's *Símbolos y números,* cited in Schneider, *La novela mexicana* 69.

56. In Mexico the English term "gay" is frequently used, particularly to refer to gay rights politics. See Lumsden 63–80.

57. Despite Roumagnac's obvious desire to attract a wide readership, his *bricoleur* style of criminology demonstrated his breadth of knowledge of the field (Buffington 66–67). His texts were, in fact, to remain influential among Mexican criminologists for generations (Buffington 135).

58. "Mayate," a term of classical náhuatl origin ("mayatl," brightly colored beetle) has historically been used to refer to ostentatiously dressed men, although its primary modern usage has been to refer to heterosexually identified men who have sexual relations, playing the "male" role, with effeminate homosexuals.

59. This brief anonymous portrait was reprinted in *Máscaras de la Revista Moderna* 112.

60. Martí was known for obsessing about the virility of his writing and his own virility as a poet. See J. Ramos, "The Repose of Heroes"; Molloy, "His America, Our America"; Montero, "Martí y el lenguaje del gabinete."

61. Recall, however, the ambiguous reference in Ceballos's "Un adulterio."

62. This term actually was in use at the time. Argentine Carlos Octavio Bunge employed it to describe an affliction of "hombres de genio" [men of genius] and saw it as indicative of a society's decadence. See Salessi 188–89.

63. Literary gossip has it that Gamboa's *Santa* is based on the real-life Mexico City prostitute "la Malagueña" (Buffington and Piccato 419n71) with

whom Gamboa had "conversed" the night before she was murdered by a rival prostitute. His visit to the morgue to view her cadaver is recounted famously in his diaries (Buffington and Piccato 417–23).

64. According to Palou, it was Mexico's first "best-seller." A rare profitable book in its day—certainly the most successful novel of the era—which permitted Gamboa the luxury of living off his earnings as a fiction writer, it was frequently reprinted even in the early years of the century and was one of the first Mexican literary works to be adapted for the cinema (*La casa* 46–47).

65. Salvador Oropesa interestingly reads Jarameño's romantic conquest of Santa as an allegory of the Spanish conquest of Mexico, with Santa cast in the role of la Malinche ("Hacia una identidad" 630–31).

66. Major studies of El Ateneo de la Juventud are few. See García Morales, Curiel (*La Revuelta*).

67. There would also appear an Ateneo Mexicano de Mujeres in 1934, a society of professional women of different fields, "el primer grupo de mexicanas que en este siglo se dedican a algo más que a obras piadosas y las consabidas 'labores propias de su sexo' " [the first group of Mexican women that in this century dedicated themselves to something other than charity and the usual "labor appropriate to their sex"] (Granillo, "La cuestión de las mujeres que supieron latín" 61).

68. Arenales was one of many pseudonyms of Miguel Ángel Osorio, better known to the literary world as Porfirio Barba Jacob. See Piedad Bonnett's introduction to his *Poesía completa*.

69. For a detailed look at this genealogy, see Bartra.

3. Virile Literature and Effeminate Literature

1. On "hero cults" and the mythification of the Mexican Revolution, see O'Malley.

2. See also Balderston, "Poetry, Revolution, Homophobia," Schneider, "Ruptura" 159–89, and Sheridan, *"Contemporáneos"* 124–34, 254–62.

3. See Parker, and also Montero's "Before the Parade Passes By."

4. See Díaz Arciniega, 58–60, 87–88 for commentary on Gutiérrez Cruz. For a complete list of articles published as part of this debate, see his bibliography, especially 173–79.

5. For a brief biographical essay on María Enriqueta Camarillo y Roa de Pereyra (who published under the name María Enriqueta), see Fiscal.

6. Loreley, journalist, poet, novelist, and temperance activist, published her best known novel, *La novia de Nervo*, in San Antonio, Texas.

7. *The Underdogs* is the established title of *Los de abajo* in English translation, although a more precise translation is "those below," whose implications range from the literal (a physical position of troops in a valley) to a range of figurative connotations (the most obvious being that of social class) including the sexual.

8. For a complete recounting of the reception of *Los de abajo,* see Ruffinelli.

9. See the bibliography of the critical edition of *Los de abajo* for a list of key Spanish language editions as well as translations of the text.

10. For a fascinating autobiographical sketch of Azuela, see Leal, *Mariano Azuela.*

11. Personal interview, May 1994.

12. Luis Cervantes is nicknamed "curro" by the troops, a term that refers to an elegant city slicker.

13. La Pintada, a nickname given to a particularly tough and sexually bold *soldadera,* literally translates as "the painted woman." *Soldaderas* perform an institutionalized role in the Mexican army of the revolution, following the troops, dedicating themselves to feeding and caring for their lovers, and sometimes even participating actively in combat. See Leal's "La soldadera en la narrativa de la revolución" in *Aztlán y México,* 185–93.

14. A nickname given to soldiers wearing caps.

15. Although Luis Cervantes, being an educated city slicker and a possible homosexual, is tainted by an implicit effeminacy, the only time any issue at all is made of his possible effeminacy is when Camila is first attracted to him: "el fresco y radioso rostro de Luis Cervantes, aquellos ojos glaucos de tierna expresión, sus carrillos frescos y rosados como los de un muñeco de porcelana, la tersura de una piel blanca y delicada que asomaba abajo del cuello, y más arriba de las mangas de una tosca camiseta de lana, el rubio tierno de sus cabellos, rizados ligeramente" [the fresh and radiant face of Luis Cervantes, those green tender eyes, his fresh and rosy cheeks like those of a porcelain doll, the smoothness of a white and delicate skin that peeked out from under his collar and from the sleeves of his rough wool undershirt, the tender blondness of his slightly curled hair] (36–37). However, his effeminacy apparently escapes his male friends, who never note anything unmanly about him except his possible homosexuality.

16. According to Sheridan, by 1932, Gide's name was synonymous with "pederasty" in Mexico (*Los Contemporáneos* 92n29). Ironically, nonvirile Contemporáneos poets like Villaurrutia identified with the more masculine Gide over another popular icon of homosexuality, Oscar Wilde, the effeminate dandy.

17. "Tropa vieja" alludes to the common term, "ropa vieja," or "old clothes," which calls up the image of ragged old unwanted clothes given up to the "ropa vejero" or "old clothes man" who wanders from neighborhood to neighborhood with a mule drawn cart collecting and reselling cast-off junk.

18. I refer here to *The History of Sexuality,* vol. 1 (92–102).

19. "Madrugar" literally means to get up early, or to do something earlier, as "the early bird catches the worm." However, this latter meaning, with its feeling of competitiveness, is taken a step further in Mexican slang to imply a violence, as in to draw first blood, or even to kill first.

20. Margo Glantz interprets Aguirre as a statuesque, neoclassical, heroic male beauty and sees his heroism as inspired by a gorgeous jai alai player. She sees a strong link between ethics and (male corporeal) aesthetics in the novel (*Esguince de cintura* 49–60).

21. Compadres are "co-fathers," a father and the godfather of the same child; however, the term is also used sometimes between friends to imply a friendship so strong that it emulates these family ties.

22. The fact that her protagonist is masculine, but a child, links Enriqueta's writing to a trend in women's writing in Latin America in her day, which Molloy has called "aniñamiento" [infantilization], or the reduction of women to the status of children. The same occurs, of course, in Campobello's *Cartucho.* See "Dos lecturas del cisne."

23. In her entirely anti-Mexican attitude, Enriqueta uses peninsular Spanish verb forms and vocabulary (Fiscal 195).

24. Eugenics was a topic of serious scientific as well as popular debate in Mexico from as early as 1910. Regarding its early status in Mexico, see Stepan, especially 55–75. A late essay by Nervo himself (1916) mocks eugenics (*Ensayos* 186–99).

25. See Auguste Villiers de l'Isle Adam's *L'Eve future.*

26. See especially Sheridan, *Los Contemporáneos* and *México en 1932;* Monsiváis, *Amor perdido* (especially 273–77), "Ortodoxia," and "El mundo soslayado."

27. Note that beyond the rhetoric, efforts to treat the mentally ill took on a form of their own in these years in Mexico. According to Rivera-Garza's fascinating study of Mexico's General Insane Asylum, la Castañeda, "The management of mental health was continuously shaped and reshaped by the idiosyncrasies of the very characters the regulations attempted to control—administrators, members of the medical staff, and inmates themselves" ("A Routine of Mental Health" 12)

28. The best of several literary biographies of Cuesta is that of Panabière; also interesting, but homophobic, is that of Katz.

29. Bradu identifies Lorenzo as Salvador Novo (277).

30. See Artaud's article on Van Gogh's mental instability.

31. Bradu writes, "Es curioso observar cómo Jorge Cuesta se desentendió de la 'locura' de su mujer cuando, años después, se dedicaría con tanta minuciosidad a examinar los síntomas de la suya. La misma credulidad que le reclamaría al doctor Lafora se la negaba a Lupe. Ni siquiera la curiosidad intelectual que lo atenazaba lo llevó a indagar en el 'caso' de su esposa. Parece que aceptó con demasiada prontitud, y tal vez con alivio, la solución propuesta por los médicos: encerrar a Lupe en un manicomio" [It's interesting to note how Jorge Cuesta feigned ignorance of his wife's "insanity" when, years later, he would dedicate himself to examining his own symptoms in

such minute detail. The same credulity that he demanded of Dr. Lafora, he denied Lupe. Not even the intellectual curiosity that normally gripped him led him to inquire into the "case" of his wife. It would seem that he accepted too readily, perhaps with a sense of relief, the solution proposed by her doctors: to lock Lupe up in an insane asylum] (*Damas* 270).

32. One of his best-known publications was *La educación sexual y la reforma de la moral sexual* (1933).

33. The letter, first published in *Vuelta* in 1977, was republished by Capistrán in *Los Contemporáneos por sí mismos*. It appears again with an English translation in Irwin, "The Legend of Jorge Cuesta" (45–52).

34. According to one rumor, Cuesta had married Marín only at the provocation of Novo, who wanted to make a mockery of her ex-husband, Diego Rivera (Bradu, *Damas* 258).

35. On the Contemporáneos, see Sheridan (*Los Contemporáneos ayer*), Capistrán, Palou (*La casa del silencio*), Olea Franco and Stanton, Blanco (*La paja en el ojo* 53–132), Monsiváis ("Notas sobre la cultura mexicana en el siglo XX" 1435–41), Paz (*Xavier Villaurrutia en persona y en obra*), and Schneider (*Fragua y gesta del teatro experimental en México*) to give but a few examples of the recent scholarship on the group as a whole.

36. Fernando Curiel, who has published extensively on the Ateneo de la Juventud, senses that the links between the two groups are stronger than is generally realized and calls for more research on the topic ("Notas para una edición" 57); some work has looked at the relations between the Contemporáneos and Alfonso Reyes, who at times appears to be something of a mentor. See Capistrán 11–44, 103–29, and Sheridan, *México en 1932*, especially 49–55, 94–103. Villaurrutia, however, plays down questions of influence: "Fueron y son hombres cultos y en este sentido, y sólo en este sentido, son un antecedente de la generación nueva" [They were and are cultured men and in this sense, and only in this sense, are they precursors of the new generation] (quoted in Sheridan, *México en 1932* 155).

37. While major critics such as Monsiváis ("Notas sobre la cultura") and Blanco (*La paja*) present the Contemporáneos as Mexico's major *vanguardista* movement of their era and Unruh does not hesitate to include them in her *Latin American Vanguards*, Schneider ("Los Contemporáneos: la vanguardia desmentida") denies the validity of this characterization, and Escalante ("Sobre los espejismos de la crítica") goes so far as to claim that the Contemporáneos have been canonized as the Mexican vanguard of their day above all because contemporary critics are offended by the blatant homophobia of the *estridentistas,* the more obvious though short-lived rival *vanguardista* movement of the twenties.

38. While their reputation was as anti-nationalists, in actuality, their po-

sition toward national culture has been interpreted somewhat differently. Sheridan makes a convincing case that the journal *Contemporáneos*, in fact, strongly promoted Mexican artists (*Los Contemporáneos* 343–45). Moreover, the group was consistently supported by the Mexican government, and some of them even got their start thanks to the father of postrevolutionary nationalist cultural production, José Vasconcelos (Sheridan 99–105).

39. Francisco Rojas González's contribution to the polemic of 1932 was that the Contemporáneos were not vanguardist poets and moreover, "no diré... que existe entre ellos la crisis, sino que advirtiendo en el fondo del asunto un gris y pesado sedimento de fracaso, me felicito de que su aventura no haya influido en la generación que ahora se levanta" [I won't say that there is a crisis among them, but that noting at the heart of the matter a heavy gray sediment of failure, I applaud the fact that their adventure has not influenced the generation now emerging] (quoted in Sheridan, *México en 1932* 207–8). Nonetheless, not only is their influence clear in future generations of writers, but their work comes to play a lasting role in debates on national culture and national identity. For example, the poetry of Villaurrutia is central to Reyes Nevárez's *El amor y la amistad en México* along with Paz's discussion of death in *El laberinto to la soledad* (56). Debra Castillo argues for a link (via Paz) between Villaurrutia and Rulfo (73), and Blanco traces Villaurrutia's influence to Revueltas, for whom Villaurrutia is "su contrario gemelo" [his twin opposite] (*Crónica literaria* 307).

40. In addition to Bradu's biography (1991), see Rivas Mercado's *Obras completas*, edited by Schneider (1981), including her account of Vasconcelos's election campaign, and also her *87 cartas de amor y otros papeles*, edited by Rojas Rosillo (1975). See also Unruh, "Una equívoca Eva moderna" and Franco's *Plotting Women* (112–28).

41. In his prologue to *La poesía mexicana del siglo XX*, Carlos Monsiváis refers to the *estridentistas* as "la parodia a pesar suyo de la vanguardia" [a parody of the avant garde in spite of itself] (48). Blanco completely excludes the *estridentistas* from his *Crónica de poesía mexicana*, and Jean Franco, in *An Introduction to Spanish-American Literature*, writes, "The *estridentistas* of the early twenties filled their poems with contemporary vocabulary and revolutionary slogans, but they were soon eclipsed by an altogether more serious movement —that which centered round the magazine *Contemporáneos* (263). On the other hand, Schneider ("Los Contemporáneos: La vanguardia desmentida") and Escalante ("Sobre los espejismos") argue against the canonization of the Contemporáneos at the expense of the *estridentistas*.

42. See Balderston, "Poetry, Revolution, Homophobia" and *El deseo, enorme cicatriz luminosa* (27–39), and Irwin, "As Invisible as He Is" on

how a hostile, homophobic environment forced Villaurrutia to veil the homo-eroticism of his poetry by not allowing bodies to appear as more than shadows or fragments.

43. *Nostalgia for Death* provides a bilingual version of Villaurrutia, with Eliot Weinberger's excellent translations. Here, however, for the purposes of this particular analysis, that requires a more literal understanding of the poems' content, I use my own translations, which appear, save for a few minor corrections, as they did in a more complete form in "As Invisible as He Is."

44. See Bergmann 229–34.

45. It was not until the late seventies that it became acceptable among serious literary critics to make overt reference to Villaurrutia's homosexuality. Prior to Paz's *Xavier Villaurrutia en persona y en obra*, the subject was not broached, whether due to embarrassment on the part of the critics or their respect for the memory of the poet whose reputation they did not wish to tarnish. For a summary of literary criticism of Villaurrutia, see Irwin, "As Invisible."

46. See, for example, an anonymous commentary in *Nexos* (December 1993): 81 under the heading "NAFPA."

47. The only published autobiographical writings explicitly addressing sexual issues are the *Cartas de Villaurrutia a Novo,* which came out in the sixties, censored. For uncut versions of some of the censored letters, see Novo's *La vida en México en el periodo presidencial de Miguel Alemán* 443–47.

48. Cardoza y Aragón is quoted in Bradu, "Presencia y figura de Xavier Villaurrutia" (56). See also Novo's *La estatua de sal.* Also recall Marín's gossip about going out to pick up soldiers quoted in Bradu's *Damas de corazón* (254). All these are fragmentary anecdotes. More substantial is Palou's *En la alcoba de un mundo;* however, it is a novel based on Villaurrutia's life, and many of its insinuations, particularly those concerning the relationship between Villaurrutia and Agustín Lazo, are clearly speculative. Even Villaurrutia's death remains a mystery. His doctor, Elías Nandino, suspects suicide but was not there when he died, and since an autopsy was never performed, he can only guess what happened (Nandino 67–69).

49. Vasconcelos was a friend of several of the Contemporáneos during his years as education minister in the early twenties. In fact, as late as 1939 in *El proconsulado,* the fourth and final volume of his autobiography, he refers to Manuel Rodríguez Lozano, his homosexual "rival" for the affections of lover Antonieta Rivas Mercado, as a "caballero sin tacha" [gentleman without fault] (718); however, in *La flama,* a later "novel of the revolution"/ "autobiography," which recounts many of the same events, he changes his tune, invoking Gide in blaming Rivas Mercado's suicide partly on her immoral friendships and the "literatura invertida" [invert literature] she read (121–23). Jean Franco sees one of the main goals of *La flama* as an attempt "to prove the deadly effects of women's and gay emancipation" (*Plotting Women* 127).

50. On Vasconcelos, see especially Blanco, *Se llamaba Vasconcelos.*

51. Ironically, Vasconcelos, who had himself claimed to be *mestizo* in *Indología*, his sequel to *La raza cósmica*, by the thirties when he writes his autobiography, *Ulises criollo*, had somehow become a pure-blooded Spanish creole (Blanco, *Se llamaba Vasconcelos* 17–18). On Vasconcelos's "muralistic" process of autobiography, see Molloy, *At Face Value* 186–208.

52. Recall that Vasconcelos had been a leading member of the Ateneo de la Juventud, who were responsible for introducing Rodó into Mexico in 1907 (García Morales 119).

53. On Mexican racism and its effects on immigration, particularly of blacks and Asians, in the same era, see Stepan 150–53.

54. See, for example, Barjau, González Navarro, *"Mestizaje."*

55. See Irwin, "La homosexualidad cósmica mexicana."

56. Oropesa reads a queer triangulated desire in the screenplay ("Deseo homosocial" 635–37).

57. Salvador Novo's exploits with the well endowed Fink, recounted in *La estatua de sal,* are examined below.

58. On homosexuality in Gide, see Lucey.

59. For information on Hughes in Mexico, see Rampersad. Note that if Rampersad knew of any of Hughes's homosexual adventures in Mexico or with Mexicans, he did not include them in his biography, most probably due to homophobia. For an angry but very interesting critique of Rampersad, see Berry (359–67).

60. Hughes was a good friend of Novo, who quite possibly introduced Villaurrutia to him at some point (Nandino 72).

61. Specifically, in "Nocturno eterno" [Eternal nocturne] (*Obras* 51–52): "cuando los ojos cierran sus ventanas" [when the eyes close their windows]; and in "Cuando la tarde...." [When the evening...] (*Obras* 61–62): "Cuando la tarde cierra sus ventanas remotas" [When the evening closes its far-off windows].

62. Not counting *Los 41*, Castrejón's 1906 sensationalist novel, the first such Mexican novels came out in the early sixties, Paolo Po's *41, o un muchacho que soñaba en fantasmas* and Miguel Barbachano Ponce's *El diario de José Toledo.*

63. Excerpts were published both in the gay liberation journal *Política Sexual* and in the Gay Sunshine Press anthology *Now the Volcano*, edited by Winston Leyland.

64. Novo's effeminacy is ridiculed by Nandino, who considered Novo "horrendamente feo" [horrendously ugly] (71): "Su afeminamiento era un poquito ridículo, como si un elefante quisiera hacer jotería" [his effeminacy was a bit ridiculous, as though an elephant wanted to perform faggotry] (72).

65. Barrera, *Salvador Novo* (106); see also González Rodríguez (30).

66. Monsiváis points out, however, that this spirit is not all playful: "En estos grupos hay reglas semejantes a las de cualquier país, según revelan las historias de la sexualidad. Entre ellas: el que huye de la norma heterosexual aleja en definitiva la felicidad y la vida amorosa; el 'perreo' (el habla de las denigraciones mutuas) es el recordatorio incesante del menosprecio de los de afuera; el 'travestismo verbal' es obligatorio porque lo más próximo a la esencia de los 'raritos' es la identidad femenina por contagio" [In these groups there are rules similar to those of any country, according to what is revealed in histories of sexuality. Among them: those who flee from heterosexual norms distance themselves definitively from happiness and love lives; "bitchiness" (speaking to each other using mutual denigrations) is the incessant reminder of heterosexuals' scorn; "verbal transvestism" is obligatory because the closest thing to the essence of the "queers" is feminine identity by contagion] (*Salvador Novo* 34).

67. On the apparent naturalness of gender norms, see Lamas. On performativity and gender subversion, see Butler, *Gender Trouble* (134–49) and *Bodies That Matter* (230–42).

68. Speculation on this topic is difficult as men are not likely to admit such feats to sociologists or anthropologists. There is another school of thought that says that such acts are looked down upon out of a belief of contagion, a fear that one might become homosexual by growing to enjoy them (see Prieur 188–207).

69. On varying roles, lack of clear roles, and variety of sexual practices, see, for example Zapata, Barbachano Ponce, Po, the orgy scenes of Teruel; intergenerational coupling is a major theme of modern "queer" novels in Mexico such as those of Ceballos Maldonado, Teruel, Ojeda, and Blanco (*Las púberes canéforas*).

4. Homosexual Panic

1. Granillo Vázquez, in her critique of Paz, writes, "Si en un primer momento el ensayista escribe un informe de lo que observa a su alrededor, en un segundo tiempo, el discurso del escritor informa y conforma al lector, llega incluso a 'organizar la experiencia'" [If at first the essayist writes a report of what he observes around him, later the discourse of the writer informs and shapes the reader, it even succeeds in "organizing experience"] ("La abnegación maternal" 233).

2. Aramoni, who considers Mexican machismo to be a form of paranoia, sees women's participation as a sort of "folie à deux" (276–77).

3. Fromm and Maccoby claim to find statistical support for Paz's theories a couple of decades later: "Our results tend to confirm the picture, which has been described so eloquently by Octavio Paz, of the Mexican male's resistance to being touched, to being made open and vulnerable" (145).

4. Recall Ceballos's misogynistic representation of female sexuality as "the incurable bleeding wound, the stinking wound, the rotting, contaminating, killing wound, the damned wound, the wound" (22).

5. The notion of homosexuality being a latent quality of Mexican machismo is confirmed by numerous investigators of *lo mexicano* including González Pineda (166) and Aramoni (276). While beyond the scope of this text-based study, Mexican cinema of the same era has recently been read in terms of the homoerotic overtones of machismo; see De la Mora.

6. Schneider reports that Barbachano Ponce wrote *El diario de José Toledo* in 1962, but it was not published until 1964, and while he lists it as coming out prior to Po's *41*, the latter was in fact published in 1963 (see "El tema homosexual" 73–74). Schaefer and M. Muñoz both list *José Toledo* as being the first, but are apparently unaware of the existence of Po's book. Neither Schneider, Schaefer, nor Muñoz seems to have been familiar with Castrejón.

7. Early critics were confused and disappointed by the ending of the novel (Tarica 6); interestingly, the 1949 film version, directed by Matilde Landeta, allows Angustias to remain a macho war hero, although her character in general is less transgressive than in the novel. Tarica writes, "in Landeta's film, although Angustias remains a fighter to the end, she looks a lot more like the familiar portrait of the Revolutionary *soldadera*, and a lot less like the *marimacho* she is in the book—in the movie, for example, she always wears a skirt" (7).

8. Zea refers to Mexicans' inferiority complex as a feeling of being "amputados, divididos, cercenados" [amputated, divided, clipped] (106).

9. See J. Sommers concerning the influence of Paz's *El laberinto* on Fuentes. Campbell sees Páramo as "la gran metáfora del poder mexicano" [the great metaphor of Mexican power] (44). J. Franco examines the machismo inherent in the attempts of the military men of *Los recuerdos del porvenir* to dominate their women (*Plotting* 135). See also D. Castillo on Rosas and his motivations to possess and control women (77–99).

10. Patricia Ramírez Buendía and Mauro Rodríguez Estrada, *Psicología del mexicano en el trabajo,* quoted in Granillo Vázquez, "La abnegación maternal" (203).

11. "El hombre del destino" (1970) (*El uso de la palabra* 204–8).

12. Escalante argues the opposite, that patricide is the most important theme of the novel (*La intervención* 40).

13. Balderston also notes a connection between Villaurrutia and Rechy ("Poetry" 66).

Conclusion

1. See D. Castillo, who links Rulfo to Villaurrutia via Paz and Maurice Blanchot, evoking a Mexican notion of death (73).

Bibliography

Adler, Alfred. *The Individual Psychology of Alfred Adler.* New York: Harper Torchbooks, 1964.

Almaguer, Tomás. "Chicano Men: A Cartography of Homosexual Identity and Behavior." In *The Lesbian and Gay Studies Reader,* ed. Henry Abelove, et al., 255–73. New York: Routledge, 1993.

Altamirano, Ignacio M. *Clemencia.* 14th ed. México: Porrúa, 1989 [1869].

———. *La literatura nacional.* Vol. 1. Ed. José Luis Martínez México: Porrúa, 1949.

———. *El Zarco* [1901], *La navidad en las montañas* [1871]. México: Porrúa, 1995.

Anderson, Benedict. *Imagined Communities.* Rev. ed. London: Verso, 1991.

Anonymous. "Amado Nervo." In *Máscaras de la Revista Moderna,* intro. by Porfirio Martínez Peñaloza, 110–13. México: Fondo de Cultura Económica, 1968.

Anzaldúa, Gloria. *Borderlands/La frontera: The New Mestiza.* San Francisco: Aunt Lute Books, 1987.

Aramoni, Aniceto. *Psicoanálisis de la dinámica de un pueblo.* México: UNAM, 1961.

Artaud, Antonin. "Van Gogh: Le suicide de la societé." In *Oeuvres completes,* 13:9–64. Paris: Gallimard, 1974.

Azuela, Mariano. *Cien años de novela mexicana.* México: Botas, 1947.

———. *Los de abajo.* Edición crítica. Ed. Jorge Ruffinelli. Buenos Aires: Colección Archivos/UNESCO, 1988 [1915].

Balderston, Daniel. *El deseo, enorme cicatriz luminosa.* Caracas: eXcultura, 1999.

———. "Poetry, Revolution, Homophobia: Polemics from the Mexican Revolution." In *Hispanisms and Homosexualities,* ed. Sylvia Molloy and Robert McKee Irwin, 57–75. Durham, N.C.: Duke University Press, 1998.

Balderston, Daniel, and Donna J. Guy, eds. *Sex and Sexuality in Latin America.* New York: New York University Press, 1997.

Barajas, Rafael. *La historia de un país en caricatura: Caricatura mexicana de combate 1829–1872.* México: Consejo Nacional para la Cultura y las Artes, 2000.

Barba Jacob, Porfirio. *Poesía completa.* México: Consejo Nacional para la Cultura y las Artes, 1998.

Barbachano Ponce, Miguel. *El diario de José Toledo.* México: Premiá, 1988 [1964].

Barjau, Luis. *No somos mestizos: Castas e identidad nacional.* México: Colección Imaginaria, 1987.

Barragán de Toscano, Refugio. *La hija del bandido o Los subterráneos del Nevado.* México: Editorial México, 1934 [1887].

Barrera, Reyna. *Salvador Novo: Navaja de la inteligencia.* México: Plaza y Valdés, 1999.

Barrera López, Reyna. "Novo en la memoria." *Del Otro Lado* 14 (1994): 40–41.

Bartra, Roger. *The Cage of Melancholy: Identity and Metamorphosis in the Mexican Character.* Trans. C. Hall. New Brunswick, N.J.: Rutgers University Press, 1992 [1987].

Bastos, María Luisa, and Sylvia Molloy. "La estrella junto a la luna: Variantes de la figura materna en *Pedro Páramo.*" *MLN* 92, no. 2 (March 1997): 246–68.

Beattie, Peter. "Conflicting Penile Codes: Modern Masculinity and Sodomy in the Brazilian Military, 1860–1916." In *Sex and Sexuality in Latin America,* ed. Daniel Balderston and Donna J. Guy, 65–85. New York: New York University Press, 1997.

Bederman, Gail. *Manliness and Civilization: A Cultural History of Gender and Race in the United States, 1880–1917.* Chicago: University of Chicago Press, 1995.

Bem, Sandra Lipsitz. *The Lenses of Gender: Transforming the Debate on Sexual Inequality.* New Haven: Yale University Press, 1993.

Benítez-Rojo, Antonio. "Nacionalismo y nacionalización en la novela hispanoamericana del siglo XIX." *Revista de Crítica Literaria Latinoamericana* 19, no. 38 (1993): 285–93.

Bergmann, Emilie. "Abjection and Ambiguity: Lesbian Desire in Bemberg's *Yo, la peor de todas.*" In *Hispanisms and Homosexualities,* ed. Sylvia Molloy and Robert McKee Irwin, 229–47. Durham, N.C.: Duke University Press, 1998.

Bergmann, Emilie L., and Paul Julian Smith. *¿Entiendes? Queer Readings, Hispanic Writings.* Durham, N.C.: Duke University Press, 1995.

Berry, Faith. *Langston Hughes: Before and Beyond Harlem.* New York: Citadel, 1992.

Blanco, José Joaquín. *Crónica de la poesía mexicana.* México: Katún, 1983.

———. *Crónica literaria.* México: Cal y Arena, 1996.

———. "Ojos que da pánico soñar" [1979]. In *Función de medianoche,* 181–90. México: Era, 1984.

————. *La paja en el ojo*. Puebla: ICUAP/Centro de Estudios Contemporáneos/ Editorial Universidad Autónoma de Puebla, 1980.

————. *Las púberes canéforas*. México: Cal y Arena, 1991 [1987].

————. *Se llamaba Vasconcelos*. México: Fondo de Cultura Económica, 1977.

Bonfil, Carlos. "Los cuarenta y uno." In *Mitos mexicanos*, ed. Enrique Florescano, 219–24. México: Aguilar, 1999 [1995].

Bonnett, Piedad. "Presentación." In Porfirio Barba Jacob, *Poesía completa*, 11–18. México: Consejo Nacional para la Cultura y las Artes, 1998.

Bourdieu, Pierre. *Masculine Domination*. Trans. Richard Nice. Stanford: Stanford University Press, 2001 [1998].

————. *Outline of a Theory of Practice*. Trans. Richard Nice. Cambridge: Cambridge University Press, 1993 [1972].

Bradu, Fabienne. *Antonieta*. México: Fondo de Cultura Económica, 1991.

————. *Damas de corazón*. México: Fondo de Cultura Económica, 1994.

————. "Presencia y figura de Xavier Villaurrutia en la crítica mexicana." *Vuelta* 137 (April 1998): 55–58.

Bruce-Novoa, Juan. *Retrospace: Collected Essays on Chicano Literature: Theory and History*. Houston: Arte Público Press, 1990.

Buffington, Robert. *Criminal and Citizen in Modern Mexico*. Lincoln: University of Nebraska Press, 2000.

Buffington, Robert, and Pablo Piccato. "Tales of Two Women: The Narrative Construal of Porfirian Reality." *The Americas* 55, no. 3 (January 1999): 391–424.

Burg, B. R. *Sodomy and the Pirate Tradition: English Sea Rovers in the Seventeenth-Century Caribbean*. New York: New York University Press, 1995 [1983].

Burroughs, William S. *The Letters of William S. Burroughs 1945–1959*. Ed. Oliver Harris. New York: Viking/Penguin, 1993.

————. *Queer*. New York: Viking/Penguin, 1987 [1952].

Butler, Judith. "Actos performativos y constitución del género." *Debate feminista* 9, no. 18 (October 1998): 296–314.

————. *Bodies That Matter: On the Discursive Limits of "Sex."* New York: Routledge, 1993.

————. *Gender Trouble: Feminism and the Subversion of Identity*. New York: Routledge, 1990.

Calderón de la Barca, Frances. *Life in Mexico*. Berkeley: University of California Press, 1982 [1842].

Calva, José Rafael. *Utopía gay*. México: Oasis, 1983.

Camarilla de Pereyra, María Enriqueta. *El secreto*. Madrid: Editorial América, 1922.

Campbell, Federico. "En el país de la impunidad, Pedro Páramo es el rey." In *Juan Rulfo: Un mosaico crítico*. México/ Guadalajara: Universidad

Nacional Aútonoma de México/Universidad de Guadalajara/Instituto Nacional de Bellas Artes, 1988: 39–46.

Campe. *Eufemia ó la mujer verdaderamente instruida.* Paris/México: Librería de la Viuda de Ch. Bouret, 1902.

Campo, Ángel de. *Ocios y apuntes, La rumba.* México: Porrúa, 1981 [1890–91].

Campobello, Nellie. *Cartucho: Relatos de la lucha en el norte* [1931]. In *La novela de la revolución mexicana,* ed. Antonio Castro Leal, 1:927–68. México: Aguilar, 1960.

Campos, Rubén. *El bar: La vida literaria de México en 1900.* México: Universidad Autónoma de México, 1996.

———. *Claudio Oronoz.* México: Publicaciones y Bibliotecas/Secretaría de Educación Pública/Premiá, 1982 [1906].

Campuzano, Juan R. *Ignacio Altamirano: Constructor de la nacionalidad y creador de la literatura mexicana.* México: Federación Editorial Mexicana, 1986.

Capistrán, Miguel. *Los Contemporáneos por si mismos.* México: Consejo Nacional para la Cultura y las Artes, 1994.

Carner, Françoise. "Estereotipos femeninos en el siglo XIX." In *Presencia y transparencia: La mujer en la historia de México,* ed. Carmen Ramos Escandón, et al., 95–109. México: El Colegio de México, 1992 [1987].

Carrier, Joseph. *De los otros: Intimacy and Homosexuality among Mexican Men.* New York: Columbia University Press, 1995.

Castellanos, Rosario. *Balún Canán.* México: Fondo de Cultura Económica, 1994 [1957].

———. *El uso de la palabra.* México: Ediciones de Excelsior, 1974.

Castillo, Alberto del. "Entre la moralización y el sensacionalismo: Prensa, poder y criminalidad a finales del siglo XIX en la Ciudad de México." In *Prensa, criminalidad y drogas durante el porfiriato tardío,* ed. Ricardo Pérez Monfort, 15–73. México: Plaza y Valdés, 1997.

Castillo, Debra A. *Easy Women: Sex and Gender in Modern Mexican Fiction.* Minneapolis: University of Minnesota Press, 1998.

Castillo, Florencio M. del. *Hermana de los ángeles.* México: Premiá/Secretaría de Educación Pública, 1982 [1854].

Castrejón, Eduardo A. *Los 41.* México: Tipografía Popular, 1906.

Ceballos, Ciro B. *Un adulterio.* México: Publicaciones y Bibliotecas/Secretaría de Educación Pública/Premiá, 1982 [1903].

Ceballos Maldonado, José. *Después de todo.* México: Premiá, 1986 [1969].

Chávez, José Ricardo. *Los hijos de Cibeles: Cultura y sexualidad en la literatura de fin de siglo XIX.* México: Universidad Autónoma de México, 1997.

Chodorow, Nancy. *The Reproduction of Mothering: Psychoanalysis and the Sociology of Gender.* Berkeley: University of California Press, 1978.

Clifford, James. "On Ethnographic Allegory." In *Writing Culture: The Poetics and Politics of Ethnography*, ed. James Clifford and George E. Marcus, 98–121. Berkeley: University of California Press, 1986.

Cocteau, Jean. *The White Book/Le livre blanc*. Trans. Peter Owen. San Francisco: City Lights, 1989 [1928].

Connell, R. W. *Masculinities*. Berkeley: University of California Press, 1995.

Cory, Donald Webster. *El homosexual en Norteamérica*. Trans. Alfredo Sánchez Luna. México: Compañía General de Ediciones, n.d. [1951].

Couto Castillo, Bernardo. *Asfódelos*. México: Premiá/Instituto Nacional de Bellas Artes, 1984 [1897].

Cruz, Jacqueline. "La moral tradicional y la identidad mexicana vistas a través de los personajes femeninos de *El Zarco*." *Explicación de Textos Literarios* 22, no. 1 (1993–94): 73–86.

Cuéllar, José Tomás de. "Baile y cochino." In *La linterna mágica*, 1–146. México: Universidad Nacional Autónoma de México, 1992 [1886].

———. *Historia de Chucho el Ninfo*. México: Porrúa, 1975 [1871].

———. *Los mariditos*. México: Secretaría de Educación Pública/Premiá, 1982 [1890].

Cuesta, Jorge. *Poesía y crítica*. México: Consejo Nacional para la Cultura y las Artes, 1991.

Cuesta, Jorge, ed. *Antología de la poesía mexicana*. México: Fondo de Cultura Económica/Secretaría de Educación Pública, 1985 [1928].

Curiel, Fernando. "Notas para una edición: La correspondencia Torres Bodet/ Alfonso Reyes." In *Los Contemporáneos en el laberinto de la crítica*, ed. Rafael Olea Franco and Anthony Stanton, 55–65. México: El Colegio de México, 1994.

———. *La Revuelta: Interpretación del Ateneo de la Juventud (1906–1929)*. México: Universidad Nacional Autónoma de México, 1998.

DeJean, Joan. *Fictions of Sappho: 1546–1937*. Chicago: University of Chicago Press, 1989.

De la Mora, Sergio. "Pedro Infante y el culto al cuate." Trans. Frederic Chaume and María Teresa Albero. *Archivos de la Filmoteca* 31 (1999): 88–104.

de Lauretis, Teresa. *Alice Doesn't*. Bloomington: Indiana University Press, 1984.

El Diario del Hogar, November 19–24, 1901.

Díaz Arciniega, Víctor. *Querella por la cultura "revolucionaria" (1925)*. México: Fondo de Cultura Económica, 1989.

Díaz Dufóo, Carlos. *Cuentos nerviosos*. México: J. Ballescá, 1901.

Díaz-Guerrero, Rogelio. *Psychology of the Mexican: Culture and Personality*. Austin: University of Texas Press, 1975 [1967].

Domecq, Brianda. "La virginidad en la literatura mexicana." In *Acechando al unicornio: La virginidad en la literatura mexicana*, 24–39. México: Fondo de Cultura Económica, 1992 [1988].

Domenella, Ana Rosa, and Nora Pasternac, eds. *Las voces olvidadas: Antología crítica de narradoras mexicanas nacidas en el siglo XIX*. México: El Colegio de México, 1991.

Enriqueta (María Enriqueta Camarilla de Pereyra). *El secreto*. Madrid: Editorial América, 1922.

Epstein, Julia. "Either/Or—Neither/Both: Sexual Ambiguity and the Ideology of Gender." *Genders* 7 (1990): 99–142.

Escalante, Evodio. *La intervención literaria*. Sinaloa/Zacatecas: Alebrije/Universidad Autónoma de Sinaloa/Universidad Autónoma de Zacatecas, 1988.

———. "Sobre los espejismos de la crítica: El caso del estridentismo." Unpublished conference paper, University of California–Irvine, April 1996.

Fanon, Frantz. *Black Skin, White Masks*. Trans. Charles Lam Markmann. New York: Grove Press, 1967 [1952].

Fernández de Lizardi, José Joaquín. *La Quijotita y su prima*. 2d ed. México: Porrúa, 1990 [1818, 1831–32].

———. *Vida y hechos del famoso caballero don Catrín de la Fachenda*. 7:533–619. México: Universidad Nacional Autónoma de México, 1980 [1832].

———. *Vida y hechos de Periquillo Sarniento, escrita por él para sus hijos*. México: Proxema, 1979 [1816].

Fernández Perera, Manuel. "El macho y el machismo." In *Mitos mexicanos*, ed. Enrique Florescano, 179–84. México: Aguilar, 1999 [1995].

Ferrer Torrents, F., and Joan D'Oc. *Sodoma pide fuero: ¿Es respetable un país con veinte millones de homosexuales?* México: F. Ferrer, 1959.

Fiedler, Leslie A. *Love and Death in the American Novel*. Normal, Ill.: Dalkey Archive Press, 1997 [1966].

Fiol-Matta, Licia. *A Queer Mother for the Nation: The State and Gabriela Mistral*. Minneapolis: University of Minnesota Press, 2002.

Fiscal, María Rosa. "Reencuentro con María Enriqueta." In *Las voces olvidadas: Antología crítica de narradoras mexicanas nacidas en el siglo XIX*, ed. Ana Rosa Domenella and Nora Pasternac, 181–99. México: El Colegio de México, 1991.

Foucault, Michel. *The History of Sexuality*. 3 vols. Trans. Robert Hurley. New York: Vintage Books, 1988–90 [1976–84].

Franco, Jean. *Critical Passions: Selected Essays*. Durham, N.C.: Duke University Press, 1999.

———. *An Introduction to Spanish-American Literature*. 3d ed. Cambridge: Cambridge University Press, 1994 [1969].

————. *Plotting Women*. New York: Columbia University Press, 1989.

Freud, Sigmund. *Civilization and Its Discontents*. Trans. James Strachey. New York: W. W. Norton, 1989 [1929].

————. "On Narcissism: An Introduction." In *The Standard Edition of the Complete Psychological Works of Sigmund Freud,* ed. James Strachey, 14:67–102. London: Hogarth Press/Institute of Psycho-analysis, 1957 [1914].

————. "Psychoanalytic Notes upon an Autobiographical Account of a Case of Paranoia (Dementia Paranoides)." In *Three Case Histories,* 83–160. New York: Collier, 1993 [1911].

————. "Three Essays on the Theory of Sexuality" In *The Freud Reader,* ed. Peter Gay, 239–92. New York: W. W. Norton, 1989 [1905/24].

Frías, Heriberto. *Tomóchic*. México: Editorial Offset, 1983 [1893–95].

Fromm, Erich, and Michael Maccoby. *Social Character in a Mexican Village*. New Brunswick, N.J.: Transaction Publishers, 1996 [1970].

Fuentes, Carlos. *La muerte de Artemio Cruz*. México: Fondo de Cultura Económica, 1985 [1962].

————. *La región más transparente*. México: Fondo de Cultura Económica, 1997 [1958].

Gamboa, Federico. *La novela mexicana*. México: Eusebio Gómez de la Puente, 1914.

————. *Santa*. México: Grijalbo, 1979 [1903].

García Morales, Alfonso. *El Ateneo de México (1906–1914): Orígenes de la cultura mexicana contemporánea*. Sevilla: Escuela de Estudios Hispano-americanos de Sevilla, 1992.

Garro, Elena. *Los recuerdos del porvenir*. México: Joaquín Moritz, 1996 [1963].

Garza, María Luisa ["Loreley"]. *Alas y quimeras*. México: Cvltvra, 1924.

————. *La novia de Nervo*. San Antonio, 1922.

Gide, André. *Corydon*. Trans. Julio Gómez de la Serna. Madrid: Alianza, 1971.

————. *La escuela de mujeres*. Trans. Xavier Villaurrutia and Antonieta Rivas Mercado. México: La Razón, 1931.

————. *L'immoraliste*. Paris: Mercure de France, c. 1902.

————. *El regreso del hijo pródigo*. Trans. Xavier Villaurrutia. México: Séneca, 1942.

————. *Si le grain ne meurt*. Paris: Gallimard, 1993 [1955].

Gilmore, David D. *Manhood in the Making: Cultural Concepts of Masculinity*. New Haven: Yale University Press, 1990.

Glantz, Margo. "*Astucia* de Luis G. Inclán, ¿Novela 'nacional' mexicana?" *Revista Iberoamericana* 63, no. 178–79 (January–June 1997): 87–97.

————. *Esguince de cintura*. México: Consejo Nacional para la Cultura y las Artes, 1994.

Gonzalbo, Pilar, et al. *Historia de la lectura en México*. México: El Colegio de México, 1999.

González, Aníbal. *Journalism and the Development of Spanish American Narrative*. Cambridge: University of Cambridge Press, 1993.

González Méndez, Guillermo. "Los estados intersexuales y la disforia de género." In *Antología de la sexualidad humana*, 3:123–72. México: Consejo Nacional de Población/Porrúa, 1994.

González Navarro, Moisés. "*Mestizaje* in Mexico during the National Period." In *Race and Class in Latin America*, ed. Magnus Mörner, 145–69. New York: Columbia University Press, 1970.

———. "El porfiriato: la vida social." In *Historia moderna de México*, ed. Daniel Cosío Villegas. Vol. 4. México: Hermes, 1957.

González Pineda, Francisco. *El mexicano: Psicología de su destructividad*. México: Pax-México, 1961.

González Rodríguez, Sergio. "Lectura y censura sexual en México, 1900–1990." In *Los amorosos*, ed. Sergio González Rodríguez. México: Cal y Arena, 1996.

Granillo Vázquez, Lilia. "La abnegación maternal, sustrato fundamental de la cultura femenina en México." In *Identidades y nacionalismos,* ed. Lilia Granillo Vázquez, 195–255. México: Universidad Autónoma Metropolitana-Azcapotzalco/Gernika, 1993.

———. "La cuestión de las mujeres que supieron latín." *Sociología* 4, no. 10 (May–August 1989): 61–80.

———. "Las tretas del fuerte: Escribir 'para, por y en lugar de el bello sexo.'" *La otredad: Los discursos de la cultura hoy: 1995,* ed. Silvia Elguea Véjar, 83–92. México: Universidad Autónoma Metropolitana-Azcapotzalco/Centro de Cultura Casa Lamm/Universidad de Louisville, Kentucky, 1997.

Gruzinski, Serge. "Las cenizas del deseo: Homosexuales novohispanos a mediados del siglo XVII." In *De la santidad a la perversión: O de por qué no se cumplía la ley de Dios en la sociedad novohispana,* ed. Sergio Ortega, 255–81. México: Grijalbo, 1986.

Guerrero, Julio. *La génesis del crimen en México*. México: Porrúa, 1977 [1901].

Guillén, Laura. *Soy homosexual*. México: Ediciones del Milenio, 1994.

Gutmann, Matthew C. *The Meanings of Macho: Being a Man in Mexico City*. Berkeley: University of California Press, 1996.

Guzmán, Martín Luis. *La sombra del caudillo. Obras completas,* vol. 1 [1961]: 499–650. México: Fondo de Cultura Económica, 1984 [1929].

El Hijo del Ahuizote. November 24–December 1, 1901.

Hocquenghem, Guy. *Homosexual Desire* [1972] Trans. Daniella Dangoor. Durham, N.C.: Duke University Press, 1993 [1978].

Huerta, Fernando. "Poder y masculinidad en el deporte." Unpublished conference paper. Las expresiones del poder: IV Coloquio Paul Kirchoff. Instituto de Investigaciones Antropológicas, Universidad Nacional Autónoma de México, 1998.

Illades, Carlos, and Adriana Sandoval. *Espacio social y representación literaria en el siglo XIX.* México: Universidad Autónoma Metropolitana: Unidad Iztapalapa/Plaza y Valdés, 2000.

El Imparcial. November 23–November 25, 1901.

Inclán, Luis G. *Astucia.* 7th ed. México: Porrúa, 1987 [1865].

Irwin, Robert McKee. "As Invisible as He Is: The Queer Enigma of Xavier Villaurrutia." In *Reading and Writing the Ambiente: Queer Sexualities in Latino, Latin American, and Spanish culture,* ed. Susana Chávez-Silverman and Librada Hernández. Madison: University of Wisconsin Press, 2000: 114–46.

———."La homosexualidad cósmica mexicana: espájos de diferencia racial en Xavier Villaurratia." *Revista Iberoamericano* 187 (April–June 1999): 293–304.

———. "The Legend of Jorge Cuesta: The Perils of Alchemy and the Paranoia of Gender." In *Hispanisms and Homosexualities,* ed. Sylvia Molloy and Robert McKee Irwin, 29–53. Durham, N.C.: Duke University Press, 1998.

Irwin, Robert McKee, Edward J. McCaughan, and Michelle Rocío Nasser, eds. *The Famous 41: Sexuality and Social Control in Mexico, c. 1901.* New York: Palgrave, 2002.

Issorel, Jacques, trans. "Neuf interviews de Xavier Villaurrutia." In *Intellectuels et état au Méxique au XX siècle,* ed. GRAL Institut d'Études Mexicaines—Perpignan, 113–24. Paris: CNRS, 1979:

Izquierdo Albiñana, A. *Andréïda: "El tercer sexo."* México: Botas, 1938.

Katz, Alejandro. *Jorge Cuesta, o la alegría del guerrero.* México: Fondo de Cultura Económica, 1989.

Krafft-Ebing, Richard von. *Psychopathia Sexualis: A Medico-Forensic Study.* New York: G. P. Putnam's, 1965.

Lafora, Gonzalo R. *La educación sexual y la reforma de la moral sexual.* Madrid: Revista de Pedagogía, 1933.

Lamas, Marta. "Cuerpo: diferencia sexual y género." *Debate Feminista 5,* no. 10 (September 1994): 3–31.

Lancaster, Roger. "Guto's Performance: Notes on the Transvestism of Everyday Life." In *Sex and Sexuality in Latin America,* ed. Daniel Balderston and Donna J. Guy, 9–32. New York: New York University Press, 1997.

Leal, Luis. *Aztlán y México: Perfiles literarios e históricos.* Binghamton, N.Y.: Bilingual Press/Editorial Bilingüe, 1985.

———. *Mariano Azuela.* New York: Twayne, 1971.

Leduc, Alberto. *Un calvario: Memorias de una exclaustrada.* México: Tipografía T. González, Sucesores, 1900.

Leland, Christopher Towne. *The Last Happy Men.* Syracuse, N.Y.: Syracuse University Press, 1986.

Lemaire, Ria. "Relendo *Iracema* (o problema da representação da mulher na construção duma identidade nacional)." *Organon* 16 (1989): 257–79.

Leñero, Vicente. *Los albañiles.* México: Planeta/Seix Barral, 1995 [1964].

Lewis, Oscar. *The Children of Sánchez: Autobiography of a Mexican Family.* New York: Vintage, 1961.

Lozano Armendares, Teresa. *La criminalidad en la ciudad de México 1800–1821.* México: Universidad Nacional Autónoma de México, 1987.

Lucey, Michael. *Gide's Bent: Sexuality, Politics, Writing.* Oxford: Oxford University Press, 1995.

Ludmer, Josefina. *El género gauchesco.* Buenos Aires: Sudamericana, 1988.

———. "Mujeres que matan." *Revista Iberoamericana* 62, no. 176–77 (July–December 1996): 781–97.

Lumsden, Ian. *Homosexualidad: Sociedad y estado en México.* Trans. Luis Zapata, México/Toronto: Solediciones/Canadian Gay Archives, 1991.

Macedo, Miguel S. *La criminalidad en México: Medios de combatirla.* México: Oficina Tip. de la Secretaría de Fomento, 1897.

Macías, Ana. *Against All Odds: The Feminist Movement in Mexico to 1940.* Westport, Conn.: Greenwood Press, 1982.

Manrique de Lara, Juana, and Guadalupe Monroy Baigen, eds. *Seudónimos, anagramas e iniciales de escritores mexicanos, antiguos y modernos.* 2d ed. México: Secretaría de Educación Pública, 1954.

Maples Arce, Manuel, ed. *Antología de la poesía mexicana.* Rome: Poligráfica Tiberina, 1939.

Marañón, Gregorio. *La evolución de la sexualidad y los estados intersexuales.* 2d ed. Santiago de Chile: Nueva Época, 1933 [1930].

Marín, Guadalupe. *La única.* México: Editorial Jalisco, 1938.

Martin, Gerald. "Literature, Music, and the Visual Arts, 1870–1930." In *A Cultural History of Latin America,* ed. Leslie Bethell, 47–130. Cambridge: Cambridge University Press, 1998.

Martínez, José Luis. *La expresión nacional.* México: Oasis, 1984.

Martínez Peñaloza, Porfirio. Introduction to *Máscaras de la Revista Moderna.* México: Fondo de Cultura Económica, 1968.

Masiello, Francine. *Between Civilization and Barbarism: Women, Nation, and Literary Culture in Modern Argentina.* Lincoln: University of Nebraska Press, 1992.

———. "Estado, género y sexualidad en la cultura del fin de siglo." In *Las culturas de fin de siglo en América Latina,* ed. Josefina Ludmer, 139–49. Rosario: Beatriz Viterbo, 1994:

———. " 'Gentlemen,' damas y travestis: ciudadanía e identidad cultural en la Argentina del fin de siglo." In *La imaginación histórica en el siglo XIX,* ed. Leslie Area and Mabel Moraña, 297–309. Rosario: UNR Editora, 1994.

———. "Horror y lágrimas: sexo y nación en la cultura del fin de siglo." In *Esplendores y miserias del siglo XIX,* ed. Beatriz González Stephan, et al., 457–72. Caracas: Monte Avila, Latinoamericana, Equinoccio, Ediciones de la Universidad Simón Bolívar, 1995.

Mirandé, Alfredo. *Hombres y machos: Masculinity and Latino Culture.* Boulder, Colo.: Westview Press, 1997.

Molina, Roderick. *Amado Nervo's Poetic Ethos.* New York: New York University Press, 1956.

Molloy, Sylvia. *At Face Value: Autobiographical Writing in Spanish America.* Cambridge: Cambridge University Press, 1991.

———. "Dos lecturas del cisne: Rubén Darío y Delmira Agustini." In *La sartén por el mango,* ed. Patricia Elena González and Eliana Ortega, 57–69. Río Piedras: Ediciones Huracán, 1984.

———. "His America, Our America: José Martí Reads Whitman." In *Breaking Bounds: Whitman and American Cultural Sudies,* ed. Betsy Erkkila and Jay Grossman. New York: Oxford University Press, 1996.

———. "La flexión de género en el texto cultural latinoamericano." *Revista de Crítica Cultural* 21 (November 2000): 54–56.

———. "The Politics of Posing." In *Hispanisms and Homosexualities,* ed. Sylvia Molloy and Robert McKee Irwin, 141–60. Durham, N.C.: Duke University Press, 1998.

———. "Too Wilde for Comfort: Desire and Ideology in Fin-de-Siècle Latin America." In *Negotiating Lesbian and Gay Subjects,* ed. Monica Dorenkamp and Richard Henke, 35–52. New York: Routledge, 1985.

Molloy, Sylvia, and Robert McKee Irwin, eds. *Hispanisms and Homosexualities.* Durham, N.C.: Duke University Press, 1998.

Monges Nicolau, Graciela. "El género biográfico en *Mujeres notables mexicanas* de Laureana Wright de Kleinhans." In *Las voces olvidadas: Antología crítica de narradoras mexicanas nacidas en el siglo XIX,* ed. Ana Rosa Domenella and Nora Pasternac, 357–78. México: El Colegio de México, 1991.

Monsiváis, Carlos. *Amor perdido.* México: Era, 1990 [1977].

———. *Escenas de pudor y liviandad.* México: Era, 1988 [1981]. .

———. *Los iguales, los semejantes, los (hasta hace un minuto) perfectos desconocidos (A cien años de la Redada de los 41).* México: Consejo Nacional para la Cultura y las Artes/Instituto Nacional de Bellas Artes, 2001.

———. "Los que tenemos unas manos que no nos pertenecen." *Debate feminista* 8, no. 16 (October 1997): 11–33.

———. "El mundo soslayado." In Salvador Novo, *La estatua de sal,* 11–41. México: Consejo Nacional para la Cultura y las Artes, 1998,

———. "Notas sobre la cultura mexicana en el siglo XX." In *Historia general de México,* ed. Daniel Cosío Villegas. 2:1377–1548. México: El Colegio de México, 1976.

———. "Ortodoxia y heterodoxia en las alcobas." *Debate Feminista* 6, no. 11 (April 1995): 183–210.

———. "Prólogo." In *La poesía mexicana del siglo XX,* ed. Carlos Monsivías. México: Empresas, 1966.

———. *Salvador Novo: Lo marginal en el centro.* México: Era, 2000.

Montero, Oscar. "Before the Parade Passes By: Latino Queers and National Identity." *Radical America* 24, no. 4 (1990): 15–25.

———. "Julián del Casal and the Queers of Havana." In *¿Entiendes? Queer Readings, Hispanic Writings,* ed. Emilie L. Bergmann and Paul Julian Smith, 92–112. Durham, N.C.: Duke University Press, 1995.

———. "Martí y el lenguaje del gabinete." *Nómada* 1 (April 1995): 67–71.

Mora Escalante, Sonia Marta. *De la sujeción colonial a la patria criolla: El Periquillo Sarniento y los orígenes de la novela en Hispanoamérica.* Heredia, Costa Rica/Montpellier, France: Editorial de la Universidad Nacional/Institut de Sociocritique, 1995.

Moretta, Eugene. *The Poetic Achievement of Xavier Villaurrutia.* Cuernavaca: CIDOC Cuaderno, 1971.

Mulvey, Laura. *Visual and Other Pleasures.* Bloomington: Indiana University Press, 1989.

Muñoz, Mario. "En torno a la narrativa mexicana de tema homosexual." *La Palabra y el Hombre* 84 (October–December 1992): 21–37.

Muñoz, Rafael F. *¡Vámanos con Pancho Villa!* [1931]. In *La novela de la revolución mexicana,* ed. Antonio Castro Leal, 2:687–778. México: Aguilar, 1960.

Murray, Stephen O. "The 'Underdevelopment' of Modern/Gay Homosexuality in Mesoamerica." In *Modern Homosexualities,* ed. Ken Plummer. London: Routledge, 1992.

El Nacional. April 9–May 3, 1895.

"NAFPA." *Nexos.* December 1993: 81.

Nandino, Elías. *Juntando mis pasos.* México: Aldus, 2000.

Nervo, Amado. "Andrógino." In *Prosa y verso,* 180–81. México: Patria, 1984 [1896].

———. "El bachiller." In *Prosa y verso,* 83–107. México: Patria, 1984 [1895].

———. *El castillo de lo inconsciente.* México: Consejo Nacional para la Cultura y las Artes, 2000.

———. *El donador de almas.* México: B. Costa-Amic, 1976 [1904].

———. *Ensayos: Obras completas.* Vol 26. Madrid: Biblioteca Nueva, 1928.

————. *Fuegos fatuos y pimientos dulces*. México: Porrúa, 1951.

————. "Hermafrodita." In *El castillo de lo inconsciente*, 118–19. México: Consejo Nacional para la Cultura y las Artes, 2000 [1895].

————. *Prosa y verso*. México: Patria, 1984.

————. "El ser neutro." In *Obras completas*, vol. 25, *Crónicas*, 169–71. Madrid: Biblioteca Nueva, 1928.

————. "Victoriano Salado Álvarez." In *Máscaras de la Revista Moderna*, intro. by Porfirio Martínez Peñaloza, 162–65. México: Fondo de la Cultura Económica, 1968.

Nouzeilles, Gabriela. "Ficciones paranoicas de fin de siglo: Naturalismo argentino y policía médica." *MLN* 12 (1997): 232–52.

————. "Narrar el cuerpo propio: Retórica modernista de la enfermedad." *Revista de Investigaciones Literarias* 5, no. 9 (1997): 149–76.

————. "Políticas médicas de la histeria: Mujeres, salud y representación en el Buenos Aires del fin de siglo." *Mora: Revista del Instituto Interdisciplinario de Estudios de Género* 5 (October 1999): 97–112.

Novo, Salvador. *La estatua de sal*. México: Consejo Nacional para la Cultura y las Artes, 1998.

————. *La vida en México en el periodo presidencial de Manuel Ávila Camacho*. México: Consejo Nacional para la Cultura y las Artes/Instituto Nacional de Antropología e Historia, 1994.

————. *La vida en México en el periodo presidencial de Miguel Alemán*. México: Consejo Nacional para la Cultura y las Artes/Instituto Nacional de Antropología e Historia, 1994.

————. "Prólogo" [1966]. In Luis G. Inclán, *Astucia* [1865], 7th ed. México: Porrúa, 1987.

Núñez Noriega, Guillermo. *Sexo entre varones: Poder y resistencia en el campo sexual*. 2d ed. México and Sonora: Universidad Nacional Autónoma de México, Miguel Ángel Porrúa, El Colegio de Sonora, 1999.

Ojeda, Jorge Arturo. *Octavio*. México: Premiá, 1987 [1982].

Olea Franco, Rafael, and Anthony Stanton, eds. *Los Contemporáneos en el laberinto de la crítica*. México: El Colegio de México, 1994.

Olivier, Guilhem. "Conquérants et missionnaires face au 'péché abominable,' essai sur l'homosexualité en Mésoamérique au moment de la conquête espagnole." *Caravelle* 55 (1990): 19–51.

O'Malley, Ilene V. *The Myth of the Revolution: Hero Cults and the Institutionalization of the Mexican State, 1920–1940*. New York: Greenwood Press, 1986.

Oosterhuis, Harry, and Hubert Kennedy, eds. *Homosexuality and Male Bonding in Pre-Nazi Germany*. New York: Harrington Park Press, 1991.

Oropesa, Salvador. "Deseo homosocial y representación homosexual en Agustín Lazo y Xavier Villaurrutia: *El caso de don Juan Manuel* y *La mulata de Córdoba*." *Romance Languages Annual* 9 (1998): 635–40.

———. "Hacia una identidad nacional: La relación México-España en *Santa* de Federico Gamboa." *Romance Languages Annual* 8 (1997): 627–32.

———. "Novelista de la modernidad: Guadalupe Marín." In *Modalidades de representación del sujeto auto/bio/gráfico femenino,* ed. Magdalena Maiz and Luis Peña, 213–24. San Nicolás de los Garza: Universidad Autónoma de Nuevo León, 1997.

Oyarzún, Kemy. "Deseo y narrativa disciplinaria: *El Periquillo Sarniento.*" *Acta Literaria* 16 (1991): 21–39.

El País. November 21–27, 1901.

Palacios, Adela. *El hombre.* México: Instituto México-Cubano de Relaciones Culturales, 1956 [1948].

Palaversich, Diana. "Caught in the Act." *Chasqui* 28, no. 2 (1999): 60–75.

Palou, Pedro Ángel. *La casa del silencio: Aproximación en tres tiempos a Contemporáneos.* Zamora, Michoacán: El Colegio de Michoacán, 1997.

———. *En el alcoba de un mundo.* México: Fondo de Cultura Económica, 1992.

Panabière, Louis. *Itinerario de una disidencia: Jorge Cuesta (1903–1942).* Trans. A. Castañón. México: Fondo de Cultura Económica, 1983.

Paredes, Américo. *Estados Unidos, México y el machismo.* Austin: University of Texas Institute of Latin American Studies Offprint Series, n.d. [1967].

———. *George Washington Gómez.* Houston: Arte Público Press, 1990.

Parker, Patricia. "Virile Style." In *Premodern Sexualities,* ed. Louise Fradenburg, 201–22. New York: Routledge, 1996.

Pasternac, Nora. "El periodismo feminino en el siglo XIX: *Violetas del Anáhuac.*" In *Las voces olvidadas: Antología crítica de narradoras mexicanas nacidas en el siglo XIX,* ed. Ana Rosa Domenella and Nora Pasternac, 399–418. México: El Colegio de México, 1991.

La Patria. November 20–23, 1901.

Payno, Manuel. *Los bandidos del Río Frío.* México: Porrúa, 1996 [1891].

———. *El fistol del diablo.* 6th ed. México: Porrúa, 1992 [1845–46].

———. "Memorias sobre el matrimonio" [1843]. In *El álbum de la mujer: antología ilustrada de las mexicanas,* ed. Julia Tuñón, 3:117–27. México: Instituto Nacional de Antropología e Historia, 1991.

Paz, Octavio. *El laberinto de la soledad.* México: Fondo de Cultura Económica, 1989 [1950].

———. *Sor Juana Inés de la Cruz o Las trampas de la fe.* Barcelona: Seix Barral, 1982.

———. *Xavier Villaurrutia en persona y en obra.* México: Fondo de Cultura Económica, 1978.

Pérez Monfort, Ricardo, ed. *Hábitos, normas y escándalo: Prensa, criminalidad y drogas durante el porfiriato tardío.* México: Plaza y Valdés, 1997.

Piccato, Pablo. *City of Suspects: Crime in Mexico City, 1900–1931*. Durham, N.C.: Duke University Press, 2001.

———. " 'No es posible cerrar los ojos': El discurso sobre la criminalidad y el alcoholismo hacia el fin del porfiriato." In *Hábitos, normas y escándalo: Prensa, criminalidad y drogas durante el porfiriato tardío,* ed. Ricardo Pérez Monfort, 75–142. México: Plaza y Valdés, 1997.

Po, Paolo. *41, o un muchacho que soñaba en fantasmas.* México: B. Costa-Amic, 1964.

Popoca y Palacios, Lamberto. *Historia de el [sic] bandalismo en el estado de Morelos.* Puebla: Tipografía Guadalupana, 1912.

El Popular. November 20–December 1, 1901.

Pratt, Mary Louise. "Women, Literature, and National Brotherhood." In *Women, Culture, and Politics in Latin America,* ed. Emilie Bergmann, et al., 48–73. Berkeley: University of California Press, 1990.

Prieur, Annick. *Mema's House, Mexico City: On Transvestites, Queens, and Machos.* Chicago: University of Chicago Press, 1998.

Quevedo y Zubieta, Salvador. *México marimacho.* México: Botas, 1933.

Quiroga, José. *Tropics of Desire: Interventions from Queer Latino America.* New York: New York University Press, 2000.

Rama, Ángel. *La ciudad letrada.* Hanover, N.H.: Ediciones del Norte, 1984.

Ramírez, Ignacio. *Obras.* 2 vols. México: Editora Nacional, 1952.

Ramos, Julio. *Desencuentros de la modernidad en América Latina.* México: Fondo de Cultura Económica, 1989.

———. "The Repose of Heroes." *Modern Language Quarterly* 57, no. 2 (June 1996): 355–67.

Ramos, Samuel. *Perfil del hombre y la cultura en México.* México: Universidad Nacional Autónoma de México/Secretaría de Educación Pública, 1987 [1934].

Ramos Escandón, Carmen, et al. *Presencia y transparencia: La mujer en la historia de México.* México: El Colegio de México, 1992 [1987].

———. "Señoritas porfirianas: Mujer e ideología en el México progresista, 1880–1910." In *Presencia y transparencia: La mujer en la historia de México,* ed. Carmen Ramos Escandón, et al., 143–62. México: El Colegio de México, 1992 [1987].

Rampersad, Arnold. *The Life of Langston Hughes,* vol. 1, 1902–1941: *I, Too, Sing America.* New York: Oxford University Press, 1986.

Rechy, John. *City of Night.* New York: Grove Weidenfeld, 1988 [1963].

Reed, John. *Insurgent Mexico.* New York: International Publishers, 1969 [1914].

Revueltas, José. *Los errores.* México: Era, 1980 [1964].

———. *El luto humano.* México: Era, 1981 [1943].

Reyes Nevárez, Salvador. *El amor y la amistad en el mexicano.* México: Porrúa y Obregón, 1952.

Riva Palacio, Vicente. *Los piratas del Golfo.* 2d ed. 2 vols. México: Porrúa, 1974 [1869].

Rivas Mercado, Antonieta. *87 cartas de amor y otros papeles.* Xalapa: Universidad Veracruzana, 1981 [1975].

Rivera-Garza, Cristina. "Dangerous Minds: Changing Psychiatric Views of the Mentally Ill in Porfirian Mexico, 1876–1911." *Journal of the History of Medicine and Allied Sciences* 56, no. 1 (January 2001): 36–67.

———. "A Routine of Mental Health: Life Inside the General Insane Asylum *La Castañeda,* Mexico 1910–1930." Unpublished manuscript.

Rojas, Marcial. "Xavier Villaurrutia, entrevisto." *Revistas literarias mexicanas modernas: Ulises 1927, 1928; Escala 1930,* 276–78. México: Fondo de Cultura Económica, 1980 [1930].

Rojas González, Francisco. *La negra Angustias.* 2d ed. México: EDIAPSA, 1948 [1944].

Roumagnac, Carlos. *Crímenes sexuales y pasionales: Estudios de psicología morbosa.* México: Librería de Ch. Bouret, 1906.

———. *Los criminales en México: Ensayo de psicología criminal.* México: Tipografía El Fénix, 1904.

———. *Matadores de mujeres.* México: Librería de Ch. Bouret, 1910.

Rubin, Gayle. "The Traffic in Women." In *Toward an Anthropology of Women,* ed. Rayna Reiter. New York: Monthly Review Press, 1975.

Ruffinelli, Jorge. "La recepción crítica de *Los de abajo.*" In Mariano Azuela, *Los de abajo,* edición crítica, ed. Jorge Ruffinelli, 185–213. Buenos Aires: Colección Archivos/UNESCO, 1988.

Ruiz de Burton, María Amparo. *The Squatter and the Don.* Houston: Arte Público Press, 1997 [1885].

Rulfo, Juan. *Pedro Páramo.* Barcelona: Bruguera, 1986 [1955].

Sagredo, Rafael. *María Villa (a) La Chiquita, no. 4002: Un parásito social del porfiriato.* México: Cal y Arena, 1996.

Said, Edward. *Culture and Imperialism.* New York: Vintage, 1994 [1993].

Salado Álvarez, Victoriano. *Cuentos y narraciones.* México: Porrúa, 1953.

Saldívar, José David. "Nuestra América's Borders: Remapping American Cultural Studies." In *José Martí's "Our America": From National to Hemispheric Cultural Studies,* ed. Jeffrey Belnap and Raúl Fernández, 145–75. Durham, N.C.: Duke University Press, 1998.

Saldívar, Ramón. *Chicano Narrative: The Dialectics of Difference.* Madison: University of Wisconsin Press, 1990.

Salessi, Jorge. *Médicos maleantes y maricas.* Rosario: Beatriz Viterbo, 1995.

Santamaría, Francisco J. *Diccionario de Mejicanismos.* 5th ed. México: Porrúa, 1992.

Schaefer, Claudia. *Danger Zones: Homosexuality, National Identity, and Mexican Culture.* Tucson: University of Arizona Press, 1996.

Schneider, Luis Mario. "Los Contemporáneos: La vanguardia desmentida." In *Los Contemporáneos en el laberinto de la crítica,* ed. Rafael Olea Franco and Anthony Stanton. México: El Colegio de México, 1994: 15–20.

———. *Fragua y gesta del teatro experimental en México.* México: Universidad Autónoma de México/Equilibrista, 1995.

———. *La novela mexicana entre el petróleo, la homosexualidad y la política.* México: Nueva Imagen, 1997.

———. *Ruptura y continuidad: La literatura mexicana en polémica.* México: Fondo de Cultura Económica, 1986 [1975].

———. "El tema homosexual en la nueva narrativa mexicana." In *La novela mexicana entre el petróleo, la homosexualidad y la política,* 65–88. México: Nueva Imagen, 1997.

Schopenhauer, Arthur. *The World as Will and Representation.* Trans. E. F. J. Payne. 2 vols. New York: Dover, 1966.

Sedgwick, Eve Kosofsky. *Between Men: English Literature and Male Homosocial Desire.* New York: Columbia University Press, 1985.

———. *Epistemology of the Closet.* Berkeley: University of California Press, 1990.

Sesto, Julio. *El México de Porfirio Díaz.* 2d ed. Valencia: F. Sempere, 1910.

Sheridan, Guillermo. *Los Contemporáneos ayer.* México: Fondo de Cultura Económica, 1993 [1985].

———. *México en 1932: La polémica nacionalista.* México: Fondo de Cultura Económica, 1999.

———. "Villaurrutia habla dos veces." *Vuelta* 222 (May 1995): 58–59.

Sifuentes Jáuregui, B. "The Swishing of Gender: Homographetic Marks in *Lazarillo de Tormes.*" In *Hispanisms and Homosexualities,* ed. Sylvia Molloy and Robert McKee Irwin. Durham, N.C.: Duke University Press, 1998.

Silverman, Kaja. *Male Subjectivity at the Margins.* New York: Routledge, 1992.

Sinfield, Alan. *The Wilde Century: Effeminacy, Oscar Wilde, and the Queer Moment.* New York: Columbia University Press, 1994.

Sommer, Doris. *Foundational Fictions.* [1991]. Berkeley: University of California Press, 1993.

Sommers, Joseph. *After the Storm: Landmarks of the Modern Mexican Novel.* Albuquerque: University of New Mexico Press, 1968.

Spackman, Barbara. *Decadent Genealogies: The Rhetoric of Sickness from Baudelaire to D'Annunzio.* Ithaca, N.Y.: Cornell University Press, 1989.

Stanton, Anthony M. "Incesto y parricidio: Estructuras antropológicas en *Pedro Páramo.*" *Juan Rulfo: Un mosaico crítico,* 147–55. México: Universidad Nacional Autónoma de México/Universidad de Guadalajara/Instituto Nacional de Bellas Artes, 1988.

Staples, Anne. "La lectura y los lectores en los primeros años de vida independiente." In *Historia de la lectura en México,* ed. Pilar Gonzalbo, et al., 94–126. México: El Colegio de México, 1999.

Stepan, Nancy Leys. *"The Hour of Eugenics": Race, Gender, and Nation in Latin America.* Ithaca, N.Y.: Cornell University Press, 1991.

Tablada, José Juan. *La feria de la vida.* México: Consejo Nacional para la Cultura y las Artes, 1991 [1937].

Tarica, Estelle. *"La negra Angustias, Mestizaje,* and Sexual Normalization in the Name of the Revolution." Unpublished conference paper. Latin American Studies Association Congress, Miami, March 2000.

Taylor, Clark L., Jr. "Mexican Gaylife in Historical Perspective." In *Gay Roots: Twenty Years of Gay Sunshine,* ed. Winston Leyland, 190–202. San Francisco: Gay Sunshine Press, 1991.

Teruel, Alberto X. *Los inestables.* México: B. Costa-Amic, 1968.

El Tiempo. November 19, 1901.

Trexler, Richard C. *Sex and Conquest: Gendered Violence, Political Order, and the European Conquest of the Americas.* Ithaca, N.Y.: Cornell University Press, 1995.

Tuñón, Enriqueta. "La lucha política de la mujer mexicana por el derecho al sufragio y sus repercusiones." In *Presencia y transparencia: La mujer en la historia de México,* ed. Carmen Ramos Escandón, et al., 181–89. México: El Colegio de México, 1992 [1987].

El Universal. April 9–April 21, 1895; November 19–23, 1901.

Unruh, Vicky. "Una equívoca Eva moderna: Performance y pesquisas en el proyecto cultural de Antonio Rivas Mercado." *Revista de Crítica Literaria Latinoamericana.* 24, no. 48 (1998): 61–84.

———. *Latin American Vanguards: The Art of Contentious Encounters.* Berkeley: University of California Press, 1994.

Urbina, Luis G. *Crónicas.* México: Universidad Autónoma de México, 1995 [1950].

———. *La vida literaria mexicana.* Madrid: Creer-Crear, 1917.

Uriquizo, Francisco L. *Tropa vieja* [1931]. In *La novela de la revolución mexicana,* ed. Antonio Castro Leal, 2:371–486. México: Aguilar, 1960.

Urzaiz, Eduardo. *Eugenia: Esbozo novelesco de costumbres futuras.* Mérida, 1919.

Valdés, María Elena de. *Shattered Mirror.* Austin: University of Texas Press, 1998.

Vanderwood, Paul J. *Disorder and Progress: Bandits, Police, and Mexican Development.* Wilmington, Del.: Scholarly Resources, 1992 [1981].

Vasconcelos, José. *La flama.* México: Continental, 1959.

———. *El proconsulado. Memorias.* Vol. 2. México: Fondo de Cultura Económica, 1984 [1939].

———. *La raza cósmica.* 21st ed. México: Espasa-Calpe, 1986 [1925].

Villarreal, José Antonio. *Pocho*. New York: Anchor/Doubleday, 1989 [1959].

Villaurrutia, Xavier. *Cartas de Villaurrutia a Novo [1935–36]*. México: Instituto Nacional de Bellas Artes, 1966.

———. *Obras*. 2d ed. México: Fondo de Cultura Económica, 1991.

Villaurrutia, Xavier/Octavio Paz. *Nostalgia for Death/Hieroglyphs of Desire*. Trans. Eliot Weinberger and Esther Allen. Port Townsend, Wash.: Copper Canyon Press, 1992.

Villiers de l'Isle Adam, Auguste. *L'Eve future. Oeuvres complètes*. Vol. 1. Genève: Slatkine Reprints, 1970.

Vogeley, Nancy. "Defining the 'Colonial Reader': *El Periquillo Sarniento*." *PMLA* 102, no. 5 (October 1997): 784–800.

———. *Lizardi and the Birth of the Novel in Spanish America*. Gainesville: University of Florida Press, 2001.

La Voz de México. November 23, 1901.

Yáñez, Agustín. "Estudio preliminar." In José Joaquín Fernández de Lizardi, *El Pensador Mexicano*, vii–liii. México: Universidad Nacional Autónoma de México, 1940.

Yingling, Tom. "Homosexuality and Utopian Discourse in American Poetry." In *Breaking Bounds: Whitman and American Cultural Studies*, ed. Betsy Erkkila and Jay Grossman, 137–46. New York: Oxford University Press, 1996.

Zapata, Luis. *El vampiro de la colonia Roma*. México: Grijalbo, 1993 [1979].

Zea, Leopoldo. "Dos ensayos sobre México y lo mexicano" [1952]. In *Conciencia y posibilidad del mexicano, El occidente y la conciencia de México, Dos ensayos sobre México y lo mexicano*, 103–26. México: Porrúa, 1992.

Index

Robert McKee Irwin is assistant professor and director of undergraduate studies in Spanish and Portuguese at Tulane University. He is the coeditor (with Sylvia Molloy) of *Hispanisms and Homosexualities* and (with Edward J. McCaughan and Michelle Rocío Nasser) of *The Famous 41.* He is currently at work on a book-length project entitled *The Other Borderlands: Mexicanizing Nineteenth-Century Border Studies.*